Burma Redux

Burma Redux

Global Justice and the Quest for Political Reform in Myanmar

Ian Holliday

Columbia University Press
New York

Columbia University Press
Publishers Since 1893
New York   Chichester, West Sussex
cup.columbia.edu

Library of Congress Cataloging-in-Publication Data
Holliday, Ian.
Burma redux : global justice and the quest for political reform in Myanmar / Ian Holliday.
p. cm.
Includes bibliographical references and index.
ISBN 978-0-231-16126-8 (cloth : alk. paper) — ISBN 978-0-231-16127-5 (paper : alk. paper) — ISBN 978-0-231-50424-9 (ebook)
1. Burma—Politics and government—1948– 2. Burma—Foreign relations. 3. Democracy—Burma. 4. Human rights—Burma. I. Title.
DS530.4.H65 2011
959.105'3—dc23
2011034580

Columbia University Press books are printed on durable acid-free paper.
This book is printed on paper with recycled content.
Printed in the United States of America

c 10 9 8 7 6 5 4 3 2 1
p 10 9 8 7 6 5 4 3 2 1

Contents

Acknowledgements

This book was written toward the end of a five-year Deanship of Social Sciences at The University of Hong Kong. While that made for many early mornings and long weekends at the keyboard, it was also utterly dependent on a professional environment in which research could sometimes be combined with administration. For that, I am grateful to colleagues throughout the Faculty of Social Sciences, and particularly to the Faculty Office staff who interacted with me on a daily basis. Special thanks go to colleagues who worked alongside me throughout my Deanship: Amy Tsang, Vanessa Sit, Ann Lee, Eric Yeung, Simon Yung and Meimi Wong. I also pay tribute to Associate Deans and Heads of Department in the Faculty.

An initial airing of some of the book's core themes took place in three lectures delivered at the 2006 Southeast Asian Studies Summer Institute at the University of Wisconsin-Madison. For feedback and comradeship I am especially grateful to students in U Saw Tun's Burmese language class who kept in touch after we all returned to normal life: Teri Allendorf, Heather MacLachlan, Jayde Lin Roberts and Matthew Walton. I also thank participants in the Myanmar symposiums I have organized annually since 2007. Konrad-Adenauer-Stiftung has been a consistently generous sponsor. Li Chenyang, my co-host for the past three years, has been a willing collaborator.

The very great collegiality of many Myanmar watchers in academia and beyond has always been a major source of stimulation and encouragement. I trust that most of my intellectual debts are clear from materials cited in the text. Informal conversations with diplomats, educators, aid agency workers and business people operating on the ground inside Myanmar or along its lengthy borders have also been tremendously helpful.

My enthusiasm for all things Burmese has been fuelled by many people, but perhaps above all by the colleagues and students who in summer 2008 helped launch the Faculty's MOEI program of intensive English-language teaching in Mae Sot, Thailand. Glenn Shive and Daniel Siegfried played important early roles, and the late Hugh Cory was a truly inspirational trainer. Serena Yang provided essential financial support for an untried and untested initiative. Critically, the first cohort of teachers was exceptional and generated many stalwarts of later programs: Anushri Alva, Carl Browne, Ray Chan, Steve Gomersall, Grace Ip, Winnie Kwan, Diana Parker, Priscilla Sham, Peggy Wong and April Yeung. Sincere thanks to everyone.

From Myanmar friends, acquaintances and strangers both inside the country and in the diaspora I have learned more than they or I know. It has always been a great pleasure and privilege to talk, and I am enormously appreciative of the time and trust accorded to me. I am especially thankful to recent generations of Myanmar students at The University of Hong Kong. The fact that I do not name names here in no way diminishes my gratitude. I hope that through this book I can give something back.

Several colleagues read some or all of the draft manuscript and in each case provided valuable comments that undoubtedly made for a better book. Very great thanks indeed to Daniel Bell, Romain Caillaud, Ian Carter, Roman David, David Skidmore, David Steinberg, Derek Tonkin, Paul Wilding, Garrath Williams and two anonymous readers approached by the publisher. The usual disclaimer applies.

At Columbia University Press, I am grateful to Anne Routon and Brad Hebel for their enthusiastic and timely support of this project. At the originating publisher, Hong Kong University Press, I thank Michael Duckworth and Jennifer Flint.

For permission to draw on material previously carried elsewhere in developing several chapters, I thank the editors and publishers of the following journal articles: Ian Holliday, "When Is a Cause Just?", *Review of International Studies* 28:3 (2002), 557-75 (Chapter 7); Ian Holliday, "Ethics of Intervention: Just War Theory and the Challenge of the 21st Century," *International Relations* 17:2 (2003), 115-33 (Chapter 7); Ian Holliday, "Doing Business with Rights Violating Regimes: Corporate Social Responsibility and Myanmar's Military Junta," *Journal of Business Ethics* 61:4 (2005), 329-42 (Chapter 8)Roman David and Ian Holliday, "Set the Junta Free: Pre-transitional Justice in Myanmar's Democratization," *Australian Journal of Political Science* 41:1 (2006), 91-105 (Chapter 4); Ian Holliday, "Voting and Violence in Myanmar: Nation Building for a Transition to Democracy," *Asian Survey* 48:6 (2008), 1038-58 (Chapter 4).

Last but by no means least, for belief and support across many years I thank Wesley Chan and Mary, Kathryn, Brian and Marjorie Holliday.

Ian Holliday
Hong Kong
April 2011

Author's note

Myanmar names usually cannot be separated into a family name and given names. Other than in a small number of ethnic nationality languages, they function as an indivisible whole and are presented that way here.

Honorifics are still commonly used in Myanmar. In the dominant language, respect for successively older males is indicated by *Maung*, *Ko* and *U*. For successively older females, it is denoted by *Ma* and *Daw*. However, such titles are used as sparingly as possible here. Only major historical figures such as U Nu and U Thant are given honorifics, chiefly because they would be unrecognizable without them. Their actual names were Nu and Thant.

Myanmar's currency is the *kyat*, which not only fluctuates in value against other currencies, but also has multiple official exchange rates. Broadly, US$1 = 1,000 *kyats*.

Acronyms

ADB	Asian Development Bank
AFPFL	Anti-Fascist People's Freedom League
AI	Amnesty International
AIDS	acquired immune deficiency syndrome
ASEAN	Association of Southeast Asian Nations
BBC	British Broadcasting Corporation
BGF	Border Guard Force
BIA	Burma Independence Army
BNA	Burma National Army
BSPP	Burma Socialist Programme Party
CIA	Central Intelligence Agency
CPB	Communist Party of Burma
DSI	Defence Services Institute
DVB	Democratic Voice of Burma
EU	European Union
GDP	gross domestic product
HIV	human immunodeficiency virus
HRW	Human Rights Watch
ICC	International Criminal Court
ICRC	International Committee of the Red Cross
ICS	Indian Civil Service
IMF	International Monetary Fund
INGO	international nongovernmental organization
IT	information technology
KNU	Karen National Union
LDC	least developed country
LIFT	Livelihoods and Food Security Trust Fund
MI	Military Intelligence

MSF	Médecins Sans Frontières
NDF	National Democratic Force
NGO	nongovernmental organization
NLD	National League for Democracy
NUP	National Unity Party
ODA	official development assistance
PDC	Peace and Development Council
PVO	People's Volunteer Organization
RC	Revolutionary Council
SLORC	State Law and Order Restoration Council
SPDC	State Peace and Development Council
3D Fund	Three Diseases Fund
UK	United Kingdom of Great Britain and Northern Ireland
UN	United Nations
UNDP	United Nations Development Programme
UNICEF	United Nations Children's Fund
US	United States of America
USDA	Union Solidarity and Development Association
USDP	Union Solidarity and Development Party
UWSA	United Wa State Army
WTO	World Trade Organization

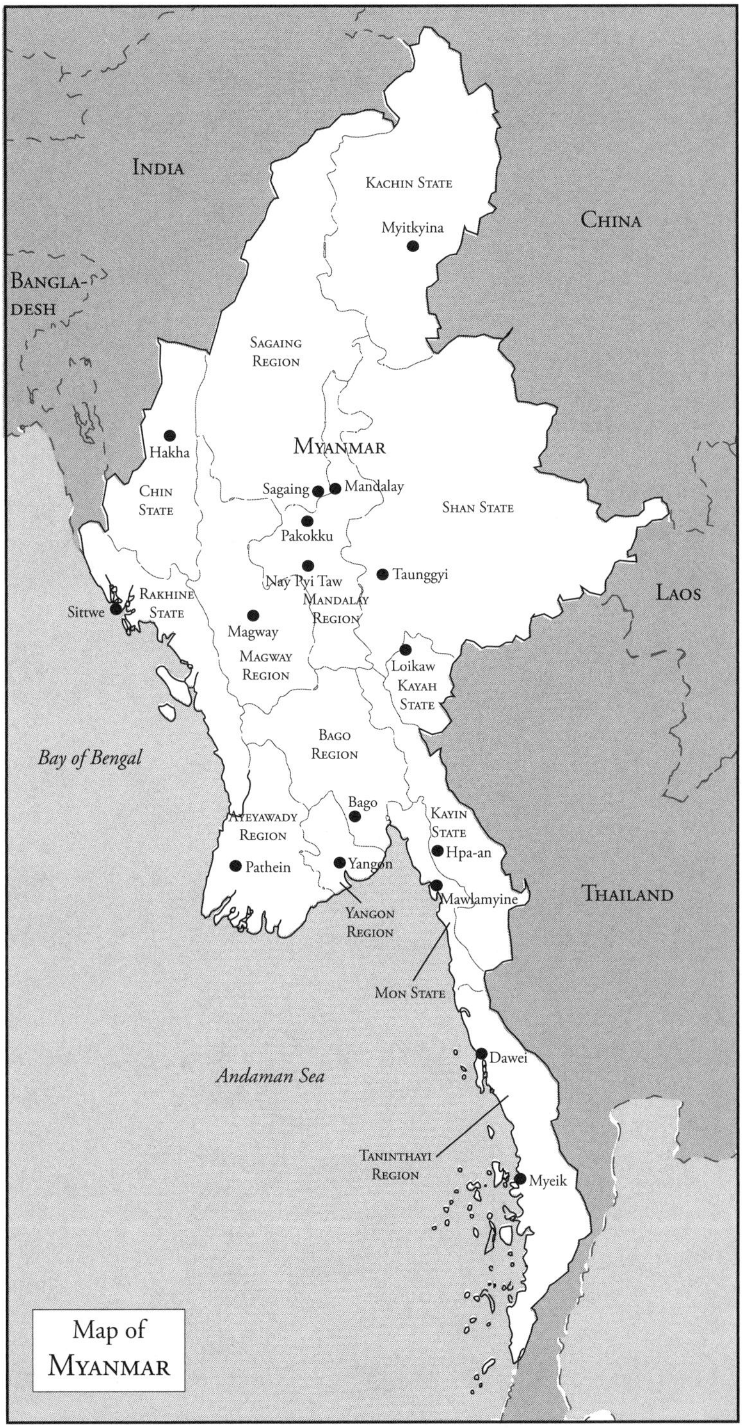
India
China
Kachin State
Myitkyina
Bangla-desh
Sagaing Region
Hakha
Myanmar
Sagaing
Mandalay
Chin State
Shan State
Pakokku
Nay Pyi Taw
Taunggyi
Rakhine State
Sittwe
Mandalay Region
Laos
Magway
Magway Region
Loikaw
Kayah State
Bago Region
Bay of Bengal
Bago
Ayeyawady Region
Kayin State
Hpa-an
Pathein
Yangon
Thailand
Mawlamyine
Yangon Region
Mon State
Dawei
Andaman Sea
Taninthayi Region
Myeik
Map of Myanmar

Introduction

For nearly 25 years since a brief eruption of mass pro-democracy protests in the middle months of 1988, Myanmar has been governed by an entrenched military machine that centralizes power, enforces rigid control, projects an abrasive nationalism, wages war on its own people, commits widespread human rights abuse, fosters systemic corruption, enriches itself and its associates, and drastically curtails the life chances of the vast majority of its citizens. For more than a quarter-century before that, from 1962 to 1988, the country then known as Burma was ruled by an autocratic regime installed by military coup and dominated by a xenophobic and quixotic general who first sketched the pattern of harsh repression that continues to this day. For 18 months before that, from 1958 to 1960, the state had a fleeting experience of praetorian politics under a caretaker government led by the same top general. In six and a half decades since the collapse of British colonialism in 1948 there have been occasional brushes with democracy, including a tightly managed 2010 election designed to attach a flimsy civilian façade to an inflexible garrison state. Mostly, however, grinding authoritarianism with a stern martial stamp has been the daily reality in this Texas-sized Southeast Asian country of, currently, 55–60 million citizens.[1]

By and large, the record of military supremacy has been abysmal. Unlike other Asian despotisms, notably South Korea and Taiwan for three decades to the late 1980s and China and Vietnam today, the country has not witnessed an economic miracle under its oppressors.[2] Rather, it has endured relative and even absolute decline, and a strategic state sandwiched between India and China and blessed with extensive natural resources and a wealth of additional advantages has seen its economy fall prey to predatory racketeering devised by leading generals and replicated by their friends and enemies. The social impacts of martial law have been mainly devastating, and with human security routinely at desperately low levels Myanmar today finds itself at the wrong end of most global rankings. As a result, the vibrancy, vigor and hope found in booming parts of the region are often attenuated or absent here. Furthermore, stretching across almost all of the period since independence, episodic and increasingly peripheral civil war has taken tens of thousands of lives and destroyed countless communities.[3] Minority ethnic nationalities living chiefly in hill country surrounding Myanmar's large central plain and intricate southern delta, and collectively making up about one third of the total population, have suffered in particular at the hands of generals determined to impose a narrow and constraining vision of national unity on the diverse population they command.[4] Chased from their homes and forced off their land, millions are now internally displaced, living as border-zone refugees and migrants, or resettled in distant parts of a growing diaspora.

As the 2000s gave way to the 2010s, a measure of political renewal passed through the country when military rulers choreographed a step-by-step transition to "discipline-flourishing democracy." An election of sorts was held in November 2010, parliament convened in January 2011, fresh executive positions were filled in February, and the junta created close to a quarter-century earlier was formally dissolved in March.[5] Sealing this final move, paramount leader Senior General Than Shwe ceded power to a new civilian government headed by President Thein Sein. However, since every part of the 2011 polity was controlled by individuals from or close to the outgoing regime, and since Than Shwe himself remained a key figure behind the scenes, it was hard to see what had changed.[6] Moreover, even after this flurry of institutional renovation critical issues long dominating national politics remained largely unaddressed. Some relate to the role of the democratic movement animated by opposition leader Aung San Suu Kyi, but also stretching beyond her influence as additional forces surface to contest austere military rule. Others concern a patchwork of ethnic nationality groups and their varying demands for autonomy. Still others focus on modernization strategies for a decrepit state, economy and society. At a time of both ongoing military rule and some structural reform, the pathways that might one day be threaded through this fractured political landscape are therefore anything but visible.[7]

Viewed from outside in an age of bracing and often unforeseen popular challenge to entrenched despotism in disparate parts of the world, the sense that real change must one day come to Myanmar nevertheless remains palpable. Indeed, in a post-Cold War era of humanitarian engagement driven by generic notions of global justice, this problematic state has for years looked to be a prime candidate for political reform, and the main task facing the rest of the world has long seemed crystal clear: helping to make it happen.

Put very broadly, that is the line taken by this book. The core aim here is to identify practical ways for foreigners motivated by mandates of global justice to facilitate real institutional change inside the country and return it to the path of democracy and diversity envisaged at independence in 1948, pursued for most of the 14 years down to General Ne Win's 1962 coup, glimpsed for several weeks in 1988 when large masses of people rose in revolt against authoritarianism, and present today in the hearts, minds and acts of many citizens.

At the same time, however, the book seeks to situate itself solidly in reality, acknowledging that colonialism had negative impacts on a subject people, that actually existing democracy for most of the long 1950s was fractious and fragile, that military control since the early 1960s has been powerfully and pervasively oppressive, that an adequate settlement between distinct ethnic communities remains a distant prospect, and that reform proposals floated by political leaders across the political spectrum are multiple and contradictory. Surveying the scene in 2006, Thant Myint-U, expatriate grandson of former United Nations Secretary-General U Thant, accepted that the country had become a "poster child" for "nightmarish twenty-first century ills."[8] In a lyrical account blending personal and national histories, the points he sought to stress though were that more needs to be said, that this is a far more complex state than most public discourse will allow, and that patient efforts to understand it must be made.

Still more importantly, the book recognizes that Myanmar's future course can be set by nobody other than Myanmar citizens, and in examining potential roles for outsiders seeks above all to develop strategies that empower local people to realize their hopes for change. Returning to public life in November 2010 after many years of enforced silence through house arrest, Aung San Suu Kyi had much to say to her compatriots and the wider world. However, her central message picked up on an argument made throughout her political career: that nothing can be achieved without active participation across society.[9] When regular citizens are given a chance to speak, they too emphasize the need for foreigners to work with and through individuals currently living inside the country. Interviewed in 2008, a staff member from a local organization focusing on gender and women's rights noted that "Many people talk of women as being victims but they have agency."[10] The point also applies to much global engagement with Myanmar. While outsiders are right to point to widespread suffering at the hands of an obdurate and rapacious military machine, they must also accept that people throughout the land are determined to shape their own destinies.

To the extent possible for an analysis written by a foreigner, and perhaps likely to be read mainly by foreigners, this book thus attempts first and foremost to get to grips with the many challenges confronting contemporary Myanmar. Only thereafter does it move to consider the demands of global justice, and the contribution outsiders prepared to acknowledge its mandates might make to domestic political reform. To this end, it focuses particularly on means by which indigenous preferences might be articulated, grassroots leadership enhanced, and the sphere of local politics expanded. Alongside a commitment to principled foreign engagement thus stands a dual insistence that outsiders willing to perform duties of global justice take a deep rather than surface interest in Myanmar, and never lose sight of local agency. On the rare but important occasions that listening projects are undertaken inside the country, they routinely transmit this kind of message. Asked in 2009 what he wanted from the international community, a middle-aged Kayah man gave this response: "Come and be in our place. Feel it and help us."[11] This modest injunction has major implications for all outsiders seeking to get involved with Myanmar, and must be fully heard, appropriately weighed and duly respected by any proponent of cross-border action informed by often abstract notions of justice. It stands as something of a direction marker for this book.

Before turning in its second half to debates about global justice and what it calls interactive intervention animated by constructive transnational partnerships for political reform, the book thus explores in its first half the situation in which Myanmar citizens currently find themselves. In such a layered and labyrinthine case, indeed in any case, this is a necessary basis for examination of means by which foreigners might reach across a recognized international frontier to facilitate political change. To get to that first main part and establish a context for analysis of a far away country about which outsiders typically know little, this introductory chapter looks at controversy surrounding its name, ways in which the current reality inside its borders might be framed, means by which its politics might be examined, and initial possibilities for rebuilding from the ruinous state that is Myanmar a place that might properly be called Burma.

Naming a nation

A standard starting point for debate, whether explicit or implicit, is a dispute about the name of the country that opened in the middle months of 1989 and continues to this day.[12] It can be traced notably to Law No. 15/89, issued on June 18, 1989, which decreed that "The expression 'Union of Burma' and the expression 'Burma' or 'Burman' or 'Burmese' contained in the existing laws enacted in the English language shall be substituted by the expressions 'Union of Myanmar' and 'Myanmar' respectively."[13] In parallel, Notification No. 5/89 provided a brief list of new names for nationalities, states, divisions, cities and rivers across the land. Order No. 2/89 held that "since the term 'Bamar' used in the National Anthem of the Union of Myanmar refers only to the 'Bamar nationality,' it has been replaced with 'Myanmar' to refer to all the nationalities."[14] The quarrel unleashed by these edicts is an appropriate place to begin this analysis.

One feature worth noting at the outset is that the decrees affected peoples and places known to the outside world chiefly through colonialism. Indeed, it was largely because something had been lost in transliteration that changes in English terminology were deemed necessary in June 1989. The city the British called Rangoon, bureaucratic heart of their Burma and first capital of the postcolonial nation, was thus renamed Yangon to reflect local pronunciation as faithfully as possible. The Irrawaddy River, cast by Rudyard Kipling in 1890 as an imperial road to Mandalay, became the Ayeyawady.[15] Maymyo, a hill station named in 1887 for Colonel James May and frequented by colonial officials, entrepreneurs and traders as refuge from monsoon heat and humidity in Burma's central plain, became Pyin Oo Lwin. To the east, Karen State, lodged on the border with Thailand and fiercely loyal to Britain in the Second World War, became Kayin State. Its administrative capital switched its spelling from Pa-an to the aspirated Hpa-an. To the south in Mon State, port city and governance center Moulmein, setting in 1926 for George Orwell's shooting of an elephant, became Mawlamyine.[16] In these many ways, the Burma captured in stages by Britain through wars fought in 1824–26, 1852 and 1885, and ruled as part of the Empire on which the sun never set to 1948 save only for three years of Japanese control from 1942 to 1945, became a rather unfamiliar place to outsiders.

In principle there was little wrong with that, for it is hard to object to local people devising a set of changes designed to improve the mapping of English to indigenous usage. Indeed, in the context of postcolonial Asia such exercises have taken place repeatedly, and rarely have they generated sustained criticism. Among former British possessions alone, parts of India have experienced parallel revisions since independence in 1947, with colonial Bombay, Madras and Calcutta all taking new names as Mumbai, Chennai and Kolkata between 1995 and 2000. Changes have also been made in Bangladesh (itself East Pakistan until independence in 1971), Malaysia (Malaya until a set of 1965 reforms), and Sri Lanka (Ceylon until 1972). Elsewhere, a classic instance is the switch from Peking to Beijing mandated by China's adoption of the *pinyin* transliteration system in 1958. Although Beijing was rarely used by people speaking and writing in English during the early years of Communist rule, it became common linguistic currency from the 1980s onward as Chinese leaders promoted it more insistently. Other than in fixed historical contexts, such as Peking University in Beijing or Peking Road in Hong Kong, it is now the standard term across the English-speaking world, and Peking strikes a jarring note. Guangzhou (Canton), Nanjing (Nanking) and Tianjin (Tientsin) are also approved contemporary usages.

In the Myanmar case, however, objections to the name changes soon surfaced, though at the time the foreign press displayed little interest. In the United Kingdom, for instance, *The Times* took three days to report the news and on June 21 ran only a 20-word item supplied by the Reuters office in Bangkok. In the United States, *The New York Times* carried a 100-word piece from the Associated Press one day earlier, on June 20. In Hong Kong, Britain's last Asian colony, the *South China Morning Post* also mentioned the change from Burma to Myanmar on June 20. Tellingly, it buried the item at the end of a story on political talks between regime officials and student leaders: "Meanwhile, the country officially changed its name in English yesterday."[17] With the passage of time, however, this early indifference became atypical as varying degrees of opposition took root.

One challenge was technical. Containing only two linguists among more than 20 members and convening for no more than a few weeks, the Commission of Inquiry into the True Naming of Myanmar was widely held to have done a poor job. On the headline issue of country name, for example, several criticisms surfaced. One was that Myanmah would be a better English rendition than Myanmar, as it would more successfully generate the soft tonal ending found in the indigenous language.[18] Another was that Myanma was preferable, and that the "r" added to produce a final long "a" sound was ineffectual outside southern British English. In the wake of the changes, and indeed for some years thereafter, academic articles from a wide range of disciplines and on an eclectic mix of topics devoted lengthy footnotes to technical flaws in the new transliterations.

Ultimately, however, the greater challenge was political. At base, this focused on naming rights for a composite country that in 1948 gained independence as a functioning democracy with explicit protections for at least some minority groups, but in 1989 was subject to martial law. Many noted that when formed by military leaders on September 18, 1988, precisely nine months prior to release of the name changes, the State Law and

Order Restoration Council had pledged to be no more than temporary. The *tatmadaw*, or defense service, Chairman General Saw Maung declared, had "no desire to hold on to state power for a prolonged period."[19] Rather, the junta intended to stabilize the polity and then sponsor a transition to fully elected government. Its first decree, issued as Declaration No. 1/88 on its initial day in control, thus set out four objectives: first, maintain law and order; second, provide secure and smooth transportation; third, ease the material needs of the people; and fourth, once all the other measures were complete, oversee multiparty democratic general elections. On September 21, it followed up by promulgating Law No. 1/88 to set the stage for nationwide polls. On September 27, it issued Law No. 4/88 to permit political parties to register. In this transitional setting leading to a planned election, many felt SLORC had no mandate to change English names across the country.

This critique was reinforced by evidence of widespread repression undertaken by SLORC both before and after its renaming exercise. Declaration No. 2/88, also issued on its first day, placed major constraints on civil liberties, declaring that "Congregating, walking, marching in procession, chanting slogans, delivering speeches, agitating and creating disturbances on the streets by a group of more than five people is banned regardless of whether the act is with the intention of creating disturbances or committing a crime or not."[20] Notification No. 8/88, issued on October 10, 1988, imposed strict limits on political parties, notably restricting their ability to address issues relating to the *tatmadaw*. Martial Law Order Nos. 1/89 and 2/89, promulgated on July 17–18, 1989, authorized the Yangon and the Central and Northwest Military Commands to conduct summary trials and executions. Within three months, 100 people had been sentenced to death.[21] On July 20, Aung San Suu Kyi and other top opposition figures were detained under house arrest.

Objections deepened still further when SLORC eventually allowed a reasonably free and fair general election to take place on May 27, 1990, but then tightened its stranglehold on power when the opposition won in a landslide. In a stunning result, the National League for Democracy took some 60 percent of the national vote, 80 percent of the parliamentary seats, and 90 percent of the seats for which it stood candidates. Even military towns voted NLD in large numbers. By contrast, the National Unity Party and its allies, widely seen as close to the generals, won little more than 20 percent of the vote and 2 percent of the seats.[22] Faced with this unexpected outcome from a poll in which more than 200 political parties initially surfaced to compete for votes, the junta again exhibited its repressive instincts. Rather than transfer power to the NLD and deliver on the undertaking given in 1988, or even set up the constitutional convention to which military leaders pointed toward the end of a campaign evidently not going to plan, SLORC proceeded as if little had changed.[23] In Declaration No. 1/90, issued on July 27 by Secretary-1 and Military Intelligence chief General Khin Nyunt, it insisted that it was "not an organization that observes any constitution." Rather, it was common knowledge that SLORC was "governing the nation as a military government and that it is a government that has been accepted as such by the United Nations and the respective nations of the world."[24] The junta amplified this response by reasserting harsh control, notably through harassment, imprisonment and sometimes torture of opposition leaders, many of whom had won seats in the general election.

In this context, a set of name changes always viewed with skepticism around the globe came to symbolize the brutal rule of a military machine that brazenly ignored the will of the people and persisted for years thereafter in centralizing power within a tight elite. Inside the country, the NLD long argued that any changes must be endorsed by an elected legislature, specifically the parliament chosen by the people in May 1990, and many other opposition figures supported this position. Leaders of minority ethnic nationalities also questioned the imposition of fresh English transliterations derived from the language of the dominant ethnic group, and mainly resolved to stick with colonial usage for both their territories and the country as a whole.[25] Outside, the UN acting in accordance with practice and precedent at once accepted the switch from Burma to Myanmar. Most states in international society also fell into line. However, a small number continued to hold firm to the old practice. Chief among them remains the US, which expresses solidarity with opposition to military rule by refusing to use the revised terminology.[26]

Two and a half decades on from the late 1980s, when a broad-based democracy movement was crushed, a military-backed single-party state was replaced by a formal junta, a landslide electoral victory was blithely ignored, a broad swath of civil rights was trampled and, at the same time, a set of changes was made to place-names throughout the country, the term Burma thus continues to represent, for many, more than just customary usage for the largest country in peninsular Southeast Asia. It also signals thoroughgoing opposition to the military machine that introduced the name Myanmar, and fierce commitment not only to the democratic cause of the opposition movement, but also to the identity claims of minority ethnic nationalities likewise preferring, on the whole, to speak of Burma. Clearly there is some irony in this, for the Burma erased from the map by dictatorial fiat in June 1989 was in no sense democratic and to no satisfactory degree multicultural, and had not been so for decades. Rather, throughout the period since the 1962 coup it had been a highly centralized authoritarian state exhibiting scant regard for minority nationalities, many of which it had long fought in alternately hot and cold civil wars.

In these circumstances, what gives the term Burma a democratic spin and at the same time hints at real ethnic diversity is its association with a series of democratic thrusts and inter-communal accords scattered across many decades of history. On the democratic side, the link is above all with the late 1980s conflict between a genuinely mass movement bent on thoroughgoing political reform and prepared to take to the streets to argue, fight and not infrequently die for it, and an entrenched dictatorship determined to cling to power by whatever means necessary. Additional ties bind in those who struggled in the long 1950s to turn the democracy created on British withdrawal in 1948 into a workable system of government, and movements launched from the 1920s to the 1940s to campaign openly for a sovereign and democratic Burma. On the side of ethnic diversity, the association is chiefly with a legendary inter-ethnic agreement struck at the Shan town of Panglong in 1947, and a series of largely unknown individuals who subsequently struggled to resist a remorseless military machine bent on imposing its will throughout the land.[27] Before that, it is with an assortment of princely leaders and peasant militias who fought loyally with the Allies in the Second World War, and believed they would one day be rewarded with meaningful degrees of territorial and cultural autonomy. To some extent it is also with romantic notions of tribal communities untouched by the rigors of modern life and skilled in evading the ever more insistent demands of the nation state.[28] When, in the late 1980s, the authoritarian strand in Burmese politics opted for Myanmar and other name changes as correct English terms, contending strands in the democracy movement and minority nationalities chose to hold fast and defiantly to the traditional nomenclature. For many, then, Myanmar and Burma most fully capture the broad national forces that for years have set the main parameters of political discourse and action across the country.[29]

Throughout, this book joins many others in taking Burma to signal aspirations for democracy and diversity. In rejecting the authoritarian path of repression and despair signposted Myanmar, down which military leaders have driven the nation, it simultaneously indicates a commitment to the democratic path of freedom and hope marked Burma for which citizens mobilized in 1988. At the same time, however, the book consciously makes use of the official terminology in referring to the years since the late 1980s. In all that follows, Myanmar is the label applied to the nation subjected to rule by junta until 2011 and to military-dominated ersatz democracy thereafter, for it neatly encapsulates much that has happened in the past two decades and more.[30] Deviations from official usage are made only in cases of ethnic nationalities that prefer to retain the old terms. As a prime example, the book thus refers to Karen State and the Karen people, rather than Kayin State and the Kayin people. Moreover, for the period prior to 1989, the old lexicon is kept in play. This runs counter to military policy and also to some current scholarly practice, both of which reach back into history to read recent name changes even into the colonial period, when standard English usage was Burma, Rangoon, Irrawaddy and so on. Such an anachronistic approach, though politically correct in military circles, is not taken here.

Finally, in the whole of this analysis Burmese (since 1989 Myanmar people) designates citizens of the country and is blind to ethnicity, whereas Burman (since 1989 Bamar) identifies members of the main ethnic group. While this conforms to current practice, it conflicts with imperial convention. This is, for instance, what colonial official, educator, scholar and post-independence adviser J. S. Furnivall wrote: "'Burman' connotes all the indigenous inhabitants of Burma together with permanent residents of alien origin who have come to regard themselves as natives of the country; this leaves 'Burmese' for use as a distinctively racial term."[31] Precisely the opposite usage is adopted here.

Framing a situation

Once a position is taken on terminology, a larger issue is how to frame Myanmar's current situation. In a history of the past 125 years published in 2009, Michael W. Charney identified several themes that have "transcended the phases of the Burmese experience ... and contribute to something that might be called the rhythm of Burmese history."[32] He listed them as first the relationship between Burmans and non-Burmans (or Bamars and non-Bamars), second impoverishment of the general population, third confrontation between democracy and authoritarianism, fourth fear of foreign domination, and fifth monastic participation in politics. For an analysis centered on promoting political reform inside the country, however, it is perhaps acceptable to focus on three main features.

Two were most visibly on display in the seismic events of 1988. The first part of a grim dialectic unleashed then was popular protest fueled by economic mismanagement and hardship, triggered by official incompetence and brutality, and detonated as the 8-8-88 democratic movement. The second part was the reassertion of military power undertaken six weeks later, which reflected and indeed consummated the decisive 1962 coup by setting in place a formal junta.[33] Other events of the past quarter-century, including the abortive 1990 general election, student strikes in 1996 and 2002, the 2007 march of the monks widely known as the saffron uprising, the criminally mismanaged 2008 Cyclone Nargis, the 2010 general election, and even the installation of notionally civilian government in 2011, were little more than somber footnotes. Two defining features of Myanmar's situation can therefore be found in what became in 1988 a violent clash between popular demands for democracy, and entrenched military rule.

Alongside these twin features, the third essential dimension is the series of increasingly localized civil wars bleeding the country's borderlands since independence in 1948. In the early decades, sporadic fighting mainly pitted the ever more Burman *tatmadaw* against both a force raised by the Communist Party of Burma, and a series of militias and ragtag bands of soldiers put together by ethnic nationalities, giving civil conflict ideological and racial strands. However, the CPB's abrupt splinter and collapse in April 1989, when anti-communist revolution was also sweeping East-Central Europe, left only ethnic conflict in place.[34] To this day fighting sometimes erupts in peripheral parts, and even zones not subject to overt violence endure deep insecurity.[35] Indeed, the state of nature described by Thomas Hobbes in *Leviathan* nearly four centuries ago, in which the life of man is "solitary, poor, nasty, brutish, and short," is often nothing other than a precise description of desperate daily conditions in frontier lands.[36] In such areas a multitude of distinct political dynamics plays out.[37]

However, within this broad context of democratic aspiration, military repression and ethnic conflict, not everything has been static during the past 20 years and the country is in no sense trapped listlessly in a late 1980s time warp.[38] Then, the political environment was characterized chiefly by a junta that held power by coercion but had no clear strategy for retaining it, and opposition groups, both democratic and ethnic, with immense moral authority but no viable program for seizing control. In the heartland, tense standoff was the order of the day. In peripheral parts, sporadic skirmishing continued to take place. Thereafter, though, the opposition's resolute push to secure full recognition of its 1988 street presence and above all its 1990 electoral triumph was obliged through force of circumstance to become more responsive and reactive to moves made by military leaders. For the NLD, one consequence was official liquidation of the political party in 2010 as senior figures decided not to contest the junta's managed election.

Across the same period, the wider society also experienced substantial change as local organizations emerged in many parts of the country to tackle problems faced by ordinary people in their everyday lives, notably during the emergency situation generated by Cyclone Nargis. Clear signs of a revival of civil society created much greater communal complexity and gave a further twist to political development.[39] Similarly, in the borderlands a decline in actual fighting took place in the early 1990s as a set of ceasefire deals was struck by the *tatmadaw* and most of the ethnic militias that for decades had confronted it.[40] The political space created by these agreements enabled local people to pay at least some attention to rebuilding shattered communities. It also allowed many individuals to play an important role in the wider national push for democracy and human rights, and ensured that by the time of the generals' 2010 election ethnic nationality activists were a key part of the peaceful political opposition.[41]

In addition, major changes have taken place on the side of the military machine. In the immediate aftermath of the September 1988 restoration of *tatmadaw* control, the junta lived from day to day with little more than a sharp survival instinct to sustain it. There was no grand strategy, and shocks like popular repudiation in the 1990 general election were dealt with strictly on an *ad hoc* basis. For a decade thereafter, serial attempts were made to stabilize the political situation. At home, a National Convention was established in January 1993 to draft a constitution to replace the 1974 charter abrogated at the time of the 1988 coup, ceasefires were agreed with ethnic nationalities, and from time to time talks, secret or otherwise, were held with opposition leaders. In November 1997 the junta renamed itself the State Peace and Development Council, indicating that Than Shwe, dominant figure from April 1992, intended to retain power for a long while. Abroad, bilateral links with China were reinforced following massacres in Rangoon in 1988 and in Beijing in 1989, and multilateral ties were developed through membership of the Association of Southeast Asian Nations, to which Myanmar was controversially admitted as a full member in July 1997. However, while these policy strands succeeded in their minimal aim of keeping the junta in power, they did not enable it to seize the political initiative.

Soon after the turn of the millennium, though, military leaders registered greater progress. In August 2003, Khin Nyunt, incoming prime minister and key regime strategist, unveiled a seven-point roadmap to a "discipline-flourishing democratic state." Built on drafting work commenced more than a decade earlier, the map traced a path to a constitutional referendum, a general election and installation of civilian government. Although Khin Nyunt himself was purged in October 2004 and placed under a long term of house arrest, the roadmap remained in place. Notwithstanding major challenges, it created an opportunity for the generals to take the lead in political development and pursue a game plan looking beyond the immediate future. In the margins, they displayed growing self-assurance by starting in November 2005 to transfer government functions to Nay Pyi Taw, a brand new fortified capital located 250 miles north of the restive city of Yangon.[42] By releasing Aung San Suu Kyi from house arrest six days after the 2010 election, they signaled further belief that politics in their garrison state were firmly under control.

Analyzing a society

Democratic aspiration and authoritarian reaction, witnessed most clearly in 1988 but viscerally present since 1962, did not emerge from nowhere. Similarly, ethnic contestation and revolt, a scar on the landscape since 1948, have profound social roots. To understand contemporary Myanmar, it is thus necessary to investigate the forces that have shaped it. Within a body of English-language scholarship amassed mainly by outsiders, many options are available.[43] Among political scientists, however, two broad clusters predominate.[44] One is a cultural approach looking to underlying modes of social integration and interaction and employing methodologies from anthropology and sociology. The other is a historical approach tracing social and political development into the past and seeking thereby to comprehend present-day society. While there are clear overlaps, the two have different reference points and dynamics.

Under the British, cultural approaches were a popular means of tapping into a distant territorial possession to understand what colonial administrator James George Scott, in a remarkable analysis published in 1882 under the pseudonym Shway Yoe, called *The Burman: His Life and Notions*. In 64 chapters, the human cycle is presented from first years to death and burial, with domestic life, religion (including Burma's famous *nats*), village life, and governance all examined.[45] *The Soul of a People* (1898) and *A People at School* (1906) by British official H. Fielding-Hall also probed political culture.[46] After independence, though, surveys penned by informed outsiders operating on an immersion basis were less common as foreign engagement tailed off. In their place came occasional cultural analyses written in the emergent idiom of political science, notably Lucian W. Pye's pessimistic analysis of political trust in *Politics, Personality, and Nation Building: Burma's Search for Identity*

(1962).[47] Modern anthropological studies were also launched by E. R. Leach in *Political Systems of Highland Burma* (1954), F. K. Lehman in *The Structure of Chin Society* (1963) and Manning Nash in *The Golden Road to Modernity* (1965).[48] In Burma's years of great isolation from 1962 to 1988, however, little fieldwork was possible.[49] Only later did ethnographic accounts of politics in part or all of the society reemerge. Christina Fink's *Living Silence* (2001) and Monique Skidmore's *Karaoke Fascism* (2004) both address Myanmar as a whole.[50]

More commonly in recent decades, scholars of national politics have turned to history. Arthur P. Phayre in 1883 and G. E. Harvey in 1925 both drew on direct local knowledge to write pioneering books under the title *History of Burma*.[51] The late colonial and early postcolonial periods then witnessed wide debate as former officials and academics trained their attention on the war-torn colony and emergent state. Among erstwhile administrators, Furnivall, already mentioned in passing and soon to be encountered again, was preeminent. Set within a broad range of study, *An Introduction to the Political Economy of Burma* (1931), *Colonial Policy and Practice* (1948) and *The Governance of Modern Burma* (1958) most fully displayed his deep understanding.[52] F. S. V. Donnison, Chief Secretary to the Government of Burma in 1946, also drew on intimate experience to write *Public Administration in Burma* (1953) and *Burma* (1970).[53] Among professional historians, examinations of the modern state informed by long or short surveys of the past came notably from D. G. E. Hall in *Burma* (1950), Hugh Tinker in *The Union of Burma* (1957), John F. Cady in *A History of Modern Burma* (1958), Dorothy Woodman in *The Making of Burma* (1962), Frank N. Trager in *Burma, from Kingdom to Republic* (1966), and Maung Htin Aung in *A History of Burma* (1967).[54]

The position taken by early postwar writers was picked up by many subsequent analysts. As Tinker put it roughly a decade after independence, this was that "The old Burma has bequeathed much to the new, but not in the sphere of government; the origins of the representative institutions of today must be sought in the British period."[55] Some 45 years on, Thant Myint-U made much the same point in *The Making of Modern Burma* (2001): "the end of the [nineteenth] century witnessed the birth of Burma as we still know it today."[56] In *The River of Lost Footsteps* (2006), he identified 1885 as the "watershed year," marked by "a break with the ideas and institutions that had underpinned society in the Irrawaddy Valley since before medieval times."[57] Charney also endorsed this approach by opening *A History of Modern Burma* (2009) in 1886.[58]

The line taken by Cady in 1958 was different, however, making reassertion of the past the core theme. "Generally speaking, the structure of governmental administration in newly independent Burma follows closely the improved patterns developed in British times, but the spirit of the exercise of authority owes much to pre-British custom as popularly recognized."[59] In this way he identified vital cultural and political traditions as important conditioning factors in the contemporary state. Later, this departure from the established focus on the colonial period was endorsed and extended by Cady's student, Robert H. Taylor. In a book that appeared as *The State in Burma* in 1987, and in a revised and extended edition as *The State in Myanmar* in 2009, Taylor reached decisively into the past to argue that "the contemporary state in Myanmar cannot be understood other than through an appreciation of the nature of the early modern pre-colonial state."[60] He thereby made a case for a very deep historical understanding of Myanmar's current political situation.

Taylor did not argue for analysis to go all the way back through more than 1,000 years of recorded history. For him, Burma's first chronicled centuries, corresponding to the medieval period in Europe, are best viewed as prehistory. They contain the revered Pagan Dynasty, founded in 1044 and maintained until 1287.[61] They feature the legendary King Anawrahta, who ruled from 1044 to 1077 and was identified as a founding father by Hall, sometime Professor of History at Rangoon University: "He was the first king of Burma and with him Burmese history proper begins."[62] They span a mix of kingdoms and tribal societies marked by shifting forms of government and patterns of alliance. Thus, while the Pagan Dynasty managed for more than two centuries to dominate not only the plains at the heart of the territory, but also parts of the surrounding hill country and delta lands, it was equally possible for central control to break down and peripheral leaders to extend their dominion into the heartland. Shan people to the east and Mon people to the south both boast long-dead monarchs able to project power from the periphery into the core.[63] Indeed, as Victor B. Lieberman noted in *Burmese Administrative Cycles* (1984), "the waxing and waning of royal power constitutes a major theme in the political history of the region."[64]

Rather, Taylor argued that in a context of fluid patterns of control stretching across many centuries, Burmese political history became settled in the late 1500s. The key figure in implanting a more consistent and ultimately modern pattern was King Bayinnaung, who from 1551 to 1581 consolidated the Toungoo Dynasty, which ruled from 1486 to 1752. Subsequently, from 1752 to 1760, King Alaungpaya formed the equally important Konbaung Dynasty, which exercised power for more than a century. Taylor demonstrates that for some 300 years down to the late 1800s the Burman state sustained reforms that considerably enhanced its capacity to exercise control over a broad range of territory. In his words, "the power of the state relative to society increased because of more effective taxation and greater military strength; increased and centralized military strength was also a consequence of advances in technology, together with an altered external political and economic environment, the result of increasingly rapid changes occurring in Europe and in neighbouring areas."[65] One consequence was that when, in the late eighteenth century, East India Company officials looked beyond Bengal into lands to the south and east, the Burma they encountered had a coherent core dominated by an established state and underpinned by a pervasive Buddhist faith. That state was also able supervise, regulate and exact tribute from much of its mountainous periphery.

An additional move is critical. Having shown that a competent Burman state was constructed in the centuries preceding British imperial rule, Taylor argues that pre-colonial governance patterns and political culture exercised a decisive shaping power over every succeeding polity down to the present day. "Both the colonial state and the contemporary state developed in the same geographical and ecological condition as the precolonial state, and there are significant cultural continuities between the periods of the state's existence."[66] He thereby holds that a full understanding of the state established by Burma's unifying Toungoo and Konbaung Dynasties across 300 years from the late sixteenth century onward is necessary to any attempt to capture contemporary governance. At the start of this book, the validity of this important methodological claim requires careful examination.

When that is done, it looks decidedly problematic. The first part relates to geographical conditions, for Taylor unchanging across pre-colonial, colonial and postcolonial states. In the broad sense of brute facts, there may be some truth in this. However, it was only by British officials that an entity corresponding to contemporary Myanmar was first mapped, and even then its borders were no more than rough approximations of those that exist today. Additionally, abundant change in the past 200 years, comprising something like a tenfold population increase, the rise of new urban centers, major population movements, and a revolution in the technological underpinnings of state-society relations, further undermine the idea of constant conditions. Any human geographer can show that in many important respects they are radically different, and anthropologist James C. Scott demonstrates that dramatic change in the control capacity of the modern state has drastically reduced space available to "the art of not being governed."[67] The second part states that ecological conditions have also been the same across the past two centuries. However, that is not the case either. In a largely rural setting, modes of agricultural production shifted markedly in many parts of the country. In particular, the opening of a new rice frontier in the second half of the nineteenth century had a wide impact.[68] The final part argues for significant cultural continuities, and is bolstered by Cady's original contention. For Taylor, political dynamics have always been established by a controlling state. "It is the nature of the state and its personnel which provides meaning to [Burma's political history since the late sixteenth century], for it is the state which has been the dominant institution in shaping economic, social and other opportunities for the population."[69] This state-centric claim is distinct from society-centric arguments reaching much the same conclusion by the different route of the country's allegedly authoritarian political values.[70] Taylor argues not that local people have long got the government they deserve, but rather that local rulers have always felt the need to adopt a maximalist, assertive conception of their role. Under threat, elites project power.

There is much to be said for this interpretation. Throughout history, state leaders have sought to boost central command, and often they have succeeded. Looking to this heritage, Michael Aung-Thwin argues that Burmese independence came not in 1948 when authority was vested in an elite shaped by colonialism and beholden to western powers, but rather in 1962 when Ne Win destroyed a crumbling democracy, shrugged off external influence, and asserted full national sovereignty through a centralizing state.[71] Moreover, it is strictly within this tradition that military leaders operated in 1988, that Than Shwe worked in the 1990s and 2000s, and that disciplined democracy is intended to function under Thein Sein in the 2010s. Nevertheless, it is stretching the point to argue that broader ecological conditions remain sufficiently unchanged for analyses of the pre-colonial political system to be centrally relevant today. The very year after Taylor's book was first published witnessed the four eights uprising.[72] In turn, this mobilization for democracy also looked to tradition as individuals walked consciously in the steps of protesters from every decade since the 1920s. Thus, while the state certainly remains what Taylor calls "the determining partner" in relationships with civil society, in modern times its authority and legitimacy have been fiercely contested.[73]

Indeed, once the focus of inquiry shifts from a persistently dominant state to the larger context in which it is embedded, many features of the political landscape exhibit clear discontinuity. Already noted is the development of democratic aspirations among a broad spectrum of citizens and evident at many points since at least the 1920s. Alongside it is politicization of ethnic identity across the country, triggered in colonial times and painfully present thereafter. Also significant is the absence prior to British rule of anything remotely resembling the modern nation-state successive elites have sought to impose on the country. Moreover, many attributes associated with such a construct were also missing in the pre-colonial period. Infrastructure and communications were poor, and interaction between people in the central plains and surrounding hill country was fundamentally different from what is witnessed today. Internal trade was chronically underdeveloped. Outlying parts now and then fell under Chinese, Indian or Siamese control. Crucially, there was no sense of a notionally unified Burma spanning core and periphery. Largely for this reason, the ethnic identities that in many ways have come to define the modern state, and have also come close to tearing it apart, are also modern constructs.[74] The firm boundaries that mark them out are often located in different places from the informal borders existing in the pre-colonial period, and both are distinct again from the frontiers set in place by the British.

In 1958, Furnivall wrote that "Burma, secluded from the outer world by mountains and the sea, appears destined for political unity by nature." However, his argument was that only rarely has unity been realized.[75] Furthermore, it was under the British that a single legal entity was definitively marked out and established on the map of the world. "Burma, as we know it with its present boundaries," wrote Bertil Lintner in 1994, "is a colonial creation rife with internal contradictions and divisions."[76] Indeed, Taylor himself made the same point some two decades on from his 1987 analysis: "Though this flies in the face of the official nationalist historiography of the country, it is no exaggeration to say that the British made modern Myanmar." Only under the British were demarcated "the internal conceptual and administrative structures of the modern state."[77] If, then, the colonial period was decisive in creating the contemporary state, it is to British rule and the consequences flowing from it that analysis should chiefly turn, and not to earlier eras and the procession of indigenous monarchs that dominated them.

For these reasons, the analytical orientation underpinning the next four chapters is a variant of orthodox scholarship, with one modification. First, it endorses the need to look to the past. "The most striking aspect of the Burma debate today is its absence of nuance and its singularly ahistorical nature," wrote Thant Myint-U in 2006.[78] Both are to be avoided. Second, it acknowledges that Britain's colonial adventure was decisive. "The speed with which Burma changed after the arrival of the British was alarming," wrote Aung

San Suu Kyi in 1990.[79] Third, though, it looks back not to 1886, when full imperial rule was imposed, but rather to the 1850s, when dramatic reshaping of a traditional society began to be registered both internally and externally. Inside, annexation of Burma's large southern delta in 1852 and formal creation of a new province within the British Raj in 1862 were key landmarks enabling colonial officials to embark on purposeful exploitation of their new possession. Outside, the opening of the Suez Canal in 1869 transformed the territory's place in the global economy. "During the forty years prior to the outbreak of World War I, Burma was caught up in a maelstrom of worldwide commercial and industrial activity far in excess of anything the country had ever before experienced," writes Cady.[80] As he also notes, the economic dynamic unleashed by these developments was at least as revolutionary as the extensive administrative reforms introduced after 1886. The social impact was enormous.

Chapter 1 examines what colonial officials liked to call the British connexion, focusing on the years from the 1850s to 1948.[81] Its twin themes are political dependence and social disintegration. Chapter 2 investigates the prehistory of modern Myanmar in independent Burma from 1948 to 1988. Its core themes are the drive for dominion sought by the *tatmadaw*, and the dissent triggered among many citizens. Chapter 3 analyzes government by junta from 1988 to 2011. Its central themes are the dictatorship to which the country was subjected for more than two decades, and the deadlock into which it slid at the end of the 1980s and struggled for years thereafter to break. Chapter 4 looks beyond the sham democracy set in place in 2011 to consider domestic political futures. Taking democratization and dialogue as twin themes, it focuses on transitional process, national reconciliation and transitional justice, drawing evidence and insights not only from Myanmar's own history and path dependence, but also from the abundant resources of comparative political science. The intention is not to prescribe, but rather to set out as clearly as possible the challenges the country is likely to face if it embarks on real political reform, as well as options for channeling them in a constructive direction.

Rebuilding a country

The major reason for looking in detail in the first half of the book at historical Burma and contemporary Myanmar is to build a secure foundation for analysis of foreign engagement with this problematic state. Ultimately, that is the core aim of everything written here. In the second half, attention thus turns squarely to outside actors and action, and in particular to debates about global justice that for the past two decades and more have infused much analysis of international politics. Again some contextual work is required through examination of existing external efforts to shape the country's political development. Only when that has been accomplished can fresh possibilities be explored.

Chapter 5 surveys how foreigners have dealt with Myanmar since the late 1980s. The twin poles of debate are inattention and involvement. Taking the major camps in global society, it finds that a case for engagement is made most forcefully in Asia. Practised both by regional powers such as China and India, and by regional bodies such as ASEAN, it is also supported by growing numbers of INGOs. By contrast, a case for isolation is made above all by a bloc of countries led by the US and vociferous activist groups. Citing repression of the country's democratic opposition and violence against ethnic nationalities, the US eventually ratcheted up sanctions to onerous levels. Alongside economic measures, it has also long placed embargoes on the country to outlaw arms sales, visas for senior officials and their families, and many forms of humanitarian assistance. The European Union and other US allies also impose sanctions. Furthermore, almost all companies with visible trade names in western markets have for years declined to do business in and with Myanmar because of negative consumer reaction and a generally difficult business climate.[82] The chapter finds that current strategies have registered only limited success and are now openly disputed among policymakers and activists outside Myanmar, and politicians and citizens inside.

Chapter 6 begins to explore new ways forward by considering the extent to which foreigners are implicated in injustice in Myanmar, and thereby carry corresponding obligations to engage with it. Picking up on debates about global justice where this issue is most fully examined, it investigates duties of both historical injustice and universal justice in an attempt to determine how the demands of justice might be framed in this context. Rejecting radical cosmopolitan approaches as inapplicable in a world of sovereign states located behind generally secure international frontiers, and indeed of sub-state communities committed to vibrant minority identities within those sovereign domains, it also dismisses fully state-centric views leaving citizens entirely at the mercy of their rulers. In between, it sketches a realm of possibility in which outsiders can confront injustice while paying necessary respect to local agency. Crucially, though, it finds that in the Myanmar case analysts of global justice are unable to specify the demands of justice in anything other than very provisional terms.

Chapter 7 thus follows up by examining how individuals prepared to acknowledge mandates of global justice might properly become involved in the political affairs of a jurisdiction other than their own. Specifically, it draws on the plentiful resources of the just war tradition to develop a typology of intervention configured chiefly by discursive and assertive forms, a framework for evaluation, and a procedure for hearing contributions to debate. In this final context it builds on calls for local control surfacing repeatedly within Myanmar to argue that insiders must be given priority, amounting to an effective veto, and that only on this condition can the views of foreigners be considered. Terming the resultant approach interactive intervention, it sketches the implications for Myanmar of this reading of justice across borders.

Chapter 8 completes the analysis by switching from procedural to substantive matters, and investigating the practical contributions outsiders willing to follow the dictates of global justice might make to political change in Myanmar through intercession and investment. Seeking both to listen to local voices as fully as possible and to learn from elsewhere, it surveys current possibilities for external action and considers prospects for political reform. It argues for an expansive notion of investment spreading beyond financial and commercial undertakings to committed and purposeful engagement designed to help build capacity at grassroots levels, boost indigenous agency and expand political space throughout the society. Alongside analysis of the fundamental role played by international aid organizations, it therefore explores the implications of a growing sense that global corporations are critical in triggering the broad social renewal essential to sustainable political reform. It incorporates each of these elements into the case for intercession made here.

While these four chapters all form part of a structured argument for political change in Myanmar, they also engage in set-piece debate with contemporary global issues. Chapter 5 on inattention and involvement evaluates existing policies of engagement and isolation. How successful are these divergent strategies? Chapter 6 on injustice and implication taps into analysis of global justice. How can injustice be confronted in the still strongly statist conditions of today's world? Chapter 7 on intervention and interaction extends just war theory to complex cross-border challenges. When intervention takes so many more forms than simply warfare and is pursued by an increasingly diverse range of actors, how should it be framed? Chapter 8 on intercession and investment focuses on somewhat parallel debates about the aid business and corporate social responsibility to examine what to do in the context of a difficult yet potentially rewarding case for engagement. In toxic circumstances, how might external action properly be fashioned?

Finally, the Conclusion pulls together the threads unraveled in preceding chapters. The core argument acknowledges the strength of opposition claims. Notwithstanding Myanmar's 2011 praetorian transition, the political situation remains dire and necessitates substantial reform. National reconciliation embracing all strands of political opinion and all ethnic groups is also essential. For foreigners, the critical question is how to deliver on the demands of global justice by making an effective contribution to change sought and driven by local people. The chapter thus focuses on how insiders might unmake Myanmar and remake Burma, and how outsiders might support their endeavors. Looking on this basis at strategic issues generated by external engagement with Myanmar and a future Burma's reintegration into international society, it argues for an agenda that can be supported by neighboring states and at the same time chime with global opinion. How that might happen is spelt out in some detail, with both state and non-state actors brought within the analytical frame.

Throughout, the main interest is how principles of global justice might inform a quest to create the multiethnic democratic order that the very notion of Burma has come to symbolize in the hearts and minds of both insiders and outsiders. That Burma, the country many seek to build in place of contemporary Myanmar, could come into being by a multitude of routes and may indeed never be fully realized. Even if it is, it will clearly not be a literal reconstruction, but rather a new creation informed by the changed circumstances of a world that has moved on considerably in the 50 years since Burma last came close to measuring up to the expectations many now have for it.[83] While the concept of Burma redux that brands this analysis conveys a sense of bringing back, reviving or restoring a Burma long written off global maps, it contains no suggestion of strict replication.

Still, however, inspiration can be drawn from the past. On the side of democracy, the link is with those who fought and in many cases died for an ideal in the tumultuous year of 1988, those who challenged Ne Win's autocracy after 1962, those who helped create a rather rickety new state in Burma's long 1950s, and ultimately those who in one way or another made the case for popular rule in struggles against British colonialism and Japanese fascism. Looming iconically over this parade of Burmese democrats is the father-daughter pairing that above all symbolizes the fight: General Aung San, independence hero and prime minister in waiting, assassinated in cabinet at age 32 in July 1947, and Aung San Suu Kyi, 1991 Nobel Peace Laureate, motivating force behind the NLD and moral leader of the nation for two decades, detained under house arrest for a total of 15 years from 1989 to 2010.[84] On the side of ethnic pluralism, the connection is with countless anonymous people who have suffered for years at the hands of a domineering and at times belligerent central state. Although there are no well-known names, no events or dates with wide resonance, and no instantly recognizable images, the need for change in interethnic relations is just as pressing.

Invigorated by the efforts of individuals past and present, this book seeks to contribute to global debate about Myanmar, and about ways forward for those who embrace a desire to wrest it from the iron grip of its military leaders and return it to a Burmese path of democratic development. One animating belief is that much current analysis does not provide a very full or balanced perspective.[85] A 2009 examination of the civilian response to Cyclone Nargis noted "a trend which sees news stories about Myanmar narrowly focus on: the brutality of the military regime, deep divisions between Myanmar people of different religious and ethnic backgrounds; emphasising its isolation within the international community."[86] Later, when ethnic people spoke, they made similar remarks. A young Shan INGO worker put it this way: "Things are not that terrible, though of course they are not good. The media paints the country in a bad light and people fear for our country. The impression given internationally is that it is very risky and dangerous to live and work here; but that is not the case."[87] A young Bamar female journalist said this: "Foreigners always think it is oppressed, not safe, and dark in Myanmar; they are afraid. But when they come here they realise the situation is different; communities are OK and survive."[88] The conclusion reached by the researchers was that "along with the stories of horror and destruction" there must be room to "acknowledge and explore the positive and negative parts of this tragedy."[89] This argument merits wide application.

Perhaps more basic still is a sense that there is simply not enough Burma talk of any kind in today's world. In 2009, one local person had this to say: "It is difficult to access data and facts on Myanmar. External organisations can help out by keeping the issues alive. They need to talk, analyse and discuss what has been written and publicised."[90] The implication is that any news item, op-ed journalism or documentary feature, any academic book, lecture or conference, any parliamentary debate, summit meeting or UN session, any film, novel or play, any painting, sculpture or performance art, indeed any routine daily conversation that makes a sincere attempt to place Myanmar and the concerns it generates at the center of at least part of the world's attention is welcome. That is the spirit in which this book is written.

1

Dependence and disintegration

Contemporary Myanmar cannot be understood by focusing solely on a quarter-century of heightened global attention since pro-democracy protests were crushed by a brutal military machine and a landslide general election victory generated no perceptible change in domestic politics. Rather, the nationwide uprising and violent crackdown witnessed in the middle months of 1988 and the vacuous political contest staged in May 1990 need to be set in the context of what went before: not only 40 years of sovereign Burma from 1948 to 1988, but also the struggle against both imperialism and fascism that preceded independence, the experience of colonial rule under the British, and so on. At the same time, however, it is not necessary to reach all the way back into Burmese history. The decisive break registered by British colonialism makes examination of the past 150 years or so broadly sufficient. This chapter investigates the period of close to a century from the 1850s to 1948 when Britain first established pervasive sway over much of the territory and then asserted full imperial control, seeking ultimately to introduce the economic, political and social reforms required by a liberal power intent on opening its new possession to global markets. Starting with a brief overview of British Burma, it then looks inside the colonial experience at liberal imperialism and the nationalist reaction it provoked. The final section examines Burma in flux in the 1940s, tracing Japanese command from 1942 to 1945 and the dying embers of British Burma from 1945 to 1948. The twin themes, inspired above all by the work of Furnivall, are the political dependence to which Burma was subjected, and the social disintegration that resulted.

British Burma

Britain's entanglement with Burma's final Konbaung Dynasty, which governed land to the east of territory accumulated by the East India Company in the eighteenth and nineteenth centuries, initially took place through exploratory and often defensive moves on the part of company officials. Although a common frontier was established in 1784 when Burma secured control of Arakan and thereby confronted British rule in Chittagong, tensions did not arise until after 1811.[1] Still the imperial preference was for some sort of informal control, rather than outright annexation. "In the eighteenth century, Britain had achieved supremacy in India by diplomacy where feasible, by war when necessary," writes Trager. "During the nineteenth century, British rule was extended to Burma in the same way."[2]

As in India, however, diplomacy eventually did fail and wars fought in 1824–26, 1852 and 1885 saw the full might of the imperial state incrementally gain total control of the territory. In the first engagement, coastal strips of Arakan to the west and Tenasserim to the south were taken. In the second, what the British called Lower Burma around the Irrawaddy Delta and Rangoon fell, placing the entire seaboard under colonial rule. In the third, Upper Burma, including Mandalay, historic heart of the territory and last regal capital, was seized.[3] The expulsion of Burma's final monarch, King Thibaw, and his two principal queens into the long Indian exile captured by Amitav Ghosh in *The Glass Palace* took place on November 29, 1885.[4] On New Year's Day 1886, Britain's complete annexation of Burma was proclaimed by Lord Dufferin, Viceroy of India, acting through Secretary of State Lord Randolph Churchill and by command of Queen-Empress Victoria. Parliamentary delays consequent on the British general election of November-December 1885 meant that formal legislative ratification came in February 1886.

In the early years, Britain's new imperial possessions were not only assembled but also governed piecemeal. At the start, in the mid-1820s, Burmese territory was administered from Penang in Britain's Straits Settlements. Quickly, however, Burma was brought within British India, of which it remained part until 1937. Even then, though, Britain ran its initial holdings as "backwaters of the Bengal presidency" for which it had no particular vision or plan.[5] In this period, Harvey writes, "Burma was governed by post from Calcutta."[6] More purposeful development set in only after the second round of conquest in 1852 and subsequent creation of a unified Indian province of Lower Burma in 1862.[7] Then, particularly after the province filled out to its full extent in 1886, widespread administrative reform took place. For many years, however, this did little more than institutionalize a subordinate position within the British Raj. Rarely was Burma viewed by its imperial masters as anything other than a marginal colonial possession, and never did it wholly erase the stigma of the fateful decision to make it an appendage of British India.

One important consequence was that self-government came slowly to Burma. Only in 1897 was a Legislative Council created with nine nominated members. In 1909 the principle of election was established when the Rangoon Chamber of Commerce was allowed to vote one person on to the 15-member Council. Not until 1923, however, was anything resembling a popular poll introduced. Then under a system of dyarchy the Legislative Council was expanded to 103 members, of whom 79 were elected through household suffrage at age 18 with no gender discrimination, and some aspects of public policy were ceded to local control.[8] Eventually, the Government of Burma Act 1935 provided for the territory to be separated from India on April 1, 1937, and given a distinct colonial status and identity. While ultimate authority in the British Crown Colony of Burma rested with the Governor and, through him, with the Secretary of State for India and Burma located in London, a measure of home rule could henceforth be exercised through a prime minister, cabinet and legislature.[9] In the late 1940s, Furnivall's assessment remained scathing: "the [Legislative] Council had no root among the people …; in reality it represented only the western superstructure divorced from national life."[10]

British rule in Burma is often seen as a vintage case of liberal imperialism. Initially of interest to agents of the East India Company, Burma had a colonial experience driven throughout by a forceful commercial logic. In 1931, Furnivall echoed themes already explored more broadly by J. A. Hobson and V. I. Lenin in holding colonialism in Burma to be a machine driven by economic motives.[11] In 2011, Neil A. Englehart qualified this interpretation by showing that in the first phase of imperialism after 1824 British engagement was so slight that local practices inevitably prevailed, and that in the second phase after 1852 officials drafted from India read that colonial model into Burma. Only after 1886 was a full market orientation imposed, and by then a considerable body of constraining precedent had built up. Furthermore, some globalization impacts registered in Burma in the nineteenth century were largely independent of British action.[12] Indeed, as colonial administrator Maurice Collis wrote in 1956, "it can be argued that the Burmese did not learn anything from us which they could not have learned had they been lucky enough to remain independent."[13] Nevertheless, liberal imperialism did have lasting effects, and was certainly seen as momentous by the socialist officials and intellectuals who dominated Burmese public life for much of the twentieth century.[14] While there were some positive sides, the eventual impact on the society was profoundly negative.

Liberal Burma

Colonialism started to reshape Burma in significant ways as soon as the delta region to the south was incorporated into the British Empire in 1852. Changes made from the 1850s onward built to a "high tide" that for Cady came within years of the imposition of full imperial control in 1886, and lasted for some three decades thereafter.[15] Indeed, from 1890, when pacification was judged complete, to 1920, when the nationalist reaction developed in earnest, the British attained many of the objectives invigorating their colonial adventure.[16] Five stand out. First, they secured a measure of order across the territory. Second, they mapped their new possession. Third, they rationalized administrative structures in its core. Fourth, they set it squarely on the path of economic development and growth. Fifth, they opened it up and located it firmly in global society. While every one of these achievements was ultimately to turn bad, the period from 1890 to 1920, prefigured by an equally successful interlude in Lower Burma from 1852, cast them chiefly in a good light.

Order was enforced in Burma through a series of pacification campaigns designed to impose passivity and security. In 1912 Sir Charles Crosthwaite, Chief Commissioner from March 1887 to December 1890, described "the methods by which a country of wide extent, destitute of roads and covered with dense jungle and forest, in which the only rule had become the misrule of brigands and the only order systematic disorder, was transformed in a few years into a quiet and prosperous State."[17] Formally concluded in 1890, pacification gave way to nothing other than a permanent military occupation that saw villagers especially in the Burman core subjected to an alien form of direct rule that could turn arbitrary and violent when necessary. Vested in the person of the colonial official was a striking amount of power.[18] In a province widely reputed to be the most lawless part of a sprawling Empire, this generated sufficient order for the core purposes of liberal imperialism.

Mapping Burma was a large exercise undertaken through an extension of the Great Trigonometrical Survey of India to the new province.[19] It involved not only negotiating external frontiers, notably with China and imperial France, but also establishing internal boundaries.[20] In a territory containing a variety of ethnic and linguistic groups never before treated as a single political entity, the British solution was to carve out a Burman core and a patchwork periphery of minority groups. For years colonial officials termed the central plains Burma Proper, and the surrounding hill country the Excluded Areas. However, as political institutions were developed and a Legislative Council was established in Burma Proper, the additional designations Ministerial or Parliamentary Burma came into use. Similarly, to reflect their separate status and the schedule of the 1935 Act in which their distinct political arrangements were listed, the Excluded Areas took on the label Scheduled Areas. At the end of the colonial period they were often known as the Frontier Areas. From the start, the divisions created by the British were rough and ready. In Burma Proper lived most of the country's Burman majority population, though some minority communities such as lowland Karens in the Irrawaddy Delta were also present and still others including Mons in the south were slowly being assimilated. In the Excluded Areas lived chiefly a complex mosaic of minority ethnic groups adapted in diverse ways to neighboring civilizations.[21] However, so intermingled were individual and group identities even across lowland and highland areas that in many parts it was difficult to specify ethnic composition with any clarity.[22] Of the two major mapping exercises, the external frontiers turned out to be more durable than the internal boundaries. Although contemporary Myanmar does not have precisely the same borders as were given to colonial Burma in 1886, the differences are small. Internally, by contrast, quite substantial changes have been made. In particular, several new minority ethnic territories have been carved out of what for Britain was Burma Proper.

The colonial attempt to rationalize administrative structures was variegated and partial. Within the complex and essentially artificial entity created in 1886, the British tailored their governance practices to the different physical terrains they encountered. In Burma Proper, traditional authority structures were largely destroyed following the expulsion of Thibaw at the end of 1885. "The monarchy, the nobility, royal agencies, the army, all disappeared, virtually overnight," reports Thant Myint-U. "In the countryside, local ruling families, many of whom had governed their charges for centuries, lost their positions as all hereditary status effectively came to an end."[23] Colonial reform thus stretched down to an unusually local level and village life, long the vibrant core of social organization, was substantially disrupted as customary relations were transformed by imposition of a novel administrative system in Upper Burma in 1887 and Lower Burma in 1891.[24] "The old categories … all dissolved into a new and undifferentiated pool of Burmese peasants."[25] Codification, regulation and rule by paper became widespread.[26] By contrast, in the mountainous Excluded Areas ringing the Burman core, existing authority structures were kept in place and Britain adopted a form of indirect rule through local princes, notables and village chiefs mirroring imperial practice in other parts of Asia. Throughout, many border lands remained "largely forgotten by the colonial state."[27] At the extreme, some almost impenetrable areas were never fully conquered.[28] In these margins of empire, soon after the final British victory in the mid-1880s, Daniel Mason set *The Piano Tuner*.[29]

Perhaps the most stunning change introduced by the British was the rapid economic development witnessed in the early decades of Burmese dependence. The key zone was analyzed by Michael Adas in *The Burma Delta*.[30] Located in Lower Burma and captured by Britain in 1852, this rice frontier was an engine of colonial economic growth throughout the second half of the nineteenth century and well into the twentieth. Adas argues that the British introduced to Burma both the liberal economic framework found across the whole of India, and specific measures designed to accommodate or stimulate capitalist expansion. Considerable infrastructure investment was made, with a national railway system built mainly between 1870 and 1915.[31] Coupled with external changes, notably the opening of the Suez Canal in November 1869, these reforms exposed the enormously fertile yet underdeveloped region of Lower Burma to both domestic and foreign exploitation. One result was a shift to "peasant exports and the growth of the money economy."[32] Another was "economic growth and social change on a scale and at a speed unequaled in Southeast Asian history."[33] In half a century from 1855 to 1905–06, the area of Lower Burma under cultivation increased from 700–800,000 acres to nearly six million, and annual rice exports grew from 162,000 tons to two million. Indeed, in the early part of the twentieth century, economic growth above all in the delta turned Burma into the rice basket of Asia. At the same time, social change saw substantial internal migration chiefly from Upper to Lower Burma, boosting the delta population from roughly one million to more than four million in the half-century from 1852 to 1901.[34] So substantial was the process of relocation in a province of broadly 10 million that "By the end of the nineteenth century the Burman heartland had grown to include most of Lower Burma."[35] The other great imperial industries, never close in size to rice but still important, were mining (mainly oil) and forestry (mainly teak), romanticized by J. H. Williams in *Elephant Bill*.[36]

Finally, Britain took what for generations had been a rather closed and isolated place and exposed it to global society. In this regard, the simple act of making Burma part of British India was decisive, for it immediately created a single colonial market not only for goods and services, but also for labor. At a stroke, Burma was opened for business on many fronts that enabled both entrepreneurs and workers to seek their fortune. Sweeping away traditional restrictions on population movement, fusing the territory with its far larger Indian neighbor, and creating attractive conditions for capitalists from around the world, British officials in the space of a generation or two utterly refashioned much of the land. Small numbers of Europeans settled, with entrepreneurs and traders far outnumbering civil servants and establishing what Cady terms "the tone of European sentiment." "They favored a *laissez faire* policy by government, strong police control, easy money, and abundant Indian labor and were generally opposed to political or economic reforms. Few of them associated with the Burmese people or knew anything about Burma except as a place to do business."[37] Alongside them came many Chinese and still more Indians. By the time of the 1931 census, the last surviving survey of colonial Burma, a population of roughly 14.5 million people included slightly more than 30,000 Europeans and Eurasians, around 200,000 Chinese, and in excess of one million Indians.[38] Major cities were transformed, or more accurately created, and Rangoon was effectively taken out of a Burmese orbit and turned into a global commercial center populated by outsiders, marked by a range of social vices, and linked by sea to a network of ports in Britain and its other Asian colonies. As early as 1901, 51 percent of its inhabitants were Indian.[39] Charney argues that "Rangoon was a mimeograph of dozens of port cities scattered throughout colonial South and Southeast Asia. A person only had to squint to be confused as to whether he or she was standing in Singapore, Penang, Calcutta, or elsewhere."[40] By the late 1930s, no more than about 30 percent of Rangoon residents were Burmese. It was "a foreign city on Burmese soil."[41]

At its peak, liberal imperialism registered broad success in British Burma, introducing changes that enabled the territory to realize much of its hitherto untapped economic potential. In 1964, I. R. Sinai wrote that "As an achievement in settlement and economic development, Lower Burma ranks with Canada or the Argentine as an immense Victorian triumph."[42] In 1967, nationalist scholar Maung Htin Aung noted that in the years from 1890 to 1920 local people were "dazzled" by economic development and the restoration of law and order.[43] In 1974, Adas wrote that "The expansion of the Delta rice industry in the last half of the nineteenth century represents one of the most impressive examples of sustained economic growth under the aegis of a European colonial regime."[44] Built on a base of primary commodity exports, above all rice, oil and teak, Burma was in many ways an impeccable variant of the imperial enterprise celebrated by Niall Ferguson.[45] At the same time, however, colonialism contained problems that ultimately were to trigger its demise, and considerably disrupt the emergence of a stable sovereign state.

Nationalist Burma

In British Burma the core triumphs of liberal imperialism were also the source of its destruction. Indeed, each of the five main domains of colonial achievement down to 1920 came to play a part in the subsequent breakdown of British rule. The imposition of order never succeeded in generating social support for an alien regime. The mapping exercise driven above all by administrative convenience and paying only limited attention to local conditions entrenched intense ethnic cleavages. The rationalization of administrative structures in the heartland destroyed much important social ballast. Economic development and growth set the stage for recession and tension. The opening of the territory to the world made for a virulent nationalist backlash that had strong aftershocks long into the postcolonial period. Looking back on British Burma from the vantage point of 1953, Furnivall wrote that "As a business concern it flourished, but as a human society it collapsed."[46]

Pacification of Burma ensured that state-society relations became "coercion-intensive."[47] Many people, Mary P. Callahan writes, "met the modern state for the first time at the end of a rifle."[48] Notwithstanding British claims to the contrary, violence remained from start to finish a feature of colonial life. Thant Myint-U notes that the effect was not unlike that witnessed in Iraq under US occupation after 2003, with an external power seeking to subdue a subject people very nearly by force alone.[49] On a personal level the imperious nature of much officialdom and the "ornamentalism" imposed on Burma by the British served only to exacerbate the situation.[50] Among colonial administrators, it came in for devastating critique in the "stifling, stultifying world" portrayed by Orwell in *Burmese Days* after five years of service as a sub-divisional officer in the Indian Imperial Police.[51] Among outsiders, it was all too apparent to Cady, who during a Rangoon residence toward the end of the 1930s was appalled by "the aloofness of the average Britisher."[52] Some years after independence, it was recalled in Pye's critique of "The colonialists' casual but ceaseless stress on class, on style, on form, and above all their inflexible self-assurance, even when dead wrong."[53] British officials in the Indian Civil Service were not all detached and uncaring. Maung Maung, president in the dark days of 1988, notes that many were sympathetic characters attuned to local circumstance: "The British bureaucracy was not, therefore, completely devoid of human warmth."[54] Especially in Burma Proper, however, the imperial state created a "peculiarly unrooted colonial regime, one which started (and ended) as a military occupation with little popular support."[55] In Burma, Aung-Thwin argues, Britain imposed "order without meaning."[56]

In mapping their new possession, colonial officials were conscious of ethnic and tribal divisions, and sought to respect established social boundaries. At the same time, however, they are widely held to have tried to set distinct groups in tension. Against this, Thant Myint-U argues that separate administrative practices in core and periphery were a reflection "less of a divide-and-rule policy and more of a cheap and easy policy."[57] Either way, imperial officials created internal conflict between peoples with many centuries of interaction and diverse customs of allegiance. The result, desired or otherwise, was that Britain played a key role in exacerbating racial divisions within the boundaries of the land brought together as Burma, and in sowing the seeds of a nationalist reaction that would destroy colonialism.[58] Christian missionary activity, stunningly successful in the hill country but of marginal impact in the Burman core, had a reinforcing effect by creating fresh religious cleavages.[59] It is no historical accident that early instances of organized resistance to British rule took religious forms. Benedict Anderson notes that the Young Men's Buddhist Association was built in Rangoon in 1906 by "English-reading schoolboys."[60] It was superseded in 1920 by the more populist and effective General Council of Burmese Associations. Inspired by Gandhian resistance in India and led by U Ottama, Burma's first great nationalist hero, a new generation of political monks rose to challenge imperialism.[61]

Precisely because it was variegated and partial, the rationalization of administrative structures undertaken by colonial officials had no more than limited social impact in peripheral parts. In the Burman core, by contrast, the destruction of traditional institutions, both formal and informal, was deeply resented. Furthermore, because Burma remained part of the Raj until 1937, there was always a real sense that it was dependent not only on Britain, but also on India. Elite administrators came from the ICS, and the repressive arm of the state was represented above all by the British Indian Army. While senior positions were taken by Europeans, other ranks were filled frequently by Indians and sometimes by minority ethnic peoples from the periphery. Indeed, until Burma was given separate colonial status, Burman participation in the state was distinctly limited, and in the army virtually non-existent. Before 1937, the Indian Army contained hardly any Burmans, though some Chin, Kachin and other minorities were recruited. Although a British Burma Army was then established, by April 1941 less than 20 percent of a total force of 10,000 men was classified as Burman alongside large Chin, Kachin and Karen contingents. Even in the Territorial Army, formed for homeland defense, only some 35 percent of a force of slightly more than 3,000 men was Burman.[62] In consequence, there was a large gulf between state and society in Burma Proper. Harvey, an ICS official, wrote that "what we gave Burma was not a government but an administration. Political direction, so far as there was any, came from the Indian government, with the British parliament in the dim background. It was a curiously impersonal system."[63] Donnison, ultimately a very senior colonial official, also wrote of the "impersonal administration" that characterized British rule.[64] Reinforcing nationalist divisions were the different paths along which administrative developments in core and periphery moved.[65] The exclusion of Burmans from military service was especially calamitous for, as Thant Myint-U notes, it ate away at national pride and fueled dangerous aspirations. "Soon a powerful ethnic nationalism, based narrowly on the idea of a Buddhist and Burmese-speaking people, one that saw little need to accommodate minority peoples, took root. At the center of this nationalism would be a desire for a new martial spirit."[66]

Rapid introduction of capitalism across Burma, while beneficial for many in the early decades, was in true Marxist fashion perhaps the most destructive force unleashed by British imperialism. In 1953, Fabian socialist Furnivall wrote that "the annexation of Upper Burma in 1886 was a milestone in the process of political and social disintegration."[67] However, it is clear from the work of Adas that the critical move was the mid-1850s opening of the southern rice frontier. What Furnivall termed "Industrial Agriculture" was most fully developed in this part of the territory.[68] From the start capitalism wrought dissolution of traditional modes of life with its wildfire spread, relentless focus on commerce and enterprise, and exploitative orientation. For Simon Schama in 2000, "Burma was a paradigm of plunder."[69] Near the end of the colonial period in 1939, Furnivall was equally critical: "Normally, society is organised for life; the object of Leviathan was to organise it for production."[70] More than once he noted that British Burma placed almost no value on culture and the arts. "Even in Rangoon there was no museum or art gallery, and, one may almost say, no public library."[71] Throughout, he contended that Burma had few resources to counteract social dislocation. Unlike India, for instance, it did not have a caste system for protection against the "solvent influence of western thought and economic forces."[72] Thus, capitalism long promoted a nationalist reaction, and at a time of decaying social order and widespread criminality Furnivall was fully supportive.[73] Moreover, after the First World War Burma's economic miracle turned sour, and the economy was essentially stagnant for the next two decades.[74] Bearing the brunt of downturn were local people, with high rates of disease and mortality taking a heavy toll.[75] In the 1920s and

1930s, the role of Indian Chettiars in lending money with land as collateral and then reaping the benefit through property transfers was especially controversial, even if exaggerated.[76] What had been a vibrant frontier became a zone of land alienation and immiseration, with close to half of all agricultural land owned by non-native absentee landlords.[77] In 1948, Furnivall wrote that "Under Burmese rule the Burman was a poor man in a poor country; now he is a poor man in a comparatively rich country."[78] This part of the problem, explored in *Man, the Wolf of Man*, a novel written in Insein Prison in the early 1940s by Nu, later to become first prime minister of independent Burma, built anti-capitalist sentiment and support for socialism and communism.[79]

Finally, opening Burma to the world had negative impacts on a hitherto rather settled, traditional society. For many years immigration, especially from South Asia, was extensive, and in the late 1920s Rangoon briefly outran New York as a reception center. "For many Indian families," Thant Myint-U notes, "Burma was the first America."[80] When the Depression hit, entrepreneurs and traders from Britain and Europe and moneylenders and laborers from India and China became especially unwelcome.[81] Nobody doubted that Burma had witnessed spectacular economic development. "But the industry was in British hands, the commerce in British, Indian and Chinese hands, and the labour force was largely Indian," Furnivall noted in 1945.[82] In 1940, Virginia Thompson reported that 75 percent of unskilled laborers in Burma's 1,048 factories were Indian, as were 95 percent of unskilled laborers and 70 percent of skilled laborers in Rangoon. "Even the postmen are Indian," she wrote, echoing Furnivall's observation from a decade earlier.[83] To a society isolated by extensive coasts and mountain ranges and with little knowledge of races other than neighboring ethnic groups, rapid economic and social change was profoundly shocking and destabilizing. In the 1930s race riots were often fatal, with serious Indo-Burman violence in 1938–39 resulting in 200 deaths, chiefly of Indian Muslims, and creating much racial bitterness. When construction of the 530-mile Yunnan-Burma Railway started on Christmas Day 1938, fear of Chinese migration spread through society.[84] In 1941, similar concerns animated opposition to the newly-built Burma Road.[85] Fundamental to this tension was the emergence in Burma of what Furnivall famously called a plural society. "It is in the strictest sense a medley, for they mix but do not combine. Each group holds by its own religion, its own culture and language, its own ideas and ways. As individuals they meet, but only in the market-place, in buying and selling."[86] As Taylor later noted, the plural society is more like a firm than a family, its foundation is utilitarian rather than organic, and it develops no common will.[87] The impact on indigenous individuals and communities was especially great. In the spirit of Furnivall, Maureen Aung-Thwin and Thant Myint-U were later to write that "Rangoon became an overseas suburb of Madras, and the average Burmese citizen no longer felt at home in his own house."[88] Later still, Charney held that Rangoon was "not so much a melting pot as a pressure cooker, where Burmese witnessed both the positive and, mostly, the negative consequences, direct and indirect, of the growing colonial economy and foreign rule."[89]

With the exception of a small number of officials of whom Furnivall is the exemplar, colonial administrators were largely heedless of the nationalist reaction building across Burma in the interwar period. Indeed, the arrogance of imperial power comes across very clearly in what Cady called "British preachment."[90] In 1931, Furnivall cited the British Liberal statesman Sir John Simon: "I do not know of any boundary of the British Empire where the Englishman may say with more confidence that here is a place where British enterprise and leadership have brought blessing to a land which needed such guidance and enterprise."[91] In 1932, Sir Harcourt Butler, first Governor of Burma 1923–27, followed up by sharing with readers of *Foreign Affairs* pious sentiments about a still limited experiment in self-government. "It may be hoped that [the Burman] will make the best of the opportunity now generously offered him."[92] In the course of the 1930s, however, many Burmese came to look for more than imperial munificence, and began to take a close interest in compelling regional developments that might aid their cause.

Burma in flux

For almost all of the colonial period, the part of Asia with the greatest impact on Burmese political development was India. Joined at the hip until 1937, and closely associated for the decade thereafter, India and Burma inevitably experienced aspects of a common political fate. From the closing months of the First World War onward, however, shared features became ever less evident and clear differences started to emerge. In July 1918, the British Government's Montagu-Chelmsford Report proposed to reward India's substantial wartime contribution with moves toward self-rule enacted in the Government of India Act 1919. At the same time, however, the report found the Burmese to be "another race in another stage of political development," and declined to endorse parallel moves.[93] Such obvious discrimination, allied with growing economic problems and smoldering racial tension, ensured that the province would take a new path. For Cady, "World War I clearly constituted … a dividing point in Burma's political history."[94] An early marker was student protest in Rangoon in 1920 that was to reverberate down the decades. Although reforms in 1922–23 were in many respects substantial, prompting Harvey two decades later to identify 1923 as "the parting of the ways," they still did not match change introduced in India.[95] As a result, nationalist reaction grew throughout the 1920s, and with the Depression became even stronger in the 1930s. In 1930–32, a peasant rebellion led by millenarian monk Saya San resulted in the arrest or capture of 9,000 rebels, the death or wounding of 3,000, and the conviction and hanging of 350.[96] Across the decade, the *Dobama Asiayone* (We Burmans Association) fed student and worker protest.[97] Formed around 1930, it encouraged members to add the honorific *thakin* (master) to indigenous names to ridicule British official insistence on formal modes of address.[98] In 1938, the *Dobama* leadership at Rangoon University and among local labor organizations led a year of revolution to mark the year 1300 in the Burmese calendar.[99]

As an increasingly militant stance prompted a search beyond India for vanguard action, Burmese leaders' gaze turned to other parts of Asia. Eventually, reactive nationalism fed into Japanese recruitment of a group of young radicals. Led by Aung San, they enacted a ritual of loyalty in Bangkok in late December 1941 that was later to stoke the legend of "the famous Thirty Comrades, the Knights of the Round Table of Burmese independence and its evergreen heroes."[100] This group formed the core of a Burma Independence Army that fought alongside the Japanese in 1942 and helped in a matter of months to destroy the colonial state and expel British officials and armed forces from most of the territory. When the Second World War enveloped Burma, Rangoon fell on March 9 and Mandalay was taken on May 2, signaling Japanese control of the entire colony. In these months of conquest there were dark sides to BIA action, for as the overwhelmingly Burman force moved northward together with the invading Japanese, Indians and Chinese were singled out for persecution. Indigenous racial conflicts that were to leave deep scars also erupted, notably between spreading Burman forces and lowland Karen communities.[101] By contrast, Burma's hill country was scarcely touched by the major battles of 1942. Thereafter, the bewildering array of battalions, forces and levies raised by the British in the frontier regions, notably through the Special Operations Executive and other clandestine services and paramilitary bodies, consistently fought on the side of the Allies.[102]

On August 1, 1943, Burma was awarded a form of independence that turned out to be both illusory and enticing. While offering little autonomy under *Adipati* Ba Maw, it whetted the appetite for full control.[103] As vicious Japanese dominion became ever more intolerable and Allied success in regaining control from the north mounted, nationalist leaders thus sought not to recreate the situation from which Japan had released them, but rather to eliminate all forms of imperial rule. Under the leadership of Aung San and the storied group of Thirty Comrades, the BIA and succeeding forces, the Burma Defence Army, the Burma National Army and the Patriotic Burmese Forces, while by no means wholly Burman, were vibrant expressions of nationalist fervor. To the British they were deeply suspect for having fought alongside the Imperial Japanese Army in 1942, served under the Japanese military regime from 1942 to 1945, and embraced the ideal of the Greater East Asian Co-Prosperity Sphere.[104] Nevertheless, when on March 27, 1945 Aung San led a BNA revolt and joined the Allies in driving the Japanese from Burma, the stage was set for the endgame of colonial rule.[105] At the close of the "longest war," Burma was recaptured by forces marshaled outside the territory in India, inside it by services active in the hill country, and within the occupation itself by Burmese resistance forces and the BNA contingents that followed Aung San into rebellion.[106] Japan suffered a devastating defeat that in little more than three years brought death to 180,000 of the 305,000 soldiers who served in Burma.[107]

When thoughts turned to the postwar order, the colonial division between Ministerial Burma and the Scheduled Areas surfaced as a critical issue. In May 1945 a British White Paper, modeled on a November 1944 Conservative Party Blue Print, floated a two-Burma principle.[108] Envisaging a general election by December 9, 1948, it provided for a constitution to be drawn up thereafter, and foresaw the Scheduled Areas gaining separate administration until such time as they clearly expressed a desire to join Burma. In July 1945 an army reorganization agreed by Aung San and the British similarly adopted a two-wing solution.[109] Indeed, in every early debate about the independence most knew was coming, a touchstone of colonial policy was protection of the minority peoples who had remained loyal to the British when Japan overran the territory in 1942. Against this, Burman leaders "began from the assumption that Burma was one nation with a multiplicity of ethnic and linguistic groups that had been artificially separated from the Burmans by British rule."[110] In May 1946 the Anti-Fascist People's Freedom League, heir to a united front Anti-Fascist Organization formed in August 1944, seized the initiative by calling for "a conference of representatives of all the peoples — namely, Burmese, Shans, Karennis, Kachins, Chins, etc., for the purpose of discussing freely the establishment of a Union of Burma."[111] Moreover, in the wake of a Japanese occupation that forced the colonial government into exile in Simla, India, there was little public sympathy for the returning British and as the Right Reverend George Appleton, Anglican Archdeacon of Rangoon 1943–46, wrote in 1947 "a deep distrust of our motives."[112] In a context of heightened nationalism set against a backdrop of exploding communal tension in India and other parts of Asia, *tats*, or pocket armies, were created to secure independence and gain partisan advantage.[113] Preeminent among them was Aung San's People's Volunteer Organization, formed in November 1945.

One result was a far more condensed independence schedule than envisaged by Britain.[114] Another was a set of accords signed by the British government, AFPFL leaders and representatives of minority peoples. In London on January 27, 1947 British Prime Minister Clement Attlee and AFPFL President Aung San agreed that independence would take place within a year. In Panglong in the Shan States less than three weeks later on February 12, Aung San joined representatives of the Shan, Kachin and Chin peoples to sign a brief document formally recognizing some of the autonomy claims of these three minorities.[115] Although Aung San and six cabinet ministers were then assassinated on July 19, 1947 in "one of the most dastardly political crimes of modern times," progress toward independence continued.[116] In the constitution approved by a constituent assembly on September 24, 1947 and effective on British withdrawal, Shan, Kachin, Karen and Karenni (from 1951 Kayah) States were fully acknowledged, allowed enhanced representation in Rangoon, accorded devolved powers within their localities, and given the option of secession a minimum of 10 years later.[117] A Special Division of the Chins was also formed. To secure passage of the constitution, incoming AFPFL leader Nu made a personal pledge to the minority peoples regarding future fair dealings.[118] Finally, in an agreement signed by Attlee and Prime Minister designate Nu in London on October 17, 1947, the transfer of sovereignty was set for January 4, 1948. Secession clauses notwithstanding, the emphasis was now increasingly on the Union of Burma, rather than on separate status for non-Burman peoples. This was simultaneously a clear triumph for nationalist leaders, and a potential source of deep controversy after independence.[119]

In the years from 1945 to 1948, nationalism was often Burmese rather than strictly and narrowly Burman. Appealing to distaste for occupation, whether British or Japanese, it focused on issues bringing people together, instead of tensions driving them apart.[120] In this way it sought to build a platform from which Burman leaders could reach out to other ethnic groups. However, nested within this broad and inclusive nationalism were more focused and exclusive dynamics. Indeed, present by the end of the colonial period and aggravated by warfare sweeping the land in its sunset phase was a series of militant ethnic nationalisms. Prominent among them was a Burman attempt to reassert identity and dominion, with a strong tendency to look back to a glorious monoethnic past rather than forward to a complex multiethnic future. This nationalism, though submerged in the prospect of imminent colonial withdrawal once the Second World War ended, was a critical British bequest to the sovereign state.[121] Equally present throughout was a series of minority ethnic identities that would emerge to challenge Burman dominion in the postcolonial years.

The institutional landscape in which these forces played out was strikingly empty. For Furnivall, a central theme was always the dissolution of local institutions and the social dislocation that resulted. Thant Myint-U also places institutional weakness alongside ethnic nationalism as a key colonial legacy. The British destroyed much, but put little of lasting value in its place. "With the exception of the Sangha [Buddhist monkhood], one is hard pressed to identify any supra-local institution which carried over from pre-colonial through colonial times."[122] In contrast to the Thai case, where imperial rule was never fully imposed, established institutions like the monarchy were not maintained to provide equilibrium and continuity in turbulent times. By comparison with the British imperial record in other parts of Asia, such as Ceylon, India and Malaya, colonial structures in the army, police, civil service and judiciary were "singularly fragile," with a history of barely 50 years in the Burman core.[123] They were largely brushed aside by the Japanese in 1942. In consequence, one of the most potent legacies of British rule was recourse to violence to subdue a restive population, overt during pacification campaigns but always present.

As Burma moved from dependence to sovereignty in the late 1940s, the disintegration long identified by Furnivall as the determining factor for its future prospects shifted to center stage. Britain, he contended in 1931, had boxed in anarchic capitalism in Burma through an application of force assembled outside the territory, building not a steel frame for a social order, but rather steel bars for an economic system.[124] His own paternalistic proposal of transitional foreign mentorship was already outdated by the time it was made in the late 1940s, and power passed decisively into the hands of indigenous leaders.[125] The central task facing them in January 1948 was to build both the nation and the state so visibly absent by the twilight of the colonial period.

2

Dominion and dissent

At 4:20 on the morning of January 4, 1948, amid fanfare and expectation, Burma threw off the dependence that for decades had been its political condition and confronted the world as a sovereign state. Dominion no longer rested in British hands or Japanese, and the country was not even a member of the British Commonwealth. In formal political terms, the future was now a matter for Burmese people alone to determine. At the same time, however, the new Union of Burma was ravaged not only by warfare conducted on its territory in brutal and devastating campaigns that saw first Japan drive out Britain and then Britain evict Japan, but also by social disintegration occasioned by colonialism and capitalism. The task facing political leaders was thus substantial and complex, for as well as guiding the ship of state they needed to build a nation to provide ballast and stability. This chapter examines the 40 years from 1948 to 1988 that saw them largely fail on both counts. It looks first at democratic Burma from 1948 to 1962, second at revolutionary Burma from 1962 to 1974, third at socialist Burma from 1974 to 1988, and finally at Burma in revolt in the middle months of 1988. It argues that the campaign for dominion that properly exercised the political class was pursued so aggressively by governing elites that far from unifying the nation in the state, it ultimately had the opposite effect of provoking widespread dissent and triggering both regime collapse and still greater social dislocation.

Democratic Burma

At the start of its democratic journey, Burma was identified as one of the most promising postcolonial states in Asia with good political and legal institutions, plentiful natural resources, solid infrastructure, and excellent human capital.[1] In April 1948, Thompson's conclusion to a balanced survey was upbeat: "Storm clouds undoubtedly hang on Burma's horizon, but at the moment they seem neither very near nor very black."[2] In 1965, Nash set a detailed analysis of village life against a backdrop of the country's great "potential of success."[3] In 1979, William L. Scully and Frank N. Trager wrote of "This once potential Camelot."[4] However, the destructive effects of warfare that leveled much of the country, plus partisan tension expressed tragically in the assassination of wartime leader and independence hero Aung San, indicated that development was always going to be difficult.[5] At a superficial level, AFPFL Prime Minister Nu, student protester in the 1930s and nationalist leader in the 1940s, could not hope to fill the void.[6] As Donnison put it in 1956, Aung San "alone was able to unite his people, speak for them, and give expression to their spirit as no one else had done since the days of Alaungpaya."[7] Tinker wrote in similar terms.[8] At a deeper level Burma, a new country of some 17 million people, simply faced enormous political, economic and social challenges. In April 1947, a correspondent for *The Times* predicted that "Only some form of dictatorship, either of a man or a party, can bring order to Burma and maintain it."[9] In 1949 Furnivall wrote that, "the members of the new Government were just ordinary men, bubbling over with ideas and good intentions, but representative of modern Burma under British rule and with the inevitable limitations of their education and environment."[10]

In actual fact it took fewer than three months for the new state to be threatened by what Maung Maung called an "epidemic of insurrections," and less than six months for it to become embroiled in civil conflict.[11] In key respects this was merely an extension of colonial experience, marked throughout by violence and in the final years by a proliferation of *tats*. Extensive militarization in the Second World War left Burma awash with arms and greatly compounded the problem, making nascent democratic authority subject to contestation on a broad front. By the time Aung San was killed, even the PVO had veered toward communism and away from the more moderate position taken by AFPFL leaders. Clearly not everything was bleak for Burma's emergent establishment, and across much of the land local militias played critical roles not in challenging the state, but rather in defending it. Indeed, in many places government-sponsored "peace guerrillas" were agents of order.[12] Nevertheless, from the moment of independence two major internal challenges threatened destruction. One was communist mobilization with parallels in other parts of postcolonial Asia. The other was ethnic rebellion, also found elsewhere but taking a notably complex form in Burma.[13]

The first major revolt flourished an ideological banner. In March 1946 the important CPB split into Red and White Flag factions, and in July of the same year Red Flag leaders went underground to launch an insurgency.

However, the more potent CPB challenge came at the end of March 1948, when the White Flag faction also moved into insurrection. From mid-1948, Muslim Arakanese, Karen, Kachin and Mon forces also fomented rebellion, with the Karen National Defense Organization in the vanguard.[14] In 1948–49 it succeeded in capturing key territory and communications facilities. At the end of January 1949 it even closed in on the capital city, and Nu was said derisively to head only the "Rangoon government."[15] Furthermore, army mutinies feeding many insurgencies depleted military forces charged with defending the young democracy. Callahan writes that "by the time Gen. Ne Win assumed the position of armed forces commander in chief in February 1949, he commanded fewer than two thousand troops, many of whom were of questionable reliability."[16] While not every insurrection posed a mortal threat, some did. Evaluating the situation in August 1949, Furnivall argued that "There is little danger that Burma will go Communist, but great danger that it may go to pieces."[17]

During the course of 1949 and into 1950, however, government units and local leaders managed to turn the tide on the fragmentary and divided forces they faced.[18] "Rebel bands are still at large in the hills, but they do not now threaten to disrupt the Union," wrote Edward M. Law Yone and David G. Mandelbaum in October 1950.[19] They argued that Burma was poised to become "a model of reconstruction in southern Asia."[20] Callahan notes that across much of the nation "alliances between center and upcountry leaders to pacify the countryside led to accommodational processes that began bringing more and more rural and local politicos into Rangoon on a regular basis."[21] The stage was apparently set for a more assured period of political and institutional consolidation. Norman Lewis's *Golden Earth*, a 1952 travelogue, reports on this moment in Burmese history.[22]

Indeed, as the 1950s unfolded, many parts of the state registered significant progress. Tolerably fair general elections were held in 1947, 1951–52, 1956 and 1960. Parliaments assembled and governments were formed.[23] A state bureaucracy was rebuilt and an indigenous judiciary put in place. In reaction to the perceived ravages of liberal imperialism, efforts to construct the kind of social democracy envisaged by Aung San and other independence leaders were made through nationalization of some of the economy, creation of a string of government agencies, and installation of cooperatives in urban and rural areas.[24] In many policy domains, state functions were revived and set to work. Growth eventually took the economy back to prewar levels of activity, and education and social sectors experienced expansion. A Burmese welfare state began to emerge.[25] Civil society developed through a vibrant associational culture.[26] Village life picked up, and essential land reforms were implemented.[27] Surveying the scene in 1953, Maung Maung pointed to encouraging factors associated with Nu's August 1952 *pyidawtha* (happy land) program of welfare reforms.[28] In 1956, Janet Welsh testified to the "astounding progress" registered by Nu's AFPFL government.[29] In 1957, Tinker argued that "Of the nations of South East Asia Burma offers the most hope for the eventual foundation of a successful social democracy in the years that are to come."[30]

However, behind this façade of progress the harsh reality was that the political and administrative spheres both functioned poorly, and each was marked by corruption and popular distrust.[31] Furthermore, over time party and government structures became increasingly divided, and constantly exhibited only limited capacity to perform routine functions.[32] Local implantation of political parties remained haphazard.[33] In peripheral parts, ethnic claims made chiefly by Karen leaders in the late 1940s came to equal prominence elsewhere in the mid-1950s.[34] In particular, both Arakan on the western seaboard and Shan State in eastern uplands bordering China, Laos and Thailand, were riven with demands for either autonomy or secession.[35] Hostility to Burmanization policies associated with the AFPFL often played a key part. Against upbeat assessments made by other contemporary writers, Furnivall wrote that it was a miracle Burma survived down to 1953, and Cady's conclusion was little different.[36] Planning a fieldtrip in the closing months of 1957, Pye sensed that the country was "entering its time of crisis," and on the ground a few months later found people "anxious to talk politics, to express their concerns with the fate of their land."[37] At the end of 1958, when political problems were all too visible, John H. Badgley held that Burma's constitution was in danger of collapsing under the pressure of rapid change, and that control could pass to "the most unified social element." His evaluation was that "Only the military and the Communists now have such national-oriented, disciplined groups."[38]

In fact, the military was already in much the stronger position, notably as a result of the historical accident that saw part of the Cold War played out on Burmese territory in the wake of China's October 1949 Revolution.[39] Although Mao Zedong's victorious Red Army drove most of Chiang Kai-shek's nationalist troops to Taiwan, a large contingent trapped in southwestern Yunnan Province in 1951 took refuge across the border in Shan and Kachin States. As fears of communist contagion mounted, US technical advisers employed by the Central Intelligence Agency offered support. Formal Burmese complaints to the UN in 1953 were ineffectual.[40] In consequence, the Nu government sought urgently to create a force capable of protecting Burma's borders and securing national sovereignty. Callahan sees this as the key factor in setting the stage for *tatmadaw* rule. Noting that India, Malaysia and the Philippines had similar experiences of colonialism, war and independence, she asks why only Burma was left with ingrained military control. Her answer is that "As the Cold War threatened to swallow up Burma, military and civilian leaders had few choices but to reinvigorate and redeploy the colonial security apparatus to hold together a disintegrating country during the formative period of postcolonial state transformation."[41]

Gradually the *tatmadaw* positioned itself as the critical institution in the state, and built a cohesive core group dedicated to defense of the nation. "Over the 1950s the Burma Army turned itself from a small politicized and factionalized hybrid force, half British and half Japanese by training, into a more professional and more coherent military machine, loyal only to itself," writes Thant Myint-U.[42] One key step was incorporation of many *tats*, "village defense units, forest guards, power station guards, and in a few places, the Union Military Police," into the *tatmadaw*.[43] Another was the creation of a solidly Burman military. With time, a Cold War effect became decisive. For Callahan, "The military solution to internal crises crowded out other potential state reformers, turning officers into state builders and citizens into threats and — more characteristically — enemies."[44] Moreover, as the *tatmadaw* began to secure both the state and its own interests, it started to branch out. In 1951, a Defence Services Institute was set up to run canteens for servicemen. Broadly, its early functions were similar to those of the Navy, Army and Air Force Institutes formed by the British government in 1921 to supply goods, provide catering facilities and meet troops' recreational needs. As early as May 1952 the DSI opened a retail store in Rangoon, however, and outlets in Mandalay and elsewhere followed. In the late 1950s, it expanded into major economic sectors and was often the dominant actor, operating banks, shipping lines and a range of import-export businesses. As these agencies were exempt from tax, they were both competitive and profitable.[45]

In parallel with this commercial activity, military leaders sought to deepen their social engagement. Internally, the Directorate of Psychological Warfare, formed in 1952, published a contemptuous analysis of Burmese people as apathetic, prone to manipulation and in need of reshaping.[46] Some molding was launched through required use of Burmese in schools and parliament, Burman dominance of newspapers and film, and internal migration by the majority ethnic group.[47] The Directorate also led efforts to inoculate the people against communism. "Billboards in conspicuous places have proclaimed the danger in which Buddhism finds itself, over one million pamphlets in more than half a dozen languages have pointed to communist excesses and the newspapers have continually reported mass meetings called to denounce atheistic communism," reported Fred von der Mehden in 1960.[48] In addition, the military elite openly criticized the 1947 constitution. Externally, a 1955 *tatmadaw* report, "Yugoslavia: Similarity with Burma," noted many shared features in two artificial nations, including intensive wartime struggle, complex ethnic composition and strategic location in the shadow of Cold War powers.[49] Senior generals also expressed frank admiration for tough militaries in, for instance, Israel and Pakistan. They were "frequently courted by British, Yugoslav, Czech, and U.S. arms manufacturers and dealers, who paid for many of the purchasing and study missions that inspired army leaders to expand military influence in domestic, nonsecurity realms."[50]

Direct political impacts of *tatmadaw* emergence as the preeminent force within a nation subject to widespread institutional destruction during the colonial era began to be felt little more than 10 years after independence. In September 1958, personal conflict split the governing AFPFL.[51] Maung Htin Aung, then Rector of Rangoon University, later put it this way: "The monster that really killed the parliamentary democracy was the bitter acrimony that discoloured the struggle for power between the two factions of the broken A.F.P.F.L."[52] In consequence, Ne Win, chief of staff of a *tatmadaw* of some 70,000 men, served as prime minister for 18 months from October 1958 to April 1960 with a mission to restore law and order and revive the country's still young democracy.[53] This intervention, though sometimes identified as the first coup against Burmese democracy, was technically constitutional. At the time, strenuous attempts were made to distinguish it from praetorian government in other parts of Asia. "It should be borne in mind that the armed forces in Burma have achieved a most respected position," wrote Trager in January 1959. "Unlike in Pakistan and Thailand, the military leaders have never evidenced dictatorial ambitions."[54]

Nevertheless, this experience further bolstered the army's position within both state and society, largely because of the efficient and effective work undertaken during its interregnum. "The caretaker administration has set standards of competence and integrity that the politicians will have to try to live up to if they are to win the support of the educated public (including the military)," noted Richard Butwell in February 1960, just before the return to party government. He judged that it was "unquestionably likely that for several months and probably some years to come decisions will partly be made by the politicians on the basis of how they will be received in top military circles."[55]

However, a subsequent coup, performed on March 2, 1962 with the loss of a single life, removed that likelihood by setting the *tatmadaw* in total control of national politics. This coup was entirely unconstitutional. One trigger was Nu's religious commitment, which saw him win the February 1960 general election on a promise to make Buddhism the state religion, and pass the relevant legislation in August 1961.[56] Several observers argued that Nu's growing immersion in Buddhism rendered him unfit for political leadership.[57] A second trigger was a concomitant drift away from socialism, long axiomatic for the entire political class. A third was fear of national disintegration, generated notably by a "federal seminar" convened by Nu to discuss with Kayah and Shan representatives ways forward for a unified state facing federalist pressures. Airing much criticism of the *tatmadaw*, the forum prompted Ne Win to seize power, abrogate the 1947 constitution, and rule by decree.[58]

Essential to the opening provided to the military was perceived economic failure, and a pervasive sense that despite a plethora of plans the country was failing to modernize.[59] In 2009, Charney had no hesitation in characterizing Nu's Burma as "from the start an economic nightmare."[60] In fact, annual growth of 5.3 percent for the 14 years of the democratic period was very respectable. Indeed, Myat Thein argues that in comparison with Indonesia, the Philippines and Thailand, Burma was possibly the "front runner" in 1962.[61] However, such progress did not enable an expanding population even to regain the standard of living experienced under the British, for while total GDP moved above prewar levels, per capita GDP in 1961–62 was still 14 percent below the 1938–39 figure.[62] Also contentious were the trappings of modernization. In 1952–53, the presence of no more than a few dozen American advisers became controversial when clandestine CIA activity in the eastern borderlands suggested that the era of foreign control was not yet over.[63] Moreover, the good lives the advisers were able to lead symbolized a growing gulf between elite and mass and cast the AFPFL as insufficiently nationalistic.[64] In March 1953, the Nu government thus announced that US assistance would end within months. Later, under Ne Win's caretaker administration, the contracts of all remaining advisers were abruptly terminated.[65]

By the late 1950s Burmese soldiers viewed themselves as state builders in three key respects. First, it was their task to secure the territorial integrity of the nation. Second, it fell to them to shape the institutions of government. Third, by them alone could the patriotic spirit of the people be cultivated.[66] Ironically, military leaders at the same time constructed not only a state within a state, but also a society within a society. To this day, parallel structures of military hospitals, schools and welfare services exist across the country, and can be readily observed in major cities. Also by the late 1950s an increasingly Burman nationalism had come to the fore, promoted by Ne Win's attempt to assert central control and curtail splittist tendencies. Always the greatest failing of Burmese democracy under Nu is judged to be its failure to engender national unity.[67] In 2009, Callahan drew a contrast with Indonesia: "[President] Sukarno spent the 1950s assiduously travelling the archipelago to forge a common national identity while the multi-ethnic uprising against the Dutch was still fresh in living memory.... The problem of bridging historically exacerbated ethnic and religious differences was never a priority for the Nu government."[68] Rather, the route taken in Burma was projection of an aggressively Burman identity to tie together a manufactured nation. Driving it was the fight for dominion that emerged among Burman leaders toward the end of the colonial period. This found its fullest expression in the *tatmadaw*, which not only led the independence struggle, but also held the country together in the difficult early years of *de jure* sovereignty and *de facto* disintegration.

Taking the long view, Burma's 14-year democratic interlude from 1948 to 1962 is atypical, and debate continues about whether contemporary opposition leaders can learn from it.[69] That democracy collapsed in 1962 was the result of historical contingency, much of which originated outside Burma. No less decisive for that, it provided an opening for the militaristic, nationalistic and centralizing state formed in the 1960s and still in place today. In 1950, Nu wrote a play entitled *The People Win Through* to appeal for peace and democracy in a strife-torn land.[70] By the end of Burma's long 1950s, however, it was the military that had the upper hand.

Revolutionary Burma

The March 1962 coup saw an overtly authoritarian 18-member Revolutionary Council, headed by "Big Number One" Ne Win, dismantle the democracy created jointly in the late 1940s by outgoing British officials and the incoming AFPFL government.[71] Nu and other ministers who had won a clear majority at the 1960 general election were imprisoned, several Shan leaders were incarcerated, and moves to censor all opposition were made.[72] Heartbreaking accounts of those bleak days, written from the perspective of ethnic leaders subject to centralizing control, can be found in Inge Sargent, *Twilight over Burma*, Patricia W. Elliott, *The White Umbrella*, and Sao Sanda, *The Moon Princess*.[73]

Initially, the coup plotters were broadly given the benefit of the doubt. Many years later, Maung Maung reported that "People heard the announcement without surprise, for they had for some time been expecting, almost hoping for, a change."[74] From a man who spent a lifetime working for Ne Win, this evaluation comes as no surprise. Yet it was also the assessment of contemporary scholars. Badgley wrote that the coup was greeted with "reserved approval by most articulate Burmese." The caretaker regime of 1958–60 was generally felt to have done a decent job, the new leaders were "well-known and respected for their integrity," and the Nu government had lost its way.[75] Trager, who visited Burma at the end of March 1962, concurs: "there seemed to be little surface or undersurface expression of hostility to the coup. If anything, there was a feeling of relief: at least the slide downward would be stopped."[76] A little later, David W. Chang noted that the domestic situation was similar to that which had generated military coups in Pakistan and South Korea in the late 1950s and early 1960s.[77] In some circumstances, he argued, "The coup is a necessary link in the process of modernization."[78]

Soon, however, Burma's RC proved to have a radical agenda congruent with extreme variants of left-wing nationalist sentiment formed during the independence struggle. Buddhism's status as state religion was quickly rescinded, and on April 30, 1962 the RC promulgated a vague *Burmese Way to Socialism*.[79] Although federal features survived in the peripheral patchwork of ethnic nationality states, power rapidly shifted to a control system of Security and Administration Committees headed by military commanders and reaching to ward and village level.[80] As Cady notes, "Organizationally, Ne Win's government was patterned on Eastern European practices; ideologically it borrowed from the People's Republic of China."[81]

On July 7, 1962 the RC revealed clear repressive intent by killing dozens of protesting and then rioting Rangoon University students, and detonating the students' union building on campus.[82] In the same month it also formed a Burma Socialist Programme Party (or *Lanzin* Party) to exercise single-party rule under RC guidance and signal a formal break with capitalism.[83] In 1962–63, real attempts were made to nationalize major business enterprises. In March 1963, a *New York Times* article reported on "total socialism in Burma."[84] Less than 12 months later, Josef Silverstein noted that "experiments and modifications continued as the drive to socialize the economy pressed blindly ahead and social tensions and terror mounted as efforts to end insurgency and disunity failed."[85] Looking back from 2006, Thant Myint-U wrote that "With the racetrack shut, the beauty pageants over, jobs lost, scholarship opportunities gone, and only beer from the People's Brewery and Distillery left to drink, it was as if someone had just turned off the lights on a chaotic and often corrupt but nevertheless vibrant and competitive society."[86]

From the outset the new politico-military elite was ardently nationalistic, with close ties to agrarian Buddhist Burmans forming the core of a *tatmadaw* of just over 100,000 men, and a "proclivity ... to encourage a Burmese way of life [that] suggests a revulsion from western ways."[87] In 1962, Ford, Fulbright and Asia Foundation activities were terminated.[88] In 1963–64, an estimated 300,000 Indians fled following nationalization of their small trading and manufacturing concerns.[89] Many Chinese and Pakistanis also left.[90] It was not unlike President Idi Amin's expulsion of Ugandan Asians in 1972.[91] Serious race riots, directed mostly at the remaining Chinese community, scarred Rangoon in June-July 1967. Abandoning political discussions with ethnic nationality leaders in 1963–64 and focusing on military responses to insurgency, the RC at the end of the 1960s unleashed a "four cuts" strategy designed to eliminate the supply of food, funds, intelligence and recruits from villagers to militias.[92]

Policies of aggressive autarky ensured that the country quickly turned in on itself. Large-scale joint ventures with private foreign firms ended in January 1965 when the Burma Corporation and Burma Unilever were nationalized. Supplementing a 1964 ban on English-medium instruction at all levels of the education system, elite private schools were taken into public ownership in April 1965, and libraries run by India, Russia, the UK and the US were closed in September 1965. Visas for western tourists were limited to a transit time of 24 hours, and visitors rarely made trips beyond Rangoon.[93] In early 1965, Badgley noted that the colonial legacy had been largely obliterated. "The men of commerce, the civil service, the law schools and Sandhurst were the source of support and means of rule for the British colonialists, as well as the AFPFL. Such men govern India and Pakistan today. But in Burma we are witnessing the recreation of a new Burman dynasty."[94] Tinker's optimism entirely evaporated: "Burma in 1966 is a hermit land... While the storm blows in South-East Asia, Burma closes the door and hopes that one day the sun will shine."[95]

Soon the dominant issue was economic calamity induced by the command economy. The critical rice sector was placed under strict control. While collectivization programs were limited, leaving production mainly in private hands, trade nationalization was extensive, compelling farmers to sell their entire marketable surplus to the state through a low-price procurement system. The intention was to channel significant profits from rice exports into broad-based modernization through an import substitution industrialization policy.[96] However, ideological rigidity combined with rank incompetence and a measure of official greed and corruption made the outcome quite different. Never was full control established, and where it was farmers had little incentive to boost yields.[97] Exports thus collapsed from more than 1.4 million tons in 1963–64 to fewer than 0.4 million tons in 1967–68. After a brief revival, they fell still further to just over 0.1 million tons in 1973–74.[98] The decline was 72 percent in four years, and 93 percent in 10 years. What had been a 28 percent share of the global rice trade in the early 1950s shrank to 2 percent in 1970.[99] At the same time, Burma slipped from high-quality to low-quality shipments. In place of booming official exports came restricted production, illegal domestic and cross-border trade, hoarding and waste. Peter John Perry writes that "export rice was the great failure of Ne Win's economic policy."[100] Burma's other two major sectors, minerals and timber, fared less badly, but were still major disappointments. Moreover, industrialization never took off, and only inefficient state-owned enterprises littered the landscape.[101]

Yet greater problems were experienced in meeting people's core needs. Noting that the regime's record on the production side was "dismal," Perry argues that "When it comes to distribution catastrophe is a more appropriate word."[102] Informal markets in basic goods spread rapidly as problems of allocation through people's stores mounted. Shortages became legion and by the mid-1960s Trade Corporation 23, code for a thriving black market covering both domestic and imported goods, was a standard feature of daily life.[103] Indeed, here and in the unregulated small business and transportation sectors was the core of the real economy.[104] Riots were reported in 20 towns in 1968, and further disturbances followed.[105] The result was never anything more than nominally socialist. Rather, the system became a harshly authoritarian, highly centralized and deeply dysfunctional form of state capitalism.[106] Moreover, the plentiful information flows and invisible-hand signaling mechanisms generated by capitalism rarely functioned because of bureaucratic ineptitude and fear of sending bad news up the government hierarchy. The situation was not unlike that reached in East-Central Europe by the 1980s, with rigid ideology, dull centralization and systemic incapacity combining to smother human innovation and energy.

Already at the end of 1965 Ne Win stated publicly that the economy was "in a mess." "If Burma were not a country with an abundance of food we would be starving."[107] Landless agricultural laborers, long some 30–40 percent of rural households, were very badly affected.[108] However, the regime ascribed visible shortfalls to teething problems, and decreed no major change. Instead, a corrupt system of concealment at grassroots levels and graded forms of relative privilege at higher levels was allowed to develop, again similar to that witnessed under Soviet-style communism. Perhaps Burma's sole distinction was the speed with which decline spread. The economy taken over in 1962 provided the RC with quite a fragile base. Before long many essential supports had been destroyed.

Socialist Burma

In the late 1960s the extent of economic malfunction obliged the regime to relax some controls, and the early 1970s saw military government given a civilian makeover. In June-July 1971 the BSPP, latterly changed from a small vanguard party to a nascent mass party with nearly 75,000 full members, held its first national congress.[109] On April 20, 1972, General Ne Win reverted to civilian status as U Ne Win, and 20 senior aides followed suit. Following a successful December 1973 referendum, a new constitution for the Socialist Republic of the Union of Burma was promulgated on January 3, 1974. It created a unicameral People's Assembly and a network of People's Councils, all nominally elected, and formally imposed legislative control on an already emasculated judiciary. On this basis, the RC was dissolved in March 1974, and power passed to the new socialist institutions. The 1974 constitution also partially reconfigured territorial politics through seven ethnic nationality states (Arakan, Chin, Kachin, Karen, Kayah, Mon and Shan), and seven Burman divisions. Subsequently, the Burma Citizenship Law 1982 identified 135 ethnic groups couched within eight major national races.[110]

Slowly the country began to open up. In 1971 "mutually beneficial economic relations" between foreign firms and the Burmese public sector were permitted, though only West German armaments manufacturer Fritz Werner, with personal contacts to Ne Win, was allowed to enter.[111] Bridges were also rebuilt with neighbors.[112] Economic aid resumed through World Bank assistance in 1972 and Asian Development Bank membership in 1973. Pointing to the future, contracts for oil exploration and production were signed with foreign companies in April 1974. Already from July 1969 tourist visas of up to 72 hours were issued, with visitors encouraged to look beyond Rangoon in the still limited time available.[113] By the mid-1970s, though, when one-week visas were issued, arrival numbers had only climbed to 1,500 per month.[114] Counted among them was Paul Theroux, who in *The Great Railway Bazaar* recorded his train journey from Rangoon via Mandalay and Maymyo to Gokteik Gorge close to the Shan border with China.[115] In late 1974, student and worker protests erupted when no more than perfunctory funeral rites were performed for U Thant, UN Secretary-General from 1961 to 1971.[116] Open dissent flared again in 1975 and 1976.[117] In 1976–77, young army officers were sentenced for plotting a coup.[118]

At the end of the decade there were increased aid flows, fresh exploitation of oil fields, and in October 1979 official blessing for English to return as a medium of instruction alongside Burmese.[119] In June 1979, a European diplomat sardonically remarked that "the economy has now improved to the point of mere stagnation."[120] In August 1981, Ne Win announced his intention to step down from the state presidency, but said he would remain head of the BSPP, now a mass organization with 1.5 million members.[121] Putting everything together, it looked as if transition would be the theme of the 1980s, and it was clear that it might not be smooth.[122] However, the middle years of the decade turned out to be rather quiet.[123] Although annual reviews in *Asian Survey* convey a sense of calm before the storm, they give no indication of where turbulence might come from.

Across the years hints of reform were occasionally noted by Burma watchers. In 1971, Badgley argued that modernization belied the common emphasis on economic malaise: "the sense of historic movement [is] powerful."[124] In 1980, Scully and Trager held that "While prophets of doom still apparently prevail, particularly among journalists covering the Burma scene, there were increasingly favorable reports in 1979 indicating not only that substantive improvements have been recorded, but also that a general reversal of past stagnating trends may well be materializing." They noted "an encouraging developmental outlook."[125] In 1981, Silverstein maintained that "prospects for the future are painted brightly against dark clouds."[126] Throughout, however, what Trager called "Burma's chronic insurrectionary activity" continued. "Each day the Burmese press published some item of rebel activity, as it has for almost twenty years. A day's news in 1967 was like that of 1957."[127] Butwell made much the same point: "If secessionist tendencies were contained in the years 1962–72, the extent of government control of the country was probably no greater on March 2, 1972 than it had been on that morning 10 years earlier when Ne Win ousted U Nu as Burma's constitutionally chosen leader."[128] In 1980, the government did attempt to entice dissidents back to legality. However, while its amnesty policy "succeeded in winning back individuals, it failed to end insurgent movements."[129]

Still the underlying economic performance was weak. In the early 1970s, some reform of the rice sector boosted production, notably through a large increase in government procurement prices from 172 *kyats* per ton in 1971–72 to 431 *kyats* per ton in 1973–74.[130] Later in the decade, a growing adoption of modern high yield varieties and limited liberalization measures enabling the sector to be "unleashed from a sluggish state" generated further improvement.[131] A Whole Township Special Rice Production Programme implemented in the late 1970s bore some fruit through close government supervision and application of modern methods. When a Green Revolution was then belatedly introduced from 1979 to 1986, exports experienced a resurgence. While a dramatic jump from less than 0.2 million tons in 1978–79 to more than 1.7 million tons in 1979–80 looks anomalous, an average export tonnage of 0.7 million tons was sustained for seven years from 1980–81 to 1986–87.[132] More generally growth rates from 1970 to 1982, though of dubious validity, were among the best in Asia.[133]

In the end, however, enhanced performance was unsustainable. The Green Revolution tailed off when export markets shrank and foreign exchange earnings collapsed.[134] Public confidence dissipated as economic crisis spread in the mid-1980s, presaging the beginning of the end for Ne Win. "There was no bread, but there was also little circus," writes Thant Myint-U.[135] Genuine liberalization of the rice sector in September 1987 removed many government regulations, allowing farmers to select which crops to grow and to sell most of their produce in the market rather than to the state. However, the reform arrived too late. Furthermore, broad-based material hardship was dramatized by a September 5, 1987 demonetization exercise, the third and most severe of the period. At a stroke, 25, 45 and 75 *kyat* notes were withdrawn without compensation, and 90 *kyat* notes were issued in their place. Some 70 percent of all currency disappeared from circulation, and many life savings were obliterated. In December 1987, "the Burma Road to poverty" registered the humiliation of least developed country designation by the UN General Assembly.[136]

Burma in revolt

The revolt, when it came, was the product of economic discontent spreading across the land at the end of 1987 and finding a political vehicle in student protest. Soon after the 1962 coup, when dissent was brutally suppressed, Josef Silverstein and Julian Wohl held that "With the nation's political leaders either in jail or unwilling to lead any active opposition to the military government of General Ne Win, and with the Revolutionary Council bent on administering the country without the aid of the other élites, the students remain as a potential force to fill the political vacuum."[137] A quarter-century on, the prescience of the remark was revealed when, on March 12, 1988, a fracas in a Rangoon teashop spilled over 24 hours into provocative and bloody repression by riot police, and the death of one student, Maung Phone Maw. During the following week, further student protest was met with more brutality. In a scandalous March 16 White Bridge incident by Rangoon's Inya Lake, hundreds died, thousands were arrested, and allegations of gang rape of female students surfaced. On March 18, all schools and universities were closed.

After campuses reopened on May 30, further clashes between protestors and riot police led in mid-June to the imposition of fierce emergency restrictions. At this time, though the focal point of dissent remained Rangoon, open rebellion was also starting to spread to other urban centers. In addition, disorder was beginning to develop a racial tinge as communal violence was directed against the country's Muslim population, almost certainly at the instigation of the government. However, when these measures failed to deflect attention from the long record of failure and stark instances of naked brutality on the part of Ne Win's regime, an announcement was made that an extraordinary congress of the BSPP would convene on July 23. In his authoritative account of the 1988 uprising, *Outrage: Burma's Struggle for Democracy*, Lintner writes that "Burma by the end of July was so tense that any minor incident could be the spark that started a blaze."[138]

At the BSPP congress, Ne Win in his opening speech made a number of dramatic announcements, proposing a referendum on a multiparty system, tendering his resignation from the party chairmanship and indeed the party, and reporting the resignations of several other top leaders, including San Yu who was both state president and BSPP vice-chairman. Ne Win also closed his address by issuing a warning: "I want the entire nation, the people, to know that if in future there are mob disturbances, if the army shoots, it hits — there is no firing into the air to scare."[139] In a subsequent speech delivered by a senior member of his inner circle, thoroughgoing economic reform was promised. While the congress declined to endorse the referendum proposal or Ne Win's resignation from the BSPP, it did accept his resignation from the party chairmanship and San Yu's resignation from the state presidency.[140] The choice to fill both positions, announced on July 26, was former Brigadier General Sein Lwin, widely reviled as the Butcher of Rangoon for his role in bloody crackdowns on Rangoon University students in both July 1962 and March 1988.

Despite its rejection, Ne Win's referendum proposal was significant as it provided a set of rather inchoate student protests with a clear rallying point. Lintner quotes the later comment of a western diplomat: "Up to then, the student movement and the sympathetic reaction of the masses was completely unfocused. It was in essence anti-government; protest against brutality, a frustrated reaction against the inane policies, the demonetisation, the hopelessness of the students, the lack of any future… Ne Win, unwittingly, provides a focus by calling for a multi-party system, and from there on in, the student cry is for democracy."[141] The subsequent culmination of many months of unrest was the four eights uprising bringing students, workers and ordinary people to the streets to call for democracy. "At 8 minutes past 8 on 8.8.88," writes Lintner, "the dockworkers in Rangoon port had walked out. That was the auspicious moment, and as soon as the word spread that the strike was on, people began marching towards the city centre."[142] Parallel events took place elsewhere. In *From the Land of Green Ghosts*, Pascal Khoo Thwe, working in a Mandalay restaurant in 1988, tells the story from a second-city perspective.[143]

The *tatmadaw* started firing at 11:30 or 11:45 on the night of August 8 in Rangoon, and did not stop until 3:00 in the morning. It continued to shoot demonstrators on August 9, 10 and 11, and even targeted nurses at Rangoon General Hospital. Deaths at the hands of soldiers were also recorded in other cities, notably Sagaing to the west of Mandalay. On August 12, however, the resignation of Sein Lwin prompted a lull in the violence. One week later, on August 19, he was replaced by Ne Win's confidant Maung Maung, who pledged to organize multiparty elections within three months. This offer was rejected by the emergent opposition leadership.[144] In a festive setting laced with uncertainty and tension, strikes, demonstrations and protest meetings continued and gradually much of the nation was consumed by a pro-democracy movement spreading from Rangoon to distant parts. "On the 22nd, a nationwide general strike was proclaimed to press the demands for the formation of a new, interim government that could rule the country pending general elections," writes Lintner. "The entire country ground to a halt."[145]

It was in a context of daily strikes and mass meetings that Aung San Suu Kyi took to the political stage.[146] Having spent the whole of her adult life in exile, Suu Kyi returned to the family home at 54 University Avenue, Rangoon at the start of April 1988 to care for her ailing mother, Khin Kyi. Turning 43 in June, she had no prior experience of active political engagement, but as the daughter of Aung San was a figure to whom many looked for leadership. Her first public response came on August 24 in a brief address at Rangoon General Hospital, the focal point for many rallies. However, there she merely announced that a more important speech would follow two days later at Shwedagon Pagoda, Rangoon's major landmark. On the morning of August 26, hundreds of thousands were present on open ground to the west of the temple to witness her call repeatedly for unity and discipline, and articulate the emphatic demands of the people: "namely that we have no desire at all for a referendum, that the one-party system should be dismantled, that a multi-party system of government should be established, and we call for free and fair elections to be arranged as quickly as possible."[147]

Throughout these weeks, opposition figures reinforced the demand for an interim government, but to no avail. Instead, *tatmadaw* leaders started to implement a successful strategy of fomenting civil disorder and confronting the mass of the population with a stark choice: dictatorship or anarchy. Jails were emptied, protests turned violent through rioting, pillage and destruction aided and abetted by government forces, lynchings and public executions took place, and water supplies were tainted.[148] Lintner writes that a "carnival atmosphere" gave way to "fear, paranoia, and anger."[149] In effect, military leaders set before the Burmese people what Federico Ferrara terms Hobbes's dilemma. In a late-twentieth-century state of nature created by government suspension of a key public good, maintenance of social order, citizens were "compelled to choose between anarchy and an inept, obtrusive, and hideously repressive Leviathan."[150] The bulk of the population opted to defect from an opposition movement that sought but failed to impose its own form of order through general strike committees of senior community figures, monks and students. While a defiant sense still hung in the air that things really might change for the better, increasingly mixed with it was a desperate fear that they could readily change for the worse.

In the event, worse triumphed over better as *tatmadaw* leaders seized the chance to re-impose a brutal and crushing form of social discipline. At 4:00 on the afternoon of September 18, a radio announcement was made: "In order to bring a timely halt to the deteriorating conditions on all sides all over the country and in the interests of the people, the defence forces have assumed all power in the state with effect from today."[151] At 6:00, news of a junta formed under Chief of Staff Saw Maung was released. Again the constitution, this time of 1974, was abrogated, and rule by decree was instituted. Within days, a ruthless army clampdown had restored military order. On October 3, all government officials were required to return to work and pick up the pieces of their lives under the refurbished dictatorship. In Mancur Olson's terms, rather than find themselves at the mercy of capricious "roving bandits," the Burmese people had reluctantly chosen to be ruled by a somewhat predictable "stationary bandit."[152]

From the outset, the dominion returned to Burmese hands in 1948 provoked militant dissent on the part of minority groups, first communist and soon also ethnic. However, a decisive political turn was taken in 1962. Both product of and reaction to colonialism, it had three key aspects. First, while a Leninist structure with Buddhist gloss never cohered, it did succeed in creating a garrison state. Second, behind all the rhetoric, state socialism was rarely more than an elaborate front for personalized military rule. Third, *tatmadaw* government lodged a fierce nationalist dynamic at the heart of the polity. It is in this sense that Michael Aung-Thwin holds formal independence in 1948 to be a "myth," placing power in the hands of the westernized elite itemized by Badgley.[153] Only in 1962 was a fully Burmese political identity reasserted, and interaction with the outside world severed. When chronic failure finally fomented a mass movement for democracy that for several months in 1988 spread open street protest to almost every corner of the country, military leaders extended their supremacy by reviving each of these three core features of the state.

3

Dictatorship and deadlock

The directorate that brutally restored military power in September 1988 subjected the country it was soon to call Myanmar to fresh dictatorship. Initially taking the name SLORC before nearly a decade later becoming the SPDC, the junta comprehensively reaffirmed military supremacy. Not until 2011 was any attempt made to give state structures some detachment from the military machine. For analytical purposes, then, the years of junta rule can be treated as a fairly unified, though by no means static, interval. At the outset, however, it is important to be clear that drawing boundaries around this era is not to overlook ample continuities flowing into and out of it. State socialism before 1988 was defined by the firm grip of military control imposed in 1962. At least in the early phases discipline-flourishing democracy after 2011 seems likely to be little different, with political practices honed by SLORC and the SPDC carried wholesale into the new era. Nevertheless, government by junta did generate significant change in national development, and in key respects did recast the political landscape. Moreover, examining the period in some detail makes possible an audit of Myanmar at the start of its experiment in praetorian democracy, and enables it to be more than a mere snapshot. This chapter looks at political dispute, economic malaise and social control under the generals before closing with an evaluation. Its twin themes are the dictatorship that dominated the country for more than two decades, and the deadlock that was a direct political consequence.

Political dispute

Throughout its ascendancy, the junta's priority was to control political space and curtail opposition to its rule.[1] The heady days of 1988, when political possibilities opened up and individuals were free to assemble, make speeches, air views and demand change, were soon a distant memory. In their place came an intensification of authoritarian control under army leaders with initially no grand plan beyond imposition of militaristic order. Many speculate about what might have been had the democratic opposition been more unified, strategic and assertive either before the September 1988 clampdown or during the subsequent standoff. On these grounds Aung San Suu Kyi's leadership of a fragmented movement is sometimes questioned.[2] Instead, the generals regrouped around what Charney terms a process of "perpetual delay" and slowly found their feet.[3] While the NLD landslide in the May 1990 general election was a major challenge, SLORC nevertheless succeeded in diverting national politics into the constitutional meanderings of the 1990s. Ultimately, these took shape as a roadmap to democracy in 2003, a constitutional referendum in 2008, a general election in 2010, and a revival of notionally civilian government in 2011. In the other main sphere of low-grade civil war in ethnic minority territories, the ceasefire deals of the early 1990s also gave the generals breathing space and allowed them eventually to take the initiative in rolling out plans for incorporation of militias into the *tatmadaw*. Rule by junta was always contested, however, and on occasion key flashpoints ignited. At no point was dictatorship able wholly to break the twin forms of deadlock it faced. One saw democratic forces marshal immense moral authority against the generals' Weberian monopoly of violence.[4] The other saw armed conflict flare in peripheral parts, and when ceasefires were agreed found a degree of control ceded to ethnic nationality groups.

At the apex of the military-state complex little is known about how the junta went about its business, as the internal operations of SLORC and the SPDC were shrouded in secrecy. Initially SLORC had 19 members under Saw Maung, who held the chairmanship until a string of bizarre public outbursts triggered his retirement on April 23, 1992. Than Shwe, hitherto Vice-Chairman, then remained paramount leader until the revival of civilian government in March 2011.[5] Partway through his long term, on November 15, 1997, SLORC was relaunched as the SPDC, with generally about a dozen members. Throughout it supervised the work of prime minister and cabinet, though overlapping memberships in high-level policy committees generated a fusion of power at the center. For his first decade in control Than Shwe was junta chairman, prime minister and defense minister, and a US evaluation at the time of Cyclone Nargis that "all roads lead to [the] Senior General" was long valid.[6]

Even within its own tight membership the junta rarely established total unity.[7] Always it presided over an unwieldy and fractured structure with frequent breaks in a chain of command stretching down to 65,000 village units.[8] As Skidmore wrote in 2005, "despite the entrenchment of military rule, there is no all-powerful military state here, no black-and-white understandings, and certainly no monolithic Orwellian entity overseeing all the Burmese people."[9] Nevertheless, ruling generals did succeed in building enough cohesion to sustain the position of the *tatmadaw* as the dominant institution within the state. Kyaw Yin Hlaing examines competing explanations for this conspicuous achievement. Rationalist accounts focus on utility maximizers. Cultural accounts emphasize traditional attitudes toward power. Formal institutional accounts look to a series of internal reforms. Agency framework accounts point to the success of hardliners in seizing control. Without dismissing any of these perspectives, he notes that two informal institutional mechanisms established under Ne Win played critical roles. One was a "tradition of discrete domains," whereby members at all levels were careful to respect internal boundaries and not interfere in others' business. The other was a policy of "mobilizing worthy insiders," whereby good care was taken of members who fell in line, and bleak ostracism was imposed on those seen as causing trouble. He argues that these shared understandings enabled the junta and the wider *tatmadaw* to withstand considerable internal and external challenge.[10]

Focusing on the SPDC's rather settled governance practices, four notionally separate and parallel hierarchies coalesced at many points. They sought to generate control in four overlapping domains: military, political, administrative and social. In the military sphere, the *tatmadaw* hierarchy combined at the top with the SPDC itself. Below that it was divided into a series of critical regional commands overseen by the junta. Following a purge of Khin Nyunt in October 2004 and a dismantling of the MI apparatus he headed, many surveillance functions were brought under core control.[11] In the political sphere, Peace and Development Councils mapped on to and usurped socialist People's Councils established at state, division, township, ward and village tract levels. In the administrative sphere, a decrepit state bureaucracy headed by a prime minister, cabinet and functional ministries supervised routine government operations.[12] Incapacity was common.[13] In the social sphere, the Union Solidarity and Development Association, formed on September 15, 1993 under SLORC Law No. 6/88, attempted to outflank opposition forces and dominate communal life. Again there was overlap, as senior SPDC figures were leading USDA patrons and PDC officials were close USDA collaborators. After the dismissal of Khin Nyunt, the USDA may also have taken on some MI functions. Assessing this edifice in 1998, Tin Maung Maung Than identified it as a prime example of the "national security state."[14]

Throughout the period there was always some grassroots support for authoritarianism even beyond the many individuals who did quite well out of it.[15] By consistently emphasizing its Buddhist credentials, casting itself as the defender of rural interests in a country where some 65 percent lived off the land, and delivering small benefits to peasants and farmers, the junta built "islands of favorable attitude" and "pockets of legitimacy."[16] Indeed, retaining the loyalty of Myanmar's large majority of rural dwellers was always central to its governance strategy. Moreover, the disaggregated nature of the state and the dynamic form taken by local interactions with it meant that "multiple images" of the regime emerged, with struggle and accommodation existing side by side in a single national context.[17] At village and ward levels, where attitudes to the regime were mediated by local officials from state bureaucracies, low-grade PDCs and the USDA, diverse responses to military rule played out. Sometimes, poor rice farmers valued central authority as protection from petty abuse and exploitation.

Nevertheless, the very fact of state fragmentation meant that problems were constantly encountered in holding together a large control edifice, and key parts were colonized to reinforce command. On seizing power, SLORC abrogated the 1974 constitution, ruled by decree and in principle could mandate anything. As Khin Nyunt put it in May 1991, "Martial Law means no law at all."[18] On the whole, however, the generals preferred to cloak their rule in legality by using codes from earlier times. One serviceable statute was the Emergency Provisions Act 1950, which outlawed "false news" and criminalized disruption of "the security or ... stability of the union."[19] Each offence carried a maximum jail term of seven years. Similarly, the State Protection Law 1975 was employed to target citizens alleged to endanger state sovereignty and security. It was often cited by the junta to hold Aung San Suu Kyi under house arrest. The Unlawful Associations Act 1908 allowed the head of state to declare any organization illegal. The Official Secrets Act 1923 provided for jail terms of up to 14 years for anyone found in possession of information deemed prejudicial to state interests.[20] In postcolonial Asia it was not unusual for states to retain draconian laws from imperial times. Perhaps most obviously, Singapore has always done that to limit the reach of democracy.[21] In Myanmar, though, the practice was taken to tyrannical heights. Furthermore, to fill any gaps the junta issued its own repressive codes, was prepared to act outside the law, and routinely made a mockery of due process.[22] The farce of Aung San Suu Kyi's May-August 2009 trial, which saw her house arrest extended after a nocturnal swim and brief stay by uninvited guest John Yettaw, is lavish testament.

Animating the junta's governance agenda was the core theme of unity. Its Three Main National Causes were non-disintegration of the Union, non-disintegration of national solidarity, and perpetuation of sovereignty.[23] Its four-point "People's Desire," made up of "three opposes and one crush," mandated resistance to perceived threats to national integrity.[24] Its four political objectives voiced parallel concerns. All were reproduced daily in the regime's major media outlets and had to be carried in other publications, including many books. Large billboards stating the People's Desire in either the Myanmar language or English were erected at strategic points. In Yangon, they were placed across the street from the US Embassy, on the main road from Mingaladon Airport to the heart of the city, close to major tourist attractions such as Shwedagon Pagoda, and so on. During set-piece mobilizations on Independence Day (January 4), Union Day (February 12) and Armed Forces Day (March 27), the discourse became especially elevated, and patriots were urged to cultivate "strong Union spirit" and hew closely to the junta's political path. Often the USDA played a key mobilizing role, commonly requiring households to send at least one member to mass events designed to celebrate the regime's achievements.

From language used in the junta's most emblematic statement, the "one crush" from the People's Desire, it was always clear that top leaders did not intend to foster unity in diversity. "Crush all internal and external destructive elements as the common enemy" does not have that spin, and neither did the drift of policy. Rather, unity was set within a Bamar straightjacket formed both by ongoing military action against minority populations, and by policies prioritizing the junta's reading of Buddhist culture throughout the nation.[25] In this way, political discourse was dominated by regimental calls for discipline, strength and vigilance in defense of territorial integrity: nationalism as political paranoia.[26] Indeed, the generals pursued unity so intensely and purposively, notably through persistent reference to the perils that awaited the nation should it fail in its collective task, that room for competing political values was reduced to insignificance.[27] The core theme of *tatmadaw* government was not, then, the harmony talk emanating from Beijing at the start of the twenty-first century, but rather a militant unity discourse insisting that a diverse nation fall in line with a martial vision of social peace and economic development.[28] Top generals argued that this was the only route to salvation for a fractured nation that ever since independence had exhibited fissiparous and chaotic tendencies.

Closing down the public sphere was therefore a central objective. In the months prior to the May 1990 general election, some political activity and debate were possible. In total, 235 parties registered, and 93 stood candidates. From an electorate of nearly 21 million, more than 15 million voted in 485 constituencies. In a result that was to haunt the regime, 392 seats went to the NLD, 23 to the Shan Nationalities League for Democracy, 11 to the Arakan League for Democracy and 5 to the Mon Democratic Front. The NUP, aligned with the junta though gaining little active backing from it, took only 10 seats. Once this outcome was known, however, the generals fell back on their repressive instincts. Already Aung San Suu Kyi was serving her first term of house arrest, imposed on July 20, 1989. Now the democracy movement was brought under tight control. Following a two-month standoff, the NLD planned to meet at Gandhi Hall, Yangon on July 28–29, 1990 to demand an immediate power transfer. On July 27, however, SLORC issued Notification No. 1/90 to repudiate any competing claim.[29] On January 9, 1993, when a National Convention set in motion a tightly managed and glacially slow constitutional process, it reneged further on its promises by ensuring that among 702 delegates only 99 had been elected in 1990, and around 500 were handpicked township officials.

As a backdrop, almost all major NLD figures were held for years under house arrest or in jail, and other members suffered every form of abuse up to and including death. Aung San Suu Kyi's three periods of house arrest came in 1989–95, 2000–02 and 2003–10, with restricted movement in between.[30] As she often pointed out, however, this confinement was merely the most visible aspect of a systematic campaign of coercion. One notorious instance came on May 30, 2003, when USDA vigilantes ambushed an NLD convoy at Depayin, Mandalay Division. Some 70 people were murdered, and Aung San Suu Kyi was taken into "protective custody" lasting for seven and a half years.[31] If anything, there was subsequently a rise in USDA violence spearheaded by its *Swan Arr Shin* militia, "well-trained thugs, who operate with impunity alongside riot-control army and police units."[32] Despite several mass pardons, human rights organizations estimated that the total number of political prisoners, put at around 1,100 in mid-2007, grew to some 2,200 by the end of 2008 and stayed at that level through to 2011.[33] In jails up and down the country, living conditions were systematically subhuman.[34] Rights violations were routine.[35] Ever present was the chance of being sent to a labor camp, a fate so terrible that prisoners sought help from fellow inmates to mutilate themselves and avert the possibility. Htein Lin's *Six Fingers*, painted secretly in Myaungmya Prison in 2001, speaks directly to this practice.[36] Karen Connelly's *The Lizard Cage* is an agonizing fictional account of prison life under the junta.[37]

By the end of the period the NLD had been significantly weakened. After its September 1988 launch, the party amassed 2–3 million members and opened branches throughout the land. By 2011, however, only its dilapidated Yangon office functioned, and surviving members faced harassment in almost every aspect of life touching the state, including education, healthcare, employment and multiple forms of registration and permit.[38] Moreover, because renewal was so hard, the party was dominated by an aging group of "uncles." In a poisonous political climate, leaders were criticized for perceived elitism, endorsing sanctions, opting not to contest the 2010 poll, and projecting a Bamar identity.[39] In 2010 Khin Zaw Win, pro-democracy activist jailed from 1994 to 2005 and later grassroots political leader, argued that the NLD had become "virtually a single-issue party" focused on democracy. It dealt with key issues of economic development "in a cursory, cavalier fashion," and was in danger of making a similar response to the ethnic nationalities question. "This shirking of national responsibility will no doubt add to the long list of developments that will happen without the NLD."[40] While core democratic principles retained considerable latent support and Aung San Suu Kyi was held in reverence and capable of drawing huge crowds when allowed to undertake political tours, by the close of the period the party had almost none of the organizational capacity required by a serious competitor for office.[41] Indeed, by 2011 it had become an extra-parliamentary opposition and social welfare body. Over the course of two decades, one of the junta's most salient achievements was to diminish the reach and power of the NLD.

Predating the party's formation was the 1988 student movement. When SLORC took power, systematic *tatmadaw* repression ensured that leaders not killed on the streets were hunted down relentlessly. Some 10,000 fled to ethnic nationality areas and soon congregated in border camps in India and above all Thailand to plan counter-offensives.[42] Others were arrested and sentenced to jail terms of 15 years or more. Activism, though visible in student strikes in Yangon in 1996 and 2002, was quelled.[43] However, in the mid-2000s most 88 Generation leaders were released and in late 2006 orchestrated small civil disobedience campaigns. In mid-August 2007, they led street protests in Yangon against a withdrawal of fuel subsidies and a large rise in transport fees, set in a context of grinding rural and urban poverty. Key figures, including Min Ko Naing and Ko Ko Gyi, were arrested and sentenced to long prison terms.[44]

In the event, however, this action was the stimulus for the saffron uprising.[45] On September 5, when Buddhist monks led a demonstration against the high cost of living in the central monastery town of Pakokku, several were roughed up by the USDA. Soon after, dissent spread to major cities. On September 22, monks filed past Aung San Suu Kyi's house in Yangon, and in the confusion that occasionally gripped street-level military commanders at that time the tall metal gate to her compound was opened for her to pay silent tribute.[46] On September 24, more than 50,000 marched in Yangon, and parallel protests took place elsewhere. The crackdown, feared for some time, came on September 26. Order was soon restored, and allegedly "fake" monks were run to ground across the country. At least 30 are known to have died and Kenji Nagai, a Japanese photo-journalist, was shot by a soldier at point-blank range in Yangon. Many surviving monks were rounded up in detention centers and banished from the *sangha*.[47] The film *Burma VJ*, directed by Anders Østergaard, is one of the best evocations of those days.[48]

In peripheral regions, about two dozen ethnic armies continued to fight the *tatmadaw* after the CPB splintered into ethnic battalions in 1989. However, from 1989 to 1996 most major militias reached ceasefire deals with SLORC, sometimes under duress.[49] Often neither actually signed nor made public, these were informal agreements typically amounting to little more than a loose truce. Around 15–20 groups thereby "returned to the legal fold," though the pivotal Karen National Union did not.[50] Always there were tensions, particularly when the 2008 constitution provided for ethnic militias to form a Border Guard Force within the larger *tatmadaw* and subject themselves to central direction. By the time discipline-flourishing democracy was instituted in 2011, BGF clauses had thus been only patchily implemented. Nevertheless, it was clear that ceasefire deals had changed the landscape quite considerably, with the junta consolidating power, ethnic nationality leaders often turning to commercial ventures, and ethnic political identities and commitments fragmenting in perplexing ways.[51] In 2011, Ashley South argued that the long-term prognosis was for "a decline of insurgency," with the once powerful KNU in "deep crisis."[52] Challenged by a breakaway group from 1994 and unable to represent all shades of Karen opinion in a nuanced social, political and religious setting, its authority was in a state of disintegration.

In a few ethnic nationality areas local elites continued to exercise power.[53] Regime strategists split the territory into white areas under military control, brown areas accessible to government and insurgent troops, and black areas controlled by enemies of the state. In 2007 Callahan also made a tripartite division, identifying extensive devolution of power in the Wa and Kokang parts of Shan State, brutal military occupation in northern Rakhine State and parts of Karen, Kayah and Shan States, and coexistence between central and local leaders in parts of Kachin, Karen, Mon and Shan States.[54] However, as she and others noted, the situation on the ground was often still more complex.[55]

In 2011, South wrote that "In reality, areas of disputed authority and influence blur into each other, with frontiers shifting over time in accordance with the season and the dynamics of armed and state-society conflict."[56] In variegated ways, then, *tatmadaw* government remained a grim reality in much hill country, secure in some places, bitterly contested in others. Throughout the period, abundant reports testified to the oppression felt by ordinary people caught in the crossfire of civil conflict.[57]

Economic malaise

By the end of the BSPP years the Burmese economy was close to collapse, giving SLORC little option but to build on the partial agricultural reforms implemented in 1987. Prompted especially by Japan, which long saw economic development as the trigger for political change, it opted for further market opening both internally and externally.[58] Broadly, this comprised fresh liberalization of the dominant rural sector, a raft of additional internal reforms, some privatization of state-owned enterprises and some encouragement of domestic and foreign investment.[59] As much local capital had long been held by the military, the junta and its close associates quickly became leading players in the fragile and distorted national economy. Foreign capital also started to flow into the country, and joint ventures were formed with state agencies such as the Union of Myanmar Economic Holdings, Myanmar Economic Corporation, and Myanma Oil and Gas Enterprise.[60] Two decades on, however, the economy remained mired in corruption and inefficiency, and the country was into its third decade on the UN's LDC list. Further privatization in the run-up to the 2010 general election saw more state firms sold to military leaders and associates at fire-sale prices.

On the domestic front, the rice sector that remains the base of the rural economy was no longer viewed as the foundation for broad-based modernization, but rather as a critical tool for regime maintenance. Ikuko Okamoto notes that ever since the late 1980s the principal policy thrust has thus been "stable supply of rice at a low price," designed to deliver political security.[61] For this reason, a lifting of the ban on private export of agricultural produce in 1988 did not extend to rice. Indeed, compulsory procurement was partially revived in 1989, though at reduced volumes. When further reform followed in April 2003, it freed up the domestic market but retained regulation of the export trade. The overall effect was to reanimate private milling and trading, such that by the late 1990s, a decade on from the initial reforms, some 30–40 percent of all yield was traded in the market. Furthermore, total production increased by roughly 50 percent over the same time span, and nearly doubled from the late 1980s to the mid-2000s.[62] By and large, the regime succeeded in its core aim of ensuring a stable supply of rice throughout the country, and though prices fluctuated a great deal they stayed broadly within the realm of affordability. Prices of other basic foodstuffs were also kept at low levels.[63]

In the early years of SLORC control, chaotic entrepreneurship on the part of senior officials and military commanders was common. Ministries might get involved in almost any business, and frequently did. While much activity was cleaned up in 1997 with the shift to the SPDC, there was still extensive corruption.[64] Always the junta had elements of kleptocracy, and the more open economic system created after 1988 was one of the most extreme forms of crony capitalism found anywhere in the world.[65] Indeed, as the period unfolded, the predatory nature of the ruling elite was revealed in manifold ways, from deals with opium kingpin Khun Sa to routine appearances of junta family members and associates at the fancier clubs and hotels in Yangon. Rarely were the perks of power more flagrantly displayed than in the infamous July 2006 wedding of Than Shwe's youngest daughter, Thandar Shwe, and Major Zaw Phyo Win, Deputy Director of the Ministry of Commerce. Filmed on bootleg video and widely circulated, the gold-encrusted ceremony fully encapsulated the vulgar opulence and rapacious extravagance of the military hierarchy.[66] At the same time, there was always quasi-official authorization for illegal business.[67] For many years a grave problem was narcotics production in parts of Shan State controlled either by the *tatmadaw*, or by ethnic militias such as the United Wa State Army formed through mutiny in the CPB.[68] Although kickbacks tended to flow into the pockets of military personnel at all levels, central and regional commanders were especially favored.[69] Less visible, but undeniably important, was the tentative emergence of small and medium enterprises in, for instance, the fisheries sector.[70]

On the side of inward investment, Myanmar witnessed some high-profile cases in the late 1980s and early 1990s. However, almost all mobile western capital left within a few years, driven out by consumer boycotts of major brands and a generally difficult business environment.[71] Tourism was also affected by activist campaigns, though it is not unusual for political violence to drive people away.[72] A Visit Myanmar Year 1996 was a failure, and in 2010 international visitor arrivals were put at only 311,000 against 16 million for neighboring Thailand.[73] Formal sanctions, imposed late in the day and only ever partial, served mainly to confirm individual and corporate decisions taken years previously. By the end of the period, the major western investors were in resource extraction, and even they were few in number.[74]

Less visible Asian investment, sometimes illegal, was harder to document. Approved foreign direct investment as of March 2006 shows that Thailand was by far the largest investor with a 55 percent stake. However, the extent of Chinese inward investment, put at 1.5 percent of the approved total, was clearly understated.[75] China and Thailand were also the two major trading partners.[76] The signing on November 2, 2010, days before the general election, of a $10 billion Thai deal to create a vast industrial complex at Dawei, deep in the south of Myanmar, looked set to transform investment patterns, stimulate local economic development, and even have broad political impacts.[77] In January 2011, this strategic initiative was formalized in a Dawei Special Economic Zone Law, patterned on Shenzhen in southern China and the first of its kind in Myanmar.

Underpinning some of this activity was ongoing infrastructural investment. From the start, the junta built part of its claim to legitimacy on economic growth stimulated by road, bridge, dam, hydropower, school, hospital, communication and other projects. On many days, the only real domestic news was infrastructure improvement reported at length in state media. Undoubtedly there was some achievement here.[78] At the same time, though, development was often used as one more excuse to confiscate land, displace farmers, impose taxes, and enrich military commanders and their associates.[79] Furthermore, the planning agenda was set at very high levels of government, and allowed for little or no grassroots input. As a result, priorities were skewed and projects to develop rural areas and dam major rivers had strongly negative impacts on local communities. In the late junta years, a rash of reports documented alleged abuse, and collectively built a case against military expansionism and control of contested territory. Graphic titles included *Valley of Darkness* (2007), *Turning Treasure into Tears* (2007), *Development by Decree* (2007), *In the Balance* (2007), *Damming the Irrawaddy* (2007), *Biofuel by Decree* (2008), *Drowning the Green Ghosts of Kayanland* (2008), *Laid Waste* (2009), *Robbing the Future* (2009), *Roots and Resilience* (2009), *Resisting the Flood* (2009), *Tyrants, Tycoons and Tigers* (2010) and *Poison Clouds* (2011).[80]

An additional problem with much economic activity was exploitation. At the extreme, forced labor took place, and was monitored by the International Labour Organization.[81] In rural areas USDA officials might require village households each to supply one member for manual work. If a road was being built, nearby township authorities would be asked to assist. Mark Duffield notes that "In this way 150 people can be taken out of a village for a week at a time to work on the road."[82] Those unable to comply had either to nominate someone else or pay a fine. Sometimes both penalties were applied.[83] Also pervasive was environmental degradation, no more than marginally relieved by the adoption of a National Environmental Policy in 1994, a Myanmar Agenda 21 blueprint in 1997, and a National Sustainable Development Strategy in 2009.[84] The important forestry sector, once managed as well as anywhere in the world, was in crisis with illegal logging in Kachin and Shan States a key factor.[85] The mining industry also generated grave concern about working conditions and environmental damage.[86] *At What Price?*, a 2004 report on rampant gold mining in Kachin State, noted many harmful impacts: "Pollution, degradation and destruction of large tracts of land, extremes of wealth and poverty, disturbance of communities, violence, gambling, prostitution and spread of disease."[87] Much the same could be said of gem and jade mining in ethnic nationality areas. Some quality stones were later auctioned at emporia organized roughly twice a year in Yangon by state-run Myanmar Gems Enterprise. Lesser products were sold directly by brokers in mining and border towns.[88] Corruption was easy and endemic.

At the end of more than two decades of government by junta it was difficult to assess the state of the economy, not least because systematic data were scarce and unreliable. Official statistics recorded robust development. Annual GDP growth was put at between 6 and 14 percent for the decade from 1993 to 2003, when a classic bank run prefigured a shift into recession.[89] In January 2011, *The Economist* placed Myanmar at number three on a list of the world's fastest-growing economies, with average annual growth of 10.3 percent from 2001 to 2010.[90] However, aggregate claims of roughly 10 percent growth per annum over a 20-year period cannot be taken seriously. While nobody denies that the starting point was extremely low, the notion that the economy has expanded seven-fold since the early 1990s is impossible to square with other data or grassroots experience. Across the entire period, for instance, the structure of the economy changed little. Consistently from 1990 to 2004, agriculture accounted for 55–60 percent of GDP, and manufacturing for only 7–9 percent. By comparison, other regional states such as Cambodia, Laos and Vietnam witnessed a significant shift from agriculture to manufacturing.[91] Unless Myanmar's agricultural sector was performing miraculously, its economy was not a regional leader.

More plausibly, Sean Turnell, Wylie Bradford and Alison Vicary put annual growth at 3 percent per annum, driven above all by the booming gas trade. In 2006–07, this was worth nearly 40 percent of exports by value, and forecast to bring in $2–4 billion annually for the next 20–30 years.[92] However, they noted that gas delivered scant benefit to ordinary people, and much of the revenue stream was in any case diverted into private accounts through a devious multiple exchange rate system. Beyond extraction, the economy was "essentially stagnant."[93] The core remained a collapsing agricultural sector, though a rare positive story was pulse and bean exports, successful "largely as a consequence of the absence of state intervention."[94] The team cited a 2009 GDP estimate of $280 per capita at market exchange rates, with at least 70 percent spent on food.[95] This was less than half the UN's 2008 figure of $578 per capita within a GDP of roughly $29 billion.[96] Given the fragility of all statistics, little more than extreme poverty can be read into either calculation. For many, remittances totaling more than $300 million per year in the late 2000s were critical.[97]

In short, no credible dataset or anecdotal evidence paints a rosy picture. By the late 2000s, the economy was distorted and trailing its neighbors. "Genuine economic 'development' is not taking place in Burma," wrote the Turnell team in 2009.[98] One year later, Turnell found the economy to be "grim."[99] While plentiful natural resources gave grounds for hope, they also created a classic resource curse. "Burma's state is almost wholly predatory, and it is not so much parasitic of its host as all-consuming."[100] Fundamental institutional reform was urgently needed, embracing effective property rights, basic freedoms, functioning infrastructure, rational policymaking, and market-opening policies internally and externally. "Laying the foundations of a market-centered and rule-based economy will be vital to the success of any transition strategy to lift Burma from its present 'least-developed' purgatory."[101] In December 2009, visiting 2001 Nobel Economics Laureate Joseph Stiglitz stressed the need to reform agriculture and improve farmers' access to credit.[102] Banking changes and microfinance projects were also required.[103]

All that said, few indicators pointed to a society mired in sub-Saharan African levels of distress. The Human Development Index 2010 ranked Myanmar 132 out of 169 countries, with gross national income of $1,596 per capita in 2008 dollars using purchasing power parities.[104] This made it the only ASEAN state in the bottom category, below Cambodia at 124 ($1,868), Laos at 122 ($2,321), Vietnam at 113 ($2,995) and Indonesia at 108 ($3,957), but kept it out of the lowest 20 percent globally.[105] Nevertheless, given what might have been expected, the performance was clearly disastrous. In 1982, David I. Steinberg drew a comparison with South Korea and Thailand, arguing that in the mid-1950s Burma was "the potential economic and political leader of the three."[106] It was exporting food and fuel and had extensive natural resources, good transport infrastructure, high literacy rates, widespread use of English, and a modern legal system. Half a century later, however, the 2010 index placed Thailand at 92 ($8,001) and South Korea at 12 ($29,518). Whereas both had passed through lengthy periods of military control and repression to create functioning democracies, Myanmar remained authoritarian.

Social control

The society shaped by two decades of junta government was heavily though not totally controlled by a state operating through propaganda, surveillance and fear. Callahan notes that in the early days citizens believed MI had spies everywhere. "Still today," she wrote in 2007, "people regularly whisper in public when their conversations turn to senior officials or politics, although less obviously so than in the early 1990s."[107] In 2010 she held that the unpredictability of power made citizens "the object of punitive, extractive, capricious and indifferent" public action.[108] In *Secret Histories*, an alluring account fusing past and present, Emma Larkin reports similar surveillance while retracing Orwell's footsteps across the country.[109] Although there may not have been a systematic *Stasi*-style network of informers, citizens were obliged to negotiate much street-level red tape. Every household had to register members and visitors with PDC authorities liable to trigger random nighttime checks. Roadblocks were set up on major routes to track and tax civilian travel, and movement between the country's 14 states and divisions was monitored.[110] For a person seeking a job, enrolment in school, college or university, access to healthcare, official documentation, or mere release from intimidation, joining the USDA was nearly compulsory. In November 2005, membership was officially recorded as 22.8 million.[111] Moreover, reinforcing petty control was terror. Ground down by fear, individuals became programmed to avoid political controversy.[112] Many people simply left the country.

Still more critical not only politically but also socially was the dominant *tatmadaw*. Total enlisted personnel stood at around 200,000 in 1988, rising to about 400,000 in 2002 before falling back to 300–350,000 by 2011. At least 90 percent of all men served in the army, with air force and navy numbers only very small.[113] Some 20 percent of recruits were allegedly not men at all, but boys.[114] In remote parts, army divisions were often required to live off the land through extortion and foraging.[115] Always faced with structural problems, including desertion, low morale and false reporting, the *tatmadaw* was nevertheless the essential institution. In an overwhelmingly rural society with limited employment opportunities, a career in the army was one of the few avenues for upward social mobility. Furthermore, the sheer size and constant presence of military forces meant that many individuals maintained links of one kind or another. Indeed, the parallel structure of hospitals, schools and so on created by the *tatmadaw* ensured that access to the military through extended family and friends was frequently critical for social welfare. Even basic necessities such as quality rice and cooking oil might be available only through military channels.[116]

In the wider society, restrictions on information and communication were retained and enlarged. The Burma Wireless Telegraphy Act 1933, creating an offence of possessing a telephone without permission, was supplemented in 1995 and 1996 to include fax machines and computer modems. The censorship system established by the Printers and Publishers Registration Law 1962 also grew.[117] For years, two state-run television channels and state-controlled newspapers regurgitated propaganda from the Office of Strategic Studies, and private-sector journalism was censored through the Press Scrutiny and Registration Division of the Ministry of Home Affairs. More than 100 weekly journals and news magazines operating at the end of the period were required to submit all copy one week before publication, and could lose articles or entire issues. One third of a magazine's content was often removed.[118] Non-state titles could also be required to carry stories written by or for the regime, frequently recycled from government outlets. In a 24-page issue, they would typically fill a page or two. Books were subject to censorship of the final published version.[119] Completed films were checked by the Film Censorship Board under the Ministry of Information. Videos were vetted by the Video Censorship Board. In 2006, Reporters Without Borders noted an enhancement of telephone tapping capacity, three-year prison terms for two photo-journalists who took unauthorized pictures of Nay Pyi Taw, and 19-year sentences for two young people who distributed poems supporting the NLD.[120] In 2010, it stated that special police had tried to hunt down clandestine reporters, that collapse of a pagoda near Yangon could not be disclosed because Than Shwe's wife had been involved in its dedication, and that gross intimidation of journalists was widespread. Its evaluation was damning: "Burma is a paradise for censors."[121]

While Myanmar under military rule was wrapped in a thick blanket of control, chinks of light were still able to penetrate. Despite strict censorship, literature, music and art remained vibrant and even political in major cities.[122] From outside, radio was a potent means of disseminating information. International broadcasts could be picked up on short wave, and BBC Burmese, Voice of America, Radio Free Asia (based in Washington, DC) and Democratic Voice of Burma (based in Oslo) all beamed into the country.[123] A staple of Aung San Suu Kyi's daily routine under house arrest was listening to these stations. Satellite television was increasingly accessible and popular, notably during major global events such as the 2010 football World Cup in South Africa and military action against Libya in 2011.[124] Although websites were heavily censored and owners of internet cafes were required to supply the authorities with regular snapshots of on-screen activity, many users were able to circumvent regime firewalls through proxy servers, and most owners declined to drive away business by submitting full reports.[125] By the end of the SPDC years, young people even in small urban centers of 20–30,000 people could find internet cafes and were allowed to access Gmail accounts and Facebook pages alongside Myanmar-language chat rooms and sites.[126] Thus, despite harsh junta clampdowns, news of the 2007 fuel price protests and saffron uprising were soon transmitted out of the country by citizen-reporters operating in big cities. News bulletins plus global commentary were then broadcast back in through short-wave radio services informing the population about censored items. Certainly technological advance associated with the internet was no more of a panacea in fighting this dictatorship than in opposing any other.[127] In April 2011 Freedom House reported on extensive internet control in Myanmar, finding only Iran less constrained.[128] Nevertheless, information was able to flow somewhat more freely than state leaders would have liked.

In civil society, countervailing power was for many years systematically extinguished.[129] In 1997, Steinberg wrote that "Since 1962, the military has destroyed civil society in Burma."[130] By and large the claim was valid, as state bodies ruthlessly dominated civil space. However, since then there has been a renaissance. Although the International Crisis Group argued in 2001 that civil society was "at its weakest state in decades," a small but steady growth was already disproving the claim.[131] When in 2006 an activist group held that the country was "devoid of a civil society," with only the USDA and parallel state bodies able to "mobilize the masses" and "carry out carefully scripted functions," it was wide of the mark.[132] In 2004, South had already pointed to a tentative revival.[133] In 2006, Karl Dorning, Brian Heidel and David Tegenfeldt, all in-country INGO workers, published separate analyses of local civil society.[134] Dorning noted that 62 local NGOs had a Yangon office, with 17 created in the 1990s and the rest in the 2000s. Others operated elsewhere. He reported more than 200,000 community-based organizations, though many would have been very local indeed and some may have existed in name only. Nevertheless, in 2007 Kyaw Yin Hlaing's evaluation was that while bodies deemed subversive would not be permitted, "Myanmar does have somewhat vibrant civic and social organizations."[135]

A step change in civic development then took place in the wake of Cyclone Nargis.[136] Sweeping through the Ayeyawady Delta and up toward Yangon on May 2–3, 2008, Nargis was a category 4 cyclone that devastated towns and villages with a wave surge of up to 3.5 meters, rapidly becoming the worst natural disaster in the country's recorded history. In its path, about 450,000 homes were totally destroyed, 197,000 partially damaged, 126,000 slightly damaged, and only 16,000 untouched.[137] As news of the tragedy seeped out, humanitarian agencies and governments around the world mobilized to act. However, the junta's response in the critical early days and weeks was to look first to its own security needs, and only second to human needs. While the full consequence will never be known, it is certain that some of at least 138,000 deaths resulted from constraints imposed on relief efforts.[138] Furthermore, while a May 22–23 visit by UN Secretary-General Ban Ki-moon afforded some relaxation of the lockdown placed on the delta, the junta was always wary of domestic and foreign action.[139] Indeed, some political prisoners were convicted for Nargis humanitarian work. Most famous is Zarganar, a comedian who sometimes poked fun at the regime and publicly criticized the blocking of Nargis aid. He was jailed for 59 years in November 2008, and had his term revised to 35 years in February 2009.[140]

However, Nargis did generate enhanced response mechanisms, ensuring that when Cyclone Giri hit western Rakhine State on October 22, 2010 deaths were in the hundreds rather than the hundreds of thousands. More broadly, it triggered a dynamic civic response with a lasting impact on the southern delta area.[141] In 2008, a staff member from the Local Resource Center, formed to boost capacity and forge links with donors, put it this way: "Nargis destroyed much, but it also revealed much as well. No one can any longer deny that there is an active and capable civil society in Myanmar, one that made an immeasurable life-saving contribution with minimum support from international agencies."[142] By the end of the junta years the total number of local NGOs had climbed to 82, and even official media were prepared to cover a sector once deemed highly sensitive.[143] In 2010 Paung Ku, a consortium of local and international agencies founded in 2007 to strengthen civil society, noted that the sector was generally weak and strikingly diverse across distinct local contexts.[144] Clearly, though, it was becoming increasingly substantial.

Perhaps the greatest shaping efforts in the junta years targeted ethnic nationality peoples. Myanmar, the language of the Bamar majority, remained the main medium of instruction throughout the land, though in some areas teachers were themselves unable to speak it. Especially in monastery schools that always bore a large part of the educational burden, much instruction therefore continued to take place in Chin, Kachin, Shan, and so on. Nevertheless, the policy thrust was deeply resented.[145] In a country with many devotees of Christianity, Islam and Hinduism, Buddhism was assiduously promoted. Indeed, despite religious boycotts following the abortive 1990 general election and the 2007 saffron uprising, the junta always sought to align itself closely with the Buddhist hierarchy.[146] Other religions, often with plentiful adherents in peripheral zones, were tolerated but received no financial support and were frequently harried and hounded.[147]

In the background was often overt conflict between the *tatmadaw* and ethnic militias.[148] While ceasefires brought a degree of respite and pushed some insurgency into virtual forms, they did not end all violence.[149] In 2006 alone, fighting in Karen State reportedly destroyed 232 villages plus crops and food stocks, and displaced 27,000 villagers.[150] People also faced resettlement campaigns designed to herd them into controlled areas and assert military dominion. In 2006, Human Rights Watch claimed that there were half a million internally displaced persons in eastern Myanmar. For Christian Solidarity Worldwide, the number was twice that.[151] Similar statistics appeared to the end of the period.[152] The result was less fighting, but no decline in militarization, no real peace, and little concord.[153] Callahan describes "a kind of post-civil-war, not-quite-peace environment."[154] Tom Kramer writes of an uneasy situation of "neither war nor peace."[155] Additional impacts were felt across Myanmar's frontiers as ethnic nationality groups fled army action to live "between sovereigns" in refugee camps or endangered migrant communities, notably in Thailand.[156] Shelby Tucker's *Among Insurgents*, Zoya Phan's *Little Daughter* and Mac McClelland's *For Us Surrender Is out of the Question* all provide raw accounts of borderland conflict.[157]

Further forms of abuse are also well documented. Muslim minority Rohingya people living mainly in Rakhine State in western Myanmar were rendered stateless by successive governments and persecuted by officials and citizens alike.[158] They experienced an extreme form of human rights violation, with rights to property, marriage, education and employment all curtailed.[159] Pushed into Bangladesh or taking to the high seas in flimsy boats to seek sanctuary, many suffered extensive abuse and some inevitably died.[160] More widely, detailed reports of rape, mutilation and extrajudicial killing were too numerous to be dismissed. *Women in and from Conflict Areas of Burma* (2000), *License to Rape* (2002), *Shattering Silences* (2004), *Dignity in the Shadow of Oppression* (2006), *State of Terror* (2007), *Unsafe State* (2007), *In the Shadow of the Junta* (2008) and *Walking amongst Sharp Knives* (2010) all describe *tatmadaw* violence against women.[161] Scorching human rights reports often surfaced. In many years Amnesty International alone released a dozen bulletins, and every one was highly critical. Annual US State Department briefings generally held that the government's human rights record had again worsened, and backed the claim in harrowing detail. Annual HRW reports took a similar line.[162] Even genocide claims were made, with Benedict Rogers in 2004 citing attacks on the Karen people and Guy Horton in 2005 lodging a claim of "slow genocide" against minority peoples.[163] In 2009, Barbara Harff estimated that only Sudan faced a greater genocide risk, and in 2010 a former human rights envoy reported that the UN had placed Myanmar on a monitoring list.[164]

Finally, beyond active harm was willful neglect. Public expenditure was small and at least 40 percent typically went to the military, where some was channeled into parallel welfare provision. In the civilian sphere, key social services received a fraction of public spending. Education consumed about 1 percent of GDP, teaching materials were limited, and little more than half of children completed primary school.[165] Most actual learning took place after class, as teachers sought to supplement meager monthly salaries of 30–50,000 *kyats* by instructing students whose parents could afford extra payments. Scarcely any universities worth the name existed, and all were subject to long periods of closure. In 12 years from 1988 to 2000, campuses were open for only 36 months. After the 1996 student strike, they were shut for nearly four years. At the same time, a shift to isolated suburban facilities and distance learning programs was made to hamper student mobilization.[166] Today, Yangon University has no undergraduates on its historic city-center campus. While by the end of the period many young people in a thin professional stratum had a least one degree, few had learned much from tertiary education. Even less money, around 0.5 percent of GDP, went to healthcare, confirming the World Health Report 2000 evaluation that Myanmar had the world's worst system bar only Sierra Leone.[167] Again, much treatment was paid for informally. For years the SPDC allocated little funding to diseases such as HIV/AIDS, tuberculosis and malaria, and USDA harassment prompted some INGO withdrawals. The official Nargis response was callous in the extreme.[168]

In consequence, international evaluations by the end of the junta years were often shockingly bad. The Press Freedom Index 2010 ranked Myanmar 174 out of 178 countries, ahead only of Iran, Turkmenistan, North Korea and Eritrea.[169] The Corruption Perceptions Index 2010 placed Myanmar at 176 out of 178 countries, tied with Afghanistan and ahead only of Somalia.[170] The Global Peace Index 2010 ranked Myanmar at 132 out of 149 countries.[171] The Failed States Index 2010 put Myanmar on alert at 16 out of 177 countries.[172] In 2011 Freedom House found Myanmar again to be one of a mere handful of wholly "not free" countries.[173] The Political Instability Task Force and related projects reached uniformly negative assessments.[174] Progress toward achieving the UN's Millennium Development Goals by the target date of 2015 was generally poor.[175] Duffield justly wrote of "chronic emergency in Myanmar."[176]

Government by junta

In September 1988, Burma's democracy movement was remorselessly crushed and an internal coup put a fresh cohort of military leaders in direct command of the state. Naked, unvarnished and unapologetic, *tatmadaw* government held sway until 2011. In many ways, overt martial law was little other than an intensification of pre-existing military control. The decisive political event in the country's postcolonial history remained 1962. In other ways, however, government by junta represented an important new departure.

Internally, as Callahan writes, SLORC and the SPDC oversaw a process of change whereby "the patterns that had long characterized Myanmar's social order [were] turned inside out."[177] A closed economy was opened to inward investment. Parts of the country's extensive borderlands, marked for decades by fighting, were allowed a fragile peace and limited development through ceasefire deals concluded with rebel forces. Some frontier zones even became more dynamic than the Bamar core. The *tatmadaw* itself, long pinned down and stretched to the limit by guerrilla action in peripheral areas, was doubled in size and refocused on making money either for survival at lower ranks or for personal enrichment at upper levels. What had been a broadly egalitarian slide into penury under a reasonably ascetic authoritarianism from 1962 to 1988 thereby became a tawdry winner-takes-all race for personal gain led from the top of the political system. Finally, a dead-end, one-party, quasi-socialist state challenged by communist and ethnic insurgents was dismantled and the military machine slowly turned its attention to constitution making in the shadow of Aung San Suu Kyi's looming presence and moral authority.[178] In sum, Callahan argues that the changes engineered after 1988 constituted "a massive remaking of state and society, comparable perhaps to that of the British after 1886."[179]

Externally, too, 1988 marked a breakpoint.[180] Andrew Selth notes that although Burma under Ne Win was viewed by the global community as a thinly-disguised military dictatorship, it was nevertheless "accepted in world councils." Moreover, once the rigors of socialist autarky were eased in the

1970s, significant aid was allocated. Looking out from Rangoon, "The regime saw its greatest threats coming from armed insurgent groups, pressure from Burma's larger and more powerful neighbours and, at a further remove, entanglement in the strategic competition between the superpowers."[181] It thus had an army configured for guerrilla warfare, a diplomatic stance premised on careful management of relations with China and India, and a strategic posture of strict Cold War neutralism. From the late 1980s onward, however, while domestic unrest was still a leading concern, external threat perceptions were "turned on their head." For the junta, China, India and Russia became close supporters. The US and UK, seen before as broadly helpful, were viewed as aggressors, and the UN was not trusted. Looking out from their fortified new capital of Nay Pyi Taw, the generals remained worried about internal opposition not only from rebel ethnic groups, but also from the democracy movement. By and large, however, their Asian neighbors were less menacing than the US and its allies. Under the junta Myanmar therefore built a large conventional army designed to project a credible deterrent capability, and a diplomatic stance premised above all on tight relations with China and Russia, both veto-wielding members of the UN Security Council. It also cultivated economic and security contacts in Asia and beyond. By the end of the period there were rumors that those contacts extended to a nuclear link with North Korea.[182]

Throughout, dictatorship was the dominant reality. In its founding moment in 1988, the junta revealed its true nature in a harsh clampdown that saw all traces of the four eights movement erased from the public domain. Thereafter, it reacted with repression to the NLD landslide in 1990, the saffron uprising in 2007 and many smaller, largely hidden challenges, devastating countless lives and communities along the way.[183] As Selth wrote of the saffron uprising, "Despite claims of confusion and dissension within the regime, its response to these disturbances was never in doubt."[184] That his point was applicable throughout the period was shown in the official response to Cyclone Nargis less than one year later, when regime security in a garrison state was prioritized over human security in a razed and ravaged delta. However, although the junta took the political initiative through constitutional reform in the 2000s, it never succeeded in moving decisively beyond the deadlock that visibly ensnared the country in 1988. Notwithstanding a degree of grassroots acquiescence and even support, military leaders failed to establish broad popular legitimacy in the face of democratic mobilization and taunts.[185] A lasting solution to ethnic nationality claims was even more elusive, with one clear indictment being extensive migration. By the start of the 2010s, the diaspora in Thailand alone numbered maybe 1.5 million individuals. All too many exiles were the "disposable people" chronicled by Kevin Bales.[186]

For more than 22 years, dismal impacts of military control were notably visible in the sphere of political institutions. At the outset, SLORC adopted a scorched earth policy, abrogating the 1974 constitution, either eliminating or colonizing existing structures, and making everything subject to enhanced military control. As much as possible, the generals sought to eliminate the competing sources of power that surfaced in 1988. Indeed, the very notion of dividing authority was wholly foreign to their way of thinking. In consequence, the period was characterized throughout by an austere, desolate and destitute institutional landscape in which only a core of laws and structures found helpful to government by junta remained in place. Not until the revival of parliamentary institutions in 2011 was anything done to reconstruct structures devastated in 1988, and even then the prospects for meaningful change remained highly uncertain.

The best explanation for this bleak state of affairs looks to the past. Dependence and disintegration in the colonial period implanted social tensions that a jejune political class was unable to manage, and entrenched modes of state-society relations premised on violence. Dominion and dissent in the first phase of independence were both consequences of what had gone before, and cause of much that was to follow. For sure, historical contingency and human agency played key parts. Nothing had to turn out the way it did, and choices made by elite actors were often significant. Nevertheless, there was a strong element of path dependence in this case, with most programming undertaken by the British.[187] This placed severe constraints on available courses of action and ensured that when major challenges arose, as they often did, leading figures forcefully reasserted state control and pointed the way to the dictatorship and deadlock of the junta years.[188]

4

Democracy and deliberation

Disintegration under colonial rule, dissent under military-backed state socialism and deadlock under martial law combined to create a situation in which Myanmar today faces major political challenges. For the military leaders who retain control and seized a degree of political initiative through constitutional reforms underpinning a return to civilian government in 2011, the pathway is clear and will comprise full institutionalization of discipline-flourishing democracy. For activists in the democratic camp and minority ethnic nationalities, by contrast, any attempt to return to a political track congruent with all that the notion of Burma now signifies is likely to require at least three important departures from the military roadmap. First, reformers will need to confront authoritarianism and sponsor reforms capable of entrenching and sustaining real democracy. Second, they will have to tackle issues of ethnic discord and thereby determine the shape of the political nation. Third, they may have no choice but to address difficult individual matters of truth, reconciliation and justice. This chapter begins by looking at the disciplined democracy brought into being in 2011. It then switches to a Burma redux agenda and in a speculative context of genuine democratization explores issues of transitional process, national reconciliation and transitional justice. Drawing on the considerable body of work amassed by comparative political science, it seeks not to lay down a fixed route for the Myanmar people, but rather to learn from experience elsewhere about the challenges they will in all probability encounter if they embark on large-scale institutional reform.

Disciplined democracy

Foundations for what the junta eventually called discipline-flourishing democracy were laid before the National Convention was launched in January 1993. SLORC Order No. 13/92, issued by Khin Nyunt on October 2, 1992, set out six core constitutional objectives: non-disintegration of the union; non-disintegration of national solidarity; consolidation and perpetuation of sovereignty; emergence of a genuine multiparty democratic system; development of principles of justice, liberty and equality; and *tatmadaw* participation in national leadership.[1] On September 16, 1993, delegates ratified 104 detailed basic principles in line with these objectives, covering core aspects of the state, legislature, executive, judiciary, and so on. Even though these principles strongly determined the shape of the future constitution, however, drafting work proceeded slowly. Following a November 1995 NLD withdrawal and subsequent expulsion, proceedings were formally suspended in April 1996.[2] For many years thereafter little public progress was made, though the Convention's steering committee continued to meet frequently.[3]

Only after Khin Nyunt, now prime minister as well as MI chief, unveiled a seven-point "roadmap to democracy" in August 2003 was the Convention revived in May 2004. This time, more than 1,000 delegates were corralled in an isolated purpose-built facility north of Yangon. Law No. 5/96 criminalized all public criticism. Meeting sporadically over more than three years, the Convention concluded its proceedings on September 3, 2007. On May 10, 2008, a draft constitution, with 15 chapters and 457 articles, was put to a national referendum. In 47 townships largely destroyed by Cyclone Nargis on May 2–3, voting was postponed until May 24. Turnout was reported at 98 percent, and 92 percent of voters were said to have endorsed the draft.[4] The constitution was formally adopted on May 29, 2008, with a proviso that it would come into effect when parliament assembled.[5]

Many aspects of the 2008 constitution reflect current global practice. In a bicameral national legislature, the 440-member lower house or *Pyithu Hluttaw* (House of Representatives) is formed chiefly through township constituencies adjusted for population, and the 224-member upper house or *Amyotha Hluttaw* (House of Nationalities) is formed mainly through elected representatives drawn in equal numbers from each of the country's seven regions (formerly divisions) and seven states.[6] The 14 territorial assemblies are also constituted largely by popular vote. The 664 members of the national legislature come together as an electoral college to nominate three candidates and select one as president and head of state, and the other two as vice-presidents. While candidates are required to be members of the national legislature, once selected they are deemed to have vacated their parliamentary seats. The president serves a maximum of two five-year terms, and constructs an executive drawing in individuals from any walk of life. Again, ministers cannot serve concurrently in the legislature. The judiciary is structured from townships up to a Supreme Court.

Article 11 enunciates a commitment to separation of powers and checks and balances among the major branches of government. Chapter VIII on rights and duties enshrines core values of justice, liberty and equality.

From the outset, however, the contentious sixth and final item on the junta's October 1992 list of objectives, *tatmadaw* participation in national leadership, was seen by many as a disabling distortion. Faithfully reflected in the 104 detailed basic principles, it became the animating core of the 2008 constitution. In both houses of the national parliament and in all 14 territorial assemblies, only 75 percent of members are elected. The other 25 percent are appointed by the commander-in-chief of the *tatmadaw* (Articles 109, 141, 161). In the executive, all presidential candidates must be well acquainted with military affairs (Article 59). While two candidates are nominated by elected members of the bicameral legislature, the third is named by military appointees (Article 60). Once selected, the president is effectively placed above the law by provisions ruling out answerability to parliament or the judiciary (Article 215). The commander-in-chief of the *tatmadaw* has the right to appoint ministers in the key fields of domestic and national security (Article 232). The National Defense and Security Council, chaired by the president, has pivotal powers (Articles 201, 204, 206, 213, 340, 342, and 410–32). Ethnic militias are placed under *tatmadaw* supervision (Article 338). Looking to the past, all senior junta officials are given immunity from prosecution for acts carried out in accordance with prevailing laws (Article 445). Looking to the future, provisions for military rule during a state of emergency effectively legitimate a coup (Articles 40, 410–32). Although there is, then, much of value in the 2008 constitution, clauses entrenching military control have elicited broad criticism.[7]

Popular endorsement of the constitution set the stage for a general election.[8] While 2010 was long trailed as the chosen year, it was not until August 13 that polling was scheduled for November 7, two and a half years after the referendum. Among other things, a Political Parties Registration Law of March 8, 2010 stipulated that only persons not serving a prison term could join a party.[9] Complementary laws declared the 1990 election void, and laid down a battery of restrictions on party formation and operation.[10] One early consequence was that about 160 members of the NLD, victor in the 1990 poll, met on March 29 to decide how to proceed. In the context of a statement from Aung San Suu Kyi, transmitted from house arrest by her lawyer Nyan Win, that she "would not even think of registering under these unjust [election] laws," members agreed unanimously not to contest the election.[11] In effect, the NLD ceased to exist when a May 6 deadline for party re-

registration passed, and formal dissolution was confirmed on September 14, 2010. In January 2011, a special appellant court in Nay Pyi Taw affirmed that the NLD was an "unlawful organization."[12] Nevertheless, the party's Yangon office continued to function, and following Aung San Suu Kyi's November 2010 release NLD statements and position papers were issued. Across the wider society, views on the election were quite diverse.[13]

For the 2010 general election, 1,163 constituencies were mapped: 330 lower-house and 168 upper-house seats in the national parliament, and 665 seats in the 14 state and regional assemblies.[14] At sub-national level, elected members ranged from 109 in the largest assembly in Shan State to 15 in the smallest in Kayah State.[15] Other than in Chin State, all territorial assemblies reserved a small set of elected seats for designated ethnic minorities.[16] However, problems in insecure or conflict areas meant that voting did not take place in a handful of constituencies, bringing the total down to 1,154: 325 lower-house and 168 upper-house seats in the national parliament, and 661 seats in territorial assemblies. To contest the poll, 47 parties applied for registration to the Election Commission. Five had existed since 1990, and 42 were new.[17] Constitutional provisions for *tatmadaw* control of ethnic militias always looked like being a major issue, and non-compliance by the Kachin Independence Organization and the UWSA ceasefire group meant either that party registrations were restricted or that polling did not take place.[18] Failure to field candidates in three constituencies, at a non-refundable cost of roughly $500 per candidate, triggered further non-registrations.

Ultimately, however, 37 parties were approved. Five were pre-existing and 32 were new. This was a major reduction from 1990, when 235 parties applied to contest the poll and 93 took part. Candidates per constituency also fell from 4.7 in 1990 to 2.6 in 2010.[19] Moreover, in 2010 only two parties mounted national campaigns.[20] The Union Solidarity and Development Party, formed from the USDA, stood loyalist candidates in more than 1,100 seats.[21] The NUP, successor to the BSPP and major loser to the NLD in 1990, contested about 1,000 constituencies. Each had more candidates than the other 35 parties combined. The two main opposition parties were the National Democratic Force, formed by former NLD members, which contested 163 constituencies, and the Democratic Party (Myanmar), which contested 47. The most visible ethnic challenge came from the Shan Nationalities Democratic Party, which fielded 157 candidates. Every other party stood fewer than 50 candidates, and some were very small indeed.[22] Especially in territorial assembly elections, the choice for many voters was binary: USDP or NUP.

The campaign lasted for two months, and covered the entire nation apart from the small number of border areas judged unsafe for electoral politics. In this regard there was an improvement on 1990, for then electioneering did not take place at all in many peripheral parts.[23] However, the blanket ban on ethnic parties in Kachin State and the election's failure to penetrate core Wa areas were important concerns.[24] In line with 1990 practice, the 2010 campaign was marked by a limited relaxation of free speech and assembly restrictions decreed in September 1988. Nevertheless, advance permission for party political gatherings was still mandated, unless conducted at party offices. Candidates were also required to refrain from saying or writing anything that might incite sedition or tarnish the image of the state or *tatmadaw*.[25] In August 2010, Richard Horsey, former ILO liaison officer, argued that "parties and individuals will likely exercise a considerable degree of caution in what they say, and initial indications are that the media will also be constrained."[26] An anodyne campaign fully confirmed his analysis.[27] It concluded with a quiet election day and a reported turnout of 73.8 percent. Voters cast ballots for the lower house of the national parliament, the upper house of the national parliament, and the relevant territorial assembly. Counts then took place in individual polling stations, purportedly in the presence of candidates and members of the public.

The official result of the 2010 election saw the USDP take 884 seats (77 percent), with 259 out of 325 in the lower house of the national assembly (80 percent), 129 out of 168 in the upper house (77 percent), and 496 out of 661 in territorial assemblies (75 percent). The NUP took 62 seats (5 percent): 12 in the lower house, 5 in the upper house, and 45 in territorial assemblies. The NDF secured 16 seats (1.5 percent). The most successful ethnic parties were the SNDP with 57 seats (5 percent) and the Rakhine Nationalities Development Party with 35 seats (3 percent).[28] This outcome was barely credible.[29] Substantial amounts of advance voting, estimated at 10 percent of the total, favored the USDP to an implausible degree, and other ballots were clearly coerced or bought.[30]

Nearly three months later, on January 31, 2011, Myanmar's national parliament assembled for the first time since 1988, triggering ratification of the 2008 constitution. As highly secretive proceedings unfolded, however, military rule looked to be largely undisturbed. On February 4, the electoral college backed Thein Sein, hitherto premier, for the presidency with 408 votes. Elected to the two vice-presidencies were former junta stalwart Tin Aung Myint Oo (171 votes), and prominent Shan doctor Sai Mauk Kham (75 votes). Shwe Man, also a former SPDC member, was elected speaker of the lower house, and retired general Khin Aung Myint ran unopposed for speaker of the upper house.[31] When Thein Sein later unveiled his cabinet of 30 ministers, all were either USDP affiliates or serving generals. All were also male. On March 30, the entire PDC structure from SPDC down to village tract and ward level was dissolved, and power was vested in the Union Government. Formally, Than Shwe relinquished his two key portfolios to Thein Sein, President of the Republic of the Union of Myanmar, and General Min Aung Hlaing, Commander-in-Chief of the *tatmadaw*. However, since active or retired military personnel still exercised considerable control, with Than Shwe himself clearly still a key figure, the extent of political reform appeared to be limited. The dark joke circulating locally was that Than Shwe had "indeed handed over power — from his right hand to his left hand."[32]

Several analysts noted that in a context of considerable continuity there were nevertheless areas with important potential for growth. In March 2011, an ICG report focused on five main aspects. First, a generational transition had taken place, with younger and more technocratic figures moving into some senior positions. Second, some state power had been diffused among the presidency, military, parliament and dominant party. Third, some state power had been decentralized to provincial assemblies. Fourth, the role of the military had been checked to some degree. Fifth, over time Than Shwe's influence was likely to decline to some extent.[33] The report detected opportunities for outsiders to promote incremental reform. In April 2011, Kyaw Kyaw analyzed a brief legislative session before a long parliamentary recess, and noted that alongside abundant shortfalls the two houses were beginning to deliver "a level of accountability, or at least disclosure, from the military that has probably not been present for several decades." He identified many possibilities for institutional development, and for gradually opening up a closed political system through exposure of senior military officials to civilian influences and points of view.[34] Such arguments were deeply controversial at the time, and will remain so until meaningful political change takes place.[35]

Transitional process

Notwithstanding the label attached to it and any future possibilities that might unfold, the polity created in Myanmar in 2011 is not democratic. It is true that the core concept is mutable and contested.[36] Over the years the stamp of democracy has been applied to a number of different models.[37] Moreover, at the thin end of a broad spectrum it does taper to little more than formal proceduralism in a competitive struggle for the popular vote.[38] However, even when democracy becomes this narrow the current system fails the test, for the claim that anything resembling competitive electioneering took place in 2010 is risible. More importantly, the extent of military control injected into the 2011 polity makes the entire system structurally long on discipline, and short on democracy. Back in 2004 when the National Convention resumed its work, USDA Secretary-General Htay Oo warned that "The multi-party democratic system being built in Myanmar may not be identical to those of other countries."[39] It turned out to be an accurate forecast. In these circumstances, the only viable analytical strategy is to insist that there are limits to how far the core concept can be stretched before it becomes something else entirely.[40] Standing behind this insistence is the belief that while democracy is enhanced by some adjectives, it is diminished by others. Given the damaging qualifier chosen by the generals, reformers have little choice but to pick up on the Latin American aspiration of the 1980s for a democracy "without adjectives."[41] For Myanmar to return to a path associated with all that notions of Burma now symbolize, a break with authoritarianism remains necessary.

How to make that breach and sponsor a transition to a genuinely democratic system is the biggest challenge facing reformers. Broadly, the strategic choice lies between two alternatives. Incremental change can be undertaken to roll back authoritarianism and build up democracy. While this creates the potential for seamless, peaceful reform, it also promises to take a long time. Alternatively, radical change can be promoted to sweep away all trace of praetorian democracy and construct an entirely new political system. Although this holds out the welcome prospect of a polity untainted by military influence, it is also likely to generate considerable violence. Generally, many Myanmar watchers in academia and the wider commentariat stand on the side of gradual change, as does the whole of Asian officialdom. Against them, many activist groups in global civil society promote radical change, and some western governments have sometimes taken this position.[42] For now, however, the issue of external interest and engagement is set to one side, and comparative analysis of options confronting the Myanmar people is the sole interest.

In the academic literature on transitions, two major camps in many ways map onto this strategic choice. Sheri Berman calls them preconditionists and universalists. "The former believe that democracy generally emerges from a particular set of conditions and experiences, while the latter claim that it can come about in all sorts of ways and settings."[43] Preconditionists thus generate lists of required factors. Universalists look instead to leadership and political will. By and large, preconditionists held sway in the 1950s and 1960s through studies such as Seymour Martin Lipset's *Political Man* (1960), Gabriel A.

Almond and Sidney Verba's *The Civic Culture* (1963), and Robert A. Dahl's *Polyarchy* (1971).[44] As democracy's third wave swept the globe after 1974, however, the universalist claim that democratization is triggered by politics and can take place in almost any context came to the fore.[45] With the collapse of communism in the late 1980s and the looming end of history, democracy promotion stretching from advocacy groups and INGOs all the way up to the commanding heights of the US government became the order of the day.[46] At the same time, the Kantian concept of the democratic peace took its place as received wisdom among policymakers.[47]

Only with the grave disappointment of the Bush administration's Iraq engagement did preconditionists regain the initiative. Then, Amy Chua's *World on Fire* (2003), Fareed Zakaria's *The Future of Freedom* (2003), and a body of work by Edward D. Mansfield and Jack Snyder captured attention.[48] "Of course," wrote Mansfield and Snyder of the sequencing approach presented in *Electing to Fight* (2005), "the international community and their pro-democracy allies may not be able to manage each transition in the optimal way, but if the sequence goes wrong, the world should expect trouble."[49] Likely problems are not only violence, but also diminishing long-term reform prospects by making a false start on democracy. When conditions promoted as conducive to democratization are examined, three main domains open up.

First, reaching back ultimately to Aristotle but drawing more fully on recent empirical work, modernization theorists emphasize economic factors. In the late 1950s, when Lipset examined social conditions supporting democracy, economic development came out as critical.[50] In the mid-1960s, the link was confirmed in Barrington Moore's famous dictum: "No bourgeois, no democracy."[51] Moreover, while other scholars focused on the role of the working class, economic progress remained key.[52] Later analysis by Adam Przeworski and others examined the material consequences of political regimes and held that although development does not generate democracy, it does sustain it.[53] In turn, this contention was challenged by scholars arguing that economic maturity also boosts the probability that a country will make a transition.[54] In 2005, modernization theory was comprehensively reasserted by Ronald Inglehart and Christian Welzel.[55]

Second, looking to Alexis de Tocqueville but again focusing on modern empirical work, cultural theorists argue that social factors are critical. They particularly highlight rich associational links, long viewed as the foundation for democracy in America.[56] In 1993, when Robert D. Putnam investigated the Italian case, he focused above all on the sense of civic community generated by dense networks of secondary bodies. His analysis was not comforting for would-be democrats in tough contexts, for he unearthed major historical constraints on social development. "Where norms and networks of civic engagement are lacking, the outlook for collective action appears bleak. The fate of the Mezzogiorno is an object lesson for the Third World today and the former Communist lands of Eurasia tomorrow." Nevertheless, even in a context of binding path dependence, his final words on the Italian south indicated that cultural supports remain indispensable. "Building social capital will not be easy, but it is the key to making democracy work."[57] In a later study, he lamented the collapse of civic engagement in America, and considered how to revive it.[58]

Third, a strand of debate emerging only in recent years examines the contribution of political institutions to successful democratization. Mansfield and Snyder argue negatively that "the chance of war arises mainly in those transitional states that lack the strong political institutions needed to make democracy work."[59] As positive requirements, they list an effective state, the rule of law, organized parties competing in fair elections, and professional news media. Arguing that democratization must be correctly sequenced (a contention they attribute above all to Dahl), they prescribe a three-step process.[60] At the outset, political leaders must "define the boundaries of the nation in a way that has broad legitimacy." If problems arise, "national legitimacy can only be achieved by constructing effective state institutions that begin to meet a people's needs for security and create for them a shared fate even if they do not share nationality."[61] Implied in this are state capacity and a constituency, probably from the center-right, prepared to invest in democratization. Next, leaders must work to enhance popular participation. Only when these tasks have been accomplished can attention finally turn to unleashing mass political parties.[62]

Whether Myanmar's reformers choose to take an incremental or radical approach, these issues are worth examining. On the one hand, the country's history from the long 1950s conforms closely to the preconditionist dystopia: "a failed and violent transition may leave a legacy of nationalist ideology, militarized institutions, undemocratic rules, and foreign enmities that will hinder further democratic consolidation."[63] On the other, dismal contemporary conditions of economic, social and political underdevelopment also direct attention to preconditionist analyses.

Heading the agenda is a national identity congruent with state borders. Here the chance that political transition will fragment the state must be acknowledged. Indeed, post-communist experience in East-Central Europe provides ample evidence of disintegration through democratization as central control erodes, multiple political arenas emerge, and power shifts from core to periphery.[64] In Myanmar, however, this possibility looks less likely now than in the immediate postcolonial period, not least because the region is dominated by established states that abhor irredentism. Thus, while territorial splits cannot be ruled out, it is necessary to consider how nation building might take place within existing borders. Further primary tasks require the state defensively to do all it can to contain ethnic conflict, meaning in Myanmar that the *tatmadaw* must stop intimidating individuals and communities and that militias should also be restrained. Constructively, humanitarian programs must address the worst forms of suffering, economic programs must stimulate national development, and social programs must embed cultural diversity and respect within a unified national community. The overarching aim is to create a civic safety net articulated around one nation, within which subsidiary ethnic identities and commitments can be couched. At the same time, a powerful political constituency believing democratization to be in its interest must be built. This would almost certainly mean reaching into the *tatmadaw*, one of only two institutions alongside the Buddhist *sangha* to span most of the country.

Once progress has been made on these fronts, the second step is gradual enhancement of democracy. Critically, the advice is to desist at least as much as to act. Democratic institutions should be filled out only when the first stage in the sequence is complete. Moreover, an important rider concerns the type of system to be put in place. Andrew Reynolds and colleagues advocate a polity institutionalizing power sharing mechanisms and protections for minority groups, and hold that this mandates a parliamentary system based on proportional representation and asymmetrical federalism.[65] South similarly argues for a consociational democracy comprising a grand coalition of elites, minority vetoes, and segmental autonomy.[66] While federal states are not always free from conflict, many analysts broadly concur.[67] Others add that it is necessary to prevent the formation of a dominant ethnic core, such as the Bamar heartland in Myanmar.[68] Still others argue for a multiparty system with a vigorous opposition and limited opportunities for rent seeking.[69] Finally, as a third step, once progress has been registered in this domain, and constitutional engineers have created a robust set of democratic institutions, mass political parties can be given free rein. First nation building, second democratic enhancement, third mass participation is the pattern prescribed above all by Mansfield and Snyder.

Considered in the context of contemporary Myanmar, this counsel has many unsavory aspects. The general analytical thrust points not to dramatic political change and quick-fire democratization, but rather to the kind of pacted transition seen in Southern Europe and Latin America in the 1970s and 1980s. After 50 years of oppressive *tatmadaw* rule, however, a big tent approach embracing former tyrants is hard to defend, especially when tyranny is under attack the world over. Moreover, the extent of the reformist task becomes clear when lessons from pacted transitions are examined. In a comparative study, Guillermo O'Donnell and Philippe C. Schmitter found that splits in the regime were always the point of departure. "Conversely, no transition can be forced purely by opponents against a regime which maintains the cohesion, capacity, and disposition to apply repression."[70] From Dankwart Rustow they drew the notion of democratization "on the installment plan" as collective actors with distinct objectives agree to a series of compromises.[71] From Dahl they took the concept of a "democratic bargain."[72] Overall, they noted the "extraordinary uncertainty of the transition," and held that pacted transitions are most successful if parties of the right are "helped" to do well, though not too well, in founding elections.[73] While Myanmar's 2010 election triggered hope that reform might move in this direction, rigid military control imposed on the 2011 polity indicated that it may take a long time for significant installments to feed through.

Furthermore, much evidence from fourth-wave East-Central European transitions in the late 1980s and early 1990s points in a very different direction.[74] Across nearly 30 countries, a sharp break with authoritarianism was generally most productive, popular mobilization was broadly positive in its effects, and even nationalist action could work for the benefit of democracy.[75] In these cases, however, the key success factor was a strong opposition movement able to dictate the terms of transition. By contrast, in countries where despots retained great power, dictatorship was generally the outcome. In situations of relatively balanced power between regime and rebels, unconsolidated, unstable, partial democracy was the result.[76] Contemporary Myanmar, with a dominant military machine and a weak and divided opposition movement, does not appear to be well placed.[77]

Pulling all this together, comparative experience generates perhaps three main lessons for Myanmar. One is that there is a fundamental need to invest in the underpinnings of sustainable democracy. However political change comes about, the chances of long-term success are almost certain to be enhanced by economic and social development. Moreover, the possibility of triggering political reform also then increases. Many analyses converge on this point. The second is that within this general context there is a specific need to bolster forces that can broadly be considered part of the political opposition. The central lesson of post-Cold War East-Central European transitions is that success comes to vibrant civic movements. The third is that though undeniably distasteful, the sequencing argument remains relevant. By any measure, Myanmar is an unpromising candidate for democratic reform, and taking the right steps looks to be critically necessary. Certainly the possibility of a false move harming long-term prospects suggests that a cautious approach is advisable.

In contemporary debate of the Myanmar case, such themes have a growing resonance. The need to build robust social foundations for political reform through broad-based investment has many adherents.[78] The requirement to address the structural weakness of the opposition movement is strongly supported.[79] The advice to embrace key political forces through inclusive dialogue focused on nation building for democracy is endorsed by all major dissenting groups. In this latter regard, calls from across the full span of opposition for a re-examination of the modern nation's founding myth in fresh discussion of the interethnic accord struck at Panglong in 1947 are centrally relevant.

National reconciliation

The issue of national reconciliation focuses attention on a major problem leaders in both the democratic camp and ethnic nationality groups have with Myanmar's 2011 polity: its limited capacity for constructing a true nation beneath the state formed by disciplined democracy. While the National Convention co-opted some opposition figures in both 1993 and 2004, it did so strictly on military terms and in very small numbers. The NLD was first marginalized and then excluded, and ethnic nationalities were represented only patchily. Furthermore, the entire process did little to generate a political solution to low-grade civil war partially suspended through ceasefire agreements in the 1990s, but never resolved.[80] While the new political system is neither wholly undemocratic nor totally centralized, there is thus a firm belief that it functions on a militant Bamar basis, giving opposition forces little choice but to fall in line. Indeed, sponsoring inclusive talks in a spirit of national reconciliation appears to be entirely absent from military thinking shaped by the core *tatmadaw* doctrine of "One blood, one voice, one command."[81] Rarely have dialogue initiatives been taken seriously by the governing elite.[82]

Across the complete span of opposition, all-embracing national reconciliation is thus fiercely promoted. Aung San Suu Kyi has long made this a key part of her platform.[83] On her first full day of freedom in November 2010, she renewed her commitment: "I'm going to work for national reconciliation."[84]

Among ethnic nationality leaders it has always been a staple of political discourse, and remains vibrant today.[85] Democratic parties that successfully contested the 2010 election acknowledge the importance of broad-based dialogue.[86] On rare occasions that ordinary citizens are given a chance to speak, they express similar commitments.[87] In addition, this is the position regularly endorsed by the UN General Assembly since 1994.[88] Standing behind this procedural demand is a history of complex and often disintegrative ethnic relations shaped by a plethora of factors.[89] Understandings of the past are deeply contested, and in all probability always will be.

Despite this, much contemporary debate focuses on a precise historical moment, and a brief historical document running to no more than a single page. The agreement signed by Aung San and a number of ethnic nationality leaders in the Shan town of Panglong in February 1947 established some of the main parameters for Burmese independence in January 1948.[90] Its terms were not implemented, however, and have thus become political flashpoints. Matthew J. Walton argues that, "Over 60 years later, the promises of the Panglong Agreement remain unfulfilled and ethnic conflict continues to plague the nation, but the elusive 'spirit' of Panglong still affects Burmese of every ethnicity."[91] Animating ethnic calls for national reconciliation talks is a plea to return to this "spirit." Indeed, just as Bamar luminaries stoke the legend of the Thirty Comrades in spearheading independence from imperial powers, so ethnic nationality leaders invest the Panglong agreement with iconic status in pointing the way to a plural modern state. Just before the 2010 general election, 109 ethnic leaders and politicians met in Kalay, Sagaing Division to call for a second Panglong conference. Soon after returning to public life a couple of weeks later, Aung San Suu Kyi endorsed the Kalay Declaration.[92]

However, as Walton notes, what actually happened in Panglong many decades ago is subject to diverse interpretation. The 1947 conference was in fact the second gathering in the town. In March 1946, leaders of the Shan, Kachin, Karen and Chin peoples, then seen as the key minority groups alongside the always rather special Karenni, had come together to discuss options for the postcolonial order. Ahead of both meetings they already had reassurances through the two-Burma principle enshrined in the May 1945 British White Paper that no decision on the place of ethnic minorities in a future independent state would be taken without their consent. Moving into the 1947 meeting, they were further encouraged by a statement from Aung San: "As for the people of the Frontier Areas, they must decide their own future. If they wish to come in with us we will welcome them on equal terms."[93] However, on neither side were positions entirely clear. The Burmans suspected

British skullduggery in promoting minority claims. Distinct ethnic groups took differing positions, and some were not present in Panglong. Only the Shan, Kachin and Chin peoples had formal representation, and notably important absentees were official Karen delegates who preferred to seek a separate deal with the departing colonial power. Walton writes that "A combination of false British promises, sustained Burman hostility toward the Karen, and the refusal of the Karen leadership to compromise when faced with the loss of British support led to the Karen rebellion that broke out immediately following independence and has continued to this day."[94]

The result, Walton argues, is that three distinct myths of Panglong have developed over the years since 1947. The dominant myth, institutionalized by successive military regimes, emphasizes Burmese ethnic unity in throwing off imperial shackles imposed first by the British and later by the Japanese, Burmese ethnic harmony in coming together to sign an agreement for a unified state, Aung San's genius in facilitating ethnic accord, and the essential subsequent role of the military in sustaining national unity and upholding the spirit of Panglong. Conveniently, it overlooks scant ethnic participation and disagreement even among the groups that did attend. The second myth, associated with the democratic opposition, is much the same as the first in its description of what happened in 1947, but different in its analysis of what later transpired. It argues that successive national governments betrayed the spirit of Panglong by limiting the autonomy enjoyed by ethnic minorities and condemning the country to civil war. In looking to recapture a lost unity, however, it too exaggerates the degree to which the people of Burma ever were a single fraternal community. The third myth, associated with ethnic nationality groups, provides a very different account of the events of 1947, finding in them broad-based agreement on a substantial degree of autonomy for non-Burman ethnic peoples, which then fed into constitutional provisions for minority self-government up to and including secession. In common with the second myth, the third holds that the spirit of Panglong has been undermined by state leaders in the period since independence. However, what has been lost is not historic unity, but rather respect for minority claims to self-rule.[95]

While deep conflict thus surrounds Panglong, Walton's final point is that it remains central to national reconciliation and political progress. "The myths of the conference, the agreement, and the vague 'spirit' of this event are fundamental elements of the identities of all ethnic groups… Any discussion of national unity must acknowledge the effects that Panglong has had, and continues to have, on ethnic politics in Burma."[96] He sketches five ways forward, arguing that more testimony should be gathered, limitations of the agreement should be acknowledged, positions taken in 1947 should be reevaluated, the formation of hegemonic identities among ethnic nationalities should be critically examined, and the notion of national identity should be broadly debated. His closing argument is this: "As a national myth, Panglong is crucial to deciphering the persistent ethnic conflict that has plagued Burma since independence, but it is also necessary to reinterpret this 'common history' in a way that recognizes ethnic diversity and even ethnic conflict, particularly if the 'spirit of Panglong' is to have any resonance in fostering national unity."[97] This expansive deliberative agenda looks to be a necessary component of national reconciliation.

Equally important is a supporting process of interethnic accommodation embracing not only questions of political and cultural autonomy, but also issues of economic and social development. Only when ethnic nationality people feel they are no longer targets of exploitation and violence, but rather partners in broad-based national renewal, will nation-building efforts gain traction. In this domain, activist reports commonly emphasize the urgent need for ethnic nationalities to gain release from the heavy hand of the military-state, expressed not only through straightforward repression, but also through insensitive development programs. These matters certainly need to be addressed, possibly through an enhanced role for territorial assemblies in development planning and oversight. However, there is also a need ultimately to consider the role of ethnic militias in nation-building programs. Currently most controversial is the *tatmadaw* attempt to incorporate insurgent forces into its hierarchy, captured in BGF clauses in the 2008 constitution. Such a move is anathema to several ethnic nationalities, for it will leave them defenseless against the might of the military machine. For true nation building to take place, though, it will eventually have to be addressed as part of a larger military restructuring designed to subordinate the *tatmadaw* to civilian control. Elsewhere, parallel efforts have not always been effective in building peace, though often poor implementation has been the problem.[98] In the wider society, reintegration of individuals for whom insurgency has become a way of life is also a key challenge.[99] Experience from Sierra Leone indicates that it is notably difficult to deal with combatants who are abusive, wealthy, educated, ideological, male and young.[100] So great is the deprivation in Myanmar's peripheral zones that some of these characteristics are rarely found. Wealthy and educated are not common descriptors of foot soldiers in many ragtag ethnic militias. Nevertheless, there is clearly a sizable task here. As in other spheres, creating the right incentives is essential if individuals are to renounce a life of war and take up peaceful pursuits.[101]

Finally, complementing and reinforcing elite talks will need to be programs launched at many levels to resolve and transform conflict, and build peace. In this regard, counseling and mediation are likely to be essential elements of a successful nation-building project. Many initiatives will clearly have to focus squarely on ethnic conflict, for decades central to social fragmentation across the nation. Additionally, however, it will be necessary to consider how to bridge deep divisions not merely between government leaders and opposition figures, but also between officials of an oppressive state and the citizens they have long commanded. At this point, analysis moves to the level of discrete individuals, where there is little choice but to examine issues of responsibility for half a century of oppression, and means by which transgressors might be dealt with.

Transitional justice

The umbrella term generally used to capture such matters is transitional justice. Quite how such a big and important topic might be handled in the Myanmar case will depend to a large extent on the nature of any future reform process. If democratization plays out seamlessly and slowly, then questions of transitional justice may never arise. Clearly this is what military leaders are hoping for: if the country really does have to embrace democracy without adjectives, then let it come in a gradualist way that never creates an opening for analysis of past injustice. To be on the safe side, impunity clauses were also written into the 2008 constitution. Nevertheless, if at some stage in the process there is a break point where authoritarianism is visibly left behind and democracy embraced, then such questions will emerge with some force. Indeed, it seems likely that as soon as a genuine move away from decades of military control is made, local people will have little option but to deliberate the terms on which officials tainted by involvement in gross human rights abuse are to be dealt with under the new political dispensation. Again they can turn for inspiration and guidance to vibrant global debate, for as democratization gathered pace in the closing decades of the twentieth century new mechanisms of transitional justice emerged in parallel.[102]

In a very basic sense, analysis of how to deal with abusive former officials boils down to a single issue: punish or pardon. At one extreme, individuals complicit in serious human rights violations can be indicted and, if found guilty, punished. In the mid-1940s, international military tribunals at Nuremberg and Tokyo prosecuted prominent members of the Axis powers defeated in the Second World War. At the other extreme, officials from a prior authoritarian regime can be given an amnesty and allowed to participate in the new order on the same terms as everybody else. In the mid-1970s, Spain's transition after the death of General Francisco Franco delivered transitional justice of this kind, and other third-wave democratizations also pardoned members of outgoing authoritarian regimes in order to generate a smooth reform process. On one side are then ethical imperatives and the demands of justice. On the other are practical attempts to build a functioning democracy. Kantian just desserts confront instrumental concerns.

At the same time, however, there are further issues beyond deciding how far to press complicity and guilt. Luc Huyse argues that "All policy choices involve answers to two key questions: whether to remember or forget the abuses — the issue of acknowledgement — and whether to impose sanctions on the individuals who are co-responsible for these abuses — the issue of accountability."[103] Filling things out, Stanley Cohen holds that five linked debates focus on knowledge, accountability, impunity, expiation, and reconciliation and reconstruction.[104] Many want past crimes to be recorded. Indeed, as Thomas Nagel notes, core demands often focus less on knowledge and more on acknowledgement, for fresh historical data may not be as important as official recognition that abuses long denied really did take place. Issues of both accountability and impunity are almost certain to arise once a break with authoritarianism is made. Additionally, a measure of symbolic purification is often sought. Arthur Stinchcombe notes that in antiquity Roman legions were ceremonially cleansed through lustration. "Whatever the troops had done, after the lustration they were a clean troop of the Republic or Empire." Today, some transitional practices can also be seen as "drawing a ritual boundary between a new clean democratic regime and a bad old warlike, terrorist, totalitarian, and corrupt regime."[105] Finally, in addressing past crimes there is always a linked desire to look to the future and safeguard reconciliation and reconstruction efforts. This promotes expedience and pragmatism, though Cohen notes that "the consensus is that such discretion and prudence should never be extended to genocide and crimes against humanity."[106]

In the late twentieth century, one key institution developed to address some of these many issues was the truth and reconciliation commission. Designed to document abuse under an outgoing dictatorship, such commissions also aim to foster national renewal and may offer qualified amnesty to complicit officials. By the end of the 1980s six such bodies had been created, in the 1990s a further 14 were added, and more followed in the 2000s.[107] Among the most significant were the pioneering *Nunca Más* (Never Again) truth commission on disappeared persons in Argentina (1983), and commissions in Chile (1990), El Salvador (1991) and above all South Africa (1996). A second important institution was the lustration system, seeking to deal with officials from the repressive apparatus of a prior authoritarian state and impose non-criminal sanctions on perpetrators of injustice. These systems were implemented chiefly after the collapse of communism in East-Central Europe, as many countries examined politicians, public officials, judges and others to gauge their degree of involvement with the secret police of the former regime.[108]

In general, truth and reconciliation commissions invite victims to tell their stories and give a personal account of abuse. Truth thereby serves as a proxy for justice, and challenges previous rulers' impunity. In the prototypical South African Truth and Reconciliation Commission, a novel element was that qualified amnesty became part of the process, with perpetrators required to meet key conditions such as exposing the political objectives of gross human rights violations. The Amnesty Committee could investigate, call and cross-examine witnesses to determine whether those conditions had been met. In effect, the commission gave transgressors a second chance in exchange for truth. The process is not without critics. In general, though, it is widely held to have helped overcome apartheid by creating a more reconciled society and facilitating democratization.[109] Indeed, the South African model quickly became a template for truth commissions in other countries also authorized to grant amnesty for certain types of offense.[110]

The key advantage of qualified amnesty is the basis it establishes for reconciliation and reconstruction of civic ties with former oppressors. On a public platform, transgressors are given the chance to reveal their capacity for moral development.[111] Discontinuity thereby runs through the hearts of individuals no longer portrayed as inhuman.[112] Qualified amnesty can thereby provide the opportunity of a fresh start for all, and in this regard is a suitable option for dialogue and negotiation. It can generate a break with the past, as revelation of concealed truth signals a shift in values from the old dictatorship to the new democracy, and accountability mechanisms enable a society to assign responsibility for human rights violations. It is also feasible in terms of time and cost. In four years, the South African Amnesty Committee processed more than 7,000 applications, with nearly 2,000 going through public hearings.[113] Moreover, although apartheid was declared a crime against humanity, the South African amnesty process has not been contested in international courts. Rather, the spread of commissions styled on it signifies a tacit global consensus, which becomes explicit when truth commissions complement prosecutions.[114] The major disadvantage of qualified amnesty is little different from that of amnesty itself: violation of victims' rights to justice. Nevertheless, even they may benefit from reparation programs leading to individual and social empowerment.

Lustration systems come in four basic models: exclusive, inclusive, reconciliatory and mixed. All aim to create a trustworthy and impartial public service and security apparatus. The exclusive system removes officials above a certain rank in the former regime. It was applied in Albania, Bulgaria and the Czech Republic. The inclusive system focuses on the secret police and allows complicit individuals to retain a public position provided that their hidden activities are revealed. It was applied in Hungary and Romania and partly designed for the former Yugoslavia. The reconciliatory system builds on the principle of a second chance found in the inclusive system to allow for continued public service in exchange for truth about the past. It presents officials with a dilemma: either they come clean and retain their position, or they dissemble and risk exclusion. It was applied in Poland.[115] The mixed system fuses elements of the three other types, but draws mainly on the exclusive system. It may lead to discretionary exclusion, or apply a more nuanced approach taking account of personal considerations such as motive, responsibility and skills. Alternatively, it may simply grant exceptions from a general exclusionary rule. It was applied in postwar and post-communist Germany, and by the US-led Coalition Provisional Authority in Iraq.

By and large, lustration systems are useful in processing a substantial case load within a short period of time without undermining democratization. While they are sometimes said to be tools for redistributing power in times of transition, that is not always the case. Similarly, though they have been cast as truth revelation procedures, this is not necessarily so.[116] Within the broad set of lustration models, exclusive variants are often seen as illiberal, "a collective witch-hunt rather than the pursuit of individual responsibility," since they deliver guilt and punishment by category.[117] Chiefly for this reason, they do not have broad support, and inclusive and reconciliatory systems are the major options. For countries without extensive spy networks on the *Stasi* model, the reconciliatory system is key, performing a similar function to truth and reconciliation commissions by floating qualified amnesty in exchange for truth within a larger transitional setting.

The general consensus is that truth commissions and lustration systems are only very imperfect responses to the demands of transitional justice. Cohen argues that "Each strategy, whether justice, restitution, expiation, or reconciliation, assumes that truth-telling has to take place first."[118] Yet observers note how hard it is to gain secure knowledge of the past, and raise searching questions about whether truth is actually told in truth commissions.[119] Striking a balance between justice and expediency is also fraught with difficulty, and will always be open to challenge. From a review of South American experience in the early 1990s, Margaret Popkin and Naomi Roht-Arriaza thus conclude that truth commissions can never be more than a second-best option. They often possess limited powers, may remove serious human rights abuse from the legal sphere, and may generate unrealistic expectations. However, they still find that truth commissions do a reasonable job of compiling an authoritative record, and play a part in establishing accountability and promoting reconciliation.[120] In general, then, analysts tend to argue for a strong dose of realism. As Huyse put it, "if the balance of forces at the time of the transition makes a negotiated mildness inevitable, a truth-telling operation with full exposure of the crimes of the former regime is the least unsatisfactory solution."[121]

In Myanmar, it is possible that negotiated mildness will be on the political agenda at some point in the future, for much opposition discourse points in that direction. If this were to happen, comparative experience could then be explored. One option would be to adopt an integrated approach using elements from truth and reconciliation commissions and reconciliatory lustration systems.[122] The standard grand bargain could apply: qualified amnesty in exchange for truth. Supplementing it, every official could be required to submit a public affidavit detailing involvement in past human rights abuse through circumstance, nature, chain of command, and so on. A prosecutor could then inspect affidavits, testimony and archival documentation, and refer suspect cases for cross-examination in a public forum. Individuals found to have told the truth would be allowed to retain their official positions, regardless of violations. Individuals found to have lied would be dismissed, charged with perjury and prosecuted. In this way, the affidavit would serve as a loyalty test. The dishonest would be removed and punished. The truthful would publicly disavow their prior loyalties and subscribe to the transition. Every official would thus be offered a second chance, regardless of previous involvement. Whether to take that chance would be a personal choice. Furthermore, the transformative potential of the process could dispel much criticism and foster consensus about moving on from the preceding regime. Transgressors' confessions and revelation of a change of heart would enable people to develop a better understanding of the past. Truth combined with the switch of loyalty would facilitate a normative shift toward a new democratic order.

Among officials, the offer of qualified amnesty in exchange for truth is unlikely to be uniformly enticing. On a constructive note, however, it could be used to create an incentive for members of a military machine fearful of prosecution to embrace change. Indeed, such an approach could help to reveal divisions within the *tatmadaw* and enable hidden or suppressed reformist factions to speak out. In South Africa, Joe Slovo's proposals for shared government, a sunset clause for bureaucrats, and qualified amnesty were carefully calibrated to buy off three key sectors: leading politicians in the ruling National Party, civil servants, and security personnel.[123] By and large, they succeeded. A moderate version of the South African process could replace a credible threat of prosecution for past crimes with a threat of legal sanction for present dishonesty. The focus on the present and future rather than on the past would permit individuals to come forward without fearing their revelations might later be used against them in a court of law. Positive incentives would thereby be offered to officials wishing to retain public posts, while others would be allowed simply to leave the state sector.

For members of the wider society keen not to see qualified amnesty watered down, the confessional nature of the process and the repudiation of military governance would generate an important element of discontinuity. Indeed, the sight of hitherto feared members of the military machine testifying about involvement in repression could play an important role in persuading ordinary citizens that things really had changed, that notorious practices like forced labor were a thing of the past, and that a minimal decency now defined their society.[124] By the same token, every new revelation and punishment meted out to untruthful officials could eventually persuade the public that reform was genuine and irreversible. Here would be found a necessary *quid pro quo* for amnesty provisions. Additionally, the dialogue and deliberation embedded in this process could go a long way to entrench principles that are fundamental to any meaningful notion of sustainable democratization.[125]

For sure there would be implementation problems. Crucially, a break with authoritarianism may never take place, rendering the entire issue of transitional justice moot. Beyond that, political polarization could make it impossible to launch the process. Allocating sufficient material and human resources would also be difficult. At a deep social level, a pervasive legacy of fear could undermine the enterprise. However, providing a second chance in exchange for truth is consistent with the country's dominant Buddhist culture of compassion, forbearance and unconditional forgiveness, and features in similar guises in other religious traditions. This spiritual congruence, allied with a generalized desire to move on from long years of discipline and terror, could dispel many doubts.

5

Inattention and involvement

The crushing of Burma's democracy movement in 1988 and the installation of a formal military junta ensured that the country slowly came to the attention of the wider world as a candidate for external action. Indeed, the stark contrast between revolution in many parts of the globe and reaction in this corner of Southeast Asia ultimately played a key role in establishing its international notoriety. Instead of assuming an apparently rightful place as a transitional polity, Myanmar was left out in the cold alongside post-Tiananmen China and a clutch of other renegade states. Being a lot smaller, a lot less strategic and a lot less astutely managed than the People's Republic, it has stayed there ever since. This chapter opens analysis of external responses to the Myanmar problem by examining policies adopted by outsiders over the past quarter-century. The first section provides an overview of debate. The second looks at engagement strategies associated mainly with Asian states and a range of humanitarian organizations. The third evaluates efforts to sanction and isolate Myanmar undertaken by states in the broad western camp and prominent activist groups in global civil society. The final section analyzes the degree of political leverage foreigners have been able to exercise over the dominant military machine and looks for pointers to future involvement. The argument is that while external actors can claim some success, they have generally fallen far short of their major objectives in shaping Myanmar's politics. The result is that today global policy responses are fiercely contested not only among outsiders, but also among people living and working inside the country.

Policy debate

Although global debate about Myanmar dates from the reassertion of military rule in September 1988, Burma clearly witnessed extensive foreign involvement long before that. For decades in the British case and years in the Japanese, imperial powers sought to impose distinct forms of total subjugation on the territory and its people. Later, Cold War rivalries spilled into Burma, and "sudden crowds" of US advisers blew into its nascent democracy "like a keen, fresh, bracing wind, seeking to stir up the ancient world of Asia."[1] To an unusually large degree, however, independent Burma was a nonaligned, neutralist power.[2] In the early 1950s even the Colombo Plan, an aid program promoted by Commonwealth states with US participation, was viewed with some suspicion by political leaders fearful of Cold War entanglements.[3] Moreover, in the course of the 1950s and early 1960s most external action inside the country was terminated as foreign assistance was curtailed haphazardly by Nu, and decisively by Ne Win. Throughout the years down to 1988, outside involvement in Burmese politics and policy remained marginal and insignificant.

On a positive note, Japan maintained close ties for the full extent of the Ne Win era, as a "substantial community of interests" developed between Rangoon and Tokyo.[4] More widely, several other foreign powers tried to engage with an economy reduced to ruins by the mid-1960s and kept that way to the end of the socialist period. Indeed, in the 1970s annual official development assistance expanded considerably from about $20 million at the start of the decade to some $400 million by the end. However, agreed economic reforms were only partially implemented and external influence remained slight.[5] On a negative note, China for some years backed communist insurgents fighting to overthrow the state, and in 1967 allowed Cultural Revolution turmoil to spill into Burma, though again the eventual impact was limited.[6] By and large, then, these years saw the extreme chauvinism and xenophobia of a battle-hardened military elite hold sway. Moreover, for most foreigners Burma was off the map in an almost literal sense. Largely inaccessible behind an effective wall of stringent visa restrictions, it was of little or no concern.

Inattention remained the predominant global stance even when, following on notably from the anti-Marcos People Power revolution in the Philippines in 1986, street protesters built mass mobilization around the four eights uprising. "The death knell for Burmese socialism tolled an entire year before Tiananmen Square burned and the Berlin Wall crumbled, but few outside Burma heard it. Television news teams were not present to record the extraordinary events surrounding Burma's democracy movement in summer 1988."[7] Gradually, though, the tightening of SLORC control and the global recognition conferred on Aung San Suu Kyi above all by award of the 1991 Nobel Peace Prize enabled the country to emerge from the shadows of media attention and secure a place on the list of activist concerns.[8] Other than during episodes of extreme national crisis, however, it has never fully captured outside interest. In 1993, John B. Haseman, US defense attaché in Rangoon from 1987 to 1990, registered widespread neglect: "Perhaps the world has seen too much in recent years. Massacre and repression in China, war in the Middle East, the breakup of the communist empire in Europe, and the end of the cold war have been striking events that have riveted the world's attention. In the process, however, the world has overlooked the abuses conducted against its people by Burma's military government for almost five years."[9] Much the same could be said about the decades since.

Despite this generalized disinterest, many foreign powers did recalibrate their policies in the late 1980s and several initiatives were taken. Indeed, when SLORC's internal coup gave an unwelcome twist to the Burma story in 1988, a span of specialist opinion in diplomatic circles was jolted into action, and fresh proposals for external involvement were formulated and implemented. Present from the outset was a wide range of formal and informal pressure reaching from Asia across much of the rest of the world. Far more visible were sanctions, which emerged at the end of the Cold War as the instrument of choice for western states intent on dealing with pariah regimes.[10] Imposed initially through *ad hoc* embargoes, sanctions came rapidly to dominate US policy and were deployed in differing forms by many of its allies.[11] Entrenched military control and an ersatz transition to democracy in 2011 triggered no more than limited change in foreign engagement.

Looking in the period since 1988 at how decisions driving external policy have been reached, and by whom, it is clear that little attempt has ever been made to engage or determine public opinion inside Myanmar. The primary reason is obvious. Fear spread throughout the land by ruthless military action against street protesters notably in 1988 and 2007, against opposition groups throughout the period, and against ethnic minority peoples across all of the years since independence has always made for a highly restrictive environment and placed most political discussion off-limits.[12] As far as many outsiders are concerned, in a context where the very notion of the public sphere is enervated and corrupted it is simply not possible to gauge internal views on options for external action.

In this daunting setting, foreigners with an interest in shaping Myanmar's politics tend to fall back on a series of proxies. First and foremost, they appealed for years to the events of 1988–90, and occasionally continue to do so today. They also cite aftershocks delivered by the military machine, which are documented by local journalists and activists and picked up by national and regional groups such as the Burma Campaign UK (founded in 1991), the Free Burma Coalition (1995), the Alternative ASEAN Network on Burma (1996), the US Campaign for Burma (2003), and the Burma Partnership (2006). Sometimes they turn to diaspora groups incorporated into global civil society, such as the exile National Coalition Government of the Union of Burma (based in Washington, DC), the National Council of the Union of Burma (based in Mae Sot, Thailand), and webs of ethnic minority concern. In addition, they parse the often Delphic remarks of Aung San Suu Kyi, which during long periods of house arrest were necessarily few in number and transmitted through intermediaries.[13] However, while activist voices are convincing in denouncing the litany of military abuse, there is rarely much insight into popular thinking.[14] This is a notably serious problem as the most widely cited proxy of all, more than 8 million votes cast for the NLD and its affiliates in 1990, recedes ever further into history. By the time of the generals' praetorian transition two decades later, the citizens who had participated in the 1990 poll constituted no more than a very small segment of the population.

This procedural deficiency has long stood at the heart of much substantive dispute. For countries clustered around the US and high-profile activist groups, aggressive strategies focusing on sanctions in the state sector and boycotts in the non-state sector are fully justified by the extent of military oppression, signals indicating a fervent popular desire to take a new path, abundant documentary reports, and above all the stance taken by Aung San Suu Kyi and the NLD.[15] By contrast, no Asian country has ever sought to move much beyond diplomatic engagement at least in part because evidence from inside the country is judged to rule out anything more coercive. Indeed across much of the region, the stated and possibly self-serving belief is that local people not only do not welcome tough external action, but also do not favor foreign involvement of any kind in their politics. Even here, however, close discussion with citizens is largely absent. Rather, policy preferences are projected into Myanmar on the basis of readings of regional values and practices, often reinforced by naked self-interest.

Policy debate is thus deeply flawed, with few protagonists making any attempt to determine how local people might like outsiders to help them, if indeed they seek external assistance at all. While many circumstantial explanations can be given, none is wholly acceptable. On the one hand, few outsiders make much effort to gauge grassroots feelings among regular citizens, community leaders, civil society groups, business organizations, and so on. On the other, many foreigners nevertheless take entrenched policy positions on no more than limited information. Even basic cost-benefit analyses are uniformly absent.[16] This state of affairs is highly problematic, for it means that no program of either action or inaction is secured by endorsement inside the country. This is a critical procedural context for the following survey, which first examines engagement strategies and then turns to isolation. In the absence of significant popular input from Myanmar, the evaluations made in the two sections look chiefly to the internal plausibility and coherence of distinct approaches.

Engagement strategies

In the period since military control was reasserted in 1988, many outside actors have devised engagement strategies designed to coax Myanmar's leaders down the path of reform through diplomatic pressure and a range of positive incentives. Indeed, some measure of engagement has long been endorsed in principle by every major external stakeholder, both state and non-state. From the UN down through leading powers in international society to prominent activist groups promoting human rights and political reform, the common call has long been for the military elite to open up and sponsor meaningful change facilitated by outsiders. Whether the issue is national reconciliation, response to humanitarian emergency, or monitoring of plebiscites, the wider world routinely presents itself as a key player. The UN has thus sent a stream of envoys over the years. The UN and ASEAN joined in working with the Myanmar government on post-Nargis reconstruction. ASEAN, the UK and US all offered to send monitors for the 2008 referendum and the 2010 election (and were all rebuffed).

In practice, however, engagement strategies have been advanced most vigorously by regional states led by ASEAN and China, and by humanitarian organizations working on the ground inside the country. By contrast, western states clustered around the US and prominent activist groups tend to invest so heavily in aggressive responses that options for engagement rarely gain much traction, and in any case are hard to undertake with any credibility. Some change has been registered in the past decade following recalibrations first by Australia and the EU, and eventually by the US. In October 2002, Alexander Downer, Australian Minister of Foreign Affairs, visited Myanmar to explore engagement options, and for some years his government experimented with an in-country program of human rights training for military personnel.[17] From 2002 the EU made a major effort both to construct a large aid presence and "to launch a serious dialogue with the Myanmar government aimed at accomplishing longer-term policy change, while also strengthening efforts to build social capital and civil society." By 2006 it had assembled what the ICG termed "by far the most comprehensive aid portfolio in Myanmar."[18] In 2009 the US sought to open dialogue channels with senior officials.[19] In 2011 the EU suspended some political sanctions and reiterated its willingness to talk.[20] However, conflicting signals have ensured that no major western power has significantly altered its political profile inside Myanmar. This section thus focuses on Asian nations and largely inconspicuous INGOs. The entry point is China's role in dealing with a state with which it shares a 1,350-mile border.[21]

This bilateral relationship naturally stretches back into the mists of time, and has long cast a deep shadow over all forms of foreign engagement.[22] When sovereignty resided in the person of a supreme ruler both sides operated tribute systems, and as recently as 1818 Burma was required to pay tribute to the Chinese emperor once every 10 years, with missions advised to travel through Yunnan.[23] As well as disrupting Burmese domestic governance, however, British imperialism subverted external relations. Not until the end of the colonial period were Burma and China able to build fresh ties, and by then it was as modern states that they confronted each other. Much can be read into the fact that in December 1949 Burma was the first non-communist country to recognize the People's Republic.[24] Although relations became fraught in the 1950s and 1960s, especially at the time of the Cultural Revolution, bonds were reformed in the 1970s. Later, when army repression of mass revolt in Rangoon in September 1988 was mirrored by the Beijing massacre in June 1989, they became strong.[25] In between, collapse of the CPB in April 1989 removed a contentious issue that by then was already something of a relic from a bygone age.[26] Although relations were never entirely cordial, political elites did find themselves on the same page on many questions.[27] In defiance of much western opinion, but in conformity with most Asian thought, state leaders today particularly agree that the core realist principle of national sovereignty trumps any other in the global arena, and that matters like human rights and democracy are chiefly of domestic concern.[28] Each holds firmly to a "one X" policy both at home and abroad, and projects unbending hostility and fierce resistance to any form of irredentism. Through trading links and Chinese investment inside Myanmar, citizens of the two countries also work together ever more closely.[29]

Considerable controversy surrounds some large-scale projects mounted by state-owned Chinese enterprises in recent years. One is planned development of seven dams in Kachin State by a joint venture between Myanmar's Ministry of Electric Power, crony-capitalist Asia World Company, and China Power Investment Corporation. Construction of Myitsone Dam on the

Ayeyawady River just to the north-east of Myitkyina was launched in May 2007. Work on some of the six other dams on its two main tributaries soon followed. All are being built with minimal local consultation, all will have substantial negative impacts on local communities and environments, and all are expected to transmit electricity directly to China via the Yunnan power network.[30]

Also contentious is construction of parallel 690-mile oil and natural gas pipelines, plus associated berthing and storage facilities, from a deep-water port at Kyaukphyu near Sittwe in Myanmar's western Rakhine State to Kunming in China's southwestern Yunnan Province. The entire infrastructure is being built by China National Petroleum Corporation, which inaugurated pipeline construction on June 3, 2010. On an annual basis from mid-2013, the pipelines are expected to transport to China 22 million tons of oil shipped from the Middle East and Africa, and 12 billion cubic meters of natural gas pumped from Myanmar's offshore Shwe field in the Bay of Bengal. They are therefore of great strategic importance to Beijing at a time of rising unease about energy security. The Myanmar government's revenue stream is projected to be $1 billion annually for 30 years.[31]

However, there are also many other projects, large and small, public and private, legal and illegal. In the 2000s, Global Witness issued a series of reports on illicit Chinese logging in Kachin State.[32] In 2008, EarthRights International published a survey of 69 Chinese corporations engaged in at least 90 hydropower, oil and natural gas, and mining projects.[33] Much additional activity is undocumented. One significant result is that today Chinese investment is facing unwanted attention and criticism inside Myanmar. Furthermore, many parts of the country, from Mandalay in the heartland up to Kachin State in the north and across to Shan State in the east, are dominated by Chinese entrepreneurs and traders, and major towns and cities have a clear Chinese feel.[34] In 2000, David Bachman noted that most states on its periphery were less dynamic economically, more disorganized socially, and less entrepreneurial than China. "Into these vacuums, Chinese traders have moved."[35] In a multitude of ways, expanding Chinese business networks are affecting Myanmar just as much as the rest of Asia.[36]

Despite this wealth of bilateral contact, China seeks to project an image of restrained engagement with Myanmar's internal affairs, exhibiting behavior patterns that are as accommodating to local conditions as in other global contexts.[37] In the non-state sector entrepreneurs take little or no interest in domestic politics.[38] In the state sector things are different, though overt political engagement is still limited. On the whole, Beijing remains committed to strategies designed to nudge military leaders in a reformist direction without at any point endangering internal stability and thereby threatening core Chinese interests.[39] The hope is that eventually a durable political settlement will be reached. In the meantime, Beijing is content to stay in the background as a mainly benevolent big brother providing protection for Myanmar in the UN Security Council and checking from a distance that potentially explosive issues like economic development, democratization and ethnic relations are handled quietly and effectively.[40]

For other Asian actors, Chinese support for the Myanmar junta throughout the late 1980s crisis had important ripple effects. In both Southeast Asia and South Asia, instinctive reactions were often hostile. Indeed, when protesters fled bloodshed in Rangoon and other major cities in September 1988, they found safe havens across Burma's 900-mile frontier with India to the north and 1,100-mile border with Thailand to the east. New Delhi was notably receptive to members of the democracy movement, welcoming students to refugee camps, broadcasting support for their cause back into Burma, and adopting a policy of strict rejection of the junta.[41] However, when the generals succeeded in seeing out the early storm and sustaining their rule into the 1990s, regional players became keen both to balance growing Chinese influence and to exploit any economic opportunities that might arise. In Southeast Asia, the shift was rapid. As early as the late 1980s, Thailand took a commercial interest that became especially strong when telecommunications tycoon Thaksin Shinawatra was premier from 2001 to 2006.[42] While tensions frequently flared along a border subject to sporadic fighting and occasional spillover, Thai business engagement has always been high. Other ASEAN states also acted quickly to build commercial links. In India, by contrast, the change did not come until 1993, when a Look East policy was unveiled to boost trade and diplomatic contacts across the region.[43] New Delhi also looked to Yangon for help in managing problems with Naga militants and trafficking activities along the Myanmar border.

In a rather haphazard manner, a platform was thereby built for ASEAN in 1992 to adopt a formal policy of constructive engagement.[44] Crafted mainly by the Thai foreign ministry, this sought to promote economic and political liberalization inside Myanmar and thereby serve regional business interests alongside the perceived needs of local people for development and reform. On July 23, 1997 ASEAN controversially admitted Myanmar to full membership, together with Laos.[45] Key enabling roles were played by Indonesia, Malaysia and Singapore. Subsequently, there were changes of tone as exasperation with the junta prompted ASEAN to switch to flexible engagement at the time of the 1997 Asian financial crisis, and to critical disengagement following the 2003 Depayin attack on Aung San Suu Kyi's convoy.[46] Throughout, extensive debate and perennially difficult relations exposed deep divisions about ways forward.[47] Nevertheless, ASEAN has not significantly altered its policy stance.[48] Even during the Nargis emergency, member states were reluctant to depart from the ASEAN Way of non-interference to insist on better access for aid agencies.[49] Thereafter, however, they turned engagement to good effect by forming a Tripartite Core Group with the Myanmar government and the UN to spearhead reconstruction efforts.[50]

Pragmatic concerns ensured that Myanmar was also embraced by other groupings. In 1992 it joined the ADB's Greater Mekong Subregion Economic Cooperation Program together with Cambodia, China, Laos, Thailand and Vietnam. In 1997 it was made part of what in 2004 became the Bay of Bengal Initiative for Multi-Sectoral Technical and Economic Cooperation, now spanning Bangladesh, Bhutan, India, Nepal, Sri Lanka and Thailand. In 1999 it attended the Conference on Regional Cooperation and Development among China, India, Myanmar and Bangladesh, termed the Kunming Initiative. In 2000 it enlisted in Mekong-Ganga Cooperation, alongside Cambodia, India, Laos, Thailand and Vietnam. Today the country is therefore linked into many regional networks, notably through technical forums but also at political levels.

Looking farther afield, Japan was for many years in a category of its own. Bonds formed through warfare and occupation in the 1940s were often ambiguous, with key Burmese leaders including Aung San and Ne Win fighting both for and against the new imperial master. However, the extent of Japan's military loss in Burma generated a firm foundation for postwar ties, fostered by veterans' associations.[51] In popular culture, Michio Takeyama's hit 1946 novel *Harp of Burma*, turned into major films in 1956 and 1985, fueled romantic attachment to the disastrous campaign.[52] Among specialists and officials, *Biru-kichi* (Burma crazy) enthusiasm for the country and its people triggered large reparations in a 1954 bilateral peace treaty and considerable development assistance thereafter.[53] Indeed, by 1987 Japan accounted for 71.5 percent of all ODA to Burma, and for 20 percent of the national budget.[54] On the Burmese side, reparations and aid flows, reinforced by the sheer brilliance of the economic miracle, stimulated interest.

In this context, the events of 1988 were a major challenge. Tokyo was already playing a key role in forcing some liberalization of the BSPP's command economy by threatening to withdraw financial support.[55] After the four eights uprising, though, "critical distance" became the mantra as Japan joined the US alliance in withholding recognition and suspending new aid.[56] Nevertheless, diplomatic protocol surrounding Emperor Hirohito's state funeral in February 1989 made the hiatus brief.[57] In 1989, Tokyo sought re-engagement through diplomacy, debt relief and focused aid, and in 1995 it boosted contacts with the junta after Aung San Suu Kyi's first release from house arrest. In the 2000s, it persisted with assistance programs and "quiet dialogue" designed to connect leading political figures.[58] However, the rise of China as the pivotal external actor had a major impact. In 1993, Steinberg wrote that "Burma has relied on the Japanese, virtually since independence."[59] Today that assessment is no longer valid.

From the heart of international society, engagement has been pursued by a succession of envoys sent notably by the UN on dozens of largely fruitless missions.[60] Over the years, two main patterns emerged. Since the early 1990s, four UN Special Rapporteurs on the situation of human rights in Myanmar have been appointed. Yozo Yokota (1992–96) resigned because of scant support from the Office of the High Commissioner for Human Rights. Rajsoomer Lallah (1996–2000) stepped down for similar reasons, never having been allowed to enter the country. Paulo Sérgio Pinheiro (2000–08) cut short a March 2003 visit after finding a hidden microphone taping conversations with activists in Insein Prison. Tomás Ojea Quintana (since May 2008) faced problems in visiting Myanmar, but did make three trips before informing the UN in March 2010 that the junta might be committing war crimes or crimes against humanity, and advising that it consider creating a commission of inquiry.[61] In parallel, there have also been four Special Envoys of the UN Secretary-General. Alvaro de Soto (1997-99) made five visits. Razali Ismail (2000-06) made 12 trips, though he too was denied entry for the final 23 months of his term. Ibrahim Gambari (2006-09) visited eight times, mainly to address issues generated by suppression of the 2007 saffron uprising. Vijay Nambiar (since 2010) currently holds the portfolio.

Filling out the spectrum of engagement is action taken chiefly by UN agencies and INGOs. While most humanitarian organizations reacted to the events of the late 1980s by declining to operate inside the country, some aid workers soon began to focus on manifest human need and ask whether citizens should have to pay twice for the military clampdown. Triggered notably by a 1992 UN Children's Fund analysis, leading agencies first discussed the merits of involvement and then in a small number of cases registered with the relevant line ministries to pilot in-country programs.[62] In October 2006, a multi-donor Three Diseases Fund (known as the 3D Fund), currently worth $125 million, was launched to run for five years. Now governed by a consortium of Australia, Denmark, the EU, the Netherlands, Norway, Sweden and the UK, it works through local and international implementing partners to tackle HIV/AIDS, malaria and tuberculosis.[63] In December 2006, the ICG reported that "the INGO sector grew from 30 organisations in 2001 with a total budget of $15 million to 41 in 2004 with a budget of some $30 million, and more continue to arrive."[64] While it came nowhere near to matching 200 INGOs in Cambodia, with only one quarter of Myanmar's population, it was no longer negligible.[65] Since Nargis, further expansion has taken place, particularly in Yangon and the delta area. In October 2009, a multi-donor Livelihoods and Food Security Trust Fund (known as LIFT), worth $100 million, was established to run for five years. Governed by a consortium of Australia, the EU, the Netherlands, Sweden, Switzerland and the UK, it too works through a range of implementing partners to help the poorest and most vulnerable segments of society.[66] By 2011, 86 INGOs and 13 UN agencies were operating inside Myanmar.[67]

The degree to which such assistance registers as political engagement is subject to extensive debate. At one extreme, Alex de Waal in 1997 based a major critique of the aid business on the contention that "Humanitarian action *is* political action."[68] Echoed notably by Sadako Ogata, UN High Commissioner for Refugees 1991–2000, in the oft-cited remark that "there are no humanitarian solutions to humanitarian problems" and the concomitant implication that political issues always have to be confronted, the claim is that any transnational aid mission will have political consequences.[69] At the other extreme, the International Committee of the Red Cross has always projected an image of strict impartiality. However, as David P. Forsythe writes, even ICRC policy "necessarily entails a type of politics that the rhetoric of neutrality cannot erase."[70] It is thus hard to escape the conclusion reached by de Waal, Ogata and others that reaching across a national frontier to deliver humanitarian programs does have political impacts.

Moreover, in the Myanmar context several positive instances can be cited. HIV/AIDS and maternal health programs are slowly and constructively reshaping welfare provision. Efforts to enhance local capacity through training initiatives notably in Nargis-affected areas are boosting civil society.[71] Life-saving healthcare missions in eastern parts of the country, launched clandestinely from Thailand by Back Pack Health Worker Teams, are helping to sustain communities in the face of *tatmadaw* incursions.[72] Peace building and conflict training programs in major cities and border zones are promoting national reconciliation.[73] Indeed, away from the contentious sphere of democracy, carefully calibrated strategies of pressure and incentive have prompted considerable change in a wide range of policy sectors. In 2010, David Allan detailed variable but significant progress in areas as diverse as human trafficking, narcotics control, national disability strategy, agriculture and food security, forestry policy, resettlement issues, and public health.[74]

The case for engagement is then repeatedly made, with many proponents looking beyond politics to economic and social issues such as underdevelopment, ethnic division, endemic poverty, health crisis, human insecurity, and so on.[75] Among Asian leaders, an additional concern is cross-border contagion. Indeed, it was above all to foster such unease that a September 2005 report commissioned by Václav Havel and Desmond Tutu labeled Myanmar under its junta a *Threat to the Peace*.[76] However, this argument was never persuasive in Asia. Rather, even the limited amount of democracy embodied in the junta's 2010 general election prompted leaders in China, ASEAN and other parts of the region to signal that the time had come for all members of international society to normalize diplomatic relations with Myanmar.[77]

The major criticism of engagement strategies is that they have generally had limited impact. Surveys of regional efforts routinely conclude that neighbors are unable to deliver on their policy objectives.[78] China cannot exercise much leverage.[79] India's ambitions have registered more frustration than success.[80] ASEAN has long been embarrassed by Myanmar and is now estranged from its bedfellow.[81] INGOs are allowed only constrained political space, and can do little to reshape a society subject to harsh discipline. Indeed, even within Asia, where non-interference is generally the default position, there remains a clear sense that more needs to be done to promote gradualist reform inside the country.[82] The conclusion drawn by many is thus that this clutch of policy responses has failed. While the ongoing reality of oppressive military rule means that this verdict is largely valid, there is nevertheless a small measure of grassroots success to set alongside the bigger disappointment. In particular, low-profile external action in Nargis-affected areas and beyond is slowly reshaping society from the bottom up.[83]

Isolation strategies

For close to 25 years since 1988 isolation strategies have been pursued by both state and non-state actors, with formal sanctions finding an array of complementary boycotts in campaigns sponsored by activist groups. However, state support is restricted to nations in the broad western camp grouped around the US, and has rarely gained endorsement from Asia.[84] Indeed, of the major regional players only Japan, conscious of expectations placed on it by the US security alliance, has ever made even minor moves in this direction. Its policy of critical distance, devised after the 8-8-88 uprising, began to be recalibrated after only six months. By contrast, non-state backing is broad, and activist networks are energized by exiles living in the diaspora, regional coalitions, and campaigns mounted in the UK, US and other parts of the world.[85] Preeminent in this domain is US government policy.[86]

Looking to history, this bilateral relationship was never well developed. Cady notes that "Burma was little known to Americans prior to World War II" and in the early postwar period was "regarded in Washington as a British-Indian responsibility." For years it remained "an enigma."[87] When the democracy movement was crushed in 1988, however, the US imposed sanctions. Initially, it terminated economic aid, withdrew trade preferences, imposed an arms embargo, and blocked loans and grants from global financial institutions such as the World Bank and the International Monetary Fund. In 1990, it downgraded US representation in Yangon from ambassador to chargé d'affaires. In 1996, it placed a visa ban on senior military figures and their families.[88] From the late 1990s, it applied the slew of economic measures that still defines its policy stance.[89] In May 1997, Executive Order 13047 issued by President Bill Clinton prohibited US citizens from making new investments in Myanmar or facilitating investments by foreign persons.[90] In July 2003, the Burmese Freedom and Democracy Act, together with Executive Order 13310 signed by President George W. Bush, banned imports from Myanmar, blocked the assets of named entities and individuals, and restricted financial and technical assistance.[91] In October 2007 and April 2008, Executive Orders 13448 and 13464 issued by Bush imposed targeted sanctions on named individuals in or associated with the regime.[92] In July 2008, the Tom Lantos Block Burmese Jade (Junta's Anti-Democratic Efforts) Act outlawed imports of jadeite and rubies from Myanmar via third countries.[93] All of these measures remain firmly in place today.

Nevertheless, the election of President Barack Obama did trigger some policy change. Following a seven-month review, officials announced in September 2009 that the US would boost humanitarian aid and seek direct talks with the Myanmar junta while retaining existing sanctions.[94] Although few early results were registered, Derek Mitchell was appointed special representative in April 2011 to bolster dialogue efforts in the wake of the country's praetorian transition.[95] Along the way, however, the US also signaled an interest in seeing junta members referred to the International Criminal Court for alleged war crimes and crimes against humanity.[96] In October 2010, Secretary of State Hillary Clinton said that she "would like to underscore the

American commitment to seek accountability for the human rights violations that have occurred in Burma by working to establish an international commission of inquiry through close consultations with our friends, allies, and other partners at the United Nations."[97] In 2011, the Burma Campaign UK listed a further 15 states in support: Australia, Canada, New Zealand and 12 EU members, including the UK.[98] In the background was heightened activist concern. In May 2009 a Harvard Law School report, *Crimes in Burma*, made the case for an ICC referral.[99] In March 2010 Quintana issued his advice that the UN investigate this possibility. In July 2010 one of his three predecessors, Yokota, spoke out in favor.[100] Pressure mounted still further when the Human Rights Council's four-year cycle of Universal Periodic Review brought Myanmar into the frame in January 2011. In rejecting 70 recommendations from the Council, the government among other things denied that it holds political prisoners and branded the Rohingya people "illegal immigrants."[101]

Among the broader alliance grouped around the US for Myanmar policy, sanctions regimes are also maintained. In 2007, Canada imposed the world's toughest sanctions. To an arms embargo, export ban beyond humanitarian goods and aid suspension introduced in 1988 and targeted visa bans imposed in 2003, it added full embargoes on imports and new investments, and a selective asset freeze.[102] In the EU, early measures comprised an arms embargo, suspension of aid and development programs, and expulsion of military personnel from diplomatic missions. Subsequently, a Common Position agreed in October 1996 introduced a visa ban for senior military officials and suspended high-level bilateral visits.[103] Renewed and extended at regular intervals, EU policy currently comprises an arms embargo, visa restrictions and asset freezes for named individuals, a ban on exports to businesses operating in wood and mining sectors, an import ban on timber products, metals and precious stones, a prohibition on investment in state-owned enterprises, and restrictions on diplomatic contacts. No more than a slight loosening was announced in April 2011 following Myanmar's shift to notionally civilian government.[104] Similarly, Australia maintains an arms embargo, targeted travel bans and selective financial sanctions introduced in October 2007 in response to repression of the saffron uprising.[105]

Reinforcing many bilateral sanctions, the dominant role of the US and its allies in the UN and other formal intergovernmental organizations has long resulted in embargoes on humanitarian aid and engagement. World Bank and IMF assistance continue to be prohibited, and though the UN Development Programme has operated inside Myanmar since 1993 it does so on a restricted mandate.[106] Other UN agencies are either missing from Myanmar or also working on a limited basis, with governance or capacity building work alongside state personnel and agencies generally ruled out.[107] From within the UN system, an ILO commission of inquiry in 1998 found evidence of "widespread and systematic" use of forced labor, and imposed moral sanctions in November 2000.[108]

The cumulative impact of these measures on humanitarian assistance for one of the world's most destitute countries has been considerable. One immediate result of the crackdown in the late 1980s was a reduction of ODA from $435 million in 1988 to $175 million in 1989. Until the mid-1990s, official aid flows continued to decline very nearly on an annual basis, dipping below $50 million a year by the end of the decade. Thereafter official assistance gradually picked up, and in the mid-2000s stood at around $150 million annually, rising to $197 million in 2007.[109] The extreme humanitarian emergency generated by Cyclone Nargis then boosted ODA to a record high of $477.5 million in 2008.[110] While allocations then fell back somewhat, they stayed above the 2007 figure.

Nevertheless, total aid spending remains far below levels found in comparable contexts. In 2006, a little before Nargis, Myanmar received $2.88 per person in ODA. This was the lowest figure among any of the world's 50 poorest countries, and well short of an average of more than $58 per capita assistance across the cohort. Even other countries with highly repressive governments received much higher ODA: $21 per person in Zimbabwe, $55 per person in Sudan, $63 per person in Laos.[111] By 2009, per capita aid spend in Myanmar had more than doubled to $6, but still lagged far behind $50 per person in Zimbabwe and unchanged levels in Sudan and Laos.[112] On the very broad assumption that a 2009 Myanmar population of 60 million missed out on $50 per person in aid, the total shortfall in that year alone was $3 billion. The loss continues to be of that magnitude today. Finally, within the generally pitiful allocations made to Myanmar since 1988, the profile of international assistance has changed markedly. In the mid-1990s, China replaced Japan as the major donor.[113] More recently, the UK, Australia and the US have all substantially increased their allocations to become leading bilateral donors.[114] Still the total commitment is very low.

An even larger impact of sanctions came in the business sphere. In 1988, Burma was almost devoid of inward investment. However, the incoming junta liberalized the economy through a Foreign Investment Law promulgated in November 1988, and so thorough was global inattention to the country's political problems that many major companies went in.[115] That soon changed, however, as the controversial 1990 general election confirmed

Myanmar's status as a rogue state. In consequence, the early 1990s saw Levi Strauss, Eddie Bauer, Liz Claibourne, J. Crew, Columbia Sportswear, Apple Computers, Kodak, Motorola, Disney, and PepsiCo pull out. When Levi Strauss left in 1992, it held that it was "not possible to do business without directly supporting the military government and its pervasive human rights violations." In a single week in July 1996, Danish brewer Carlsberg and Dutch brewer Heineken announced that they were halting engagement. Carlsberg had planned to invest $30 million in a bottling plant. Heineken was involved in a half-built brewery project. "Every billboard in the country will come down," declared Heineken. "Out is out."[116] Each withdrawal was prompted not by formal sanctions, which came later, but by informal pressure generated by activist groups.[117] Indeed, for years the Burma Campaign UK and Global Unions maintained "dirty lists" of companies, though after 2008 the Burma Campaign UK could no longer afford to do so.[118] The effect remains potent, and few corporations trading in western markets now do any business in or with Myanmar.[119]

The case for isolation is also frequently made, as the country has witnessed manifold human rights violations over the past 25 years. Above all, however, proponents look to Aung San Suu Kyi. The official position long taken by the NLD leader is that while she has never called for sanctions, she sees no reason to advise foreign governments to revise measures they have themselves adopted. After her release from house arrest in November 2010, the NLD thus issued short policy analyses and position papers cautioning against precipitate policy change, though at the same time promising a policy review and fresh discussions with sanctioning powers.[120] However, this line cannot be fully squared with the historical record. In June 1989, the *Bangkok Post* reported that Aung San Suu Kyi had "said that foreign countries should suspend all trade and economic relations with the junta 'until they keep their promises' to hold free and fair multi-party elections."[121] In January 1997, a commencement address delivered by her husband, Michael Aris, to the American University in Washington, and a week later carried under her own byline in *The New York Times*, made an explicit case for activist pressure: "I would therefore like to call upon those who have an interest in expanding their capacity for promoting intellectual freedom and humanitarian ideals to take a principled stand against companies that are doing business with the Burmese military regime."[122] One key reason for obfuscation is that military leaders relish any chance to charge their most famous citizen with economic subversion.[123]

As with engagement strategies, the major problem with isolation strategies is their failure to deliver. In a working paper prepared for the UN

Commission on Human Rights in June 2000, Marc Bossuyt set out a "six-prong test" to ensure that sanctions are imposed for valid reasons, target the proper parties, address appropriate goods or objects, are reasonably time-limited, are effective, and are free from public outcry in the subject jurisdiction.[124] As Derek Tonkin noted in a March 2011 analysis, EU (and other) sanctions "record an alarming negative on all counts," with only targeting proper parties registering even a hint of success.[125] Particular cases also expose the inability of sanctions to secure their objectives. After the US imposed a full export ban in July 2003, Nick Mathiason reported in January 2004 that Swift, a hi-tech financial intermediary, had created software capable of converting dealings into euros.[126] Looking in December 2003 at informal measures imposed by the UK government, Alan Boyd remarked that "BAT, the subject of intense political lobbying in the United Kingdom, simply off-loaded its 60 percent stake to a Singapore-based investor and will continue to get revenues under a licensing agreement."[127]

This is not to argue that economic sanctions have had no effect. In April 2004, the US State Department reported to Congress that the 2003 export ban closed more than 100 garment factories and eliminated 50–60,000 jobs. In May 2005, the Myanmar government put job losses at 80,000.[128] Later, Toshihiro Kudo confirmed that "U.S. sanctions seriously damaged the garment industry in Myanmar."[129] Wider opportunity costs are immeasurable. Rather, it is to hold that since sanctions are fragmentary, and even boycotts do not fully tighten the noose, they cannot deliver on their core aims. Kudo found that US sanctions introduced in 2003 "did not have as much of an impact on military-related enterprises as they did on domestic private firms," and that they "had a disproportionately greater impact on the people than … on the military regime."[130] This was a critical failure, for experience shows that to work sanctions must create sizable political costs for the ruling coalition.[131] When the target state is authoritarian this is especially difficult, for then the winning coalition is typically small.[132] In Myanmar, the stark inability to damage military interests has made economic sanctions one more instance of a failed embargo.[133] Exactly parallel points can be made about activist campaigns. Looking into the future from the perspective of 1990, Steinberg wrote that "an indefinite policy of isolation may not work."[134] So it has proven.

Political leverage

Diverse foreign policies appear to have had some shaping impact on Myanmar's domestic politics. The painfully slow transitional process currently taking place signals some acknowledgement on the part of military leaders that in governing a country long taken as their reserved domain they must indicate some conformity with global trends and values. US evaluations released by WikiLeaks claim that top generals do not like being sanctioned, and are embarrassed by their rogue status.[135] More significantly, in a resurgent civil society a still relatively small cohort of UN agencies and INGOs is able to provide solid support for local initiative. Gradually some political impacts are being registered at grassroots levels. At the same time, however, external action has long fallen far short of its major objectives, leaving ordinary citizens in a desperate state of servitude and impoverishment. Many reasons can be given for this dismal state of affairs, and in such a complex case all may be valid to some degree. In two respects, though, foreigners bear some responsibility.

One is the inattention that has generally characterized external relations with Myanmar. There have certainly been many honorable exceptions, including diplomats striving to craft effective policies, aid workers devoting their lives to assisting people inside the country and along its extensive borders, activists going to considerable lengths to bring scandalous human rights violations to global attention, business executives concerned to create real economic and social benefits for local people, and pockets of engaged individuals from other walks of life undertaking a wealth of productive action. Indeed, the past decade has seen significant reengagement with Myanmar, albeit from the tiny base maintained throughout the 1990s, and much of it has been productive. On the whole, however, the wider world has not focused on Myanmar in the years of great misery and serial crisis that have passed since the late 1980s.

China, the critical external power, has not invested in the bilateral relationship. After a state visit by President Jiang Zemin in December 2001, the only senior officials to visit in the period of junta government were Politburo Standing Committee member Li Changchun in March 2009, Vice-President Xi Jinping in December 2009, and Premier Wen Jiabao in June 2010. Many commercial agreements were signed during the trips, prompting the ICG to remark in September 2010 that "This spike in top-level visits and economic deals sends a signal to Naypyidaw about its importance in Beijing's calculations and the potential economic largesse it can offer."[136] By the same token, the long span of neglect before that also sent a powerful negative message. Similarly, India has taken little interest. In 2010, a task force of diplomats, academics and policy specialists reached this verdict: "Not a single credible person has dedicated himself or herself to studying Myanmar comprehensively as a primary interest in the so-called strategic community or in academe … More damagingly, of all of its postindependence neighbors, India has paid the least substantive attention at the official level to its relations with Myanmar."[137] Equally, Thailand was held by a 2010 task force to lack the "energy and resources to refashion [its] seemingly rudderless Burma/Myanmar policy."[138] Outside the region, US policy is determined by no more than a handful of individuals in Congress, and effectively made by Aung San Suu Kyi.[139] In the EU the situation is more complex. Nevertheless, the policy context in the UK, which as former colonial power is typically the critical voice, is akin to that in the US, though with a possibly still larger activist component.[140]

Generalized inattention is a major problem because it both feeds ignorance and reduces credibility and legitimacy. Few policymakers have much detailed understanding of conditions on the ground inside Myanmar, options for change, or popular expectations of external engagement. Developing a nuanced and balanced perspective that can inform wider policy analysis and debate is thus inherently difficult. Moreover, in very practical terms no outsider can dip into an issue every now and then and expect either to be taken seriously, or to exercise real and lasting influence. By and large, however, this is the basis on which Myanmar policy is set by key regional powers and still more so by dominant players in international society.

The other respect in which the wider world bears some responsibility for the current state of affairs is the nature of the involvement it does have with Myanmar. Notably on the side of isolation strategies, western powers and activist groups are often content to impose embargoes and lecture the governing elite on human rights and democracy. While this is not uniquely the case following the expansion of aid and willingness to engage in dialogue signaled by Australia, the EU and the US in the late 2000s and early 2010s, it remains the signature theme.[141] For a nation ruled for decades by a western power widely held to have exploited the land for its own interests and sowed deep-seated interethnic discord, this approach was always unlikely to work. Furthermore, although they seem paranoid to many outsiders, military leaders' suspicion of foreign intentions is not wholly unfounded.[142] For years, US and other western policy has effectively been premised on regime change. More widely, isolation prevents new voices and influences from registering inside the country, and limits the emergence of counterweights to military rule through a healthy civil society and a vibrant middle class with global links and perspectives. As Thant Myint-U remarked in 2009, "sanctions are extremely counter-productive, in that they've held back two forces — American soft power and global capitalism — that could have actually started to change things."[143]

Taken as a whole, one striking feature of external action is the sense of missed opportunity. Within Asia, the sense of crisis has always been underdeveloped, and business as usual has been an easy policy choice. Beyond Asia, the sense of crisis has long been overdeveloped, for once the junta stabilized control temporarily after 1988 and more permanently after 1990 it was not likely with one more heave to collapse into the abyss. Rather, the situation called for creative approaches designed to build trust across deep internal divisions and, more broadly, reshape the domestic political environment. Though hinted at in minor policy initiatives, however, no new strategy materialized in the period down to the installation of disciplined democracy in 2011. Today, only very few diplomats, aid workers, activists and corporate executives are making concrete efforts to facilitate positive political reform inside the country.

In consequence, a still more striking feature of external action is the open debate it has provoked among Myanmar people. The NLD holds firmly to isolationism, calling in a February 2011 statement for no more than an impact study and talks with the US and allied powers.[144] Interviewed a few days later, Aung San Suu Kyi said that it was too early to "reward" the generals by removing sanctions.[145] Several weeks later she insisted that "Sanctions must remain in place. Sanctions should only be lifted when something has changed here."[146] Against this, however, minor parties with elected members of parliament from both the democratic and ethnic camps articulate a frank desire to move on.[147] In March 2011, leaders of 10 such parties issued an open letter asking the EU to use its annual policy review to "rethink its current approach of isolating Myanmar."[148] This is also the message transmitted by individuals interviewed by listening projects inside the country, less through overt denunciations of sanctions than through the many constructive alternatives that are floated.[149] Furthermore, in those possibilities can be found implicit critique of anodyne engagement strategies launched during the past 25 years.

The result is that global policy responses to Myanmar's dominant military machine are in some disarray. Outsiders have registered only small success in promoting political reform, or even economic development and social stability. Insiders are fiercely divided about ways forward, manifesting little confidence in either isolationist strategies or engagement policies as currently implemented. In these circumstances, a thorough reexamination of options for external action is urgently required.

6

Injustice and implication

While Myanmar has long triggered deep concern among foreigners, policies implemented to date have registered limited success and are now openly disputed by both insiders and outsiders. It is therefore necessary to think again. In an age of humanitarian engagement driven by generic notions of global justice, this chapter seeks to do that by turning to core principles. Specifically, it looks to contemporary political philosophy to clarify the duties of justice in this case and determine not what the wider world might do to help local people, but rather what the dictates of global justice indicate it must do. The aim is to build a secure theoretical foundation for policy options in the world of practice. To this end, the chapter addresses two main issues. One is the extent to which outsiders are directly implicated in injustice in Myanmar, and the requirements that flow from that. Have foreigners visited harm on local people, and if so what must they do to rectify matters? The other is obligations owed to Myanmar citizens not because of any traceable course of action or inaction on the part of external agents, but merely through bonds entailed by universal membership of the human race. Are there claims foreigners need to deliver on purely because at least some of the injustice in contemporary Myanmar is intolerable in the world of the twenty-first century? The chapter opens with a brief survey of debate about global justice. It then examines the issue of external responsibility for injustice inside Myanmar. Following on, it considers duties of global justice with no readily identifiable historical imprint. It closes by aggregating the demands of justice in this case. The argument is that outsiders clearly do owe duties of justice to the people of Myanmar. Without taking a further analytical step, however, ways in which they might be performed can be described only very provisionally.

Global justice

Stretching back to the ancients, justice has always been at the heart of political inquiry. Of more recent vintage, however, are subsidiary strands of debate. One is the interest in social justice that emerged toward the end of the nineteenth century and came to dominate political philosophy in the twentieth.[1] Another is the preoccupation with global justice that developed at the end of the Cold War and expanded interest beyond bounded contexts. Global justice is currently a leading theoretical concern.

Landmark studies of social justice published by John Rawls and Robert Nozick in the early 1970s confined deliberation chiefly to a single society, and focused mainly on distributive matters. To argue out requirements of justice in the original position, where free and equal persons assemble behind a veil of ignorance about individual circumstance, Rawls put not the many billions of people who inhabit the earth, but rather representatives of the inhabitants of a particular place. In this thought experiment, cross-border issues of justice were scarcely considered. As Rawls wrote in the opening pages of *A Theory of Justice*, "I shall be satisfied if it is possible to formulate a reasonable conception of justice for the basic structure of society conceived for the time being as a closed system isolated from other societies."[2] Only later did he fully address issues of global justice. Similarly, although Nozick's entitlement theory of justice did not have to be constrained in this way, for in principle the "framework for utopia" created in the minimal state need have no territorial bounds, in practice it too was seen both by Nozick and his critics as generating a series of closed systems.[3] Moreover, theorists such as Peter Singer, who dispensed with territorial issues through an insistence that the justice claims of distant strangers are on an equal footing with those close by, were mainly confined to the margins of debate. While the 1971 Bengal emergency across the border from Burma in the nascent state of Bangladesh was used as a framing device by Singer, it did not reshape mainstream theory.[4] In the 1980s, the appearance of communitarian critiques, notably in the work of Alasdair MacIntyre, Michael J. Sandel, Charles Taylor and Michael Walzer, served only to reinforce the focus on specific societies and cultures.[5]

The fall of the Berlin Wall in 1989, the collapse of the Soviet Union in 1991 and the abrupt termination of the Cold War occasioned a redirection of interest, placing justice beyond borders at the heart of analysis. Combined with rapid advances in information and communication technology that saw crises in hitherto hidden and mysterious parts of the world begin to flash across television and computer screens, it triggered a significant reorientation of theoretical debate. Although Burma's 1988 uprising slightly predated this broad international shift, and in consequence was largely disregarded by the wider world, the country nevertheless soon became a staple of global concern. Though rarely at the heart of analysis, it retains a committed following in transnational activist networks.

Furthermore, the refocusing of global attention rapidly generated institutional impacts in international society. Before long, an order designed to address issues of broad global welfare was set in place alongside orders devised decades earlier to oversee global security and the global economy.[6] Clearly there were antecedents. Michael Barnett looks in the nineteenth century to abolitionist campaigns against the slave trade, missionary work, creation of the ICRC and gradual emergence of international humanitarian law, and in the twentieth to a steady accumulation of humanitarian norms, rules and institutions.[7] By contrast, Samuel Moyn holds that an understanding of rights as applicable to all and protected by the global community was not widely held before the 1970s. Then, however, in reaction to the failure of revolutionary projects, and especially of anti-colonialist struggles, a modern humanitarian turn took place, captured above all in President Jimmy Carter's pioneering late 1970s attempt to situate human rights at the heart of US foreign policy.[8] As Barnett again writes, though, only post-Cold War experience fully grounded the new order, generating both a "surfeit of conventions and treaties" designed to protect the right to life, and a "metropolis of organizations" dedicated to reducing suffering and lending a hand.[9]

The case of Burma down to 1989 and Myanmar thereafter is better explained by Barnett. Although ODA to Burma increased 20-fold in the decade of the 1970s emphasized by Moyn, it was only in the post-Cold War world that the country became a pariah state subject to the full panoply of activist concern. More widely, the trend of emergency relief aid across the span of international society also supports Barnett's interpretation. Though somewhat rough and ready, the data chart a dramatic upward trend during the 1990s and 2000s.[10] Equally, changes registered at the UN after 1990 were significant, with *An Agenda for Peace*, issued in June 1992, identifying new global challenges of preventive diplomacy, peacemaking, peacekeeping and post-conflict peace building.[11] These themes were then picked up in other reports, notably *Supplement to An Agenda for Peace* (1995), what became known as the Brahimi report (2000), and *In Larger Freedom* (2005), which embraced the responsibility to protect agenda of the International Commission on Intervention and State Sovereignty.[12] Completing an adjustment only partially checked by the dampening effects of the 2001 terrorist attacks on US targets, the 2005 UN World Summit formally acknowledged a collective responsibility "to protect populations from genocide, war crimes, ethnic cleansing and crimes against humanity."[13] When the UN Security Council debated the escalating Libya crisis in March 2011 and through Resolution 1973 authorized measures to protect civilians under Chapter 7 of the UN Charter, it took another important step by making the responsibility militarily enforceable.[14]

At the same time, INGOs have played ever more substantial post-Cold War roles in global humanitarian missions, and are now deployed in many desperate settings.[15] Though sidelined by many agencies in the 1990s, Myanmar is today a case in point. In this sphere, a dividing line is often drawn between old and new forms. Old humanitarians are impartial, apolitical and neutral, symbolized above all by the ICRC.[16] New humanitarians are openly radical, political and campaigning, with secular co-religionists assembled as "keepers of the flame" in AI to the fore.[17] The concept of *témoinage* (or bearing witness), promoted by the disaffected French doctors who in the early 1970s broke with the ICRC in Biafra to create Médecins Sans Frontières, is emblematic.[18] While the contrast is ultimately unsustainable, for even the ICRC cannot fully evade politics, there clearly has been a reorientation as INGOs increasingly prioritize human rights over human need.[19] Key steps in the broad movement of change were the formation of AI in 1961, of MSF in 1971, and of the organization that became HRW in 1978.[20] These agencies are currently at the cutting edge of global humanitarianism.

More broadly, even major corporations from a sector long wary of visible political involvement now sometimes take public positions on matters of global justice. In the Myanmar case, it is very much because of pervasive injustice, policed actively and aggressively by campaign groups, that businesses with visible brands in western consumer markets have disengaged. In international society, leading companies are today key members of human rights forums at the UN and elsewhere.[21] The UN Global Compact, articulated through 10 principles of responsibility and sustainability in the areas of human rights, labor, the environment and anti-corruption, is one of the clearest institutional manifestations.[22] In this way, the corporate sector has assumed a place in the broad humanitarian movement that partly defines contemporary global politics.

For this analysis, what is critical about the international humanitarian order is its transparent political ambition to engage with cross-border issues of justice, to address not merely local symptoms but also both local and global causes. While humanitarianism often conjures notions of emergency response to disaster, the new order extends well beyond that in being neither restricted to crisis situations nor simply focused on catastrophe.[23] In place of misfortune it finds injustice.[24] In place of humanitarian gestures it puts duties of justice. Moreover, in overseeing this transformation and endorsing a principled commitment to abrogating state sovereignty in pursuit of justice, the UN has sponsored an evolution in understandings of a key principle of international society. What was once "sovereignty as authority," implying control over territory, is now increasingly "sovereignty as responsibility," mandating respect for human rights.[25] The shift, far from complete but certainly visible, is driven by emergent conceptions of global justice.

Faced with these profound systemic changes, the challenge for the analysts of social justice in domestic settings who largely dominated political philosophy in the 1970s and 1980s was to develop ways of dealing with wider demands.[26] How could they handle the justice claims of Singer's "Bengali whose name I shall never know, ten thousand miles away?"[27] How, in the context of the Myanmar case, might they respond to the plight of individuals living in the state next to Bangladesh, equally unknown to most global theorists, and equally distant from their main bases of activity?

One response was to dispense with the focus on the local. In cosmopolitan accounts, the entire world is treated as a single place, a kind of global village in which borders have limited or zero salience for issues of justice. Thomas Pogge writes that "The central idea of moral cosmopolitanism is that every human being has a global stature as an ultimate unit of moral concern."[28] Once the individual is established as the key category, other matters such as race, nationality, citizenship, and so on become strictly secondary. Onora O'Neill explains why frontiers cannot be accorded priority: "When boundaries are taken wholly seriously … transnational justice is not just played down but largely wiped off the ethical map."[29] In *Political Theory and International Relations* (1979), Charles R. Beitz thus countered Rawls by allowing the original position to embrace the whole of humanity and trigger global redistribution.[30] Henry Shue in *Basic Rights* (1980) and O'Neill in *Faces of Hunger* (1986) reached similar conclusions.[31]

Against this, a competing response was to insist that political spaces marked by historically contingent frontiers remain key sites for justice. In this sphere Simon Caney identifies first realism with its fixation on states wedded to the national interest fighting things out in a lawless world, second the society-of-states English School focused on an "anarchical society" at the international level, and third nationalist analyses looking not to states but rather to nations as critical units in world politics.[32] However, the key distinction is frequently binary. In opposition to cosmopolitan accounts seeking at least a measure of universal justice are broadly communitarian accounts promoting diverse forms of bounded justice in states, nations or political communities.[33]

On this latter side of debate, a Burkean approach focuses on a metaphorical contract generated by fine-grained local attachments holding people together through time and space. For Walzer, the communal integrity central to this line of thinking "derives its moral and political force from the rights of contemporary men and women to live as members of a historic community and to express their inherited culture through political forms worked out among themselves."[34] While this is therefore an argument about self-government, it also points to restricted possibilities for cross-border understanding. The state, Walzer argues, is a union of people and government. "Foreigners are in no position to deny the reality of that union ... They don't know enough about its history, and they have no direct experience, and can form no concrete judgments, of the conflicts and harmonies, the historical choices and cultural affinities, the loyalties and resentments, that underlie it."[35] The result is that outsiders have no alternative but to assume that there exists "a certain 'fit' between the community and its government ... This presumption is simply the respect that foreigners owe to a historic community and to its internal life."[36]

David Miller makes a parallel case on a foundation of national responsibility. A nation is a group with a common identity, a public culture, acknowledged mutual obligations, a valued ongoing existence, and an aspiration to political self-determination.[37] Together, these elements generate a meaningful sense of national identity, which in turn entails a responsibility shared by every member in just the same way as beliefs, attitudes and benefits are held in common. National responsibility underpins an understanding of justice that cannot be faulted "for ignoring the special responsibilities we properly owe to our compatriots, for failing to take proper account of the value of self-determination, for insufficient sensitivity to cultural difference, and so forth."[38] Like Walzer, Miller maintains that outsiders must respect communal integrity. Even in acute situations, people grouped together in nations are not only needy, but also "choosing agents" keen to control their own lives.[39]

Finally, for cosmopolitans and communitarians alike the core contemporary interest is the demands of justice: not what people might want to do to help distressed individuals and societies, but rather what they must do as a duty of justice. Moreover, those duties are shaped by a series of dichotomies. While none is uncontroversial in either theory or practice, three major distinctions can be drawn. First, duties can be negative or positive. If negative, they mandate that things not be done on the principle of do no harm. If positive, they direct that things be done on the principle of actively helping the needy. Second, duties can be perfect or imperfect. If perfect, they are owed to a named person or set of named persons possessing a corresponding right against the duty-bearer. If imperfect, they are owed to no one individual or set of individuals and enable nobody to demand performance of anyone in particular. Third, duties can be special or general. If special, they are created by a verifiable historical connection. If general, their grounding has no such trace.[40]

In what follows, this final distinction is used to structure analysis of the Myanmar case. In the next section on historical injustice the focus is on special duties. Have foreigners visited harm on the Myanmar people that now demands rectification? In the subsequent section on universal justice, the focus is on general duties. Are there claims outsiders must deliver on purely because at least some of the injustice inside the country is intolerable in the world of the twenty-first century?

Historical injustice

For many theorists of global justice, corrective action based on thorough historical documentation has not been a central concern. Indeed, in much the same way as analysts of social justice have rarely traced Nozickian entitlements all the way back to something akin to the state of nature, so proponents of global justice have often declined to engage in a full unpicking of the past. Given recent experience in Africa, Asia, Europe and the Middle East, where deep historical claim and counter-claim have frequently provoked ideological and nationalist controversy, there is good reason for this neglect. Rather, when focused on the demands of global justice both cosmopolitans and communitarians have tended to frame analysis in general terms. Nevertheless, on each side there has been some interest in special duties produced by historical injustice. On this basis, an initial set of grounds for external engagement with Myanmar can be developed.

Among cosmopolitans, the requirements of justice are typically cast not only generally, but also positively and imperfectly. Without contesting this, however, Pogge also argues for negative, imperfect, special duties, holding that the rest of the world visits harm on the global poor in several ways. One is by conferring legitimacy on any elite able to sustain a monopoly of violence throughout (the bulk of) a designated territory. As Robert H. Jackson shows, quasi-states draw enormous benefit from *de jure* sovereignty in international society.[41] Another is through vesting in all governments, no matter how generated or constituted, two important privileges: an international borrowing privilege allowing rulers to borrow extensively in the country's name, and an international resource privilege enabling them to dispose freely of its natural resources. Still another is through global institutions such as the World Trade Organization that play into the hands of rich nations by denying market access to poor people.[42] The resultant duties are special because they address specific elite decisions. They are negative, and thus notably stringent, because they require the wider world to stop making matters worse by operating a system that sustains global inequality. They are imperfect because they are owed to no particular person and enable no one to demand performance. In practical terms, they mandate broad-based global institutional reform rather than targeted remedial measures. Pogge argues notably for a Global Resources Dividend requiring all governments to share a small part of the value of any resources they use or sell, and for reforms confining global borrowing and resource privileges to democrats.[43]

This is a contentious agenda. One clear challenge to the restriction of key international privileges to democrats can be found in the late work of Rawls, which rejects the exclusion of governments of other well-ordered peoples such as decent non-liberal states.[44] Moreover, at a very practical level, denying Beijing access to a range of standard privileges makes the proposal thoroughly unworkable for at least as long as China remains non-democratic. Pogge's reforms are not especially vulnerable to communitarian critique, however, for none of his suggested measures mandates the assault on communal integrity frowned upon by Walzer and others, and none overly restricts the functioning of domestic politics.

While these prescriptions are not specific to any contemporary case, they are clearly relevant to Myanmar. Indeed, the point about the role of the international community in conferring *de jure* sovereignty on almost any elite able to control national territory was made by SLORC when it declined to honor the result of the 1990 general election.[45] Furthermore, many activist reports testify to the generals' penchant in the 1990s and 2000s for making ample use of the international resource privilege, and evidence of the resource curse has long been widespread.[46] More controversially, economic sanctions imposed by the US and its major allies deny considerable market access to the Myanmar people. Implementation of even a small part of Pogge's reform agenda would thus have major consequences. First, the resource tax would certainly be applicable. Second, the denial of global privileges may well come into play, for, while Asian states beg to differ, leading western states forcefully repudiate the notion that Myanmar today is in any sense democratic. Third, the entire sanctions debate would be reopened to consider whether ongoing exclusion of Myanmar citizens from much of the global market is just.

At some distance from the cosmopolitan core, though sympathetic to many of its main commitments, Richard W. Miller argues that "People in developed countries have a vast, largely unmet responsibility to help people in developing countries."[47] Through a relational account tracing a panoply of cross-border interactions, he makes a case for special duties toward the global poor that may be negative or positive, and perfect or imperfect. Central to his analysis are rights and duties created by exploitation in the transnational economy, inequity in international trade arrangements, negligence in climate harms, and imperial irresponsibility. Critical in identifying actual duties of repair are specific links and ties. In much the same way as relationships within sovereign units generate complex webs of onerous rights and duties, so transnational interactions create parallel entanglements. When relations are abusive, they trigger demanding duties to desist and repair. In this way, a case for global civic respect, trust and friendship is made.

To some degree Miller's prescriptions overlap with Pogge's in pointing to "inequitable frameworks" imposed by the developed world on the developing.[48] This aspect of his work is thus equally relevant to Myanmar. He also makes a significant departure, however, in tracing relational rights and duties in two important areas: imperial action and business engagement in the developing world. He argues that through diverse forms of exploitation, global powers and corporations have amassed major duties of restitution. While specifying the content of such duties requires meticulous examination of the historical record, some broad evaluations of the Myanmar case can nevertheless be made.

Looking first at state action, rectification could be required of Burma's imperial masters. Here, though, Miller notes that while outsiders certainly incur liabilities to make good cross-border damage, it must also be understood that injustice "can fade and finally disappear over time, cancelling the moral debt."[49] He thus proposes a "moral statute of limitations of about two generations on the transnational duty of repair."[50] Searching no farther than Asia and focusing on only one case among many, however, the wisdom of such a move is questionable. A still vital feature of regional politics is Japanese wartime atrocities dating from the 1930s and 1940s. Brought to broad attention notably by the 1997 publication of Iris Chang's *The Rape of Nanking*, focused on events of 1937–38, Japan's record of occupation many decades ago remains a source of deep tension across East Asia.[51] Indeed, in the period from 2001 to 2006, when Japanese Prime Minister Junichiro Koizumi made annual visits Tokyo's Yasukuni Shrine, the issue of cross-border harm perpetrated more than two generations into the past and corresponding duties of repair became central to regional relations. Widely held to glorify Japanese militarism, notably because it holds the remains of 12 convicted and two suspected Class A war criminals, Yasukuni still stands as a provocative public reminder that distant moral debts may not yet have been paid.[52] Equally, looking to the future Miller's statute could tempt current or prospective transgressors to prevaricate over settling accumulated debts until the two-generation rule had eliminated them. Thus, while it would evidently be wrong to argue that no moral debt will ever be cancelled, it is also mistaken to implement a universal statute of limitations. Rather, detailed examination of actual historical episodes is preferable.

The case of Burma under colonialism is hard to judge. On the one hand, there is no doubt that British rule had deep programming effects on the society, sweeping away much that had gone before, subjecting the territory to disparate and often harmful influences, and setting in place a path dependence that remains prevalent and damaging today.[53] While Japanese imperialism did not have such a deep impact, it was also ruinous through harsh occupation and widespread destruction. On the other hand, though, duties of repair owed by the two powers were long ago acknowledged and at least partially discharged. When the British negotiated with Burmese leaders in the immediate postwar years, they were widely seen as trying to give the emergent state a fair start. All financial debts were erased, an offer of Commonwealth membership was made (and declined), and in common with withdrawals by many other democratic imperialists no overt conflict took place.[54] "We need harbour no resentment," said Prime Minister Nu in a broadcast to the nation on the day of independence. A decade later, Maung Maung wrote that "it was fortunate that Burma had finally to deal with the British and no other."[55] For years, the UK joined fellow western nations in providing aid and advice to Rangoon. For its part, Japan moved on quickly from reparations to become the leading foreign donor, and long positioned itself to advise successive regimes. Even in bad times, Tokyo tried hard to cultivate constructive relations.[56] Moreover, when British and Japanese action stopped it was often because the Burmese government indicated that foreign assistance was no longer welcome.

In these circumstances, arguments for rectification can be made either way. Certainly the considerable impact of British and to a lesser extent Japanese imperialism means that the case for positive duties of repair cannot be definitively closed. When colonial impacts still shape much that transpires in the society, the two-generation rule does not seem appropriate. At the same time, though, means by which ongoing duties might be discharged when extreme hostility to foreign engagement has long been central to domestic governance is not easy to determine.

A further argument made by Miller is that it is essential to look beyond remote instances of formal colonization to recent modes of informal imperialism, notably the global effects of the "American empire."[57] In the Myanmar case, the point already made about the role of a US-led group of nations in imposing aid, trade and investment sanctions thereby comes sharply into focus.[58] Such action has certainly harmed local people by withholding billions of dollars annually in assistance, and incalculable amounts of economic activity. Whether imperfect, special duties of justice arise is thus a critical issue. Proponents will insist that embargoes were imposed in the name of global justice, and can hardly be used now to ground a case for rectification. Critics will argue that sanctions have long been known to be ineffective and are presently maintained not for principled reasons of global justice, but rather for pragmatic reasons of domestic politics. In February 2009, US Secretary Clinton acknowledged that "Clearly the path we have taken in imposing sanctions hasn't influenced the Burmese junta." In October 2009, French Foreign Minister Bernard Kouchner was more blunt: "Sanctions are useless and everyone recognises that."[59] For years western embargoes, both formal and informal, have spectacularly failed Bossuyt's six-prong test. In this context, the negative duty to stop visiting harm on the Myanmar people becomes pressing. Positive duties of repair may also ensue.

Additionally in the sphere of contemporary state action, the role not only of isolating western nations, but also of engaging Asian governments needs to be examined. Above all since 1988 it is China, India, Thailand and the wider ASEAN membership that have ensured the survival of authoritarianism in Myanmar, less through any course of positive action than through culpable inaction.[60] In any weighing of historical injustice in this case, a significant neighborhood effect therefore needs also to be placed in the balance. Again, special duties of rectification could arise.

Turning to non-state action, charges of exploitation in the transnational economy are substantially reduced by the low level of corporate engagement with Myanmar. Certainly, western companies involved in resource extraction are ruthlessly targeted by campaign groups, but largely for this reason only very few now work inside the country. Fair and balanced scrutiny of their practices should nevertheless continue. By the same token, however, Asian businesses operating across borders in Myanmar must also be made fully accountable. At present, such companies function mainly beyond independent evaluation, even though anecdotal evidence suggests that many of their corporate practices are deeply damaging to local people, local cultures and the local environment. Reports on illegal logging have already been cited. Much criminally dangerous mining is also undertaken by Asian entrepreneurs. Chinese involvement in dam and pipeline projects is often damaging. Other forms of inward investment are equally harmful. While some adverse activity declined in the late 2000s, notably as a result of activist pressure on logging companies, wider Asian business engagement is on the increase. Not all of it is beyond moral doubt, and some of it may generate special duties of justice.

Among communitarians, scope for global justice is restricted by prioritization of communal integrity. By another route, however, these theorists do permit cross-border action since the Burkean notion of historical continuity allows for rectification of past injustice through special duties.[61] David Miller, not part of the communitarian mainstream but linked to it, argues that because a nation extends through time as well as space, it can be called to account for abuse committed by previous generations. Individuals cannot legitimately enjoy the benefits of membership of a national community, such as inherited territory and capital and a sense of pride in national achievements, "without at the same time acknowledging responsibility for aspects of the national past that have involved the unjust treatment of people inside or outside the national community itself, and liability to provide redress in whatever form the particular circumstances demand."[62] This contention is important, for it opens the door not only to global-level special duties listed by Pogge, but also to national-level special duties identified by Richard W. Miller. Indeed, lacking a moral statute of limitations, quasi-communitarian Miller traces duties of repair farther back into history than does quasi-cosmopolitan Miller. If taken seriously, his prescriptions could generate major duties of rectification of historical cross-border abuse in the Myanmar case.

Universal justice

Still wider concerns open up when attention turns to universal justice and duties owed to the Myanmar people not because of any identifiable course of action taken by outsiders, but rather by virtue of bonds entailed by membership of the human race. This switch from special to general duties moves analysis onto home territory for cosmopolitans, the ground on which much argument is pitched. Notwithstanding their focus on the local and particular, communitarians also make significant contributions.

Cosmopolitans are largely defined by a refusal to take state frontiers as given in debates about justice. "Why should the boundaries of states be viewed as presuppositions of justice rather than as institutions whose justice is to be assessed?," asks O'Neill.[63] Their argument is that justice cannot be fully captured in spatial fragments, but necessarily spans the whole world. The consequences for cross-border political action are substantial. First, all individuals have basic rights. Some 30 years ago, Shue put it like this: "One of our most appealing moral concepts, I believe, is the concept of (universal) human rights: the conviction that every person ought to be guaranteed a few basics by other people when helpless to secure them for herself."[64] This orientation is fundamental to the case made by cosmopolitans committed to positive rights. Second, political institutions must be judged, in large part, on the extent to which they uphold basic rights. Third, basic rights generate a duty in others to ensure they are safeguarded. Fourth, reaching across an established international border can be an effective way to do that.[65] Positive, imperfect, general duties are thereby mandated.

This need not be an argument for world government, however, and cosmopolitans have generally been careful not to insist on that.[66] Rather, the focus is on making global governance more responsive and accountable through democratization reforms proposed by Daniele Archibugi, Richard Falk and David Held, representation reforms outlined by Andrew Kuper, network reforms promoted by Anne-Marie Slaughter, decentralization reforms sought by Iris Marion Young, and so on.[67] Common to all cosmopolitan accounts is the need to trump the sovereignty claims of state rulers when basic rights face serious abuse within their jurisdiction. O'Neill thus acknowledges potential dangers in concentrating too much power in a borderless world, and argues instead for just but permeable frontiers. "A better set of just institutions might be one that is constructed in the light of considering carefully to whom and to what (to movements or persons, of goods, of information, of money) any given boundary should be porous."[68] Moreover, the agents who most productively cross borders in the name of justice will not necessarily be state employees, but could come from religious institutions, professions, corporations and INGOs.[69] Caney holds that global political institutions should be built to protect civil and political rights and cosmopolitan distributive principles, to enable people to affirm cultural and national commitments, and to permit citizens to make their rulers accountable.[70] He thus argues for a system of multilevel governance in which power moves from states up to global bodies, and down to local communities. He also proposes "a reformed United Nations incorporating a democratically elected second assembly," procedures that "enable people to hold powerful international institutions (such as the WTO, IMF, and World Bank) to account," and "a UN volunteer force charged with ensuring that people's civil and political rights are upheld."[71]

Although most of these proposals operate at some distance from current political reality in the UN Security Council and elsewhere, their practical implications are worth probing for they would drastically reshape Myanmar's position in the global system and considerably extend foreign involvement with the country. Looking beyond high-level reform of international institutions to measures likely to impact on the ground, Caney's UN volunteer force would be deployed to address a lengthy action agenda designed to enhance civil and political rights. Alongside it would be persons from religious groups, professions, corporations and INGOs championed by O'Neill in the name of justice. Together, these agents would be charged with reshaping Myanmar in line with contemporary human rights norms. An array of cosmopolitan theorists would fully support their engagement.

On the communitarian side there is widespread agreement that the notion of universal justice can sometimes justify cross-border action. Walzer concedes that border violations are permissible when there is evidence of "acts that shock the conscience of humankind," though he expects this to happen only rarely.[72] "The common brutalities of authoritarian politics, the daily oppressiveness of traditional social practices — these are not occasions for intervention."[73] Nevertheless, many possibilities remain: massacre, ethnic cleansing, slave labor, famine and malnutrition, and maybe even pandemic disease.[74] At a lower level of abuse, he allows for coercive measures falling short of force, such as economic sanctions, since they "still assume the value, and hold open the possibility, of domestic politics."[75] In this way, though starting from premises making it very difficult for outsiders to interfere with the politics of a community they played no part in shaping and can never fully comprehend, Walzer endorses most of the military intervention witnessed globally in the past 20 years or so. In 2007 he wrote that the list he was prepared to accept was "more or less actual in many parts of the world."[76]

David Miller similarly recognizes that obligations of cross-border justice arise when fundamental rights go unprotected: "the global minimum that people everywhere can claim as a matter of justice ... is ... respect and protection for their basic human rights."[77] He focuses particularly on core material needs: "only certain rights-violations are urgent enough to trigger remedial responsibilities in outsiders: being denied material subsistence triggers such responsibilities, whereas being denied equal participation in politics does not."[78] He also acknowledges two limits to national responsibility, each of which could justify foreign engagement. First, "where nations are subject to external or to autocratic rule, it is usually difficult to identify acts undertaken by individual members or by the state as genuinely national acts, and so it becomes inappropriate to spread responsibility for those acts throughout the population in question." Second, "where cultural divisions run deep, we may decide that talk of a single nation … is out of place."[79]

Finally, late in life Rawls looked beyond closed systems to consider how just rules might be set globally. Taking a non-cosmopolitan, non-communitarian approach focused on liberal peoples with domestic contracts, he devised a world system of bounded justice.[80] Rawls first stands firm against Beitz and others: there can be no global analogue of the original position. Instead, he posits a second-stage position in which representatives of liberal societies, again ignorant of specifics, meet to agree laws to govern the interactions of peoples. He contends that they will consent to a contract with eight principles designed to entrench political independence, civil liberties and the self-respect of a people, and to generate a duty of assistance toward peoples in need.[81] Next he acknowledges that liberalism cannot reasonably be expected of all peoples, and argues that the principle of toleration will prompt respect for decent hierarchical peoples who uphold basic human rights but do not acknowledge all of the equal political rights that characterize liberal democracy. Liberal and decent peoples will come together as well-ordered peoples, but will exclude three types of not well-ordered peoples: outlaw states prone to belligerence, burdened societies prevented by historical factors from becoming well-ordered societies, and benevolent absolutisms that deny their citizens a political voice.[82] He holds that well-ordered peoples will establish institutions and practices to guide their relations with non-well-ordered regimes, and especially with outlaw states and burdened societies. Toward outlaw states, they may direct public exposure and pressure, economic and other sanctions, and even armed intervention.[83] Toward burdened societies, they have a duty of assistance to help develop just institutions, rights-based political cultures and self-government.[84]

Even communitarians and those close to them in debates about universal justice thus encounter few problems in justifying positive, imperfect, general duties of engagement with Myanmar. Walzer, who insists on respect for communal integrity and limits on cross-border knowledge, draws up a long list of permissible and maybe required foreign action, though whether any or all of them apply to Myanmar is an open question. In the country's recent history, the most plausible causes look to be massacre, military targeting of ethnic nationalities, and forced labor. Miller, who stresses national responsibility, presents a list focused on basic material needs and suggests that arguments about indigenous national responsibility may not apply fully in Myanmar because of its autocratic regime and deep ethnic faultlines. Rawls, who builds on the contractarianism of the domestic original position, sees only limited scope for external involvement in all but a small range of circumstances. Broadly, however, Myanmar falls within that range, generating a duty of assistance as a burdened society and permitting engagement up to and including military action as an outlaw state.

On this side of the argument duties of global justice remain comparatively limited, and differences in tone are significant. Walzer stresses the importance of domestic politics, Miller prioritizes choosing agents at the local level, and Rawls insists that "well-ordered societies giving assistance must not act paternalistically, but in measured ways that do not conflict with the final aim of assistance: freedom and equality for the formerly burdened societies."[85] Nevertheless, communitarians agree with cosmopolitans in finding Myanmar an appropriate candidate for considerable external involvement.

Demands of justice

In the Myanmar case the demands of justice are undeniably and inevitably complex. An immensely tangled fabric of rights and duties has to be unpicked, and much of it stretches far beyond the country's borders. Some duties are perfect, identifying named persons or legal entities on both sides of the equation. Much damaging business engagement may be of this kind, with individuals in affected communities appearing as rights-bearers and foreign corporations engaged in exploitative practices featuring as duty-bearers. However, the isolation decreed for Burma by Ne Win after 1962 and the ringfence of sanctions imposed on Myanmar by the US and its allies after 1988 jointly ensured that transnational interactions became quite restricted. The result is that most duties are imperfect, owed to no one person or set of persons and demanding performance of nobody in particular. This is clearly the case with all general duties of universal justice. It is certainly also the case with most special duties of historical injustice, which do little more than distinguish broadly harmful impacts of decisions and actions taken or not taken by outsiders. In these circumstances, contemporary debate about global justice becomes centrally relevant.

Starting from a premise of positive rights vested in all members of international society and progressing from there to contest territorial boundaries blocking their realization, many cosmopolitans readily construct an argument for external action. Diverse individuals are authorized to enter the country and work for justice. Looking to functioning political communities held together by Burkean ties and moving from there to insist they be accorded respect and collective responsibilty, communitarians are nevertheless also able to build a case for external engagement through specific provisions applying in this case. The political community prioritized by Walzer is fragmented and the nation to which Miller appeals is fractured and beaten down by authoritarianism. Again, then, outsiders can go into the country to promote justice, though there is a clear sense that their action will be more limited, designed only to remove constraints on the proper functioning of domestic politics. Standing aside from both camps, but closer in this debate to communitarians than cosmopolitans, Rawlsians readily sign up for external engagement since the state is outlaw. Positive, imperfect, general duties are rapidly mandated on all sides.

Doubts however remain. Even in this case that seems to tick all the right boxes for all the right analysts, the notion of positive duties up to and including military action raises major questions. It is certainly hard to square such an aggressive mandate with Asian values that applaud communal harmony, prioritize economic development as the great social solvent, and work from there to repudiate cross-border involvement of almost any kind. Clearly no single set of precepts spans the whole of Asia, and at least some regional thought declines to rule out foreign engagement in all circumstances.[86] Undoubtedly, values of social harmony and sovereign integrity are more contested than elite figures such as Lee Kuan Yew and Mahathir Mohamad might think.[87] Nevertheless, the point made by Joanne R. Bauer and Daniel A. Bell in 1999 remains valid: these sorts of claims are "met by receptive audiences throughout the region."[88] Indeed, the principle of non-intervention has always been the cornerstone of foreign policy in ASEAN, to which Myanmar was admitted in 1997.[89]

Against this it could be argued that in practice Myanmar's military rulers have not delivered on their side of the implicit bargain, for both communal harmony and economic development are far below desired levels. For this reason, external engagement with the country's politics is permissible, and even among Asian states has been witnessed to some extent in recent years.[90] Nevertheless, at a time when no state within 4,000 miles is prepared to impose economic sanctions on Myanmar, and when regional leaders such as China and India find no basis for visible involvement in its domestic affairs, it is difficult to see how yet more aggressive forms of foreign engagement mandated by notions of global justice could get off the ground.[91] While communitarians are clearly likely to come closer to much Asian thinking than cosmopolitans, there is still a great divide.

That there should be doubts of this kind is all the more remarkable when Myanmar in many ways looks incapable of creating the conditions necessary for functioning domestic politics and operative national responsibility. It is on this basis that communitarians are able to endorse external action. Yet even in this case the demands of communal integrity remain at least as important as those of global justice. Partly this is because Myanmar has a still recent history of foreign dominion, exercised both by the British over many decades, and by the Japanese over just a few years. In the end neither experience turned out well, and neither features positively in the collective memory. Partly it is because in the years since 1988 the country has been targeted in many ways by foreigners, and none of this action has registered demonstrable success. Partly it is because a potent aspect of local culture, stoked by imperialist intrusions in the nineteenth and twentieth centuries and by ineffectual foreign sanctions and embargoes more recently, is a belief that people must be allowed to fashion their own destiny. In 1958, Cady paraphrased an evaluation reached half a century earlier by Fielding-Hall. Under the British, the Burman "lost his pride of being a Burman; he resented being lectured about the West, being told to learn new things and to forget his traditional ways."[92] In 1976, he wrote of "the population's deep-seated assumption of prideful superiority."[93] Such feelings remain prevalent.

In authoritarian minds beliefs of this kind assume perverse and extreme forms, as in this 1991 remark by a SLORC leader: "There is no other race that can love you except your own … foreigners can never love you. … They love us just to exploit us and because they want our natural resources."[94] Even in routine comments made by ethnic nationality people who have suffered most at the hands of Bamar xenophobes, however, the demand for local citizens to control their future is clear. In interviews conducted in 2009, the broad message was that foreigners could help local people in many ways. An important parallel theme, though, was that they should not be arrogant in delivering assistance. This is how an older Rakhine female INGO worker put it: " 'International experts' should not belittle us. Don't come with the attitude that Myanmar people are stupid or don't know anything … When you come don't think we don't know anything. There are some things we don't know, but there are things they don't know."[95] Pye's take on this cultural dimension is that when Europeans imposed nation-states on the region in the nineteenth century, Asians responded by developing a powerful form of nationalism based on paternalistic authority.[96] While the result may not be a full Millian drive for liberal freedom, there remains a strong preference for local autonomy. In Burma, this was publicly displayed in the late 1940s, and embodied above all in the person of Aung San. In the democratic interlude of the long 1950s it fed skepticism about foreign entanglements and for decades made Burma the quintessential nonaligned nation.[97] In the 1960s it was taken to extreme lengths by Ne Win's autarky. After 1988, it saw the military elite fully confirm Pye's analysis.

Quite where things now stand on other parts of the political spectrum is hard to say. For many years Aung San Suu Kyi made repeated appeals to the outside world not to visit Myanmar, not to do business, and not to invest. Indeed, putting pressure on major corporations to disengage from the country was the basis in 1997 for her most famous request: "Please use your liberty to promote ours."[98] From time to time ethnic nationality leaders echo some of her pleas. However, whether this string of negatives retains broad support, and whether there is any appetite for positive political engagement on the part of outsiders, are today issues that need to be thoroughly and systematically explored.

Perhaps at base, then, the concern is that a debate so readily reaching dramatic conclusions about external action is conducted almost wholly at a great distance, physical, emotional and intellectual, from Myanmar and its neighborhood.[99] This is not to insist that theorists of justice set up shop in the country, or even in the region. Equally, it is not to mandate that in examining the demands of global justice they focus overwhelmingly on this case. Clearly they have wider and more abstract interests. Nevertheless, at a time when Myanmar remains one of the most commonly cited targets of foreign action, greater attention might properly be paid to it. Although its designation as an "outpost of tyranny" alongside Belarus, Cuba, Iran, North Korea and Zimbabwe may have lapsed at the end of the Bush administration, for many activists it is still the "last good cause."[100] In these circumstances, there is reason to think it might be more fully studied. On a broader plane, when the evaluation reached by many theorists is that duties of direct and aggressive engagement are properly triggered in distant parts of the world, determining whether that conclusion is by and large acceptable to local people appears to be at least a requisite courtesy, and in all probability a necessary moral and practical basis for action. In the Myanmar case, the fact that so much global theorizing has generated so little foreign engagement may be tacit acknowledgement of that. Nevertheless, there remains a major shortfall.

To bridge the gap in Myanmar minimally necessitates finding a way to understand the wishes of people who continue to subsist under authoritarianism. Certainly, exile opinion should also be surveyed. However, it can be accorded no more than subsidiary status for the life choices made by individuals in the diaspora, and the interests they now have, often put them at variance with citizens still living and working inside the country.[101] Almost 25 years ago, though making a slightly different point, Judith N. Shklar wrote that "For an inquiry into the preferences of the oppressed to mean anything at all, one would have to conduct it under conditions that make it possible for the most deprived members of society to speak without fear and with adequate information."[102] Given the repressive nature of the military machine and the pervasive terror that stalks the land, that is in no sense easy.[103] Equally, however, it is not mission impossible.

One way forward might be a quasi-Rawlsian approach of identifying representatives to speak on behalf of the broader population, with political, religious, NGO and business leaders an obvious constituency. More direct and practical would be a less formal attempt to build on recent listening projects. In 2009, the Centre for Peace and Conflict Studies argued that "at the very least, those inside need to be heard as loudly and clearly as those who live and speak outside the country ... Hearing voices from the inside is paramount."[104] In 2010, it held that "international discourses on Myanmar are increasingly shaped by those 'outside' the country, while the voices of those on the 'inside' are rarely heard."[105] Moreover, when CDA Collaborative Learning Projects partnered with local and regional agencies to take an established global initiative to Myanmar in the closing months of 2009, it found that talking was easier than expected: "most of those approached were very willing to discuss [assistance] issues, in groups as well as individually, and seemed to feel comfortable in the process."[106]

As things now stand, however, support inside Myanmar for external action of any kind is only partially known. Despite clear evidence of indigenous mobilization for change, notably in 1988 and 2007, it is impossible to say with confidence how local people might react to foreign involvement in general, and how they would want to frame specific projects. At the end of a decade of difficult outside action in the equally distant and complex settings of Afghanistan and Iraq, this is a major concern. Also worrying is a broad global dismissal of regional views, notably advanced by such critical powers as China, India and Thailand. Inconvenient though it may be for some proponents of global justice, hearing voices from Asia is an essential moral and practical precondition for external engagement with Myanmar.

In this way, communitarians' argument about respect for local cultures comes to the fore. "Isn't intervention presumptuous? Aren't we just imposing our values on someone else?," Caney asks in mimicry.[107] For four reasons he thinks not. First, such questions should also be asked of oppressors. Second, in an interdependent world outside agencies will always make an impact. Third, countervailing risks of indifference and callousness must be borne in mind. Fourth, foreign action may be welcomed by some members of the target society. While each point is telling, none enables outsiders to circumvent the critical moral step of paying close attention to expressed local values and desires. Moreover, there truly is some presumption in a debate conducted primarily in the seminar rooms, conference halls, academic journals and position papers of elite western universities, policy thinktanks and state agencies, and rarely making contact with people on the receiving end of proposed action.

Communitarian prescriptions are thus centrally relevant. Even citizens of a benighted country like Myanmar are not only victims, but also agents keen to shape their collective fate. To CDA interviewers at the end of 2009, one person commented: "This Listening Project is the first time anyone has come to ask us about our experience. I am very happy about it."[108] Two men from Loikaw in the eastern borderlands made this remark: "For some NGOs, the projects come from above, top-down. They should listen to the people from the communities."[109] Still more critical than finding out what local people think about cross-border aid programs is grasping how they feel about a broad span of political action. Equally, it is important to acknowledge that regional neighbors are invested far more deeply in what happens inside Myanmar than are distant strangers with, as Walzer would note, little or no local knowledge.

In the Myanmar case, then, debates about global justice in and of themselves enable the demands of justice to be framed no more than provisionally. Some perfect duties can perhaps be picked out, enabling obligations of repair to be specified with some precision. Mostly, however, duties are imperfect and lead nowhere in particular. This is clearly true of general duties, but also the case with many special duties. While arguments for pressing duties of global justice are thus readily and compellingly made, much more needs to be said about practical implications. Exactly what are outsiders required to do, and how should they undertake their task? To what extent are local people content for foreigners to engage with their country, and what do they consider the best way forward? Which forms of action are broadly endorsed within the wider neighborhood, and which are not? In this regard, Caney's follow-up point sets a better tone: "Whether intervention is regarded as presumptuous would depend, in part, on procedural factors, such as *how* the intervention takes place (whether there is dialogue and consultation with people within the regime being intervened in) … [and] *who* intervenes."[110] Decisive here is the parenthetical remark, directing attention away from cosmopolitanism and toward the communitarian insistence that local agency expressed through domestic politics is key and must be prioritized.

In these circumstances, little can be said about substantive matters. Beyond a small number of perfect duties, the demands of justice are abstract and obscure. To make practical progress in the critical domain of imperfect duties, it is therefore necessary to construct a procedure that can be used to sort distinct modes of external action, facilitate choice between available options, and enable local and regional voices to be heard as fully as possible. Without this, theories of global justice are inadequate, for the real-world obligations triggered by them can be specified only in a radically incomplete manner.

7

Intervention and interaction

Examined from the standpoint of global justice, a prima facie case for external engagement with Myanmar is readily made. Viewed solely from that perspective, however, the demands of justice can be established only very imprecisely. While a small set of perfect duties can perhaps be identified and necessary tasks of repair specified, a much larger set of imperfect duties generates few clear pointers to action. This chapter therefore follows up by developing a procedure to help sort distinct modes of engagement and allow for justifiable choices to be made between alternatives. It also seeks to ensure that both rights-bearers and duty-bearers are brought within the frame, and that the opinions of people likely to be most affected by any cross-border action are fully heard. The opening section examines the core concept of intervention. The second turns to ethics of intervention, drawing on the long tradition of just war theorizing to develop a framework for use in wider contexts than simply warfare. The third examines how and by whom interventionist options might properly and fairly be considered. The fourth takes the resultant concept of interactive intervention and applies it to Myanmar. The argument has several strands. In today's world, intervention is multifaceted and draws in a large body of actors. Rules of engagement to embrace this diversity can nevertheless be worked out and should be respected by all agents. Extensive efforts must always be made to affirm that any actual intervention takes place as interactively as possible. In the Myanmar case, outsiders should follow these procedures to perform imperfect duties of global justice.

Types of intervention

The concept long used to capture involvement in the affairs of a society other than one's own is intervention. However, the many forms cross-border action currently assumes in the real world of international politics make it difficult to say exactly what meaning should now attach to the term. That task has been especially difficult since the end of the Cold War saw an expanding array of individuals from both public and private agencies launch a wide range of transnational action. In these challenging circumstances, the approach taken here is first to set down a broad, bedrock definition, and then to develop a conceptual framework capable of capturing the many modes falling within its parameters.[1]

Catherine Lu writes that "The very intelligibility of the concept of intervention relies on a structure that distinguishes between an internal and an external context, insiders and outsiders, private and public. The concept of intervention paradigmatically entails the situation of an outsider acting within the insider's preserved domain."[2] She further remarks that in the global realm the notion takes on a political dimension and issues of sovereignty become central. Here are encountered complex webs of Walzerian political communities, Millerian nations and Rawlsian peoples, all largely self-determining behind acknowledged international frontiers. Even for cosmopolitans the component parts of this conception have meaning, unless they really do insist on a single world government. For this reason, Lu's definition can be taken as a foundation stone: "The concept of intervention encompasses any action by an outside party in the internal affairs or jurisdiction of a distinct unit."[3] Reading into this formulation the political element fully endorsed by Lu, intervention is defined here as engagement designed to alter the governance arrangements of an alien jurisdiction.[4] More simply, it is cross-border political action.

Building on this, a full conceptualization can be constructed by focusing on three key dimensions.[5] The first is the nature of the intervening agent, where a critical matter for global politics is whether it is a state or non-state. With many agencies operating in a gray zone of partial state control and partial agency autonomy, this demarcation is not hard and fast.[6] However, problems of real-world categorization raise no major conceptual issues. Similarly, whether an intervening agency is one state or many, and in the latter case whether it is a formal intergovernmental organization such as above all the UN, may have ethical importance but is of no relevance to a conceptualization.[7] The second dimension is the mode of intervention, where an important question is whether it is non-coercive or coercive, or in slightly different language discursive or assertive. While there may again be boundary issues, the distinction is reasonably straightforward. Discursive identifies attempts to engage argumentatively and thereby facilitate local change. Assertive denotes attempts to engage forcefully and thereby compel local change. The third dimension is the domain of intervention, and whether in a physical sense action is initiated outside or inside the target jurisdiction. External indicates engagement outside relevant borders, and internal identifies action inside them. Using these three dimensions, an eight-part typology emerges. In both the state and civil sectors are four modes of intervention. Expressive pressure is discursive and external to the target jurisdiction. Consensual engagement is discursive and internal. Aggressive pressure is assertive and external. Belligerent engagement is assertive and internal.

Expressive state pressure finds an exemplar in diplomatic pressure. "Diplomacy is an instrument of governments," Adam Watson wrote 30 years ago.[8] While today it also embraces non-state actors in global corporations, INGOs, opposition movements and terrorist groups, all of these examples lie outside this statist category. Within states, diplomacy increasingly spreads beyond diplomatic corps to encompass defense, trade, environmental and other officials. Despite many changes of form and substance, diplomacy remains central to international relations, enabling states to "articulate, coordinate and secure particular or wider interests, using correspondence, private talks, exchanges of view, lobbying, visits, threats and other related activities."[9] This type requires an element of pressure because routine diplomacy, "the dialogue between states," is not intervention at all but rather maintenance of ongoing relations between long-term dialogue partners.[10] The stronger form thus becomes necessary, though to fit the category it must be non-coercive. A new dataset reported in 2009 identified 438 diplomatic interventions in 68 civil conflicts from 1945 to 1999.[11] For the UN, "preventive diplomacy" is "action to prevent disputes from arising between parties, to prevent existing disputes from escalating into conflicts and to limit the spread of the latter when they occur."[12] In the years since 1988, diplomatic pressure has been the major instrument used by states across Asia to try to shape political development inside Myanmar, with ASEAN, China and Japan in the lead.

Expressive civil pressure is a diffuse category comprising discursive forms of non-state political action undertaken in spheres external to the target jurisdiction. Letter-writing and internet campaigns, protest marches, and other events designed to raise political consciousness and increase pressure on target regimes all feature. Today, AI and HRW are the leading human rights INGOs, with AI notably adept at humanitarian pressure. Other INGOs engaging in direct aid provision also undertake such mobilization, with MSF a prime example. Some headline global issues generate their own protest groups and activity. Since 1988, Myanmar has been a major target of this form of intervention, with ongoing military control generating considerable concern among established INGOs, and also spawning single-issue protest groups around the world.

Consensual state engagement is also a broad category, for states can take discursive cross-border action in many ways. Visible recent instances are peace-keeping operations closely associated with the UN, which sends blue helmets on missions mainly to monitor ceasefires.[13] "Peace-keeping," Secretary-General Boutros Boutros-Ghali claimed in 1992, "can rightly be called the invention of the United Nations."[14] However, a UN mandate is not required. Rather, what is needed is consent, "the first principle of all peacekeeping" and the basis for its separation from peacemaking.[15] Critically important in debate about humanitarian intervention between established western powers and rising China, this distinction ensures that peace operations appear in two parts of this typology.[16] Beyond peacekeeping, states can directly provide many forms of development aid to distressed societies and thereby influence their domestic politics. Today, UN relief agencies, the EU's humanitarian aid office, the US Agency for International Development and similar state bodies make direct inputs to countries all over the world. In Myanmar, post-Nargis work undertaken with ASEAN and UN involvement falls into this category.

Consensual civil engagement can be launched by many actors and institutions in global civil society. Major corporations are, for instance, increasingly significant forces in international politics.[17] However, the main agencies in this sphere are INGOs, which commonly engage in cross-border provision of goods such as food, water and clothing, and services such as medical care, shelter and education. The focus here on political forms means that new humanitarians such as MSF are especially relevant. As even formally impartial organizations like the ICRC are rarely entirely neutral though, they too come within the analytical frame. While some of these agencies receive state funding, they act in largely or wholly autonomous ways and therefore are best viewed as part of the non-state sector. Their activities stretch from reshaping discrete policy domains to building capacity in civil society and thereby having an impact on broad political development. Sometimes they embrace conflict mediation, resolution and transformation activities. As with the parallel state form, intervention within this type must have a measure of target jurisdiction consent. In Myanmar, INGO action has been increasingly visible in recent years, spanning diverse policy sectors and a small set of conflict resolution initiatives and training programs.

Aggressive state pressure in archetypical form comprises sanctions, which can be economic or political, and can be applied by individual states or by coalitions brought together in the UN, EU and so on. In principle, embargoes can be general or directed. In practice, however, making sanctions truly "shrewd" or "smart" is inherently difficult.[18] The leading analysis finds the main mode to be economic, defined as "the deliberate, government-inspired withdrawal, or threat of withdrawal, of customary trade or financial relations."[19] Typically, the sender tries to inflict costs on the target in one or more of three ways: by limiting exports, restricting imports, or impeding the flow of finance.[20] While such sanctions can be traced to antiquity and in modern times formed part of the Wilsonian response to the First World War, they only came to the fore after the Second World War. Then the US emerged as the principal sanctioning power, imposing unilateral embargoes on Cuba, Iran, Libya, Vietnam and many other nations. In little more than 50 years after 1945 "Congress passed 61 pieces of sanction legislation as an expression of its disapproval of almost half of the countries of the world."[21] Multilaterally, the UN has in recent decades also become a major sanctioner. In the 1990s the organization, having previously imposed embargoes only on Rhodesia in 1966 and South Africa in 1977, placed full or partial sanctions on Iraq, the former Yugoslavia, Libya, Liberia, Somalia, parts of Cambodia, Haiti, parts of Angola, Rwanda, Sudan, Sierra Leone and Afghanistan. In addition, UN member states applied unilateral, bilateral or regional economic sanctions.[22] By the end of the decade, many moral and practical concerns were being raised.[23] Nevertheless, in the new millennium sanctions have retained broad policy appeal.[24] Additionally, a threatened referral to emergent institutions of global justice, notably the ICC formed in 2002 on the basis of 1990s experience in a number of countries, is best viewed as a form of aggressive state pressure. Ever since the 8-8-88 uprising was crushed, Myanmar has been the target of US and other sanctions on political ties, development aid and economic activity. Referring the junta to the ICC for alleged war crimes is also supported by states in the broad western camp.

Aggressive civil pressure is an amorphous type that captures assertive political action led by non-state agents in spheres external to the target jurisdiction. Just as sanctions are the archetype for aggressive state pressure, so activist campaigns designed to have an economic impact on the target jurisdiction are prime forms of aggressive civil pressure. Boycotts of South African goods, culture and sporting events organized by the Anti-Apartheid Movement from the 1960s to the 1990s are leading examples. However, also included in this category are attacks on diplomatic compounds and expatriate nationals, and violent demonstrations against governments held to fall under the target regime's diplomatic sway. Riotous anti-US protests in many parts of the world after the March 2003 Iraq invasion, and vehement anti-Israeli, anti-US demonstrations are all examples. In Myanmar, disengagement of leading global companies in the 1990s was driven chiefly by activist campaigns.

Belligerent state engagement has historically taken the paradigm form of war, which looks straightforward but is actually complex. A classic definition from 1952 holds war to be "a contention between two or more States through their armed forces, for the purpose of overpowering each other and imposing such conditions of peace as the victor pleases." Against this, Yoram Dinstein holds that only making war something states do is acceptable "with no demur."[25] This element is also questionable, however, as cases such as Spain in the 1930s and Yugoslavia in the 1990s quickly demonstrate. In practice, some civil movements are now treated as if they were states for the purposes of international law. Equally, some inter-state hostilities, such as the Japanese invasion of Manchuria in 1931, the early years of the Iran-Iraq conflict in the 1980s, and various US "police actions" during the Cold War, are usually regarded not as war, but merely as armed conflict because no formal cessation of diplomatic relations takes place.[26] For this analysis, though, the latter refinement is irrelevant, and Michael Howard's definition of war can stand: "all armed conflict between political entities, whether or not these are or claim to be recognised as sovereign states."[27] In the 1990s, the creative form of peace operations known as peacemaking became another instance of this type of cross-border engagement.[28] While the objectives are markedly different, the mode of intervention is similar in being both military and hostile to the target jurisdiction's political agenda.[29] In the past quarter-century Myanmar has not been subject to belligerent state engagement.

Belligerent civil engagement is most prominently represented by cross-border terrorism, currently the dominant mode of assertive non-state political action. Modes of coercive non-state action such as banditry and racketeering that operate across frontiers but are apolitical are not captured here. In this category the clearest instance is the September 11, 2001 strikes on US targets, with the 1993 New York World Trade Center bombing a further example. Both can be said to mark a switch from old terrorism, wanting "a lot of people watching, not a lot of people dead," to new terrorism, seeking "a lot of people watching and a lot of people dead."[30] However, the type is not confined to new forms, as many earlier variants also worked across borders in pursuit of political change. Less visible forms of this mode of engagement are assertive acts undertaken by foreign corporations and INGOs that run counter to the target's political agenda. Since the late 1980s Myanmar has not experienced any significant measure of belligerent civil engagement.

Even when attention is restricted to political forms, intervention is conducted by a broad range of actors and a large number of agencies in a wide variety of ways. The typology presented here orders the diversity of current interventionist experience, though the eight types remain somewhat complex and fluid. In a very loose way, the distinct modes can be viewed as parallel ladders of intervention in the state and non-state sectors. The analogy is not exact, for there are two different possibilities of escalation: from discursive to assertive, and from external to internal. Nevertheless, the notion of parallel ladders can be taken as a rough way of visualizing the eight interventionist types.

Justifying intervention

Once intervention has been sorted and classified, attention can turn to determining when it is permitted or even mandated. In many analyses, such issues are examined only at the most assertive end of the spectrum, above all when war is on the agenda. Then there is considerable interest in underlying rationales and justifications. However, it is not only at the extreme that matters of this kind come into play. Rather, if the notions of communal borders, integrity and sovereignty that infuse intervention with meaning are taken seriously, as they are not only by all communitarians but also by many cosmopolitans, then any attempt to shape politics across an acknowledged frontier must be fully justified.[31] The requirement is therefore to devise a procedure for ethical analysis that can be used at any point in the broad span of interventionist types.

At the end of the Cold War, when political practitioners began to construct an international humanitarian order and political theorists started to take an expanding interest in global justice, many ethical frameworks emerged. Indeed, in the first half of the 1990s the UN, a Wilton Park conference, Brown University in the Providence Principles, the World Conference on Peace and Religion in the Mohonk Criteria, the ICRC in a code agreed by eight major disaster response agencies, and Save the Children all issued guidelines to action.[32] Unsurprisingly, none took much interest in abstract moral principles. By contrast, when philosophers picked up on the shift in global politics they sometimes turned for inspiration to just war theory, for two millennia a vibrant western and Islamic tradition.[33] Soon discourse on humanitarian intervention actively embraced it.[34] Elsewhere, in analyses of international terrorism for instance, just war principles also became central to debate.[35] In these many ways, the revival of just war theorizing stimulated by publication of Walzer's *Just and Unjust Wars* in 1977 was taken to a new level through fresh modes of interest.[36] Today this body of theory is an obvious place to look when constructing a framework for ethical analysis of diverse contemporary forms of cross-border engagement.

At the heart of the just war tradition stand two major questions. When is intervention justified? How should it be undertaken? The first generates a concern with *jus ad bellum*, or just recourse to war, the second an interest in *jus in bello*, or just conduct of war.[37] When debate is extended beyond war, however, several issues raised under the second heading fall away. Classic *in bello* conditions include discrimination, designed to identify legitimate human targets, proportionality, focused on morally appropriate degrees of violence, and minimum force, mandating the least possible brutality, bloodshed and loss of life. Though perhaps relevant to some degree, none of these conditions translates readily into forms of intervention falling short of warfare. For this reason, the focus here is solely on *ad bellum* conditions. It is worth noting that some theorists argue that isolating one of the two classic questions in this way is not possible.[38] *Jus in bello* cannot be explored in isolation from *jus as bellum* because *ad bellum* conditions set the parameters and terms of engagement. However, while this is valid, the reverse contention is not. *Jus ad bellum* can certainly be separated out and examined on its own, for a decision to intervene is logically prior to actual engagement.

Since just war theory is vital and contested, *ad bellum* conditions are drawn up in diverse ways. Nevertheless, there is broad agreement that *jus ad bellum* has seven constituent parts: just cause, right intention, legitimate authority, formal declaration of war, reasonable hope of success, last resort, and proportionality regarding aims.[39] The theorists who subscribe to this list, or something very like it, hold these conditions to be jointly necessary and sufficient for award of *jus ad bellum*. The key issue for this analysis is the utility of the list in shaping an interventionist ethic stretching beyond warfare. Taken at face value, and cast in fresh language, there is no reason why these seven conditions should not be useful.

Analyzing just war theory initially on its own terms, several issues need to be addressed. One is quite minor. Formal declaration of war has fallen into considerable disuse, and has thus become inapplicable.[40] Since an assessment should not hang on a practice no longer widely observed, the condition is best excluded.[41] A larger issue is that just cause has always been difficult to specify clearly, and has long been problematic. "The traditional phrase 'just cause' is a vague one," writes Richard Norman, "and as it stands it might appear to give no guidance at all."[42] "For many critics," notes A. J. Coates, "... 'just cause' [is] the essential weak link in just war theory."[43] Beyond that, there is an ordinary language objection that just cause tends to be given a meaning equivalent to that of *jus as bellum*, implying that it is compromised if conditions such as right intention, legitimate authority and so on are not fulfilled. In everyday conversation, a cause is just if and only if it meets all the conditions on the list. For this reason, just cause is best equated with *jus ad bellum*.

If that happens, though, it is necessary to find a new condition to undertake the allotted function of just cause in the wider theory. What that mainly involves is kick-starting a process of deliberation and debate by pointing out that terrible things are happening in the world and that making war might be the appropriate response. Many argue that only self-defense can provide sufficient justification.[44] Wait for someone to make war on you, or in some versions reveal that they intend to make war on you, and then consider making war back is the maxim. However, that is too limiting. It rules out pre-emptive warfare, and in principle there is no reason why it should be sidelined. Something else is thus needed. In a theory premised on justice, the obvious candidate is demonstrable injustice.[45] Naturally, this does not exclude self-defense, for unprovoked attack is demonstrably unjust. On a positive note, it has the advantage of extending analysis beyond self-defense, and of grounding rights to self-defense in claims of justice.

There are therefore six conditions of just cause, and it is simply advisable to take one further step and put them in sequence. This is best done functionally, in terms of the task each is required to perform in the decision-making process generating a verdict one way or the other. Looked at like this, there are three main tasks. First, it is necessary to be clear that there exists in the world a problem to which war is the only viable solution. The twin conditions of demonstrable injustice and last resort speak jointly to this. The perceived problem can be labeled intractable injustice. Second, it is important to ensure that any proposed solution is acceptable as a response to that problem. Here legitimate authority and right intention are key. The proposed solution can be termed responsible intervention. Third, it is essential to be satisfied that resorting to war is likely to result in a better, not worse, world. Here reasonable hope of success and proportionality come into play. The risk assessment exercise can be called weighing contingent factors.

Translating all this into the larger discourse of intervention understood as cross-border political engagement, it can be argued that intractable injustice remains appropriate in provoking action. Individuals should not interfere in the politics of another jurisdiction unless they become aware of significant internal injustice. Demonstrable injustice can thus be taken unchanged from the modified version of just war theory developed here to the broader ethic. Last resort appears to be more difficult. While it makes eminent sense to argue that military engagement must be a last resort, it makes no sense to speak that way of, say, expressive state or civil pressure. Nevertheless, it is important to mandate that no foot be set on the parallel state and non-state ladders of intervention unless it is clear that citizens of the target jurisdiction are not themselves able to tackle the significant injustice they face. The remaining conditions translate almost directly from just war theory to the wider ethic. The proposed solution should certainly be responsible intervention, though here legitimate authority is best cast as appropriate authority to embrace non-state modes that may not be able to secure formal legitimacy. Right intention need not be revised. Finally, a risk assessment exercise remains imperative, and should comprise reasonable hope of success and proportionality regarding aims.

The argument is that this framework can be used to assess all eight types of intervention, and is an appropriate way to structure ethical debate. As those types combine different forms of agency, distinct modes of intervention and diverse realms of activity, the burden of proof varies across them. The injustice that provokes intervention of the most aggressive and invasive kind, war or cross-border terrorism, must be a lot more intractable than that which provokes other forms. Equally, the intervention must be embarked upon with an enhanced sense of responsibility, and the risk assessment exercise carries a heavier burden of proof. However, as cross-border political action of any kind is not to be taken lightly, the conditions listed here are always applicable. To indicate how this framework might be used in debate, it is necessary to examine the three paired sets of conditions.

Intractable injustice identifies an unjust situation that cannot readily be treated within the target jurisdiction. One of the two composite conditions is demonstrable injustice. It must be clear that injustice is real and potent. The second is exhaustion of less invasive strategies, a condition that has to be met to place state or non-state actors on the respective ladders of intervention. Ascertaining that injustice cannot readily be dealt with by the indigenous political system is the minimal respect for communal integrity required by any form of external engagement. To move up the parallel ladders, it is necessary to check that opportunities afforded at lower levels have been fully considered. Particular care must be taken when switching from external to internal action.

Responsible intervention identifies a form of cross-border political engagement combining appropriate authority and right intention. The first condition does not mean that all civic action is ruled out, but rather that in both the state and non-state sectors attention must be paid to authorization. Among states, this is increasingly held to require multilateral backing and even a UN mandate for action such as humanitarian military intervention.[46] Among non-states, authorization is harder to generate but still required through, for instance, appeal to human rights principles. Regarding the second condition, right intention is never easily determined and can only be judged case by case. However, it does not require entirely unmixed motives. As Walzer noted in discussing the 1991 Gulf War, "even just wars have political as well as moral reasons — and will have, I expect, until the messianic age when justice will be done for its own sake."[47] It may then be advisable to say that the stated moral objective should at least be prominent, and that any other intention is admissible to the extent that its objective is coextensive with the just intention.[48]

Weighing contingent factors identifies a risk assessment exercise that must be undertaken by all external agents. No cross-border political action can be launched without reasonable hope of success, and no agency can adopt strategies out of proportion to its aims. In the real world, many interventions have been able to meet these conditions, but some have not. In 1993, a UN peacemaking operation in Somalia had an overambitious mandate, and resulted in disaster.[49] In 1995, the UN's first ever "safe area" in Srebrenica, policed by 110 troops, was quickly overrun by Serbian forces perpetrating the worst atrocity seen in Europe since the Second World War.[50] In a different sphere, many sanctions regimes, including ones imposed on Myanmar, have almost no hope of success.[51]

Deliberating intervention

Since intervention will always be contentious, it will always have to be argued out in either actual or virtual forums. The first issue concerns the identity of participants in debate. Here the requirements of global justice mandate that both rights-bearers and duty-bearers be brought within the frame. Additionally, on a very practical level it is important that individuals and groups likely to be most affected by any actual intervention be allowed to speak. In all probability, many people will thereby gain entry for more than one reason. Next, once participants have been identified and assembled, it is necessary to determine how debate should be structured. Given that communal integrity is valued by cosmopolitans and communitarians alike, insiders must be accorded a privileged status amounting to a collective veto over proposals made by outsiders. In many distressed societies this is both a near-impossible undertaking, and a vital ambition. Before interfering in others' affairs, it is essential to find out what they think. Once that has been done, it is important to act in conformity with their wishes. To the fullest extent possible, this minimal respect must be granted to intended beneficiaries of cross-border political action.

Debate thus opens among citizens of the target society. Many, perhaps even all, will be simultaneously rights-bearers and individuals liable to be affected by cross-border action. On both counts, however, significant gradations may exist, and may need to be reflected in permissible contributions. In particular, abusive state officials may bear considerably fewer rights than ordinary citizens, and thereby gain less of a say. Once such matters have been decided, the literature on deliberative democracy stands as an obvious reference point in determining how discussion might unfold. Since about 1990, when what John S. Dryzek terms the "deliberative turn in democratic theory" took place, analysts have proposed a variety of mechanisms for generating authentic debate.[52] Against theorists who insist on an austere conception of public reason, Dryzek himself favors a more tolerant position allowing for "argument, rhetoric, humour, emotion, testimony or storytelling, and gossip."[53] He also proposes that discussion focus on specific needs rather than abstract values and ideals, holding that this will boost the probability of agreement. Ian O'Flynn examines possibilities for deliberative democracy in divided communities, focusing on two key procedural requirements of reciprocity and publicity. He argues that building a strong civil society is essential.[54] James S. Fishkin floats the possibility of deliberative polling, whereby people are brought together and asked for their views before and after open discussion.[55] Deliberative ideals have also been explored in non-democratic contexts such as China.[56] In addition, they have been raised to the global level through Dryzek's project of "transnational discursive democracy."[57]

In the realm of intervention, the proposal that debate be moved outside elite forums and opened to the people evidently takes on a utopian tinge. On the one hand, potential targets are frequently societies in which the voice of the people is forcibly muzzled. On the other, the need for external action often arises most pointedly in situations of extreme emergency such as war or natural disaster. Nevertheless, it remains important to aspire to broad-based discourse in which citizens are given a fair chance to express their views. Moreover, Dryzek's focus on informal modes, O'Flynn's insistence that civil society be strengthened, and Fishkin's deliberative polling are all consistent with the argument made here for either a quasi-Rawlsian approach of identifying trustees to speak on behalf of the broader population or, more practically, a less formal attempt to make use of listening projects.

In difficult but familiar settings where the government is chauvinistic, prickly and utterly resistant to dialogue of any kind, it is quite possible that the first stage of debate will generate rapid cessation of official involvement. Citing the sovereignty invested even in Jackson's quasi-states, autocrats like Myanmar's military leaders are likely to treat with disdain a proposed forum on intervention. Clearly this should not be allowed to derail proceedings, for that would be to grant a damaging veto to dictators. Equally, participants should not conclude that only assertive modes of cross-border action are viable, for that too would be to invest in the target regime a key negating power. Instead, attempts should continue to be made to develop a broad domestic consensus on discursive engagement. Only if failure is registered here should discussion switch to assertive modes.

Nevertheless, the practical consequence of official hostility will need to be evaluated, for ordinary people will very likely then be prevented from speaking out either by formal restrictions or by a culture of intimidation and fear. Creative ways of tapping into local sentiment will thus have to be found. While it may not be possible to secure either representative or scientific input, there is almost always the option of operating through outsiders working on the ground. Only very rarely are the UN and major aid agencies totally excluded, which opens up the possibility of making use of UN missions, INGO field offices, and the networks of local contacts they must develop to undertake their core functions. In this way, gathering a sense of indigenous opinion should be possible without either engaging in illegal activities or endangering lives. While the quality of the resultant data will inform the seriousness with which it is taken, there should not normally be grounds for dispensing with this step.

Once a measure of internal deliberation or consultation has been undertaken, debate switches to an external forum where it is picked up by outsiders assembled under two key headings. In one category, the central criteria are moral and backward-looking. Here are the bearers of imperfect duties of justice, both state and non-state, seeking to find acceptable ways to deliver on demands accruing either specially through harmful past action, or generally through common membership of the human race. In the other category, the decisive criteria are political and forward-looking. Here are above all neighboring states, more distant states with a significant regional presence or interest, and major INGOs and corporations with a firm commitment to engagement with the target society. Many participants, perhaps even most, will feature in both categories, being simultaneously significant duty-bearers and important foreign stakeholders.

In the external forum, considerations relating to the likely impact of any actual intervention mandate that close neighbors be allowed more of a voice than individuals living far away. This issue was at the heart of a rare discussion of Myanmar in the UN Security Council in January 2007, when a resolution was tabled by the US and UK. Against the contention that the junta might pose a danger to nearby states, Chinese Ambassador Wang Guangya asserted that "None of Myanmar's immediate neighbours, ASEAN members or most Asia-Pacific countries believed that the current situation in Myanmar posed a threat to regional peace and security." Following on, South African Ambassador Dumisani S. Kumalo noted that ASEAN "had said that Myanmar was not a threat to its neighbours." Concluding, Russian Ambassador Vitaly Churkin, speaking from the chair but in a national capacity, maintained that "a large number of States, including, most importantly, Myanmar's neighbours" shared the opinion that the situation in the country did not pose a threat to the peace.[58] All three countries thus voted against the resolution, with China and Russia applying vetoes. Intuitively, the argument about listening to neighbors makes sense. They are likely to have a good feel for conditions inside the target jurisdiction. In addition, any impacts of engagement, whether positive or negative, will almost certainly be felt more strongly in the region than many time zones away.

Outsiders' first task is to table and examine information gathered inside the target jurisdiction. Phased contributions are then heard. In one sequence, neighboring states present their views and distant stakeholders follow up. In another, major duty-bearers indicate how they can contribute to a collaborative interventionist effort. Ultimately a free flow of debate ensues. Throughout, the judgments and assessments of insiders are accorded primacy, and distinct forms of external contribution are mapped on to them. At the close of deliberations, conclusions can be drawn and an itemized action plan endorsed. As a final task, the broad balance of opinion can be made known, and every actor intending to intervene in the target jurisdiction advised to respect it. Ideally, a division of responsibilities and agreed coordination mechanisms will also be established. While some may commit to direct engagement on the ground, others may limit themselves to indirect involvement, for instance through allocation of funding.

In contexts of large-scale and potentially controversial cross-border action, a necessary component in establishing broad commitment to these procedural requirements will almost certainly be UN backing. This could be sought in three main ways. First, the General Assembly could be asked to endorse the approach in principle. Second, a body such as the General Assembly Third

Committee (Social, Humanitarian and Cultural) or a reformed version of the Human Rights Council could consider proposals for low-level, discursive engagement. Third, the Security Council could rule on proposals for high-level, assertive engagement. Additional parts of the UN system, such as the UNDP, UNICEF and the UN Global Compact, could be allocated key supporting functions both in supervising the deliberative process and in coordinating any follow-up action. For all of these agencies, such responsibilities would be no more than an incremental extension of existing activities.

Throughout, the focus of debate will be injustice inside the target jurisdiction, and means by which duties of global justice, both historically determined and universally entailed, might best be performed. The key requirements are initially to hear what rights-bearers in the target jurisdiction have to say about the injustice that has accumulated in their society, then to table for analysis and debate means by which concomitant duties might be performed, and ultimately to work out practical engagement strategies. In this way, imperfect duties of global justice can be stripped of the abstract and intangible character they readily assume, and given meaningful real-world content.

Clearly in any actual case deliberation will necessarily be rough and ready, and the process is highly unlikely to turn out precisely as outlined here. Engaging local opinion could be difficult. The role and activities of the target regime may be contentious. Determining which neighbors should join a regional forum will be open to negotiation. Detailed issues of agency participation could be hard to resolve. Securing input from key duty-bearers could be impossible. Coordination may have to be abandoned in favor of simply calling on all parties to take note of conclusions reached, and inviting them to operate in broad conformity with their main thrust. Moreover, none of this undeniably cumbersome procedure should ever be allowed to stand in the way of urgent global response to the kind of humanitarian catastrophe witnessed in Myanmar after Cyclone Nargis. Equally, however, it should be animated to the largest degree possible when any proposal for cross-border political action is made. In principle, a process of interactive intervention premised on the demands of global justice should aspire to this broad shape.

Interactive intervention

Two elements are central to the procedures of interactive intervention presented here: a leading role for insiders, and a following role for outsiders. To insiders is allotted the initial task of exposing injustice, sketching the main parameters of desirable intervention, and tabling it for external consideration and debate. To outsiders falls the consequential task of acknowledging imperfect duties of global justice, committing to cross-border political action, and deciding how to engage in ways that are consistent with insider views. While outsiders' role is thereby indispensable, it is also essentially recessive. The core process can be used to structure analysis of any form of cross-border political action, proposed or actual. It covers both the state and non-state sectors, embraces the central issues generated by intervention, and indicates how many clamorous voices are to be heard. Though not specific to the Myanmar case, it can be employed to evaluate proposals for foreigners to reach inside the country and perform duties of justice. This final section looks at how that might be done, focusing not on substantive matters, which are addressed later, but rather on the issue of procedure that is the concern of this chapter.

In an examination of imperfect duties of global justice, rights-bearers are the totality of the Myanmar people. Instances of historical injustice have been experienced by the nation as a whole. Issues now triggering universal concern equally pervade the entire society. Broadly, however, a far more weighty set of rights is borne by the oppressed citizenry, and a considerably less weighty set is held by forces of oppression focused on the military machine, for they are themselves responsible for much contemporary injustice. This distinction has significant implications for a process of interactive intervention, generating a large voice for civic actors and only a small say for officials. Duty-bearers are also multiple. Under the rubric of historical injustice, duties borne by former imperial masters Britain and Japan, and even by isolating western powers and engaging Asian powers, need to be considered. Under the rubric of universal justice, the global community represented in the UN is the key player. The major external stakeholders likely to be affected by any actual engagement are Myanmar's immediate neighbors and regional associates.

In this case, several practical ways of launching a process of interactive intervention are conceivable. Requests for external assistance in tackling injustice made above all by opposition forces and grassroots leaders could be heard by states. Conceivably, an *ad hoc* contact group could lead the response, set the ensuing agenda for engagement and oversee the entire process. Indeed, a subset of the Group of Friends of the Secretary-General on Myanmar, formed in December 2007, is well placed to do that with UN secretariat support.[59] Equally, however, non-state actors could take the lead, with the "globalization from below" currently developing in networks of cross-border citizen activism building a platform for action.[60] While major INGOs are likely to be most prominent, it would also be possible for a core group of large companies to take charge and work through bodies such as the UN Global Compact and peak international associations to devise new modes of corporate and other involvement.[61] In any of these scenarios, the core tasks for external actors remain the same: to solicit the views of local people, convene an external forum, and promote implementation of any conclusions reached.

Clearly a bleak scenario is all too plausible. Myanmar's controlling military elite may refuse to condone any form of cross-border political engagement, and attempt to derail any proposal for interactive intervention. While post-Nargis action coordinated jointly by the government, ASEAN and the UN is a positive step, official displeasure remains highly likely, making internal deliberation extremely problematic.[62] Indeed, in a country where terror remains the basis for governance, scientific approaches are difficult in realms deemed politically sensitive, with solid quantitative and qualitative social research only rarely possible.[63] Nevertheless, much information about the domestic context is already available, and a great deal more could be gathered. Inside the country, many reports are compiled by UN agencies, INGOs and local bodies.[64] Together, they provide quite a full picture of economic, social and political conditions. Beyond that is material collected by aid agencies stationed on Myanmar's frontiers. In Thailand, for instance, border town Mae Sot and regional center Chiang Mai are prime hubs for INGO activity. Further sources are vibrant journalistic networks animated by DVB, *The Irrawaddy*, Mizzima, and a host of smaller organizations. Assembling all these data, a large background dossier could be compiled.[65]

Despite this wealth of evidence, however, popular opinion about foreign engagement remains somewhat unknown. The most substantial and visible activist reports tend to address situations of extreme crisis, such as military repression of the saffron uprising, scandalous government inaction in the wake of Cyclone Nargis, and ongoing army offensives in ethnic nationality areas. These certainly trigger foreign awareness of significant problems stretching well beyond Walzer's common brutalities of authoritarian politics. Typically, however, they provide only partial insight into insider perspectives on ways forward. Although one clearly important source of views on external action can be found in statements issued by the NLD and by political parties that won seats at the 2010 general election, the body of information is still rather limited. In these circumstances, listening projects provide one way to fill the gap. There, often abstract possibilities for cross-border action could be brought to life through real-world case studies. Brief analyses of foreign involvement with post-Nargis reconstruction or wider Southeast Asian issues could be presented, ideally detailing problems and failures alongside achievements and successes. As well as enlivening debate, this would give local people an informed sense of available options.

Once the in-country exercise is complete, the external forum can convene through an assembly of major duty-bearers and key stakeholders. The first order of business will be to consider the dossier compiled inside Myanmar, and to seek broad agreement on its implications for future action. In itself this will be challenging. Thereafter, the task will be to deliberate ways forward. Throughout, the procedural point made earlier must be respected. In the external forum, views collected inside the country are privileged and voices from the neighborhood have a special status. Again, any problems encountered here should not be allowed to stand in the way of an effective response to pressing need.

The practical consequence of an Asian focus in the Myanmar case is that the reach and extent of foreign action may be significantly curtailed, and the demands of justice interpreted in a very conservative manner. Nevertheless, due process must prevail, and remote actors must find ways to secure if not active participation then at least passive acceptance and perhaps behind-the-scenes support from leading regional powers. As Zakaria argues at a much broader level, in the post-American world the US must embrace, celebrate and accommodate other powers by making them stakeholders in the new global order.[66] Major INGOs and corporations with an existing or potential stake inside the country should also be fully involved. Ideally, a broad plan of action will be agreed, as well as an understanding of who will do what, and when they will do it. As a final step, the coordinating body will plan implementation. In principle, this could comprise a published strategy spelling out in some detail agreed interventionist options, and a mechanism for monitoring action items against an approved timeline. In the messy world of practice, however, full transparency may not be possible.

Through a process of interactive intervention, foreigners can perform imperfect duties of global justice owed to the Myanmar people. At the outset, the procedure enables rights-bearing citizens inside the country to say how those duties should be framed and understood, thereby safeguarding notions of communal integrity that give intervention meaning and are valued by all communitarians and many cosmopolitans. Subsequently, it permits valid regional concerns to be heard. Throughout, it embraces duty-bearers and makes them integral to the process, allowing for obligations to be picked up and met in ways that are broadly acceptable to insiders and outsiders alike.

8

Intercession and investment

At a time when global policy responses to entrenched military control in Myanmar are failing and contested, heavy duties of mostly imperfect justice nevertheless weigh on outsiders. Using processes of interactive intervention to structure analysis, this chapter explores substantive options. The opening section surveys both discursive and assertive possibilities, and for three main reasons argues for discursive. The second section looks in some detail at practical ways forward within this domain, and outlines an agenda going well beyond business as usual for outsiders. The third section follows up by considering the external actors who might be drawn in to implement this agenda, and arguing for foreigners to invest in reform through aid agency action and calibrated corporate engagement. The final section reviews the interventionist strategy sketched here and assesses its potential political impact. It holds that significant long-term change is possible. Acknowledging that actual choices among available options must be made only after hearing the voices of Myanmar people, and accepting that existing reports on their preferences allow for no more than remote and provisional contributions to debate, the chapter nevertheless makes a cautious case for discursive intervention. Its core aim is to show how intercession and investment, designed as twinned parts of a unified and responsive strategy, can partner and reinforce indigenous pursuit of national reconciliation and sustainable democracy.

Interventionist options

Focusing first on discursive forms of intervention, foreigners have engaged extensively with Myanmar since the late 1980s. Chiefly, however, they have operated in the external realm, and have only launched a limited range of political projects inside the country. Thus, while much expressive pressure has been applied through diplomatic initiatives and activist campaigns, comparatively little consensual engagement has taken place. The reasons for this imbalance lie mainly in the difficulties put in the way of internal action by the Myanmar authorities, who have always been highly resistant to foreign engagement with the millions of citizens they view as uniquely theirs to shape and govern.

Notwithstanding the extent of expressive pressure directed at Myanmar over the past two decades, much more could still be done. In particular, ways could certainly be sought to intensify diplomatic pressure. All major external powers recognize that military rule in Myanmar is problematic, yet only rarely do they adopt a coordinated approach. Indeed, the main problems with state engagement since the late 1980s have been deep division among key players, and disappointing results flowing from their diplomatic initiatives.[1] Notable in this regard is frequent disagreement between the two dominant external powers, China and the US, which take very different positions on core issues such as human rights, democracy, economic development and national sovereignty.[2] While this strategic reality should not be viewed as a permanent blockage, it does hinder concerted action. To date, the closest international society has come to a measure of coordination is the UN Secretary-General's Group of Friends. However, that has limited interventionist aims, and in any case has not been notably effective in building a united diplomatic front.

At the next level, a long history of broad social conflict, deep political cleavage and often open civil war makes Myanmar a major concern for specialist external agencies, and an obvious target for consensual engagement. However, headline state action is seldom on the agenda. One option sometimes cited is multiparty talks on the North Korean model, which by reaching into Myanmar to embrace government leaders would move beyond expressive pressure.[3] While this proposal has been floated for years, it has not been paid much attention by leading foreign powers and is currently no more than a remote prospect. Also possible is UN peacekeeping, though this too is rarely considered, and even reports such as *Threat to the Peace*, the 2005 Havel-Tutu study, issued no call of this kind.[4] Most feasible from within the state sphere is then a wealth of development action seeking to reshape the society from the bottom up. Here options for expanding existing programs are plentiful. In the non-state sector, consensual engagement takes place through still limited INGO action. Some agencies seek to boost social welfare. Others invest in civil society capacity building. A few others conduct peace training and conflict resolution workshops in Myanmar or across the border in Thailand, where participants come mainly from migrant groups displaced by interethnic warfare in peripheral zones. There is thus both experience to build on, and scope for fresh initiative. Indeed, at a time when many important local actors point to the pressing need to boost grassroots engagement this is a prime area for new thinking.

Crossing the line into the domain of assertive strategies, foreigners have again been active since the late 1980s. Here though they have restricted themselves entirely to the external realm, and have given no serious thought to action inside the country. Thus, the repertoire of aggressive pressure, both state and civil, has been extensively mined, notably through formal sanctions and informal consumer boycotts. By contrast, there been no real support for belligerent engagement, and cross-border military action and terrorism are entirely absent from the mainstream political agenda. Given the degree of regional hostility to such extreme forms of intervention, and the absence of interest in them anywhere else, they are best excluded from analysis.

In the sphere of aggressive pressure, the case for state sanctions continues to be made. In late 2010, 1998 Nobel Economics Laureate Amartya Sen was a firm advocate, holding that embargoes should be smartened by targeting elite interests, and broadened through Asian participation.[5] However, smart sanctions have long been the main policy thrust of all major sanctioning powers, yet none has succeeded in delivering on its core aims and none ever could without substantially damaging other regional interests.[6] Similarly, tightening the global economic embargo through Asian sanctions has always been a major policy objective, but after many years of no progress must now be judged a possibility that even the moral authority of an Asian Nobel Laureate will not realize. Much the same can be said about the non-state sector, where threats of consumer boycotts have driven most major western corporations from the country, but have had little or no impact on Asian companies. Realistically, the scope for innovation here is minimal.

Nevertheless, one further assertive option remains to be explored in the emergent sphere of universal jurisdiction, where creation of the ICC as a permanent tribunal in The Hague has opened up new possibilities for states to deal with extreme forms of hitherto domestic injustice. For years a stream of analysis has built a case for referral of Myanmar's military elite to the ICC on grounds of grave human rights abuse.[7] In the course of 2010, many governments in the broad western camp indicated an interest in this agenda.[8] By the time of Myanmar's praetorian transition in early 2011 the campaign thus had some momentum, though intractable Asian resistance made it in no sense overwhelming.

In contemporary debate, universal jurisdiction is often lauded for promoting peace in conflict-ridden societies.[9] When the UN Security Council created *ad hoc* criminal tribunals in the former Yugoslavia and Rwanda in 1993 and 1994, it said that each would contribute to "restoration and maintenance of peace."[10] Similarly, the Preamble to the 1998 Rome Statute establishing the ICC held that part of the case for a permanent tribunal lay in "grave crimes [that] threaten the peace, security and well-being of the world."[11] Later, the December 2002 UN General Assembly resolution on Khmer Rouge trials took as a core aim "pursuit of justice and national reconciliation, stability, peace and security."[12] Many observers also maintain that external justice can contribute to internal peace. A common instrumental claim, found in the 1998 Rome Statute, is that it deters future abuse by challenging a culture of impunity.[13] A second argument is that it helps to uphold and strengthen the rule of law by enforcing international standards and promoting learning at the individual level.[14] A third is that it removes manipulative leaders from office.[15] A fourth is that it generates truth and a corroborated account of historical events, thereby furthering reconciliation.[16] A fifth is that it is a debt owed to victims of abuse that helps them heal and achieve closure, and also mollifies any retributive emotions they may feel toward perpetrators.[17]

To date, however, little support has been advanced for any of these claims, and much evidence runs in the opposite direction. The tribunal for Yugoslavia, with the longest track record of any international court, has been hailed as a success by participants and supporters, though even in positive accounts there is clear documentation to the contrary.[18] Indeed, in this case international justice did not deter abuse, but rather allowed violence to spread from Croatia to Bosnia and Herzegovina, and then to Kosovo. Condemnation or arrest of a wrongdoer in Bosnia and Herzegovina actually increased hostility among ethnic groups.[19] The imposition of global standards was also problematic, with insufficient attention paid to local context.[20] Ultimately, it was chiefly the prospect of EU membership that gave leaders of ex-Yugoslavian countries an incentive to prosecute international crimes domestically. Elsewhere, threatening abusive authoritarians with judicial referral has had mixed effects. In March 2009, the ICC issued an arrest warrant for Sudanese President Omar Hassan Ahmad Al Bashir on war crime charges linked to the Darfur conflict.[21] While this curtailed his global travel and created a measure of international isolation, it also prompted the immediate suspension of projects sponsored by 13 INGOs, including MSF, Oxfam and Save the Children.[22] Russia and China, which has a large stake in Sudan's oil industry, opposed the warrant, arguing that it would undermine peace-building efforts.[23]

Extensive intervention in Myanmar has been undertaken since the late 1980s, and on the whole has failed to deliver on its objectives. Nevertheless, the available options have not been exhausted. From coordinated diplomatic efforts launched by states from outside, to enhanced engagement by either states or INGOs on the ground inside, through to a state-sponsored ICC referral, the wider world can do a great deal more to shape the country's politics. While the issue of where to pitch future interventionist strategies must ultimately be decided by the Myanmar people, broad exploration can be pursued here as a distant and tentative contribution to domestic debate. For three reasons, this analysis opts for discursive intervention and rules out assertive.

The first is that it is not possible in existing data to find much support inside Myanmar for assertive strategies. Clearly this is not conclusive, for the data are partial. Nevertheless, it is striking that although the NLD continues to voice support for sanctions, there is very little other domestic backing for assertive strategies. Indeed, an ICC referral was explicitly ruled out by Aung San Suu Kyi in November 2010: "I've never said I want [junta leaders] to be brought into the international court."[24] More widely, opposition parties and local actors all look in much the same direction, seeking external assistance with peaceful political reform, broad-based economic development, and inclusive national reconciliation. These themes are at the heart of speeches given by Aung San Suu Kyi and position papers released by the NLD in 2011.[25] They form central planks of the platforms of parties that contested the 2010 general election.[26] They emerge as dominant strands in listening projects.[27] Certainly major differences of tone and emphasis cannot be overlooked, and in any case nothing definitive can be read into fragmentary evidence. Equally, though, in a context where data will never be perfect, the presence of these priorities and the absence of widespread calls for more aggressive action cannot be dismissed.

The second reason is that in contemporary Myanmar a key condition of sustainable political reform is meaningful social change at all levels. Comparative studies point decisively in this direction, and in recent years a prominent theme of much Myanmar analysis has been the need to recast the balance of political forces across the country by rolling back military dominance and creating spheres of grassroots control. In 2004, South placed local change at the heart of a new model for democratization. "While change at the national level, whether revolutionary or gradual, *is* urgently required, sustained democratic transition can only be achieved if accompanied by local participation."[28] In 2008, Duffield insisted that the key task is "to push back the boundaries of arbitrary personal power that have long been the root cause of Myanmar's chronic emergency … [and] to create a *space of possibilities*."[29] In

2009, Thant Myint-U made a case for reshaping the terrain on which politics is contested: "the most important thing is to change the landscape first."[30] In 2010, Callahan argued for "a series of initiatives carried out inside Burma to gradually expand the space, legal and political protections, and opportunities for the poor, uneducated, unhealthy, malnourished, and disenfranchised citizenry."[31] Listening projects also regularly transmit this message.[32] While there is no full consensus, much insider and outsider opinion prioritizes creating contending power centers able to challenge the status of the military machine as the essential political actor. While discursive engagement can reach inside the society to help extend political space, and facilitate moves toward political reform, it is hard to see how assertive action embracing sanctions and an ICC referral can contribute to this agenda.

The third reason is that assertive intervention has very unclear prospects. Sanctions are already known to have failed. Not only have they not delivered on their stated objectives, but also they have fueled regime hostility to the outside world and set both domestic and external relations on a battleground. On the whole, it is in such contexts that military personnel feel most comfortable. As Duffield notes from interviews inside Myanmar, putting politics on a war footing is often seen by local people as a gift to military leaders.[33] An ICC referral seems likely to be similarly unproductive. Indeed, the evidence from elsewhere is that such a move could trigger many negative impacts. An escalation of violence is one possibility. Disdain and militant non-cooperation on the part of leading generals are highly probable. Intractable problems in securing support from China and other regional states are almost inevitable.[34] While universal jurisdiction may deliver other benefits to the Myanmar people, its potential contribution to constructive political reform looks to be limited.

Interceding for change

The core substantive aim of discursive intervention is to foment meaningful social change sought by rights-bearing Myanmar citizens and needed by them to exercise political agency. In a context of disciplined democracy, this directs attention to enhancing political possibilities at all levels from the grassroots to the legislature and executive. Moreover, ways to do that do exist. Duffield argues that while fear effectively closes down the public sphere, the inability of the central state to secure full local implementation of its commands and directives opens up political possibilities. They can be seized first to build a basic social safety net for people subject to scant state provision, and second to roll back oppressive military control and create local space. In his words, the "crisis of self-reliance" can thereby be reinterpreted "in terms of a complex and multilevelled social ecology of survival and resistance."[35] Humanitarian engagement then becomes expansive, designed to embrace many aspects of social welfare, including education, health and livelihood issues. In this way, Duffield contends, the development enterprise can be made more "aspirational," not content with meeting basic needs, but also striving to facilitate social transformation.[36] As South put it several years ago, aid is "*a way into* political action."[37]

Considerable work of this kind is already being undertaken inside Myanmar, and is endorsed by many key stakeholders including the NLD, which notably since Aung San Suu Kyi's release from house arrest in November 2010 has sought to reach out to civil society.[38] The two leading local NGOs are Metta Development Foundation, formed in 1998, and Shalom (Nyein) Foundation, formed in 2000. Focused on agriculture, education, health, livelihood issues and capacity building, Metta operates through grassroots initiative, community participation, training and education, and local networks. Its global partners and donors include UN agencies, national governments and state agencies, INGOs and individuals.[39] Shalom also has development programmes in the education and forestry sectors, but works above all on peace building. With five ethnic nationalities (Chin, Kachin, Karen, Kayah and Mon) it has developed high-level mediation programs aimed at facilitating dialogue reaching all the way up to the *tatmadaw* and armed militias. In its core territories it has also responded to grassroots requests to establish peace education programs through training courses, peace committees and an interfaith youth cooperative action program. This work is also supported by a range of outside bodies.[40]

In looking for productive engagement options, outsiders can learn from and build on initiatives of this kind, which are now replicated in myriad ways throughout the society. Many obstacles undoubtedly stand in the way. Politically, a culture of hostility to foreigners is not confined to the governing elite. Socially, deep cleavages between ethnic groups, political forces and even local people and exiles living in the diaspora make for a complex setting that can be quite bewildering to outsiders. Practically, all sorts of daily hazards are sure to be encountered. Nevertheless, it is precisely in this broad domain that the most innovative external engagement is currently taking place, with aid agencies from both the state and non-state sectors working through local bodies to implement programs, boost indigenous capacity and open up political space. Standard practice in major programs like the 3D Fund and LIFT is to call for proposals from grassroots agencies and fund them to deliver on agreed objectives. Many INGOs operate similarly.

At the same time, a great deal more can still be done. Partly the task is to broaden and deepen, so that territorial coverage is extended beyond vibrant Nargis-affected areas and driven more fully into the society. Partly it is to ensure that experience from elsewhere is brought to bear on local challenges, though always the issue of cross-border transfer must be handled sensitively. When studies in the 1990s and 2000s examined community mediation in leading Asian societies, they found local practices that set each apart from the others, and all of them apart from the US.[41] Nevertheless, in an abundant literature there is much of relevance to Myanmar's circumstances.[42] For nearly 50 years interactive conflict resolution has been explored in real-world settings.[43] Specific issues such as the best time to mediate, optimal choice of techniques, and individual decisions to invest in the process have been analyzed in great detail.[44] Peace workshops in contexts such as Northern Ireland, Israel/Palestine and Sri Lanka have been picked apart for lessons.[45] From these and other studies, the need to promote empathy across social cleavages has emerged as critical.[46] In the Tibetan case, deliberative approaches have been piloted among exile communities.[47] In Northern Ireland, where political change has already taken place, social psychologists continue to experiment with ways to resolve conflict and entrench peace through positive cross-group contacts designed to promote intergroup forgiveness.[48]

Comparative analysis also has much to teach about the critical importance of boosting civil society. For Myanmar, a poignant comparison is negative. In Sri Lanka in May 2009, President Mahinda Rajapaksa ended a quarter-century of interethnic civil war by declaring total victory over the Tamil insurgency. Ominously, Than Shwe and Rajapaksa then exchanged bilateral visits in June and November 2009, triggering fear that the *tatmadaw* is eager to draw lessons from its maritime neighbor.[49] Looking back into recent history, though, Sri Lanka might well have pursued another path. From outside, first India and then especially Norway invested considerable efforts in consensual state engagement through peace facilitation.[50] Local actors sought to underpin the process by addressing ethnic division through awareness-raising programs and cross-ethnic dialogue, reducing political tension through mobilization and informal diplomacy, and confronting economic issues through reconstruction and development. However, fatal weaknesses brought about by patronage, protracted warfare and a strong top-down project orientation drove out the mass-based, grassroots action needed for success.[51] For Myanmar to take the different route desired by so many, the lesson again is that reconstruction of civil society is essential. In East-Central Europe after 1989, cross-border civic action was critical in taming ethnic hatred.[52] In Uganda, where limited democratic progress in the 1990s has latterly been halted and even reversed, external engagement with domestic civil society is critical to building a positive human rights culture.[53]

Support for a capacity-building orientation at local levels is also clear from opinions now held inside Myanmar. One NGO worker interviewed several months after Cyclone Nargis said this: "Capacity building is important. INGOs should be used for their knowledge and resource persons. They have to give and share capacity. We need to know about project management, community development and emergency responses. We want to be taught how to fish, not to be given fish."[54] Another noted that external engagement is often not supportive. "Needs and interests are different with donors sometimes. Sharing information is ok but some groups just come through and collect information and take photos and don't return."[55] Even for INGOs immersed in the local setting, apparently minor issues require focused attention, as is clear from this account of meetings convened by a large external agency: "They are held at a grand hotel. The participants of the women's organisations are from the villages in remote areas. They are worried about their dress and footwear. They have to pay at least 2000–3000 kyats to get to the location of the hotel."[56] Another person captured the views of many local NGO workers: "We need donors to have a good knowledge of our reality. We don't want to pretend with them. They must accept our reality and think about our capacity-building. Trust is really important. We want a donor to always be involved with us and working collaboratively. Good or bad, we have shared responsibility for our work. We want to develop proposals collectively and be flexible and open. It can be difficult to find donors like this."[57]

Similar expectations of external engagement were visible in interviews conducted with ethnic leaders in mid-2009 mainly on the topic of national reconciliation. Although some doubted whether the international community could do much in Myanmar, others foresaw a positive contribution provided that outsiders "create more connections with domestic actors" and "more fully understand the situation and its complexity."[58] Again, capacity building was a key theme. As an older Bamar male INGO worker put it, "NGOs need to revive and re-strengthen thinking skills and open our eyes. Help us set goals. Don't just distribute things and give charity, but also give knowledge and training."[59] In late 2009, CDA gathered similar testimony.[60] These injunctions also link back to a remark made by Aung San Suu Kyi in 1994, when Myanmar's civil society was in a much more desperate state and capacity building a far greater task: "It is not enough merely to provide the poor with material assistance. They have to be sufficiently empowered to change their perception of themselves as helpless and ineffectual in an uncaring world."[61] Here, the link with Duffield's point about extending the frontiers of political space is explicit.

Moreover, if a domestic rebuilding program of this kind does advance, a supporting role for high-level consensual state engagement will eventually be triggered. Indeed, if Myanmar is to avoid the fight to the finish witnessed in Sri Lanka in 2009, key external powers will one day need to build on local change and reach out to government officials through multiparty talks designed to entrench grassroots progress. In small collaborative steps taken by UN agencies, INGOs and local NGOs to build civil society capacity and boost space for local action, they will find a platform for engaging political leaders. It is also important that they do so, for securing local progress through institutionalization is ultimately critical, with power-sharing mechanisms, third-party security guarantees and transitional justice to the fore.[62] Once civil society reaches a point where these kinds of issues surface for attention, external powers thus become essential actors.

In the sphere of consensual engagement lies a potentially large and onerous agenda going far beyond current attempts to shape political development inside Myanmar. In no sense would implementation of these initiatives represent a minor incremental advance on current external action. Rather, it would constitute a step change in intervention. Led from the grassroots through civic action undertaken above all by UN agencies and INGOs, it would ultimately require a recasting of major power engagement. The aim would be to reset Myanmar's political trajectory through local empowerment ultimately backed by systemic reform negotiated at the elite level.

Investing in reform

The external actors on whom imperfect duties of global justice most clearly fall, and who thereby bear the greatest responsibility for delivering on a substantive agenda of this kind, can be identified only in broad terms here. Far more detailed consideration is necessary to allocate actual duties with any precision. Nevertheless, some clear pointers exist and have already been sketched out. Focusing on special duties of historical injustice, some duties of repair may still be borne by the UK and Japan as former imperial powers. While many have been discharged, others may have lapsed and yet others were in a perverse sense discounted by Ne Win, the possibility that some remain live needs to be explored. Alongside them, large duties of rectification may have been incurred in recent years through a raft of western sanctions known to be ineffective and kept in place mainly for unscrupulous domestic reasons. They could trigger stringent negative duties to stop visiting harm on the Myanmar people and important positive duties of restitution. In addition, culpable Asian inaction in dealing with the Myanmar problem could be brought within the frame. Entailed under a separate heading are general duties of universal justice that are still more difficult to apportion, and best allocated through the UN.

Even this initial attempt to list potential duty-bearers clearly injects a considerable degree of unreality into the analysis. The chance that surviving imperial duties of repair will be computed is slim. The likelihood that sanctioning powers will accept that their policies are unjust is close to non-existent. The probability that damaging Asian engagement will ever be called to account is slight. The ability of an unreformed UN to take the lead in determining duties of universal justice is compromised.[63] Nevertheless, if outsiders are one day prepared to consider the demands of justice in this case, such positive duties need to be examined. Furthermore, they do not automatically trigger direct engagement, but could rather be met through financing in-country programs implemented by others. In Tokyo in January 2002, the International Conference on Reconstruction Assistance to Afghanistan assembled a multi-billion dollar fund.[64] A parallel future initiative for Myanmar, perhaps also convened in Tokyo as part of a larger process of interactive intervention, might learn from it. Contributions could be gauged by evaluating special duties of historical injustice. External claims of interest in the country's future development could be turned into vehicles for delivering on general duties of universal justice.

Certainly, though, in the two key substantive domains of mediation and capacity building identified here, it will be necessary for some foreign agents and agencies to play a constructive role inside Myanmar. How best to do that brings two large contemporary debates sharply into focus. One concerns aid agencies, both state and non-state, which are already working on this agenda. In recent years, vibrant analysis of the international aid business, currently worth about $10 billion annually, has posed major questions for this sector. The other concerns global corporations, which though not always viewed as positive political actors in the development literature are profiled that way through notions of corporate social responsibility, and the wider contribution of business to social change. While the two debates overlap at several points, they can be separated for analytical purposes.[65]

Controversy has surrounded the aid business for decades, but can perhaps be said to have found a true voice in 1997 in de Waal's *Famine Crimes*, focused on the politics of disaster relief in Africa. The core argument made there was that "Western governments and donating publics are deluded into believing the fairy tale that their aid can solve profound political problems, when it cannot."[66] Indeed, de Waal's position was especially radical, for he argued that "the 'humanitarian international' — the transnational elite of relief workers, aid-dispensing civil servants, academics, journalists and others, and the institutions they work for" limits indigenous politics by weakening domestic accountability.[67] As he put it, reaching across a border to deliver aid triggers "a leaching of power from those who suffer."[68] While outsiders can offer support, a lasting solution to development problems can come only through domestic political action. On this basis, he held that "most current humanitarian activity in Africa is useless or damaging and should be abandoned."[69] In *Dead Aid*, published in 2009, Dambisa Moyo reiterated the point.[70]

In the past decade many others have reinforced this critique. From inside the aid industry in 2002, Fiona Terry in *Condemned to Repeat?* held that all too frequently aid is delivered in blind ignorance of political context, and ends up feeding oppression rather than alleviating suffering.[71] From outside in 2003, David Rieff in *A Bed for the Night* condemned the political naivety of much humanitarian engagement, and charted a descent into something close to modern-day colonialism.[72] Looking at the development industry, William Easterly in *The Elusive Quest for Growth* and still more in *The White Man's Burden* similarly argued that foreign action pays insufficient attention to local accountability and feedback.[73] He maintained that the world's poor do not benefit from aid, but rather become imprisoned in a trap formed by rich-country planners intent on imposing grand designs on impoverished nations. On this basis, he took aim at ambitious proposals found in Jeffrey D. Sachs' *The End of Poverty*, which marks out clear steps to the eradication of extreme poverty within 20 years, and in the aid work of global celebrities such as Bono and Bob Geldof.[74] Beyond the revisionist critique, others also acknowledge the deficiencies of much past practice, the importance of promoting what Sen calls *Development as Freedom*, and the need to adopt evidence-based ways to help what Paul Collier terms *The Bottom Billion*.[75]

In this debate are found not only the main axes of quintessentially twentieth-century dispute between proponents of planning and champions of markets, but also the broad middle ground sketched by less combative and rhetorical economists. Easterly holds that "The right plan is to have no plan," and against advocates of traditional ways ("planners") promotes new agents for change ("searchers"). "Planners announce good intentions but don't motivate anyone to carry them out; Searchers find things that work and get some reward. Planners raise expectations but take no responsibility for meeting them; Searchers accept responsibility for their actions. Planners determine what to supply; Searchers find out what is in demand. Planners apply global blueprints; Searchers adapt to local conditions."[76] However, in between two rather caricatured poles lies a vast range of potential activity that may or may not be productive depending on context and circumstance.

The task taken up by many is thus to document success and failure, and to determine how development agencies might learn from both. In a generous review of *The White Man's Burden* championing "ground-level explorations of what is feasible," Sen put it this way: "The challenge is to respond to the plight of the hopelessly impoverished without neglecting to insist that help come in useful and productive forms."[77] He agreed with Easterly that "the failure of many grand schemes results from their disregard for the complexity of institutions and incentive systems and their neglect of individual initiative, which must be societally encouraged rather than bureaucratically stifled."[78] At the same time, he wrote approvingly that Easterly is "moved by a rich vision of indigenous creativity that can flower in the absence of extraterritorial grand designs."[79]

Pulling these various arguments together, the key point is that external engagement must be undertaken within the context of domestic politics, and do all it can to ensure that its mechanisms and procedures are able to function as fully as possible. The role of outsiders is to offer facilitation and support. The orientation already taken here is thereby strongly reinforced, indicating that investing in capacity and reform at the grassroots level should be a top priority for global aid agencies in both the state and non-state sectors. As Greg Mortenson has shown by building girls' schools in remote parts of Afghanistan and Pakistan, such activity can be a distinctive and significant form of foreign engagement.[80] More widely, Easterly's searchers are precisely the kinds of people now reanimating civic action inside Myanmar, and bolstering their work is a central task for outsiders.

Equally, however, it is important to look beyond the aid business to mainstream corporate business and consider how it might also help build a platform for long-term change. Here too widespread debate opens up as proponents of globalization confront analysts of exploitation in development contexts.[81] On one side, economists and peak global agencies such as the World Bank and UN Global Compact argue that globalization can operate to the benefit of the poor.[82] On the other, many observers point to the catastrophic impact much foreign trade and investment has on local communities.[83] In parallel, while some note the development gains that can flow from corporate action even in repressive contexts, others view business engagement with rights-violating regimes as thoroughly unprincipled and impermissible. Located at the heart of much analysis is debate about corporate social responsibility, and the positive need for companies to add to the core economic value acclaimed by liberal economists an explicit commitment to morally acceptable practice.[84]

At base, corporate social responsibility mandates that enterprises make a deep rather than superficial commitment to host communities, eschew all forms of malpractice, and join local people in securing a range of broad social benefits. In Myanmar, such action has been seen only in small ways, for companies subscribing to this agenda are thin on the ground and the very concept has only recently started to gain any purchase.[85] Indeed, the best example lies in the most controversial sector of natural gas exploitation through off-shore fields and on-shore pipelines.[86] There French oil giant Total has for years been targeted by activist groups for forced labor and other abuses along a pipeline in southern Myanmar distributing natural gas to Thailand from the Yadana field in the Andaman Sea.[87] In response, the company has employed mainly local personnel, created a socioeconomic program focused on health, education, economic development and infrastructure, and formed village liaison teams to implement it. Consultants appointed by Total to conduct independent impact assessments attest that forced labor was not used on the project, and commend the outreach activities.[88] In a 2003 evaluation, Kouchner, co-founder of MSF, French health minister 2001–02 and French foreign minister 2007–10, noted that Total's engagement with dictatorship "underlies all criticism of the Group," but nevertheless held that many specific allegations were "refuted by an onsite investigation." He embraced the "real success" of the socioeconomic program.[89] At the same time, he called on all actors engaged with Myanmar to speak out: "One day, indifference or silence will be construed as guilt."[90]

Clearly evident from the Total case and others around the world is the need to ensure that companies investing in repressive settings meet the high demands placed on them, and do not backslide or free-ride. Indeed, a clear incentive in authoritarian and impoverished contexts is to draw considerable benefit from cheap labor and low operating costs, and deliver no more than minimal salaries and exploitative conditions to local people and communities. Means of changing the incentive structures facing inward investors therefore need to be found. In the Myanmar case, however, the chosen mechanism of boycotts and sanctions has gone to the other extreme of persuading most major companies to have nothing to do with the country, thereby denying local people employment opportunities and engagement with key forces of globalization. Among corporations targeted by western activism, only those with large sunk costs like Total will attempt to maintain their investments and map out a middle way guided by broad social commitments.[91]

Central to the argument made by corporate social responsibility advocates is thus the need for ethical framing of business action. In part this can take place through domestic criminalization of overseas corruption. Pioneered by the US through the Foreign Corrupt Practices Act 1977, this emergent global movement was joined by China in February 2011 when the National People's Congress outlawed foreign bribery.[92] For the Myanmar case, this was a critical move. Also necessary, however, is corporate embrace of mechanisms such as a publicly-displayed stakeholder statute, value statement, or code of conduct.[93] In authoritarian contexts, where rights violations are commonplace and there is a high possibility that business will merely reinforce existing structures of repression, measures of this kind are notably important. In the case of Total in Myanmar, the company has a code of conduct underpinned by principles drawn from the Universal Declaration of Human Rights and the ILO Charter. Appended all to subcontractor agreements, it is a legally binding document. In analogous settings around the world, this approach was pioneered in the Sullivan Principles in South Africa (1977) and later developed in the Caux Round Table Principles for Business (1994), the Global Sullivan Principles (1999), and the UN Global Compact with Business (2000).[94] Each calls for extensive consultation among a wide network of business leaders, and requires that responsible corporations deal with all stakeholders in a fair and equitable manner, act as positive and proactive change agents, and adopt compliance standards that are mandatory, transparent and subject to external validation.[95] Indeed, independent monitoring, undertaken by competent evaluators, is generally held to be essential.[96]

The Total experience demonstrates that boosting external engagement with Myanmar through direct corporate investment remains highly controversial.[97] Even getting such an approach off the ground would be difficult. On one side, it is hard to see why executives would sign up for it, as it would provoke the sanctions lobby and trigger wider exploitation charges. It would also place companies in a tough business setting, and could expose executives to illegal practices. For major corporations that have chosen to duck the international sweatshops debate and prefer not to invest in corrupt societies, there is little incentive to get involved with Myanmar.[98] On the other side, it is equally hard to imagine military leaders showing any interest in this agenda when they have successfully rebuffed all previous attempts to use investment as a lever for domestic political change.[99] Some indicators are nevertheless favorable. Among companies, long-term strategic issues come into play. "Today's operations are not commercially viable," said a representative of Japanese corporation Mitsui in 1996, "but we believe this country has big potential."[100] Other businesses recognized that potential in the late 1980s, but chose to forgo it as political problems mounted in the 1990s. Among military leaders, an awareness of the need for development has long been visible in infrastructure projects, and in attempts to boost investment and employment in defiance of sanctions. Myanmar's National Sustainable Development Strategy identifies agriculture, forestry, energy, mining, transportation, communications and tourism as priority areas for future investment.[101]

For these reasons, a requisite approach in the Myanmar context would almost certainly be group-based engagement, with participating corporations jointly making a public commitment to principled and sustainable investment. Then the chance that individual corporations might be picked off by the sanctions lobby would be reduced, and the extent of leverage over a venal military machine would be enhanced. One possible facilitator is the Caux Round Table, committed to human dignity and the Japanese *kyosei* concept of "living and working together for the common good enabling cooperation and mutual prosperity to coexist with healthy and fair competition."[102] Rooted in Confucian thought but expressive of values with currency throughout Asia, this ethic could provide a powerful foundation for engagement.[103] In particular, it is likely to be viewed positively by the Asian corporations that are leading investors in Myanmar and now have nascent corporate social responsibility programs.[104] More broadly, another potential promoter is the UN Global Compact, which already animates corporate networks in difficult settings around the world. As with INGO involvement in grassroots capacity building, external state action may well be needed to entrench this strategy. Again, political leadership could be supplied by a coalition of countries drawn from both regional and western powers.[105]

In the Myanmar case, many options now exist for delivering on imperfect duties of global justice through strategies of discursive intervention. Once the demands placed on major duty-bearers have been identified, possibilities for investing in reform can be pursued. Indeed, through both aid agency and business engagement in communities across the country, foreigners can help rebuild a society subject to many decades of devastation, and thereby construct a platform for long-term political renewal. In particular, INGOs and global corporations can take the lead in delivering on the capacity-building agenda now surfacing within domestic civil society as it slowly finds its feet in a still-hostile operating environment. In the longer term, states can play a supportive though no less important role in entrenching grassroots initiative through elite-level mediation.

Interventionist strategy

In more than two decades of engagement with Myanmar, no external agent or agency has registered much success. Indeed, even after the launch of disciplined democracy a huge governance deficit remains and widespread human rights violations continue. At local levels, however, away from most media interest, many minor triumphs have been secured. In detailing variable but significant amounts of progress in a range of disparate sectors in 2010, Allan reached the important conclusion that "opportunity is far more common than most would expect."[106] Today, then, openings for interactive intervention do exist, and must be explored by committed outsiders willing to respond to the demands of justice in this case.

The argument made here for consensual engagement through intercession and investment focuses on local capacity building by both aid agencies and responsible global corporations, and aims to empower local people to lead political change as much as possible. It thus runs counter to much current interventionist activity. While remaining within the discursive domain, it moves far beyond the mainly Asian focus on expressive state pressure through diplomacy. Though not taking up assertive options, it is also in many respects more developed than the mainly western focus on aggressive state and civil pressure through sanctions and boycotts. By reaching inside Myanmar to try to reshape political realities on the ground, it places greater demands on external agents. The first task in this final section is to determine how this fresh approach might be grafted onto existing external engagement with Myanmar. The second is to evaluate its potential political impact. The third is to examine the degree of local support it might command.

Implementing a strategy of consensual engagement in a context of expressive pressure applied above all by Asian states is reasonably straightforward. Although in the Myanmar case many domestic hurdles stand in the way of enhanced intervention, few external problems are likely to be encountered by a low-profile approach seeking to build mainly from the grassroots up and to involve states in high-profile political negotiation only at later stages in the process. By contrast, the constraints placed on consensual engagement by existing modes of aggressive pressure imposed mainly by western states are substantial. Extensive state sanctions mean that much aid agency action is either severely reduced or even ruled out. Sanctions supplemented by consumer boycotts eliminate a large spectrum of corporate investment. In these circumstances, practical options for consensual engagement need to be examined.

One way forward would be to focus on the many aid agencies and global corporations unaffected by sanctions maintained only by the US and its leading allies. Operating beyond existing global embargoes are government bodies in non-sanctioning states, INGOs, and corporations based in non-western nations and markets. Moreover, much is already being done in a quiet way by some of these organizations. State development agencies from East Asian jurisdictions such as Japan, South Korea and Taiwan are currently very active inside Myanmar. INGOs are mounting a growing array of programs. Businesses across Asia are taking another look at Myanmar as a potential investment destination, and some are prepared to embrace the notion of corporate social responsibility. Starting out on this basis is then feasible and appropriate, for low-profile humanitarian engagement and inward investment from Asia, perhaps spearheaded by dynamic businesses from China and India, offer the best chance of building a platform for long-term success.[107] Ultimately, however, it will also be necessary for the US and its allies to reconfigure their Myanmar policies. Most palatable to western governments and indeed publics is often said to be a *quid pro quo* approach, whereby sanctions are slowly removed in response to measurable political progress inside Myanmar. The Obama administration opted for what is often termed conditionality in its 2009 policy review. The EU similarly takes this position. While ongoing elite-level hostility on all sides could delay implementation, there may be no practical alternative.

In terms of political impact, discursive intervention is unlikely to generate dramatic change. In all probability, intercession and investment will not be revolutionary in their short-term consequences. However, evidence from comparable cases shows that such action can have positive long-term effects if well designed and implemented. In the sphere of intercession, mediation can deliver especially strong results if undertaken in a painstaking and involved manner from the grassroots up, rather than in a quick and easy manner at the elite level. In the sphere of investment, aid agency and corporate action focused on local capacity building can enhance a palpable sense of organic growth in contemporary Myanmar, and a strong feeling across a still emergent domestic civil society that now is the time to boost it still further. More widely, modernization theory has long drawn adherents and can be cited in support of this strategy. The further benefits socially responsible engagement might bring are a forceful additional incentive.

All that said, it is important not to press the claims of this approach too hard, for it is undeniably contentious. Indeed, doing business with a rights-violating regime, whether understood in the narrow or broad sense, can never be anything other than inherently problematic. In 1988, the year of the democracy crackdown in Burma, Norman Bowie focused on the narrow meaning to argue that "businesses have obligations to pull out of oppressive countries if there is little hope of reform."[108] After a brief flirtation with Myanmar, executives in prominent global corporations took note of the junta's response to the 1990 general election and quickly followed his advice. Taking the broader sense, many leading western powers have also focused above all on isolation strategies and clean hands. In all cases, the reasoning and the action are fully comprehensible. On the ground inside Myanmar, however, the result has been a tight concentration of power in the military-state complex to the extent that few options for challenging it now exist. It is for this reason that attempts to boost countervailing power are currently on the political agenda and promoted by local civic leaders. If implemented, Myanmar might within a few years be able to emulate processes of change witnessed in Vietnam since 1986, when *doi moi* (renovation) reforms were unveiled and substantial grassroots dynamism was unleashed.[109] If carefully designed and executed, strategies of intercession and investment can be constructive partners for indigenous pursuit of national reconciliation and sustainable democracy.

A final issue is the degree of support the strategy sketched here might command inside Myanmar. Certainly endorsement can be found in debate now taking place among civil society leaders, notably in Nargis-affected areas. Again, however, the limitations of such testimony need to be clearly stated. Existing data are not only restricted in quantity and quality, but also targeted at other matters. Thus, most reports currently in the public domain do not seek to aggregate communal preferences or represent broad social opinion, but rather to provide a snapshot of specific aspects of contemporary Myanmar. Typically, the focus is either on fast-growing community and NGO action in the Ayeyawady delta, or on the peripheral world of ethnic nationality groups, for these are the elements of present-day society with which outsiders have greatest contact and in which they have most interest. By contrast, the opinions of individuals in other groups are rarely captured. At the extreme are the powerful, the favored and those who work with and for them: military commanders, local leaders and officials, well-connected businesspeople and others who have chosen to align themselves with the military agenda and are in no hurry for political change. Across the core of the society are regular citizens eking out a living and doing their best to survive from day to day. Mostly their views are unknown, though it seems highly probable that they are more disparate than mainstream media and activist commentary allows.[110]

Furthermore, even if public opinion is on the side of those yearning for significant political renewal and change, which seems likely from all that has happened since the late 1980s, it is quite possible that the popular mood leans toward a clean break with praetorian politics. If so, it may not favor a strategy designed to build competing power nodes alongside the dominant military machine, and could instead argue for revolutionary destruction of the military-state complex. While key leaders including Aung San Suu Kyi rule out this possibility, unless and until proper consultation takes place the answer to this critical question cannot be known. More generally, a vein of proud nationalism by no means restricted to military leaders and a generalized mistrust of external action following decades of substantial disappointment could also stand in the way of foreign engagement. Always the main input must be made by local people, and before any strategy of interactive intervention is launched their voices need to be heard as fully as possible.

Nevertheless, the recorded views of many civic actors cannot be wholly discounted. Indeed, if local debate were to take the form of a series of listening projects, the grassroots social leaders who feature so prominently in this analysis would undoubtedly be a key constituency. Even if it were to cast a still wider net across the society, they would remain major contributors. While not wanting to push the issue too far, it can certainly be argued that the line taken here has some domestic support. Moreover, in arguing for consensual engagement, local NGO workers reveal a series of preferences that must be fully acknowledged by outsiders. These are for change to be driven primarily by Myanmar people rather than by foreigners, by grassroots actors rather than by top leaders, and by supportive external bodies sharing and facilitating these goals. In important ways, then, contemporary preferences run counter to the broad policy thrust of much existing external engagement, which particularly through sanctions seeks to put outsiders in the driving seat, focuses on elite politics, and subverts the emergence of civil society.

Conclusion

The twist the Burma story took in the late 1980s, when the early phases of an apparent transition to democracy were decisively curtailed by the country's entrenched military elite, is often cast as a modern variant of the morality plays that flourished in late medieval Europe. In one telling, Aung San Suu Kyi features as the protagonist embodying the core virtues and highest political aspirations of a repressed, fearful and impoverished nation. "Burma's Saint Joan" is how an October 1995 *Vanity Fair* cover put it.[1] Her antagonists are presented neither as seven deadly sins nor as a lengthy parade of vices, but rather as a unified set of largely faceless evildoers grouped together in a brutal military machine. In another more hopeful version premised on the belief that in the end good must triumph over evil, the NLD leader emerges as a Burmese Beatrice guiding her people through Dante's nine spheres of heaven to the desired destination of vibrant, peaceful and prosperous democracy. In states clustered around the US in the broad western camp, forms of these parables implicitly underpin much government policy, routinely inform media attention sporadically trained on the country, and long ago passed into popular culture through secular sanctification of the 1991 Nobel Laureate and concomitant demonization of military leaders. For years they have been a staple of activist discourse in the diaspora and transnational networks.[2]

Perhaps something is to be said for Manichean readings of Myanmar politics, for they neatly capture the dark, brooding presence of the dictatorial generals who continue to dominate the country, and the exemplary moral and physical courage of Aung San Suu Kyi in standing up to them and holding in their faces the torch of freedom. They also train attention on the single most unusual feature of contemporary politics: the sheer durability of military rule. That Burma experienced a coup and suspension of democracy in 1962 was not remarkable, and was not seen as such at the time. In Third World nations in Cold War settings, fragile postcolonial democracies routinely succumbed to strongman politics. That the country then moved into a period of destructive state socialism under a malfunctioning command economy was also not uncommon. That eventually there was a popular backlash and mass protest for democracy was par for the course. Rather, what set this case apart was the ability of obscure military leaders to hold off and resist the potent moral power of Aung San Suu Kyi and the transitional wave she personified. In a global context that saw Václav Havel, Nelson Mandela and other democratic rebels prevail at the end of the Cold War, Myanmar under its generals became atypical. Today, as military leaders take the initiative by defiantly rolling out their own praetorian version of democracy, it remains something of an anomaly in international society.

Ultimately such readings are unhelpful, though, for they impose a distorting dichotomy on a byzantine situation, and imply that most current problems can come close to being solved by the elementary expedient of returning the *tatmadaw* to its barracks and placing the democratic opposition in charge of the country. With one bound Burma was free. As Timothy Garton Ash wrote in May 2000, however, "Burmese politics are anything but a simple fairy-tale confrontation between Suu and Slorc, beauty and the beast." Missing from such a picture are above all "fiendishly complex mixtures of ethnic discontent, insurgency, and drug trade" that have shaped national development for years and vastly complicate prospects for national renewal and reform.[3] Also overlooked are further challenges strung across the economic, social and political domains. One important task for any analysis is therefore to step beyond dualistic and reductionist accounts to deliver a more realistic assessment of the current state of affairs. Then the political situation becomes in Steinberg's term "minimally triangular" as important issues facing the country are imbued with great and daunting nuance.[4]

At the same time, however, the manifold dimensions of the Myanmar problem must not be allowed to overwhelm and undermine the other key analytical task of trying to chart a way forward for a country many insiders and outsiders agree has gone badly off track in recent decades. Furthermore, although any attempt to do that must be led above all by local people through broad-based analysis and debate, foreigners can also make a positive contribution to sustainable reform. Indeed, the demands of global justice indicate that outsiders must find ways to perform the duties they now bear. Although some duties are perfect and readily identified, the vast majority are imperfect and obscure. While focusing debate on fundamental global obligations, they therefore also direct analysis to the procedural requirements of interactive intervention.

Following on from analysis in earlier chapters, this conclusion wraps things up and turns more speculatively to the future. In his 1967 history, Maung Htin Aung appended a dialogue to convey modes of narration found in classical Burmese plays, staged at night and often unfinished by dawn. "Then the leader of the troupe of strolling players comes out and gives a synopsis of the final act; afterwards he answers questions put by the more interested members of the audience."[5] While the degree of political uncertainty pervading contemporary Myanmar rules out a final act, it remains possible to consider some of the pathways that might be taken by its people. In its initial two sections this concluding chapter looks inside the country, examining prospects on the one hand for unmaking Myanmar and on the other for remaking Burma. In its final two sections it looks outside, first investigating possibilities for external engagement with internal reform efforts and then considering how a future Burma might reposition itself in the wider world from which it has for so long been largely absent. The argument does not seek to minimize the challenges confronting local people. Equally, it attempts to move beyond fatalism by marking out practical steps for an agenda of political change.

Unmaking Myanmar

For reformers intent on unmaking Myanmar, the two key political tasks above the level of the individual are a major injection of democratic principle and practice, and a reevaluation of ethnic relations. While proposals for engineering such changes are promoted in varying degrees by key figures in the democratic and ethnic nationality camps, core aspirations are broadly shared. Shortly before the November 2010 general election, prominent individuals from both main strands of opposition called jointly for a second Panglong conference for national reconciliation. When Aung San Suu Kyi returned to public life after the election, veteran politicians and ethnic leaders invited her to lead an effort to convene the conference, and she agreed to do so.[6] At the same time, however, the dynamics are not entirely the same in the two domains, and rolling reformist demands into a single catch-all plan of moving beyond military control needs some unpacking if future challenges are to be fully understood. Put another way, unmaking authoritarian Myanmar is not the same as unmaking centralizing Myanmar, and while there are clear overlaps it is important also to focus on elements of difference.

On the side of democracy, a generalized belief is that a state not underpinned by a measure of popular consent and a functioning social contract will be vulnerable to contestation and challenge.[7] In this regard the military machine clearly has much still to do. Nevertheless, the history of Myanmar and many other countries reveals that governments with apparently only limited popular support can extend their dominion for quite long periods. In *The Logic of Political Survival*, Bruce Bueno de Mesquita and colleagues seek to explain why it is that autocratic leaders manage to stay in office for roughly twice as long as their democratic counterparts. While this question differs from one addressing the sustainability of distinct political systems, the answer remains relevant to the Myanmar case. Their analysis focuses on individual incentives in building a winning coalition of support from within a broader selectorate of potential members. The argument is that in autocracies winning coalitions are relatively small and exclusive, creating strong loyalty to political leaders. In democracies, by contrast, winning coalitions are relatively large, generating a real chance that members of the current coalition will also be included in rival coalitions capable of delivering equally good benefits. The result is that bonds between leaders and coalition members are weak.[8] In Myanmar, precisely these kinds of incentive structures have long been in place, building sufficient support within the *tatmadaw* and a small circle of key figures for ongoing military control, mandating that policy decisions be driven chiefly by concerns for coalition maintenance rather than broad public welfare, and making it very difficult to trigger democratic change. When infused with the informal institutional mechanisms identified by Kyaw Yin Hlaing as critical bonding agents, military government becomes formidable.[9]

In the wider society, moreover, several structural features underpin and reinforce authoritarian control. By and large, the substantial literature on the resource curse assembled since the late 1990s predicts civil conflict and system breakdown in resource-rich contexts. In many respects, Myanmar looks to be a strong fit.[10] However, analysts also document other possible outcomes, such as emergence of a predatory state capable of imposing a measure of public order through control of natural resource revenues.[11] This is what has happened in Myanmar, with income from substantial off-shore natural gas deposits giving state leaders extensive latitude in generating a fragile but workable rentier peace throughout most of the society.[12] Similarly, the consensus is that democracies are typically far less controlling and abusive than dictatorships, meaning that revolt is always possible in a repressive state.[13] Again, though, alternatives are conceivable. During the Stalinist Great Terror of 1936–37, Soviet leaders arrested more than 1.5 million citizens and killed some 700,000. Yet imposition of a tyrannical peace was feasible because the 1936 constitution created an elaborate cloak of legality designed to suggest that everything was taking place within the rules.[14] Here too may be found parallel Myanmar concerns, for with the 2008 constitution firmly in place military leaders can claim that the rule of law is being respected throughout the land.

Looking to the future, China's model of Communist Party legitimation through economic growth charts a further option for system maintenance.[15] In 2010, Teresa Wright reported on five main social groups of private entrepreneurs, professionals, state-sector workers, private-sector workers, and farmers, showing that in the reform era of rapid economic development each has a different but no less clear rationale for "accepting authoritarianism."[16] Similarly, drawing on a 2004 survey of perceptions of inequality and distributive injustice, Martin King Whyte in 2010 exploded the "myth of the social volcano," arguing that triumphant economic resurgence has created widespread support for the political system.[17] This successful construction of an authoritarian state on a foundation of booming economic growth implies that a reasonably robust social contract need not be articulated through democracy and human rights. While the jury is still out on how long Communist Party leaders will continue to deliver sufficient prosperity to manage the incipient stresses and strains of an unwieldy social system, there does appear to be in the Chinese model a medium-term option for Myanmar's political elite. Indeed, if the level of basic state efficiency found in the People's Republic can be replicated by the increasingly technocratic officials filling senior positions under disciplined democracy, a workable authoritarian settlement may prevail.

Dramatic popular uprisings in North Africa and the Middle East at the start of 2011 clearly show that the chance authoritarianism will one day collapse can never be eliminated. After 30 years of domestic stability and global support, President Hosni Mubarak of Egypt was hustled from office by 18 days of peaceful street protest. One day tactics of nonviolent revolution developed in Serbia under President Slobodan Milošević and applied in Cairo's Tahrir Square may also fuel change in Myanmar.[18] At the same time, however, the continuing existence of long-standing authoritarian regimes in other parts of the world, including much of Asia, opens up the possibility that Myanmar's military machine will succeed in sustaining a measure of political passivity and regime longevity beneath the veneer of disciplined democracy. This is especially likely for as long as the major opposition figurehead remains above all a moral leader rather than a political strategist. In the early 1990s, Gene Sharp worked with key individuals from Burma's 1988 uprising and ongoing ethnic struggle and wrote *From Dictatorship to Democracy*, a manual for strategic nonviolent protest, as a blueprint for liberation from military rule.[19] Interviewed in March 2011, when many of his ideas were widely credited with shaping the Egyptian revolution, he argued that the failure of revolt in Myanmar resulted from a strategic deficit. "If you don't plan, if you don't have a bigger strategy, you're not going to win."[20]

On the side of ethnic relations, prospects for meaningful progress are even cloudier. Although the democratic opposition gathered around Aung San Suu Kyi has long captured global attention, in many respects the key social reality underlying military control is not confrontation with democratic forces, but rather overt ethnic division.[21] It was above all elite fear of secession, not entirely unwarranted, that prompted the military coup half a century ago and subjected Burma to dictatorship. Despite all the popular energy and hope invested in mass democratic mobilization a quarter-century later, 1962 rather than 1988 remains the decisive year in modern political development. Moreover, whereas in their struggle with democratic groups military leaders have implemented a plan to make selective use of opposition rhetoric while allowing no more than minimal political change, in their long-running battles with ethnic nationalities they have only limited strategic direction. The ceasefires of the early 1990s had very narrow aims. More recently, the 2008 constitution registered more progress by creating territorial assemblies and incorporating some militias into the *tatmadaw* through BGF provisions. Nevertheless, while insurgency now appears to be on the decline, the imagination and vision needed to craft a sustainable ethnic settlement remain absent.

Examining structural features of the current situation, Myanmar has many standard triggers for endemic inter-communal violence, with the resource curse again dominant. Economists find a direct link: abundant natural resources heighten the chance of ethnic conflict by creating malign incentives for rentier activities. Political scientists posit an indirect mechanism that is no less compelling: extensive natural resources generate weak political institutions based on patronage systems that boost the likelihood of civil war.[22] However, not all natural resources have the same disfiguring social impact. In general, oil is most damaging and is associated with civil conflict in many lands.[23] Even then, though, location is important, with off-shore holdings typically generating less violence than on-shore. In Myanmar, revenues from large-scale marine natural gas deposits contribute critically to regime maintenance through predatory rentier social order imposed on the entire country.[24] They do not drive interethnic violence, however, since they are wholly inaccessible to insurgent groups. Nevertheless, other natural resources found to have negative impacts elsewhere are relevant to this case. One analyst reported that narcotics cultivation extends civil conflict.[25] In Myanmar this is very much an issue, as above all the UWSA ceasefire group in eastern Shan State secures core funding through opium and methamphetamine production.[26] By contrast, another found that drug production can reduce the degree of violence by giving both state and rebel leaders incentives to switch from fighting to business. That too is the case in Myanmar, where the emergence of state militarization and armed opposition as a way of life has nevertheless seen actual fighting tail off in the past 20 years and entrepreneurialism pick up.[27] Still another argued that contraband activities linked to natural resource holdings tend to prolong civil conflict, a finding again confirmed in Myanmar.[28]

Looking beyond natural resources, further structural features of the contemporary state are widely held to intensify interethnic strife. Taking societies as a whole, poverty, strong cultural identities and dysfunctional institutions correlate positively with conflict.[29] Sheer demographic and military strength of rebel forces is also important, as is distance from the capital city and roughness of the terrain in which fighting takes place, with mountainous regions being especially advantageous to insurgents.[30] All of these elements are present in Myanmar. Additionally, ethnic group concentration lengthens conflict not so much by enhancing motivation and making people more likely to fight, but rather by facilitating militia coordination.[31] Finally, rebel location along a remote international border extends conflict, and rebel camps on its external side have a reinforcing effect.[32] In Myanmar, the fact that all ethnic militias are based in peripheral parts, with some maintaining clandestine bases in neighboring states, clearly prolongs combat. The long KNU fight against *tatmadaw* control is a case in point, with refugee camps in Thailand providing an important base for insurgent activity and implicitly legitimizing the struggle.[33]

There are thus many reasons to doubt whether progress will be made in managing Myanmar's convoluted ethnic relations. On the positive side, there is in Chinese practice a series of pointers to special governance arrangements for specific regions or areas. Indeed, learning from its neighbor the SPDC created many industrial zones and, more significantly, in 2011 formed the Dawei Special Economic Zone on the Shenzhen model.[34] One day, this archetype could perhaps be replicated for different purposes in peripheral parts. Additionally, scholars have floated proposals for a Tibetan Special Cultural Zone in China that could provide a useful template for Myanmar.[35] Moreover, to handle the return of Hong Kong (1997) and Macau (1999) to the motherland, Beijing created Special Administrative Regions with extensive autonomy guarantees over a 50-year period. In this array of Chinese possibilities are options that could contribute to an agenda for national reconciliation in Myanmar.

At least three darker alternatives are, however, conceivable. One is a final showdown that sees government forces use the mandate written into the 2008 constitution to push for total victory over ethnic militias. As insurgency visibly weakens throughout peripheral zones, many rightly fear this is all too probable. A second is a partial peace seeking to do little more than codify contemporary interethnic relations.[36] As an extension of established ceasefire agreements, this is also feasible. A third, related to the second, is emergence of a set of unrecognized pseudo-states as war-making gives way to profit-making in border regions.[37] In 2001, Charles King examined what he called the wars of the Soviet succession and discovered that in their wake four *de facto* states had arisen: Nagorno-Karabakh (in Azerbaijan), the Dnestr Moldovan republic or Transnistria (in Moldova), and the republics of Abkhazia and South Ossetia (in Georgia).[38] In a context of stalled or frozen conflict, each was able to field armed forces, control territory, educate children and maintain an economy to much the same degree as the larger state to which it notionally belonged. The August 2008 armed conflict between Georgia and Russia later showed that such situations are not entirely stable. Nevertheless, in Myanmar the long-running civil war of the colonial succession has prompted similar patterns of informal state building, with some ethnic nationalities creating quasi-official structures such as schools and education departments.[39]

In much popular commentary, the tendency is to view Myanmar futures as essentially dichotomous: brutal dictatorship versus pacific democracy, chaotic civil war versus tidy federal state with extensive autonomy for ethnic nationalities, and so on. By and large, one side of these binary divides is quite plausible, for there is a strong likelihood that under the banner of disciplined democracy the country will remain authoritarian and centralizing.[40] By contrast, the other side has to be judged a distant prospect. Indeed, the chance that Myanmar will move all the way from its current authoritarian political system to the other extreme of stable, federal democracy is small. Even a major fragmentation of *tatmadaw* control would still leave many competing visions of national progress in the political arena, with military, democratic and ethnic nationality groups all seeking power. In common with other developing states in Southeast Asia and beyond, Myanmar is thus likely to find that armed forces remain a visible part of the political scene for years to come. Similarly, whether or not the *tatmadaw* overwhelms ethnic militias, the possibility that the country will find a stable solution to its ethnic nationality problems is slim. The balance of probability is thus that domestic politics will be messy for years to come, and that no comprehensive unmaking of Myanmar will take place.

Remaking Burma

The many challenging features of Myanmar's current situation generate a framework within which local people must act, but do not determine what they will do. Addressing that issue, a point often made by Aung San Suu Kyi is that ultimately the task is to stimulate broad national renewal at the level of each and every citizen. To remake Burma it is necessary to develop a new generation of Burmese. With very different objectives in mind, military strategists reached much the same conclusion in the course of the 1950s and have engaged in projects of national reshaping ever since. In both cases, the ultimate aim is to evade constraints imposed by the country's many structural problems and move directly to a fresh future. Among opposition leaders, both democratic and ethnic, this line of thinking returns analysis to broad-based national reconciliation designed to bridge cleavages not only between the country's many ethnic groups, but also between the regime and the democratic opposition and, more generally, between the state and its citizens.

In ethnically-divided societies where identities rather than interests are the main issue and symbolic politics predominate, attempts to project mediation programs across communal fault lines have generated a wealth of new approaches. However, while such procedures have attracted a great deal of attention, they are in no sense a panacea. In the celebrated South African case, the available evidence shows that truth and reconciliation did contribute to change by filling out the core democratization process.[41] In other contexts, however, the record is patchier. Indeed, in Rwanda after the 1994 genocide truth telling generated widespread trauma.[42] The point made by Laurel E. Fletcher and colleagues thus looks valid: there is no evidence that any society can make an easy start over, or that truth commissions provide a happy ending for tales of violent ethnic division. In such circumstances, they argue, an ecological approach is essential and humility and openness work best.[43] In other words, reconciliation must take place at all levels of the society from the grassroots up.

Fundamental to most studies is the finding that there will always be limits to what can be accomplished by mediation. Ultimately structural attributes of dysfunctional societies have to be addressed, and incentives pointing in the direction of authoritarian system maintenance have to be recast to underpin a democratic order. In many respects this is an extension of arguments about the logic of political survival in an autocratic setting, as well as about resource curse impacts. In the Myanmar case, the reshaping tasks are legion. Above all, behavior supportive of authoritarianism and Bamar nationalism needs to be made less profitable than behavior supportive of democracy and ethnic diversity. As is widely recognized, this will not be easy. Typically the legacy of dictatorship is negative for civil society, and has a dampening effect on political agency, though type and duration are relevant mediating factors.[44] Certainly the damaging effects of Myanmar's long, controlling dictatorship are likely to be felt for years throughout society.

Again, then, for a program of remaking Burma to gather momentum an urgent need to rebuild civil society and boost grassroots action in contemporary Myanmar emerges as paramount. Moreover, after many years of limited hope that change of this kind might ever be possible, the current situation does look more hopeful. Indeed, interviews conducted with local leaders in the late 2000s in the most vibrant zones of civic action quickly turned into a paean to civil society, and supporting evidence of change, though anecdotal, was impressive. The main conclusion of a post-Nargis report was emphatic: "A dynamic, varied, active, mobilised and intelligent civil society exists in Myanmar."[45] On all sides, it was fully acknowledged that the cyclone, while devastating in its impact, had also created an opening for rapid local development. "Prior to this we had no track record. Now we manage a budget of one million dollars … We originally had 100 volunteers and now we have over 2,000 … Before Nargis, our partner had three staff and we had five. After Nargis, our organisation has 46 staff."[46] The catastrophe also energized agency workers and drove them out into the community. "We are more active than before. Before, we only sat in the office in Yangon and conducted training. After Nargis, we know our way and are able to work and mobilise more in the field."[47] Myanmar NGO Network, formed at the end of 2007, only became fully established once Nargis had struck, bringing together 20 local agencies to work in a coordinated manner. "Many more NGOs emerged after Cyclone Nargis. We are all better networked and more visible. We have over 100 civil society groups in Myanmar from different places all over the country but mainly from Yangon."[48]

The Burma subjected to authoritarian control in 1962 and subsequently written off the map by military decree in 1989 was rapidly reduced to a feeble replica of its former self. In the process, it experienced a drastic reduction in its capacity for self-renewal that today remains a major impediment to social change. The Burma to which many citizens look back, however, was characterized by meaningful political space and extensive community action. Particularly for some 50 years down to 1962, the society was plural not only in the negative sense coined by Furnivall, in which distinct races rub shoulders but do not mix, but also in the positive sense intended by political scientists from Dahl forward, in which diverse groups compete for power and none holds a dominant position.[49] If this is the Burma many local people wish to remake, then building on recent growth in a still nascent civil society looks to be essential.

The world in Myanmar

For the best part of 25 years, the world has not worked out a satisfactory means of dealing with the Myanmar problem, and both insiders and outsiders contest current strategies. At the same time, however, the country is only rarely a pressing strategic concern for any external power, and the chance that productive foreign engagement will be implemented in the years ahead is perhaps slight. Inattention is still a key problem. In these circumstances, it is therefore important to determine where the most substantial duties of global justice lie, and how this bedrock of external obligation might generate a platform of support for domestic reform efforts.

Perfect duties are almost certainly limited. Similarly, imperfect duties incurred at the international level are perhaps not the most pressing concern. Clearly, any move to implement proposals for a worldwide resource tax and rules limiting global borrowing and resource privileges to democrats, or at least to decent non-democratic states, would have an impact on Myanmar. Indeed, one task activist groups might take up is lobbying for global reform of this kind, for it would materially reshape the country's domestic political environment by removing or recasting key foundations of ongoing military power. Nevertheless, most attention remains focused on Myanmar itself. There, imperfect duties are significant. Whether amassed through injustice visited on local people in the past, or entailed by universal membership of the human race, it is in this domain that the burden of obligation weighs most heavily on outsiders.

Taking Harold D. Lasswell's classic understanding of politics, the argument made here about external engagement with domestic reform efforts addresses each of the four key elements: who, what, when and how.[50] Who? An analysis of global justice and the Myanmar case picks out several responsible outside agents. Under the heading of historical injustice are two cohorts of foreign powers: damaging imperialists from decades ago, and both isolating and engaging states in the present day. Under the heading of universal justice, the UN represents the wider global community as the critical actor. What? The case made here is for discursive intervention designed to enable aid agencies and global corporations to work with and for local people to reanimate Burma through intercession and investment. At a later stage in the process states also need to engage in elite-level mediation to solidify and institutionalize grassroots progress. When? For different reasons, both isolationists and engagers hold that now is not the time to make radical changes to their Myanmar policies. Isolationists wish to see more reform before rewarding the generals. Engagers believe Myanmar is beginning to make some progress toward political renewal. Against each broad camp, the argument advanced here is that strategies of discursive intervention should be launched as quickly as possible. How? The simple answer given to this question is by making rights-bearing local people the policy drivers and seeking to empower them as much as possible. Oppressed citizens in civil society hold far greater rights than oppressive rulers in the military machine.

The important remaining task is to consider the broad thrust of this analysis through the strategic prism of contemporary international politics. An initial point is that when viewed from the perspective of one medium-sized Asian country in a complex global system, much current debate has distant themes. In particular, the question of whether the US will remain the international hegemon well into the twenty-first century, in other respects intriguing, is largely irrelevant to this case.[51] In dealing with Myanmar, the US is not now, never has been and in all likelihood never will be the dominant external actor.[52] Only at the extreme, then, in the remote possibility that it will be usurped at the peak of international society by a very different kind of Chinese power, is analysis of the unipolar moment germane.[53] On the realistic assumption that such a dramatic change will not take place in the foreseeable future, the US will find itself largely where it always has been with regard to Myanmar. Though not uniformly evident in policy debate and choices, Washington has little option but to work with regional powers and at least for this case to come to terms with a China model in the making.[54] In this regard the age of nonpolarity dawned decades ago, and a Global-Asian Era is already apparent.[55]

For some proponents of a Burma redux agenda this is in many ways unpalatable, as in concert with regional and global allies the US has long been a leading advocate of political reform up to and including regime change. From the analytical perspective developed here, however, it is entirely appropriate that the US be required to work with and through regional powers. Indeed, after decades of sometimes highly assertive US action in distant parts of the world culminating in military interventions ordered by President Bush, it is widely recognized that a change of approach could be productive for American interests.[56] In themes sketched by President Obama and in initiatives taken by his administration can thus be found extensive strategic reorientation as Washington seeks to address global challenges through alliance and rapprochement.[57] Moreover, in making a course correction it has always been clear that the US need not abandon its most cherished ideals. In many cases, a change of tone is more necessary than a change of objective, with a focus on patient implementation of workable policies an essential ingredient.[58] Although it made no more than limited steps in this direction, the 2009 Myanmar policy review was one example of this shift.

Examination of the role the wider world might play in promoting meaningful political reform in Myanmar must therefore be undertaken above all inside the region. There the possibility of growing US disengagement following years of mixed experience raises concern.[59] Equally, rivalry among China, India and Japan is a worry, for an ideal and perhaps even necessary basis for progress is broad regional consensus.[60] At the same time, however, issues of this kind need not be disabling in this case, for core elements of a shared approach are discernible above all in fears about the negative impact ongoing authoritarianism in Myanmar might have on the wider world.[61] Indeed, the cynical view that regional states' designs on Myanmar are uniquely predatory conflicts with evidence that what they seek above all is peace, stability and strategic alliance.[62] Just as China and India worry about turmoil along lengthy borders should the domestic situation spiral out of control, so the US and its major allies are readily persuaded that state weakness and failure pose some of the greatest challenges to contemporary global order.[63] More than anything, the potentially catastrophic consequences of military government and ethnic division in Myanmar generate a foundation for collaboration among all major stakeholders in Asia and outside.[64]

In this way, however, only a limited common position emerges. While it may be enough to moderate some of the worst excesses of military rule, it cannot be expected to sustain anything approaching a full agenda for political change. For that, some degree of agreement that real power needs to be returned to the people is required. In a situation where authoritarian China is the pivotal external actor, this may seem unattainable. Even here, however, progress could be possible, for a strategy of incremental, grassroots engagement is likely to generate few concerns about pushing Myanmar too hard and risking instability. Beyond that, the governance changes sought by major powers are often quite similar, with even Beijing prepared in UN Security Council statements to condone language pointing to a key role for local people.[65] Additionally, there are broad hints that China may slowly be developing a new "dictatorship diplomacy" aimed at distancing itself from some of the world's worst pariahs and partnering with western states to deal with others.[66]

Instructive in this regard is the case of Darfur in western Sudan, acknowledged as one of the major humanitarian crises of the 2000s. Strategically, Darfur has important parallels with contemporary Myanmar. China is a key external actor through significant oil interests and a broad desire to reassert great power status. Western states, while deeply concerned about humanitarian issues, are often preoccupied with other matters and essentially inertial. As the crisis intensified in the course of the decade, Beijing was therefore able to step into the void left by western nations and become a humanitarian rule-maker. The maxims it put in place indicate that arguments about socialization into established international society need to be handled with care.[67] On one side, it was motivated by humanitarian concern. On the other, the norm to which it appealed was that of a state-based international system. It thereby developed a novel set of rules for humanitarian intervention, articulated through a triple consent mechanism embracing the host country, the relevant regional association and the UN.[68] Similarly, in March 2011 an Arab League request for the UN Security Council to impose a no-fly zone over Libya was critical in removing a potential Chinese veto.[69]

When the issue is not a distant African state in which China has a reasonably large stake, but rather a neighboring Asian state in which it has absolutely core interests, then Beijing's political primacy is assured. The lesson to be drawn from Darfur and Libya is that it will look for explicit backing and preferably energetic leadership from ASEAN as the relevant regional body. It will also seek some indication that the Myanmar government is comfortable with any proposed engagement. In the unlikely event that assertive action is on the agenda, it will want full UN endorsement. Given the geopolitics of the situation, these can be taken as the major parameters within which future foreign involvement must unfold. ASEAN, furnished since December 2008 with a Charter promoting aspirations for economic integration and good governance, will therefore have to make some hard choices with regard to Myanmar and craft a policy capable of securing support primarily from China.[70] India, though facing trenchant criticism of its Myanmar policy and attempting to redefine an increasingly anachronistic strategic posture, will have little choice but to fall in line.[71] Japan could be better placed.[72] As a benign regional power with excellent historical ties to Myanmar, Tokyo could position itself as a critical mediating force capable of shuttling between all relevant parties. In particular, it could draw in the US and may even be able to revive its Pacific alliance.[73] Moreover, since state action is likely to work best if designed to support grassroots progress facilitated by aid agencies and global corporations, it could readily embrace the full range of discursive engagement.

In this way, the new dynamics of multilateralism could be fully exploited to access the networks of non-state actors increasingly captured in foreign policy calculations.[74] In the US the importance of such individuals has been openly acknowledged through Secretary Clinton's support for "leading through civilian power."[75] This notion of citizen diplomacy reaches back to analysis promoting connectivity within networks as the key to power in the twenty-first century.[76] In Asia, these dynamics resonate strongly with regional preferences for economic development as a first step and political change in its wake, for the objective is to build not only civic but also economic capacity.[77] Looking to other positives, there is ample reason to hold that among Asian publics a regional approach seeking to facilitate political change from the ground up inside Myanmar would secure generalized assent. The available data show that Asian opinion broadly endorses liberal values, but is resistant to quasi-imperial modes of disseminating them.[78]

Attention thereby returns to local people in local communities, and the need to focus above all on their demands and agency. In this regard, western leaders currently make the right noises, but have not yet fully retuned their Myanmar policies. In Cairo in June 2009, Obama said that "No system of government can or should be imposed by one nation on any other."[79] In the Nobel Lecture delivered in Oslo in December 2009, he made the case for moving beyond sanctions on rogue states: "I know that engagement with repressive regimes lacks the satisfying purity of indignation. But I also know that sanctions without outreach — condemnation without discussion — can carry forward only a crippling status quo."[80] To date, however, his administration's Myanmar policy has taken no more than limited steps in this direction. Similarly, having visited Egypt and Tunisia in the wake of mass uprisings, EU High Representative for Foreign Affairs and Security Policy Catherine Ashton argued in February 2011 that "listening to the revolution" was critical: "We are listening now not to avoid action, but to make sure the action we take over the coming months and years is effective." Such action, she noted, would be "detailed, unglamorous, work on the ground … laying the foundations of deep democracy and then building it up, brick-by-brick."[81] Again, however, the annual policy review undertaken in April 2011 provided only limited evidence that this approach is informing the EU's Myanmar stance. Equally, the UN has not satisfactorily addressed the multiple challenges facing Myanmar. As Thant Myint-U put it in July 2009, "The UN always says security, development and human rights are interlinked. I think this is right. But where is this more complex approach when it comes to Burma?"[82]

Clearly the eventual political impact of a bottom-up approach seeking to boost grassroots agency above all through a wealth of non-state transnational engagement cannot be determined with any precision. Experience shows that "activists beyond borders" can sometimes provoke political reform in target jurisdictions.[83] Indeed, one study of the Universal Declaration of Human Rights found evidence of change in countries and regions as diverse as Kenya, Uganda, South Africa, Tunisia, Morocco, Indonesia, the Philippines, Chile, Guatemala and Eastern Europe.[84] Against this, however, another report looking directly at third-party mediation in conflict situations held that while diplomacy was generally positive in its effects, and informal workshops were also helpful if used to complement state action, non-state action on its own did not have a good record.[85] Again, though, a further study reported that non-state engagement was useful in and of itself in the South African case, and still another noted that such engagement can make an indirect contribution by triggering formal diplomatic activity.[86] On balance, then, there appears to be empirical support for the strategy sketched here. More widely, several other consequences of foreign engagement are now well established. One is that INGO human rights action inside a conflict-ridden society can assist in turning it away from violence and toward peaceful civic engagement.[87] A second is that foreign aid can be destabilizing for dictatorship.[88] A third is that subsequent peacekeeping efforts can boost human rights.[89] All of these impacts can be sought as external actors look to support reform efforts in contemporary Myanmar.

At the same time, dismal scenarios cannot be ignored. In an analysis written soon after participating in a December 2010 live video-link discussion with Aung San Suu Kyi, Garton Ash commented that "A sober analysis ... shows a constellation of forces in and around Burma less favourable than those in South Africa, or Poland, or the Philippines, or Chile, or the many other stories of eventually triumphant self-liberation over the last three decades."[90] Regional states, he noted, prioritize commercial and strategic interest above human rights. Exile activist Zarni, who also took part in the forum, advances a similar argument, holding that neighboring states have few problems with Myanmar's current political system and the unregulated access it gives them to plentiful natural resources and cheap labor.[91] Thus, what is broadly a positive record of external democracy promotion in the post-Cold War period faces real challenges in Myanmar.[92]

If the darkest assumptions about stances and motivations of regional states are correct, possibilities for outsiders to assist Myanmar's reformist cause are certainly reduced. A core principle of interactive intervention is that neighboring states occupy a special position. While not holding veto power over more distant actors, they are privileged because of physical proximity and close understanding of the target society. If it really is true that Asian states are strictly predatory in their approaches to Myanmar, then it will be difficult for more distant states to launch engagement strategies. However, there is little reason to endorse such negative assessments. Statements made by leading politicians from ASEAN, China, India and Japan, and action taken by them to coax Myanmar's military rulers out of their bunker mentality and into regional society, suggest that Asian states are positioning themselves in more complex ways than the notion of pure predation would imply.[93] The ideas and norms currently being diffused among them are not cynical.[94] Moreover, even if the bleakest assumptions were valid, it would still be possible for non-state actors to facilitate reform, thereby changing some grassroots political realities.

In these circumstances, options for building a coordinated international approach to an issue of shared concern become very feasible. To move forward, western powers would need to embrace generalized Asian preferences for low-profile engagement. In so doing, however, they would be building on studies of past intervention showing that nation-building works best if not too ambitious and pursued in a generally supportive context.[95] Equally, they would have ample opportunity to insist that any actual cross-border action took place on a clear ethical foundation. In this way, they would be able to promote considerable enhancement of aid agency action, and give a real boost to corporate social responsibility across Asia. They could also use the opportunity to reflect on the kinds of external engagement they themselves wish to promote. For many observers of Myanmar's still highly distinctive local cultures, this would preferably not be insensitive inward investment and a rapid switch to mass tourism, but rather forms attuned to local conditions. While the logic of economic globalization suggests this will probably not be possible, a coordinated regional approach could at least promote efforts likely to be welcome to many local people. A strategy of consensual engagement implemented through intercession and investment undertaken first and foremost at the local level thus looks like a viable way forward.

Burma in the world

The central aim of the argument made here is to find a way for outsiders to join with local people to open up opportunities for both individual and group action inside Myanmar. In this way, foreigners can deliver on some of the demands of justice in this case, and citizens can create space to determine their collective future rather than have it imposed on them by a small and isolated elite. For external actors, the task is thus strictly facilitative, focused on creating a political context in which internal political preferences can play out. Joining hands with individuals in communities throughout the land, their work is to help recast the framework in which political issues are addressed, deliberated and decided in Myanmar.

For local people, by contrast, no clear task can be specified by an external analyst. The belief underlying this study, picked up from listening projects and other in-country reports, is that citizens seek overwhelmingly to move Myanmar broadly in the direction of democracy, and that implicit in that shift will be attempts to entrench inter-communal diversity and cross-cultural respect. However, while there is anecdotal support for such a belief, things may play out very differently if ever a program of interactive intervention were launched inside the country. Indeed, if the economy were to boom under disciplined democracy and a measure of civic renewal, local people may choose to follow their Chinese neighbors in accepting authoritarianism, at least for a while.[96] Alternatively, they might actually decide to pursue a process of large-scale political reform designed to recapture much that is bound up in contemporary understandings of Burma. While outsiders can harbor preferences, they cannot make choices.

Although much external interest and engagement is driven by a desire for the world to be more present and active inside Myanmar, there is also a parallel motivation for Myanmar to be more present and active in the world. When full military control was imposed on Burma half a century ago, one clear consequence was international isolation. Until the end of the Ne Win period, Burma was one of the closest approximations to a hermit state known to the Cold War world. Thereafter, the military junta promoted a degree of opening through erratic economic liberalization, periodic measures designed to boost the tourist trade and a range of foreign policy initiatives centered on close contact with Beijing and ASEAN membership.[97] In return, most of the US alliance responded to grave human rights violations by cordoning off a pariah state. The result was not an extension of Burma's effective quarantine into the Myanmar years. Rather, it was skewed reengagement with the outside world as trade and other links with many parts of Asia became quite developed while ties with the western world remained strictly limited. Integral to that reemergence was a pattern of mutual distrust and fear among Myanmar leaders and their western counterparts. Indeed, the gulf that separated them in 1988 remains wide to this day.

For that there is good reason, as world views on the two sides are vastly different and disdain and contempt are often primary emotions projected across the divide. From each perspective this is understandable. Nevertheless, outsiders clustered around the US gain little by blockading Myanmar and sentencing it to a lengthy period of seclusion, for in place of a broad array of external influences playing out inside the country there is only a narrow spectrum of shared links and experience. Even communitarians can agree that for any modern state that would be regrettable. For one facing as many deep challenges as Myanmar, it is especially so. This is not to imply that the aim is to make the country a quasi-colony or clone of western powers, but rather that the desire is to see it return with confidence to the give and take that comes with active participation on the world stage.

Looking again to Burmese history, in the late 1940s and for much of the 1950s a newly independent state moved quickly beyond colonialism to become an early force in Asian regional development and, ultimately, creation of the Non-Aligned Movement. In the aftermath of the Chinese Revolution, Burma was a key player in facilitating regional responses, and a regular presence at regional conferences. In April 1954, it was a founding member of the non-interventionist grouping of Colombo powers formed by India, Pakistan, Burma, Indonesia and Ceylon at a time of growing crisis in Indochina.[98] In June 1954, when Chinese Premier Zhou Enlai introduced the landmark Five Principles of Peaceful Coexistence, he did so in collaboration with Indian Prime Minister Jawaharlal Nehru and Burmese Premier Nu.[99] At the subsequent April 1955 Asian-African Conference in Bandung, Indonesia, where in Richard Wright's contemporary report "The despised, the insulted, the hurt, the dispossessed — in short, the underdogs of the human race were meeting," Burma was a key organizer alongside the other Colombo powers.[100] Ahead of the conference, Nehru hosted Vietnamese Foreign Minister Pham Van Dong in New Delhi, and the two then traveled to Rangoon, where Nu joined them for the onward journey to Indonesia.[101] In Bandung, Nu was a leading figure keeping easy and respected company with Zhou, Nehru and counterparts from other countries.[102]

As prime minister for most of the 1950s, Nu also made other overseas trips, and for years was an active regional and international statesman.[103] Throughout, Burma was viewed as the strategic state it clearly is, lodged between India and China, located in Southeast Asia but with historical ties and contemporary links to South Asia, keen to develop alternatives to great power rivalry. As Nu remarked in the Cold War context of September 1950, "If we … thrust the Union of Burma into the arms of one bloc, the other bloc will not be content to look on with folded arms."[104] Today, however, the situation is very different. Myanmar was admitted to ASEAN in 1997 as a problematic state, and has remained an embarrassment to the organization ever since. The Asian diplomacy undertaken by Burmese leaders in the 1950s is inconceivable in current circumstances, and unlikely to reappear in the foreseeable future. One great sadness of the country's postwar experience is how thoroughly the self-assured nationalism of much of the Burmese elite of the 1950s was destroyed in the 1960s, and replaced by the uniformly mistrustful xenophobia that persists to this day.

Grounds for hope nevertheless remain. Recent years have witnessed quite substantial change in Myanmar's contacts with the outside world as technologically adept activists and young people living in cities and even small towns find ways to log on to the internet, evade regime censorship and become virtual global citizens. Most fully visible in high-profile confrontations such as the 2007 saffron uprising focused above all on Yangon, this emergent social revolution now spreads to urban centers throughout the country and embraces significant numbers of people. Conscious of opportunities available to peers around the world, including in hitherto rigid neighboring states such as communist China and caste-ridden India, connected young people in Myanmar could become a key constituency for change designed to return the country to mainstream international society. Enhanced foreign contact through grassroots aid agency and corporate engagement would considerably augment the process. As Aung San Suu Kyi said in a taped audio address to the January 2011 World Economic Forum in Davos, "We yearn to be a part of the global community … We have already missed so many opportunities because of political conflicts in our country over the last 50 years."[105]

Indeed, one eventual measure of the success or otherwise of interactive intervention in Myanmar may well be registered in the impact made on the wider world by the future Burma so many people inside and outside the country wish to see. While the current fascination with rising China and India may not be fully replicated, for both are many times bigger, broad interest in the degree to which this long hidden Asian culture offers lessons for the rest of humanity is very possible. At present, however, dynamic regional forces are all too often absent from Myanmar, and intriguing forms of Asian modernity have little or no parallel in a society only dimly and distantly aware of the challenges and opportunities of the twenty-first century. While China remains far from democratic and India may not strike everyone as a perfect exemplar for a future Burma, they nevertheless offer life chances to their people extending well beyond anything known in Myanmar.[106]

If interactive intervention could stimulate change in this regard and permit a reenergized and reconfigured Burma to move from the narrow margins into the broad mainstream of international society, it would already make an important contribution. If it could also enable local people to chart a course toward the national reconciliation and sustainable democracy urgently sought by opposition figures, it would deliver on many of the demands of global justice generated by the quest for political reform in the difficult Myanmar case.

Notes

Introduction

1. The last full census, conducted in March 1983, gave a population of 35.4 million. However, when a constitutional referendum was held in 2008 the total population was recorded as 57.5 million. Human Rights Watch, *"I Want to Help My Own People": State Control and Civil Society in Burma after Cyclone Nargis* (New York, NY: Human Rights Watch, 2010), p.63. Also see Anthony Ware and Matthew Clarke, "The MDGs in Myanmar: Relevant or Redundant?," *Journal of the Asia Pacific Economy* 16 (2011), forthcoming.
2. Oded Shenkar, *The Chinese Century: The Rising Chinese Economy and Its Impact on the Global Economy, the Balance of Power, and Your Job* (Upper Saddle River, NJ: Wharton School Publishing, 2005). Bill Hayton, *Vietnam: Rising Dragon* (New Haven, CT: Yale University Press, 2010).
3. The Human Security Report Project at Simon Fraser University measures conflict years within states by isolating specific civil conflicts and calculating their total duration. It places Myanmar at the top of global rankings with 246 conflict years from 1946 to 2008, meaning that on average each year has been marked by four civil conflicts. Human Security Report Project, *Human Security Report 2009/2010: The Causes of Peace and the Shrinking Costs of War* (Vancouver: Simon Fraser University, 2010), Table 10.2.
4. Accurate data on ethnic composition are not available. In 2011, a US estimate gave this breakdown: Bamar 68 percent, Shan 9 percent, Kayin 7 percent, Rakhine 4 percent, Chinese 3 percent, Indian 2 percent, Mon 2 percent. US Central Intelligence Agency, *The World Factbook*. www.cia.gov/library/publications/the-world-factbook. The University of Maryland tracks six endangered ethnic groups inside Myanmar: Chin, Kachin, Karen, Mon, Rohingya and Shan. Minorities at Risk, www.cidcm.umd.edu/mar.

5. The junta assumed two distinct identities in the period from September 1988 to March 2011. However, since there was considerable continuity of membership and policy, this analysis refers throughout to a singular junta.
6. *Irrawaddy*, "SPDC, R.I.P.," March 30, 2011.
7. Transnational Institute and Burma Centrum Nederland, *Ethnic Politics in Burma: The Time for Solutions* (Amsterdam: Transnational Institute and Burma Centrum Nederland, 2011).
8. Thant Myint-U, *The River of Lost Footsteps: A Personal History of Burma* (New York, NY: Farrar, Straus and Giroux, 2006), p.ix.
9. Aung San Suu Kyi, *Freedom from Fear: And Other Writings*, rev. ed. (London: Penguin, 1995), pp.192–8. In an April 2011 interview, she put it this way: "More people, especially young people, are realising that if they want change, they've got to go about it themselves — they can't depend on a particular person, ie me, to do all the work." Polly Toynbee, "Saturday interview: Aung San Suu Kyi," *Guardian*, April 16, 2011.
10. Centre for Peace and Conflict Studies, *Listening to Voices from Inside: Myanmar Civil Society's Response to Cyclone Nargis* (Phnom Penh: Centre for Peace and Conflict Studies, 2009), p.124.
11. Centre for Peace and Conflict Studies, *Listening to Voices from Inside: Ethnic People Speak* (Phnom Penh: Centre for Peace and Conflict Studies, 2010), p.202.
12. Lowell Dittmer, "Burma vs. Myanmar: What's in a Name?," *Asian Survey* 48:6 (2008), 885–8.
13. *Working People's Daily*, "Placenames law enacted," June 19, 1989.
14. *Working People's Daily*, "Change in national anthem," June 19, 1989.
15. Rudyard Kipling, "Mandalay," in Rudyard Kipling, *Barrack-room Ballads* (New York, NY: Signet, 2001), 40–2.
16. George Orwell, *Shooting an Elephant: And Other Essays* (London: Secker and Warburg, 1953).
17. *South China Morning Post*, "Burma states terms for student talks," June 20, 1989, p.12.
18. See, for instance, Mya Maung, "The Burma Road from the Union of Burma to Myanmar," *Asian Survey* 30:6 (1990), 602–24, n.1.
19. Cited in Derek Tonkin, "The 1990 Elections in Myanmar: Broken Promises or a Failure of Communication?," *Contemporary Southeast Asia* 29:1 (2007), 33–54, p.38.
20. Amnesty International, *Myanmar (Burma): New Martial Law Provisions Allowing Summary or Arbitrary Executions and Recent Death Sentences Imposed under These Provisions*, ASA 16/15/89 (London: Amnesty International, 1989), p.4.
21. James F. Guyot and John Badgley, "Myanmar in 1989: Tatmadaw V," *Asian Survey* 30:2 (1990), 187–95, p.188.
22. James F. Guyot, "Myanmar in 1990: The Unconsummated Election," *Asian Survey* 31:2 (1991), 205–11.
23. Tonkin, "The 1990 Elections in Myanmar."
24. *Working People's Daily*, "State LORC Declaration No. 1/90 of July 27, 1990," July 29, 1990.

25. Everyday usage is now quite variable, with old and new names often employed interchangeably. Nevertheless, official positions taken by leadership groups tend to stick to the old terminology.
26. The State Department puts it this way: "The SPDC changed the name of the country to 'Myanmar,' but some members of the democratic opposition and other political activists do not recognize the name change and continue to use the name 'Burma.' Out of support for the democratic opposition, the U.S. Government likewise uses 'Burma'." US Department of State, *Background Note: Burma*. www.state.gov/r/pa/ei/bgn/35910.htm.
27. Matthew J. Walton, "Ethnicity, Conflict, and History in Burma: The Myths of Panglong," *Asian Survey* 48:6 (2008), 889–910.
28. James C. Scott, *The Art of Not Being Governed: An Anarchist History of Upland Southeast Asia* (New Haven, CT: Yale University Press, 2009).
29. Dittmer, "Burma vs. Myanmar."
30. In 2010, Amartya Sen, who lived for three years as a boy in prewar Mandalay, wrote this: "The military rulers have renamed Burma as Myanmar, and the renaming seems perhaps understandable, for the country is no longer the Burma that magnificently flourished over the centuries. New Myanmar is the hell-hole version of old Burma." Amartya Sen, "We hear you, Michael Aris, loud and clear," *OutlookIndia*, November 15, 2010. www.outlookindia.com/article.aspx?267765.
31. J. S. Furnivall, *Colonial Policy and Practice: A Comparative Study of Burma and Netherlands India* (New York, NY: New York University Press, 1956), p.11, n.1. British historian Hugh Tinker held to this usage in all four editions of *The Union of Burma*, published in 1957, 1959, 1961 and 1967, explaining that he was following the practice adopted in the 1953 census. Hugh Tinker, *The Union of Burma: A Study of the First Years of Independence*, 4th ed. (London: Oxford University Press, 1967), p.xi.
32. Michael W. Charney, *A History of Modern Burma* (Cambridge: Cambridge University Press, 2009), p.201.
33. Bertil Lintner, *Outrage: Burma's Struggle for Democracy* (Hong Kong: Review Publishing Company, 1989).
34. Martin J. Smith, *Burma: Insurgency and the Politics of Ethnicity*, 2nd ed. (London: Zed Books, 1999).
35. Tom Kramer, *Neither War nor Peace: The Future of the Cease-fire Agreements in Burma* (Amsterdam: Transnational Institute, 2009).
36. Thomas Hobbes, *Leviathan: Or the Matter, Forme and Power of a Commonwealth Ecclesiasticall and Civil* (Oxford: Blackwell, 1955), p.82.
37. Mary P. Callahan, *Political Authority in Burma's Ethnic Minority States: Devolution, Occupation, and Coexistence* (Washington, DC: East-West Center Washington, 2007).
38. Michael Aung-Thwin, "Parochial Universalism, Democracy *Jihad* and the Orientalist Image of Burma: The New Evangelism," *Pacific Affairs* 74:4 (2001–02), 483–505, p.492.

39. Centre for Peace and Conflict Studies, *Myanmar Civil Society's Response to Cyclone Nargis*.
40. Zaw Oo and Win Min, *Assessing Burma's Ceasefire Accords* (Washington, DC: East-West Center Washington, 2007).
41. Amnesty International, *The Repression of Ethnic Minority Activists in Myanmar*, ASA 16/001/2010 (London: Amnesty International, 2010).
42. Donald M. Seekins, *State and Society in Modern Rangoon* (Abingdon: Routledge, 2011).
43. Andrew Selth, "Modern Burma Studies: A Survey of the Field," *Modern Asian Studies* 44:2 (2010), 401–40.
44. For a full survey and a different way of dividing the field, see Robert H. Taylor, "Finding the Political in Myanmar, a.k.a. Burma," *Journal of Southeast Asian Studies* 39:2 (2008), 219–37.
45. Scott distinguishes two kinds of *nats*. The first are "inhabitants of the six inferior heavens" of the Burmese spirit world. "Perfectly distinct from these are the nats of the house, the air, the water, the forest, — the spirits of nature, fairies, elves, gnomes, kelpies, kobolds, pixies, whatever other names they have received in other countries." Shway Yoe, *The Burman: His Life and Notions*, 3rd ed. (London: Macmillan, 1910), p.232. On Scott, see Andrew Marshall, *The Trouser People: A Story of Burma in the Shadow of the Empire* (New York, NY: Counterpoint, 2002). On the 37 *nats* in the contemporary pantheon, see Bénédicte Brac de la Perrière, "The Taungbyon Festival: Locality and Nation-confronting in the Cult of the 37 Lords," in Monique Skidmore (ed.), *Burma at the Turn of the Twenty-first Century* (Honolulu, HI: University of Hawai'i Press, 2005), 65–89.
46. H. Fielding-Hall, *The Soul of a People* (London: Richard Bentley and Son, 1898). H. Fielding-Hall, *A People at School* (London: Macmillan, 1906). Fielding-Hall also wrote books about domestic life and religion described by Maung Maung as "tender and loving and a little romantic." Maung Maung, *Burma's Constutition*, 2nd ed. (The Hague: Martinus Nijhoff, 1961), p.5.
47. Lucian W. Pye, *Politics, Personality, and Nation Building: Burma's Search for Identity* (New Haven, CT: Yale University Press, 1962).
48. E. R. Leach, *Political Systems of Highland Burma: A Study of Kachin Social Structure* (London: G. Bell, 1954). F. K. Lehman, *The Structure of Chin Society: A Tribal People of Burma Adapted to a Non-Western Civilization* (Urbana, IL: University of Illinois Press, 1963). Manning Nash, *The Golden Road to Modernity: Village Life in Contemporary Burma* (New York, NY: John Wiley & Sons, 1965). For a full survey, see U Chit Hlaing, "Anthropological Communities of Interpretation for Burma: An Overview," *Journal of Southeast Asian Studies* 39:2 (2008), 239–54.
49. Ardeth Maung Thawnghmung, *Behind the Teak Curtain: Authoritarianism, Agricultural Policies and Political Legitimacy in Rural Burma/Myanmar* (London: Kegan Paul, 2004), p.9. Selth, "Modern Burma Studies," pp.410–11.
50. The second edition of Fink's book was published as *Living Silence in Burma*. Christina Fink, *Living Silence in Burma: Surviving under Military Rule*, 2nd ed. (London/Chiang Mai: Zed Books/Silkworm Books, 2009). Monique Skidmore, *Karaoke Fascism:*

Burma and the Politics of Fear (Philadelphia, PA: University of Pennsylvania Press, 2004).

51. Arthur P. Phayre, *History of Burma: Including Burma Proper, Pegu, Taungu, Tenasserim, and Arakan, from the Earliest Time to the End of the First War with British India* (London: Trübner & Co., 1883). G. E. Harvey, *History of Burma: From the Earliest Times to 10 March 1824, the Beginning of the English Conquest* (London: Longmans, Green, 1925).
52. J. S. Furnivall, *An Introduction to the Political Economy of Burma* (Rangoon: Burma Book Club, 1931). Furnivall, *Colonial Policy and Practice*. J. S. Furnivall, *The Governance of Modern Burma* (New York, NY: Institute of Pacific Relations, 1958).
53. F. S. V. Donnison, *Public Administration in Burma: A Study of Development during the British Connexion* (London: Royal Institute of International Affairs, 1953). F. S. V. Donnison, *Burma* (London: Benn, 1970).
54. D. G. E. Hall, *Burma* (London: Hutchinson, 1950). Hugh Tinker, *The Union of Burma: A Study of the First Years of Independence* (London: Oxford University Press, 1957). John F. Cady, *A History of Modern Burma* (Ithaca, NY: Cornell University Press, 1958). Dorothy Woodman, *The Making of Burma* (London: Cresset Press, 1962). Frank N. Trager, *Burma, from Kingdom to Republic: A Historical and Political Analysis* (Westport, CT: Greenwood Press, 1966). Maung Htin Aung, *A History of Burma* (New York, NY: Columbia University Press, 1967).
55. Tinker, *The Union of Burma*, p.1.
56. Thant Myint-U, *The Making of Modern Burma* (Cambridge: Cambridge University Press, 2001), p.10.
57. Thant Myint-U, *The River of Lost Footsteps*, pp.5, 162.
58. Charney, *A History of Modern Burma*.
59. Cady, *A History of Modern Burma*, p.4. Also see Tinker's review, which dwells on this point. Hugh Tinker, review of John F. Cady, *A History of Modern Burma* (Ithaca, NY: Cornell University Press, 1958), *Pacific Affairs* 32 (1959), 213–15.
60. Robert H. Taylor, *The State in Myanmar* (Honolulu, HI: University of Hawai'i Press, 2009), p.5.
61. Michael Aung-Thwin, *Pagan: The Origins of Modern Burma* (Honolulu, HI: University of Hawai'i Press, 1985).
62. Hall, *Burma*, p.14.
63. Hall, *Burma*, pp.28–37. Ashley South, *Mon Nationalism and Civil War in Burma: The Golden Sheldrake* (London: RoutledgeCurzon, 2003).
64. Victor B. Lieberman, *Burmese Administrative Cycles: Anarchy and Conquest, c.1580–1760* (Princeton, NJ: Princeton University Press, 1984), p.3.
65. Taylor, *The State in Myanmar*, p.6.
66. Taylor, *The State in Myanmar*, p.5.
67. Scott, *The Art of Not Being Governed*.
68. Michael Adas, *The Burma Delta: Economic Development and Social Change on an Asian Rice Frontier, 1852–1941* (Madison, WI: University of Wisconsin Press, 1974).
69. Taylor, *The State in Myanmar*, p.1.

70. Maung Maung Gyi, *Burmese Political Values: The Socio-political Roots of Authoritarianism* (New York, NY: Praeger, 1983).
71. Michael Aung-Thwin, "1948 and Burma's Myth of Independence," in Josef Silverstein (ed.), *Independent Burma at Forty Years: Six Assessments* (Ithaca, NY: Cornell Southeast Asia Program, 1989), 19–34.
72. In the preface to the later edition of his book, Taylor wrote: "*The State in Burma* did not predict and I did not anticipate the dramatic events of 1988. Some reviewers and critics were happy to draw attention to that point. Whether their prediction skills were and are more acute than mine is for others to decide." Taylor, *The State in Myanmar*, p.xv.
73. Taylor, *The State in Myanmar*, p.4.
74. Scott, *The Art of Not Being Governed.*
75. Furnivall, *The Governance of Modern Burma*, p.3.
76. Bertil Lintner, *Burma in Revolt: Opium and Insurgency since 1948* (Boulder, CO: Westview, 1994), p.41.
77. Robert H. Taylor, "British Policy towards Myanmar and the Creation of the 'Burma Problem'," in N. Ganesan and Kyaw Yin Hlaing (eds), *Myanmar: State, Society and Ethnicity* (Singapore: Institute of Southeast Asian Studies, 2007), 70–95, pp.72–3.
78. Thant Myint-U, *The River of Lost Footsteps*, p.41.
79. Aung San Suu Kyi, *Burma and India: Some Aspects of Intellectual Life under Colonialism* (Shimla: Indian Institute of Advanced Study, 1990), p.33.
80. Cady, *A History of Modern Burma*, p.155.
81. Donnison, *Public Administration in Burma.*
82. Ian Holliday, "Doing Business with Rights Violating Regimes: Corporate Social Responsibility and Myanmar's Military Junta," *Journal of Business Ethics* 61:4 (2005), 329–42.
83. Ironically, those expectations were perhaps expressed most fully by Maung Maung in *Burma's Constitution*, published in 1959 and 1961. This was an extended celebration of an emergent democracy about to be crushed by a military-state complex that the author himself was to join, and indeed briefly head in the middle months of 1988. Maung Maung, *Burma's Constitution.*
84. Gustaaf Houtman, "Sacralizing or Demonizing Democracy? Aung San Suu Kyi's 'Personality Cult'," in Monique Skidmore (ed.), *Burma at the Turn of the Twenty-first Century* (Honolulu, HI: University of Hawai'i Press, 2005), 133–53.
85. Compare a remark from 2004 that hostile commentary often makes it "almost impossible or politically unacceptable to portray any positive aspects of the military regime." Ardeth Maung Thawnghmung, *Behind the Teak Curtain*, p.xii. Also see Selth, "Modern Burma Studies," pp.433–9.
86. Centre for Peace and Conflict Studies, *Myanmar Civil Society's Response to Cyclone Nargis*, p.2.
87. Centre for Peace and Conflict Studies, *Ethnic People Speak*, p.192.
88. Centre for Peace and Conflict Studies, *Ethnic People Speak*, p.196.
89. Centre for Peace and Conflict Studies, *Myanmar Civil Society's Response to Cyclone Nargis*, p.2.

90. Centre for Peace and Conflict Studies, *Myanmar Civil Society's Response to Cyclone Nargis*, p.51.

Chapter 1

1. John F. Cady, *A History of Modern Burma* (Ithaca, NY: Cornell University Press, 1958), p.67.
2. Frank N. Trager, *Burma, from Kingdom to Republic: A Historical and Political Analysis* (Westport, CT: Greenwood Press, 1966), p.19.
3. British terminology is still in use, with local people sometimes speaking in English of Lower and Upper Burma.
4. Amitav Ghosh, *The Glass Palace* (New York, NY: Random House, 2000).
5. Neil A. Englehart, "Liberal Leviathan or Imperial Outpost? J. S. Furnivall on Colonial Rule in Burma," *Modern Asian Studies* 45 (2011), forthcoming.
6. G. E. Harvey, *British Rule in Burma, 1824–1942* (London: Faber and Faber, 1946), p.77.
7. Englehart, "Liberal Leviathan or Imperial Outpost?."
8. J. S. Furnivall, *Colonial Policy and Practice: A Comparative Study of Burma and Netherlands India* (Cambridge: Cambridge University Press, 1948), pp. 71–2, 160.
9. John L. Christian, "Burma: Strategic and Political," *Far Eastern Survey* 11:3 (1942), 40–4. Robert H. Taylor, "Politics in Late Colonial Burma: The Case of U Saw," *Modern Asian Studies* 10:2 (1976), 161–93.
10. Taylor, "Politics in Late Colonial Burma," p. 165.
11. J. S. Furnivall, *An Introduction to the Political Economy of Burma* (Rangoon: Burma Book Club, 1931). Also see J. A. Hobson, *Imperialism: A Study* (London: J. Nisbet & Co., 1902), and V. I. Lenin, *Imperialism: The Highest Stage of Capitalism: A Popular Outline* (New York, NY: International Publishers, 1939).
12. Englehart, "Liberal Leviathan or Imperial Outpost?."
13. Maurice Collis, *Last and First in Burma (1941–1948)* (London: Faber and Faber, 1956), p.290.
14. Julie Pham, "J. S. Furnivall and Fabianism: Reinterpreting the 'Plural Society' in Burma," *Modern Asian Studies* 39:2 (2005), 321–48.
15. Cady, *A History of Modern Burma*, p.125.
16. For an analysis of perceptions of Burma recorded by British travelers, see Stephen L. Keck, "Picturesque Burma: British Travel Writing 1890–1914," *Journal of Southeast Asian Studies* 35:3 (2004), 387–414.
17. Sir Charles Crosthwaite, *The Pacification of Burma* (London: Frank Cass, 1968).
18. Mark Duffield, "On the Edge of 'No Man's Land': Chronic Emergency in Myanmar," School of Sociology, Politics, and International Studies, University of Bristol Working Paper No. 01-08, p.8. www.bristol.ac.uk/spais/research/workingpapers/wpspaisfiles/duffield0108.pdf.
19. Michael W. Charney, *A History of Modern Burma* (Cambridge: Cambridge University Press, 2009), p.5.

20. E. R. Leach, "The Frontiers of 'Burma'," *Comparative Studies in Society and History* 3:1 (1960), 49–68. Dorothy Woodman, *The Making of Burma* (London: Cresset Press, 1962). Woodman opens her book by noting that Burma's borders were not fully mapped until a frontier agreement was signed with China on October 1, 1960.
21. Leach, "The Frontiers of 'Burma'." F. K. Lehman, *The Structure of Chin Society: A Tribal People of Burma Adapted to a Non-Western Civilization* (Urbana, IL: University of Illinois Press, 1963).
22. E. R. Leach, *Political Systems of Highland Burma: A Study of Kachin Social Structure* (London: G. Bell, 1954).
23. Thant Myint-U, *The Making of Modern Burma* (Cambridge: Cambridge University Press, 2001), p.3.
24. Englehart, "Liberal Leviathan or Imperial Outpost?."
25. Thant Myint-U, *The River of Lost Footsteps: A Personal History of Burma* (New York, NY: Farrar, Straus and Giroux, 2006), p.181.
26. Charney, *A History of Modern Burma*, p.8.
27. Mary P. Callahan, *Making Enemies: War and State Building in Burma* (Ithaca, NY: Cornell University Press, 2003), p.16.
28. Woodman, *The Making of Burma*, pp.335–452.
29. Daniel Mason, *The Piano Tuner* (New York, NY: Alfred A. Knopf, 2002).
30. Michael Adas, *The Burma Delta: Economic Development and Social Change on an Asian Rice Frontier, 1852–1941* (Madison, WI: University of Wisconsin Press, 1974).
31. Cady, *A History of Modern Burma*, pp.162–3.
32. H. Myint, *The Economics of the Developing Countries*, 4th ed. (London: Hutchinson, 1973), pp.29–44.
33. Adas, *The Burma Delta*, p.38.
34. Adas, *The Burma Delta*, p.58.
35. Adas, *The Burma Delta*, p.57.
36. J. H. Williams, *Elephant Bill* (London: Rupert Hart-Davis, 1950).
37. Cady, *A History of Modern Burma*, p.163.
38. Virginia Thompson, "The Burma behind the Road," *Far Eastern Survey* 9 (1940), 291–300, pp.293–5.
39. Adas, *The Burma Delta*, p.99.
40. Charney, *A History of Modern Burma*, p.18.
41. Charney, *A History of Modern Burma*, p.2.
42. I. R. Sinai, *The Challenge of Modernisation: The West's Impact on the Non-Western World* (London: Chatto & Windus, 1964), p.126.
43. Maung Htin Aung, *A History of Burma* (New York, NY: Columbia University Press, 1967), p.268.
44. Adas, *The Burma Delta*, p.58.
45. Niall Ferguson, *Empire: How Britain Made the Modern World* (London: Allen Lane, 2003). In his book, Ferguson addresses the Burmese case only tangentially.
46. J. S. Furnivall, "Burma, Past and Present," *Far Eastern Survey* 22:3 (1953), 21–6, p.23.
47. Callahan, *Making Enemies*, pp.2–3.

48. Callahan, *Making Enemies*, p.14.
49. Thant Myint-U, *The River of Lost Footsteps,* pp.22–3.
50. David Cannadine, *Ornamentalism: How the British Saw Their Empire* (Oxford: Oxford University Press, 2001).
51. George Orwell, *Burmese Days: A Novel* (London: Harcourt Brace, 1934), p.69. For an analysis of British writing about Asian colonies, see Douglas Kerr, *Eastern Figures: Orient and Empire in British Writing* (Hong Kong: Hong Kong University Press, 2008).
52. John F. Cady, *Contacts with Burma, 1935–1949: A Personal Account* (Athens, OH: Center for International Studies, Ohio University, 1983), p.21.
53. Lucian W. Pye, *Politics, Personality, and Nation Building: Burma's Search for Identity* (New Haven, CT: Yale University Press, 1962), p.9.
54. Maung Maung, *Burma's Constutition*, 2nd ed. (The Hague: Martinus Nijhoff, 1961), p.5.
55. Thant Myint-U, *The Making of Modern Burma*, p.10.
56. Michael Aung-Thwin, "The British 'Pacification' of Burma: Order without Meaning," *Journal of Southeast Asian Studies* 16 (1985), 245–61.
57. Thant Myint-U, *The River of Lost Footsteps,* p.194.
58. John H. Badgley, "Burma: The Nexus of Socialism and Two Political Traditions," *Asian Survey* 3 (1963), 89–95, p.89. Parimal Ghosh, *Brave Men of the Hills: Resistance and Rebellion in Burma, 1824–1932* (London: Hurst, 2000).
59. Charles S. Brant and Mi Mi Khaing, "Missionaries Among the Hill Tribes of Burma," *Asian Survey* 1 (1961), 44–51.
60. Benedict Anderson, *Imagined Communities: Reflections on the Origin and Spread of Nationalism*, rev. ed. (London: Verso, 1991), p.119.
61. Mya Maung, "Cultural Value and Economic Change in Burma," *Asian Survey* 4:3 (1964), 757–64, p.757. Donald Eugene Smith, *Religion and Politics in Burma* (Princeton, NJ: Princeton University Press, 1965), pp.86–107. Also see John F. Cady, "Religion and Politics in Modern Burma," *Far Eastern Quarterly* 12:2 (1953), 149–62.
62. Robert H. Taylor, *The State in Myanmar* (Honolulu, HI: University of Hawai'i Press, 2009), p.100.
63. G. E. Harvey, *British Rule in Burma, 1824–1942* (London: Faber and Faber, 1946), p.30.
64. F. S. V. Donnison, *Public Administration in Burma: A Study of Development during the British Connexion* (London: Royal Institute of International Affairs, 1953), p.110.
65. Josef Silverstein, *Burmese Politics: The Dilemma of National Unity* (New Brunswick, NJ: Rutgers University Press, 1980), p.29.
66. Thant Myint-U, *The River of Lost Footsteps,* p.197.
67. Furnivall, "Burma, Past and Present," p.22.
68. Furnivall, *An Introduction to the Political Economy of Burma*, p.45.
69. Simon Schama, *A History of Britain: Volume 3: The Fate of Empire, 1776–2000* (New York, NY: Hyperion, 2000), p.459.
70. J. S. Furnivall, *The Fashioning of Leviathan* (1939), cited in Callahan, *Making Enemies*, p.21.

71. J. S. Furnivall, "The Future of Burma," *Pacific Affairs* 18:2 (1945), 156–68, p.157. Also see Furnivall, *An Introduction to the Political Economy of Burma*, p.xxi.
72. Furnivall, *Colonial Policy and Practice*, p.10.
73. Furnivall, *An Introduction to the Political Economy of Burma*, p.ix.
74. Walinsky, *Economic Development in Burma*, p.54.
75. Judith L. Richell, *Disease and Demography in Colonial Burma* (Singapore: NUS Press, 2006).
76. Sean Turnell, *Fiery Dragons: Banks, Moneylenders and Microfinance in Burma* (Copenhagen: NIAS Press, 2009), pp.13–52.
77. Adas, *The Burma Delta*. James C. Scott, *The Moral Economy of the Peasant: Rebellion and Subsistence in Southeast Asia* (New Haven, CT: Yale University Press, 1976).
78. J. S. Furnivall, cited in R. H. Taylor, "Disaster or Release? J. S. Furnivall and the Bankruptcy of Burma," *Modern Asian Studies* 29:1 (1995), 45–63, p.53.
79. See Richard A. Butwell, *U Nu of Burma* (Stanford, CA: Stanford University Press, 1963), p.81.
80. Thant Myint-U, *The River of Lost Footsteps,* p.185.
81. Furnivall, "Burma, Past and Present," p.22. Michael Adas, "Immigrant Asians and the Economic Impact of European Imperialism: The Role of the South Indian Chettiars in British Burma," *Journal of Asian Studies* 33:3 (1974), 385–401. Adas, *The Burma Delta*.
82. Furnivall, "The Future of Burma," p.156. Also see Allen Fenichel and Gregg Huff, "Colonialism and the Economic System of an Independent Burma," *Modern Asian Studies* 9:3 (1975), 321–35.
83. Thompson, "The Burma behind the Road," p.296. Also see Furnivall, *An Introduction to the Political Economy of Burma*, p.162.
84. Thompson, "The Burma behind the Road," p.292.
85. Virginia Thompson, "Transit Duty on the Burma Road" *Far Eastern Survey* 10:18 (1941), 213–15. Also see Donovan Webster, *The Burma Road: The Epic Story of One of World War II's Most Remarkable Endeavours* (New York, NY: Farrar, Straus and Giroux, 2003).
86. Furnivall, *Colonial Policy and Practice*, p.304.
87. Taylor, "Disaster or Release?," p.55.
88. Maureen Aung-Thwin and Thant Myint-U, "The Burmese Ways to Socialism," *Third World Quarterly* 13:1 (1992), 67–75, p.68.
89. Charney, *A History of Modern Burma*, p.18.
90. Cady, *A History of Modern Burma*, p.309.
91. Sir John Simon, cited in Furnivall, *An Introduction to the Political Economy of Burma*, p.v.
92. Sir Harcourt Butler, "Burma and Its Problems," *Foreign Affairs* 10:4 (1932), 647–58, p.658.
93. Montagu-Chelmsford Report, cited in Donnison, *Public Administration in Burma*, p.52.
94. Cady, *A History of Modern Burma*, p.186.
95. Harvey, *British Rule in Burma*, p.78.

96. Scott, *The Moral Economy of the Peasant*, p.149. Also see Maurice Collis, *Trials in Burma* (London: Faber and Faber, 1938), pp.213–21; and Michael Adas, *Prophets of Rebellion: Millenarian Protest Movements against the European Colonial Order* (Cambridge: Cambridge University Press, 1979), pp.99–102.
97. Aung San Suu Kyi, *Burma and India: Some Aspects of Intellectual Life under Colonialism* (Shimla: Indian Institute of Advanced Study, 1990), pp.67–8.
98. Cecil Hobbs, "Nationalism in British Colonial Burma," *Far Eastern Quarterly* 6:2 (1947), 113–21.
99. Lintner, *Burma in Revolt*, p.33.
100. Christopher Bayly and Tim Harper, *Forgotten Armies: Britain's Asian Empire and the War with Japan* (London: Penguin, 2005), p.13.
101. Andrew Selth, "Race and Resistance in Burma, 1942–1945," *Modern Asian Studies* 20:3 (1986), 483–507, pp.490–1.
102. Selth, "Race and Resistance in Burma." Jon Latimer, *Burma: The Forgotten War* (London: John Murray, 2004).
103. Maung Maung, *Burma's Constutition*, pp.57–61. *Adipati*, a Burmese term, comes close in meaning to the German *Führer* or the Spanish *caudillo*. Ba Maw rose to prominence as Saya San's lawyer in 1931, and was nationalist premier of Burma 1937–39. His memoir covers the full period of warfare and occupation. Ba Maw, *Breakthrough in Burma: Memoirs of a Revolution, 1939–1946* (New Haven, CT: Yale University Press, 1968).
104. Selth, "Race and Resistance in Burma," p.498. Bayly and Harper, *Forgotten Armies*.
105. Bayly and Harper, *Forgotten Armies*, pp.433–4.
106. Louis Allen, *Burma: The Longest War, 1941–45* (London: J. M. Dent, 1984).
107. Some of the soldiers' stories are reproduced in Kazuo Tamayama and John Nunneley, *Tales by Japanese Soldiers of the Burma Campaign 1942–1945* (London: Cassell, 2000).
108. Alice Thorner, "British 'Blue Print' for Burma," *Far Eastern Survey* 14:10 (1945), 126–8. Furnivall, "The Future of Burma."
109. Hugh Tinker, "Burma's Struggle for Independence: The Transfer of Power Thesis Re-examined," *Modern Asian Studies* 20:3 (1986), 461–81, p.465.
110. Josef Silverstein, "The Other Side of Burma's Struggle for Independence," *Pacific Affairs* 58:1 (1985), 98–108, p.104.
111. Supreme Council of the Anti-Fascist People's Freedom League, May 16–23, 1946, cited in Silverstein, "The Other Side of Burma's Struggle for Independence," p.105.
112. G. Appleton, "Burma Two Years after Liberation," *International Affairs* 23:4 (1947), 510–21, p.515.
113. Yasmin Khan, *The Great Partition: The Making of India and Pakistan* (New Haven, CT: Yale University Press, 2007).
114. Tinker, "Burma's Struggle for Independence."
115. Angelene Naw, *Aung San and the Struggle for Burmese Independence* (Chiang Mai: Silkworm, 2001). Matthew J. Walton, "Ethnicity, Conflict, and History in Burma: The Myths of Panglong," *Asian Survey* 48:6 (2008), 889–910.

116. Sir Raibeart M. MacDougall, "Burma Stands Alone," *Foreign Affairs* 26:3 (1948), 542–53, p.546. The assassins were employed by former Premier Saw, a rival for power who was convicted of the crime and hanged at Insein Prison, Rangoon in May 1948.
117. Josef Silverstein, "Politics in the Shan State: The Question of Secession from the Union of Burma," *Journal of Asian Studies* 18:1 (1958), 43–57. Maung Maung, *Burma's Constutition*, pp.167–92.
118. Hugh Tinker, "Nu, the Serene Statesman," *Pacific Affairs* 30:2 (1957), 120–37, p.125.
119. E. Burke Inlow, "The Constitution of Burma," *Far Eastern Survey* 17:22 (1948), 264–7.
120. Josef Silverstein, *Burmese Politics: The Dilemma of National Unity* (New Brunswick, NJ: Rutgers University Press, 1980), p.50.
121. Selth, "Race and Resistance in Burma." Thant Myint-U, *The Making of Modern Burma*, pp.253–4. Mary Callahan, "Myanmar's Perpetual Junta: Solving the Riddle of the Tatmadaw's Long Reign," *New Left Review* 60 (Nov/Dec 2009), 26–63, pp.38–40.
122. Thant Myint-U, *The Making of Modern Burma*, p.254.
123. Thant Myint-U, *The Making of Modern Burma*, p.254.
124. Furnivall, *An Introduction to the Political Economy of Burma*, p.xiii.
125. Julie Pham, "Ghost Hunting in Colonial Burma: Nostalgia, Paternalism and the Thoughts of J. S. Furnivall," *South East Asia Research* 12:2 (2004), 237–68. Englehart, "Liberal Leviathan or Imperial Outpost?."

Chapter 2

1. Sir Raibeart M. MacDougall, "Burma Stands Alone," *Foreign Affairs* 26:3 (1948), 542–53.
2. Virginia Thompson, "The New Nation of Burma," *Far Eastern Survey* 17:7 (1948), 81–4, p.84.
3. Manning Nash, *The Golden Road to Modernity: Village Life in Contemporary Burma* (New York, NY: John Wiley & Sons, 1965), p.1.
4. William L. Scully and Frank N. Trager, "Burma 1978: The Thirtieth Year of Independence," *Asian Survey* 19:2 (1979), 147–56, p.148.
5. John F. Cady, "Conflicting Attitudes toward Burma," *Far Eastern Survey* 15:2 (1946), 27–31. J. R. Andrus, "The Agrarian Problem in Burma," *Pacific Affairs* 19:3 (1946), 260–71. Clarence Hendershot, "Burma Compromise," *Far Eastern Survey* 16:12 (1947), 133–8. J. S. Furnivall, "Twilight in Burma: Reconquest and Crisis," *Pacific Affairs* 22 (1949), 3–20. J S Furnivall, "Twilight in Burma: Independence and After," *Pacific Affairs* 22:2 (1949), 155–72. J S Furnivall, "Burma, Past and Present," *Far Eastern Survey* 22:3 (1953), 21–6. Also see Angelene Naw, *Aung San and the Struggle for Burmese Independence* (Copenhagen: Nordic Institute of Asian Studies, 2001).
6. Hugh Tinker, "Nu, the Serene Statesman," *Pacific Affairs* 30:2 (1957), 120–37. Also see Louis J. Walinsky "The Rise and Fall of U Nu," *Pacific Affairs* 38:3/4 (1965–66), 269–81; U Nu, *U Nu, Saturday's Son* (New Haven: Yale University Press, 1975); Hugh Tinker, "Burma: The Politics of Memory," *Pacific Affairs* 49:1 (1976), 108–13.

7. F. S. V. Donnison, *British Military Administration in the Far East 1943–46* (London: Her Majesty's Stationery Office, 1956), p.369.
8. Tinker, *The Union of Burma*, p.27.
9. Cited in G. Appleton, "Burma Two Years after Liberation," *International Affairs* 23:4 (1947), 510–21, p.519.
10. Furnivall, "Twilight in Burma," pp.156–7.
11. Maung Maung, *The 1988 Uprising in Burma* (New Haven, CT: Yale University Southeast Asia Studies, 1999), p.10.
12. John F. Cady, "The Situation in Burma," *Far Eastern Survey* 22:5 (1953), 49–54, p.50.
13. Virginia Thompson, "Burma's Communists," *Far Eastern Survey* 17:9 (1948), 103–5.
14. Andrew Selth, "Race and Resistance in Burma, 1942–1945," *Modern Asian Studies* 20:3 (1986), 483–507.
15. Bertil Lintner, *Burma in Revolt: Opium and Insurgency since 1948* (Boulder, CO: Westview, 1994), pp.1–19.
16. Mary P. Callahan, *Making Enemies: War and State Building in Burma* (Ithaca, NY: Cornell University Press, 2003), p.114.
17. J. S. Furnivall, "Communism and Nationalism in Burma," *Far Eastern Survey* 18:17 (1949), 193–7.
18. Maung Maung, "Burma Looks Ahead," *Pacific Affairs* 25:1 (1952), 40–8.
19. Edward M. Law Yone and David G. Mandelbaum, "Pacification in Burma," *Far Eastern Survey* 19:17 (1950), 182–7, p.187.
20. Edward M. Law Yone and David G. Mandelbaum, "The New Nation of Burma," *Far Eastern Survey* 19:18 (1950), 189–94, p.194.
21. Callahan, *Making Enemies*, p.144.
22. Norman Lewis, *Golden Earth: Travels in Burma* (London: Jonathan Cape, 1952).
23. Josef Silverstein, "Politics, Parties and National Elections in Burma," *Far Eastern Survey* 25:12 (1956), 177–84. Lee S. Bigelow, "The 1960 Election in Burma," *Far Eastern Survey* 29:5 (1960), 70–4. Richard Butwell and Fred von der Mehden, "The 1960 Election in Burma," *Pacific Affairs* 33:2 (1960), 144–57.
24. Mya Maung, "The Burmese Way to Socialism Beyond the Welfare State," *Asian Survey* 10:6 (1970), 533–51.
25. Frank N. Trager, *Building a Welfare State in Burma, 1948–1956* (New York, NY: Institute of Pacific Relations, 1958).
26. Kyaw Yin Hlaing, "Associational Life in Myanmar: Past and Present," in N. Ganesan and Kyan Yin Hlaing (eds), *Myanmar: State, Society and Ethnicity* (Singapore: Institute of Southeast Asian Studies/Hiroshima Peace Institute, 2007), 143–71, pp.150–5.
27. Nash, *The Golden Road to Modernity*.
28. Maung Maung, "Pyidawtha Comes to Burma," *Far Eastern Survey* 22:9 (1953), 117–19, p.117.
29. Janet Welsh, "Burma's Development Problems," *Far Eastern Survey* 25:8 (1956), 113–22, p.122.
30. Hugh Tinker, *The Union of Burma: A Study of the First Years of Independence* (London: Oxford University Press, 1957), p.388. In editions of his book issued in 1959 and 1961, Tinker kept the evaluation intact.

31. Cady, "The Situation in Burma," pp.50–1. Neil A. Englehart, "Is Regime Change Enough for Burma? The Problem of State Capacity," *Asian Survey* 45:4 (2005), 622–44, pp.624–8.
32. Lucian W. Pye, *Politics, Personality, and Nation Building: Burma's Search for Identity* (New Haven, CT: Yale University Press, 1962). Kyaw Yin Hlaing, "Power and Factional Struggles in Post-independence Burmese Governments," *Journal of Southeast Asian Studies* 39:1 (2008), 149–77, pp.151–7.
33. Manning Nash, "Party Building in Upper Burma," *Asian Survey* 3:4 (1963), 197–202.
34. Hugh Tinker, "Burma's Northeast Borderland Problems," *Pacific Affairs* 29:4 (1956), 324–46.
35. Geoffrey Fairbairn, "Some Minority Problems in Burma," *Pacific Affairs* 30:4 (1957), 299–311.
36. Furnivall, "Burma, Past and Present." Cady, "The Situation in Burma," pp.49–54.
37. Pye, *Politics, Personality, and Nation Building*, pp.61-2.
38. John H. Badgley, 'Burma's Political Crisis," *Pacific Affairs* 31:4 (1958), 336–51, p.351.
39. Mary P. Callahan, "Burma: Soldiers as State Builders," in Muthiah Alagappa (ed.), *Coercion and Governance: The Declining Political Role of the Military in Asia* (Stanford, CA: Stanford University Press, 2001), 413–29, pp.417–22.
40. Cady, "The Situation in Burma," p.53.
41. Callahan, *Making Enemies*, p.5.
42. Thant Myint-U, *The River of Lost Footsteps: A Personal History of Burma* (New York, NY: Farrar, Straus and Giroux, 2006), p.275.
43. Bigelow, "The 1960 Election in Burma," p.74.
44. Callahan, *Making Enemies*, p.5.
45. Callahan, *Making Enemies*, pp.168–9.
46. Callahan, *Making Enemies*, p.189.
47. Josef Silverstein, "The Federal Dilemma in Burma," *Far Eastern Survey* 28:7 (1959), 97–105. John H. Badgley, "Burma: The Nexus of Socialism and Two Political Traditions," *Asian Survey* 3:2 (1963), 89–95, pp.91-2.
48. Fred von der Mehden, "Burma's Religious Campaign against Communism," *Pacific Affairs* 33:3 (1960), 290–9.
49. Callahan, *Making Enemies*, p.177.
50. Callahan, *Making Enemies*, p.18.
51. Frank N. Trager, "Political Divorce in Burma," *Foreign Affairs* 37:2 (1959), 317–27.
52. Maung Htin Aung, *A History of Burma* (New York, NY: Columbia University Press, 1967), p.324.
53. Frank N. Trager, "The Political Split in Burma," *Far Eastern Survey* 27:10 (1958), 145–55.
54. Trager, "Political Divorce in Burma," p.323.
55. Richard Butwell, "The New Political Outlook in Burma," *Far Eastern Survey* 29:2 (1960), 21–7, pp.25, 23.
56. Donald Eugene Smith, *Religion and Politics in Burma* (Princeton, NJ: Princeton University Press, 1965), pp.230–80.

57. Frank N. Trager, "The Failure of U Nu and the Return of the Armed Forces in Burma," *Review of Politics* 25:3 (1963), 309–28, p.320. Smith, *Religion and Politics in Burma*, pp.312–20.
58. Callahan, *Making Enemies*, p.203.
59. On planning, see Tin Maung Maung Than, *State Dominance in Myanmar: The Political Economy of Industrialization* (Singapore: Institute of Southeast Asian Studies, 2007), pp.35–9.
60. Michael W. Charney, *A History of Modern Burma* (Cambridge: Cambridge University Press, 2009), p.81.
61. Myat Thein, *Economic Development of Myanmar* (Singapore: Institute of Southeast Asian Studies, 2004), p.54.
62. Myat Thein, *Economic Development of Myanmar*, pp.17–18.
63. Frank N. Trager, *Burma, from Kingdom to Republic: A Historical and Political Analysis* (Westport, CT: Greenwood Press, 1966), pp.314–21.
64. Badgley, "Burma." Tinker, *The Union of Burma*, pp.124–6.
65. John F. Cady, *A History of Modern Burma* (Ithaca, NY: Cornell University Press, 1958), p.621. One US adviser who worked in Burma (effectively in the Prime Minister's Office) from September 1953 to February 1959 subsequently wrote up the experience. See Louis J. Walinsky, *Economic Development in Burma: 1951–1960* (New York, NY: Twentieth Century Fund, 1962).
66. Callahan, *Making Enemies*.
67. Richard Butwell, "The Four Failures of U Nu's Second Premiership," *Asian Survey* 2:1 (March 1962), 3–11.
68. Mary Callahan, "Myanmar's Perpetual Junta: Solving the Riddle of the Tatmadaw's Long Reign," *New Left Review* 60 (Nov/Dec 2009), 26–63, p.40.
69. David I. Steinberg, "'Legitimacy' in Burma/Myanmar: Concepts and Implications," in N. Ganesan and Kyan Yin Hlaing (eds), *Myanmar: State, Society and Ethnicity* (Singapore: Institute of Southeast Asian Studies/Hiroshima Peace Institute, 2007), 109–42, p.121.
70. U Nu, *The People Win Through: A Play* (New York, NY: Taplinger, 1957).
71. Kyaw Yin Hlaing, "Setting the Rules for Survival: Why the Burmese Military Regime Survives in an Age of Democratization," *Pacific Review* 22:3 (2009), 271–91, p.276.
72. John Badgley, "Burma's Military Government: A Political Analysis," *Asian Survey* 2:6 (August 1962), 24–31, p.24. John H. Badgley, "Burma," p.90.
73. Inge Sargent, *Twilight over Burma: My Life as a Shan Princess* (Honolulu, HI: University of Hawaii Press, 1994). Patricia W. Elliott, *The White Umbrella: A Woman's Struggle for Freedom in Burma*, 2nd ed. (Bangkok: Friends Books, 2006). Sao Sanda, *The Moon Princess: Memories of the Shan States* (Bangkok: River Books, 2008).
74. Maung Maung, *The 1988 Uprising in Burma*, p.28.
75. Badgley, "Burma's Military Government," p.24.
76. Trager, "The Failure of U Nu and the Return of the Armed Forces in Burma," pp.320–1.
77. S. E. Finer's *The Man on Horseback* was published several months after Ne Win's coup. In its first sentence it noted that "The year 1962 opened with brisk outbursts of

military revolt." S. E. Finer, *The Man on Horseback: The Role of the Military in Politics* (London: Pall Mall Press, 1962), p.1.

78. David W. Chang, "The Military and Nation-building in Korea, Burma and Pakistan," *Asian Survey* 9:11 (1969), 818–30, p.830.
79. Fred R. von der Mehden, "The Burmese Way to Socialism," *Asian Survey* 3:3 (March 1963), 129–35.
80. Tin Maung Maung Than, *State Dominance in Myanmar*, pp.111–13.
81. John F. Cady, *The United States and Burma* (Cambridge, MA: Harvard University Press, 1976), p.18.
82. Mya Maung, *Totalitarianism in Burma: Prospects for Economic Development* (New York, NY: Paragon House, 1992), pp.5–8.
83. Mya Maung, "Socialism and Economic Development of Burma," *Asian Survey* 4:12 (1964), 1182–90. John Badgley, "Intellectuals and the National Vision: The Burmese Case," *Asian Survey* 9:8 (1969), 598–613.
84. Sir Richard Allen, "Britain's Colonial Aftermath in South East Asia," *Asian Survey* 3:9 (1963), 403–14, p.406.
85. Josef Silverstein, "First Steps on the Burmese Way to Socialism," *Asian Survey* 4:2 (1964), 716–22, p.716.
86. Thant Myint-U, *The River of Lost Footsteps,* p.294.
87. Badgley, "Burma," p.91.
88. Badgley, "Burma," p.93.
89. John H. Badgley, "Burma's Zealot Wungyis: Maoists or St. Simonists," *Asian Survey* 5:1 (1965), 55–62, p.55.
90. Robert A. Holmes, "Burmese Domestic Policy: The Politics of Burmanization," *Asian Survey* 7:3 (1967), 188–97, pp.191–3.
91. Thant Myint-U, *The River of Lost Footsteps,* p.296.
92. Martin J. Smith, *Burma: Insurgency and the Politics of Ethnicity*, 2nd ed. (London: Zed Books, 1999), p.259.
93. Josef Silverstein, "Burma: Ne Win's Revolution Considered," *Asian Survey* 6:2 (1966), 95–102.
94. Badgley, "Burma's Zealot Wungyis," p.55.
95. Hugh Tinker, *The Union of Burma: A Study of the First Years of Independence*, 4th ed. (London: Oxford University Press, 1967), p.388.
96. Kyi May Kaung, "Theories, Paradigms, or Models in Burma Studies," *Asian Survey* 35:11 (1995), 1030–41.
97. Teruko Saitō, "Farm Household Economy under Paddy Delivery System in Contemporary Burma," *The Developing Economies* 19:4 (1981), 367–97.
98. Peter John Perry, *Myanmar (Burma) since 1962: The Failure of Development* (Aldershot: Ashgate, 2007), p.54.
99. Perry, *Myanmar (Burma) since 1962*, p.60.
100. Perry, *Myanmar (Burma) since 1962*, p.78.
101. Tin Maung Maung Than, *State Dominance in Myanmar.*
102. Perry, *Myanmar (Burma) since 1962*, p.109.

103. Frank N. Trager, "Burma: 1967 – A Better Ending than Beginning," *Asian Survey* 8:2 (1968), 110–19, p.111.
104. Perry, *Myanmar (Burma) since 1962*, p.27.
105. Jon A. Wiant and David I. Steinberg, "Burma: The Military and National Development," in J. Soedjati Djiwandono and Yong Mun Cheing (eds), *Soldiers and Stability in Southeast Asia* (Singapore: Institute of Southeast Asian Studies, 1988), 293–321.
106. Perry, *Myanmar (Burma) since 1962*, pp.28–31.
107. Silverstein, "Burma," p.95.
108. Koichi Fujita, "Agricultural Labourers in Myanmar during the Economic Transition: Views from the Study of Selected Villages," in Koichi Fujita, Fumiharu Mieno and Ikuko Okamoto (eds), *The Economic Transition in Myanmar after 1988: Market Economy versus State Control* (Singapore: NUS Press, 2009), 246–80, pp.247–52.
109. Richard Butwell, "Ne Win's Burma: At the End of the First Decade," *Asian Survey* 12:10 (1972), 901–12.
110. The 8/135 classification remains in place today. Ian Holliday, "Ethnicity and Democratization in Myanmar," *Asian Journal of Political Science* 18:2 (2010), 111-28, p.118.
111. David Steinberg, "Democracy, Power, and the Economy in Myanmar: Donor Dilemmas," *Asian Survey* 31:8 (1991), 729–42, pp.733–4.
112. Jon A. Wiant, "Burma 1973: New Turns in the Burmese Way to Socialism," *Asian Survey* 14:2 (1974), 175–82.
113. Josef Silverstein, "Political Dialogue in Burma: A New Turn on the Road to Socialism?," *Asian Survey* 10:2 (1970), 133–42, p.139.
114. Frank N. Trager and William L. Scully, "The Third Congress of the Burma Socialist Programme Party: 'The Need to Create Continuity and Dynamism of Leadership'," *Asian Survey* 17:9 (1977), 830–8, p.838.
115. Paul Theroux, *The Great Railway Bazaar: By Train through Asia* (Boston, MA: Houghton Mifflin, 1975), pp.179–206.
116. Andrew Selth, *Death of a Hero: The U Thant Disturbances in Burma, December 1974* (Nathan: Griffith University, 1989).
117. Edwin W. Martin, "The Socialist Republic of the Union of Burma: How Much Change?," *Asian Survey* 15:2 (1975), 129–35.
118. Trager and Scully, "The Third Congress of the Burma Socialist Programme Party."
119. Josef Silverstein, "Burma in 1980: An Uncertain Balance Sheet," *Asian Survey* 21:2 (1981), 212–222, p.219.
120. Cited in Perry, *Myanmar (Burma) since 1962*, p.2.
121. Josef Silverstein, "Burma in 1981: The Changing of the Guardians Begins," *Asian Survey* 22:2 (1982), 180–90.
122. David I. Steinberg, "Burma in 1982: Incomplete Transitions," *Asian Survey* 23:2 (1983), 165–71.
123. Hugh MacDougall and Jon A. Wiant, "Burma in 1984: Political Stasis or Political Renewal?," *Asian Survey* 25:2 (1985), 241–8. Hugh C MacDougall and Jon A. Wiant, "Burma in 1985: Consolidation Triumphs over Innovation," *Asian Survey*

26:2 (1986), 186–95. Robert O. Tilman, "Burma in 1986: The Process of Involution Continues," *Asian Survey* 27:2 (1987), 254–63. John B. Haseman, "Burma in 1987: Change in the Air?," *Asian Survey* 28:2 (1988), 223–8.

124. John Badgley, "The Union of Burma: Age Twenty Two," *Asian Survey* 11:2 (1971), 149–58, p.149.
125. William L. Scully and Frank N. Trager, "Burma 1979: Reversing the Trend," *Asian Survey* 20:2 (1980), 168–75, p.168.
126. Silverstein, "Burma in 1981," p.189.
127. Trager, "Burma: 1967," p.114.
128. Butwell, "Ne Win's Burma," p.907.
129. Silverstein, "Burma in 1981," p.183.
130. Myat Thein, *Economic Development of Myanmar*, p.92.
131. Teruko Saitō, cited in Perry, *Myanmar (Burma) since 1962*, p.75.
132. Perry, *Myanmar (Burma) since 1962*, p.54.
133. Perry, *Myanmar (Burma) since 1962*, p.59.
134. Perry, *Myanmar (Burma) since 1962*, p.59.
135. Thant Myint-U, *The River of Lost Footsteps,* p.317.
136. Mya Maung, *The Burma Road to Poverty* (New York, NY: Praeger, 1991).
137. Josef Silverstein and Julian Wohl, "University Students and Politics in Burma," *Pacific Affairs* 37:1 (1964), 50–65.
138. Bertil Lintner, *Outrage: Burma's Struggle for Democracy* (Hong Kong: Review Publishing Company, 1989), pp.115–16.
139. Lintner, *Outrage*, p.119.
140. Ne Win remained influential into the 1990s, but died in relative obscurity on December 5, 2002 with no state funeral and only minimal notice in state media.
141. Lintner, *Outrage*, p.126.
142. Lintner, *Outrage*, p.133.
143. Pascal Khoo Thwe, *From the Land of Green Ghosts: A Burmese Odyssey* (London: HarperCollins, 2002).
144. Derek Tonkin, "The 1990 Elections in Myanmar: Broken Promises or a Failure of Communication?," *Contemporary Southeast Asia* 29:1 (2007), 33–54, p.37.
145. Lintner, *Outrage*, p.154.
146. Zaw Oo, "Aung San Suu Kyi: Gandhian Dissident Democrat," in John Kane, Haig Patapan and Benjamin Wong (eds), *Dissident Democrats: The Challenge of Democratic Leadership in Asia* (New York, NY: Palgrave Macmillan, 2008), 241–70.
147. Aung San Suu Kyi, *Freedom from Fear: And Other Writing*s, rev. ed. (London: Penguin, 1995), p.198.
148. Aung San Suu Kyi, *Freedom from Fear*, p.204.
149. Lintner, *Burma in Revolt*, p.351.
150. Federico Ferrara, "Why Regimes Create Disorder: Hobbes's Dilemma during a Rangoon Summer," *Journal of Conflict Resolution* 47:3 (2003), 302–25, p.311.
151. Cited in Lintner, *Outrage*, p.176.
152. Mancur Olson, "Dictatorship, Democracy, and Development," *American Political Science Review* 87:3 (1993), 567–76.

153. Michael Aung-Thwin, "1948 and Burma's Myth of Independence," in Josef Silverstein (ed.), *Independent Burma at Forty Years: Six Assessments* (Ithaca, NY: Cornell Southeast Asia Program, 1989), 19–34.

Chapter 3

1. Monique Skidmore, *Karaoke Fascism: Burma and the Politics of Fear* (Philadelphia, PA: University of Pennsylvania Press, 2004). Christina Fink, *Living Silence in Burma: Surviving under Military Rule*, 2nd ed. (London/Chiang Mai: Zed Books/Silkworm Books, 2009).
2. Khin Zaw Win, "A Burmese Perspective on Prospects for Progress," in Monique Skidmore and Trevor Wilson (eds), *Myanmar: The State, Community and the Environment* (Canberra: ANU E Press and Asian Pacific Press, 2007), 18–35. Kyaw Yin Hlaing, "Aung San Suu Kyi of Myanmar: A Review of the Lady's Biographies," *Contemporary Southeast Asia* 29:2 (2007), 359–76.
3. Michael W. Charney, *A History of Modern Burma* (Cambridge: Cambridge University Press, 2009), pp.170–200.
4. John Kane, *The Politics of Moral Capital* (Cambridge: Cambridge University Press, 2001), pp.147–71.
5. Benedict Rogers, *Than Shwe: Unmasking Burma's Tyrant* (Chiang Mai: Silkworm, 2010).
6. US Department of State, "Burma: Than Shwe is the problem," May 8, 2008. WikiLeaks US Embassy Cables, ref. 08RANGOON333.
7. Win Min, "Looking inside the Burmese Military," *Asian Survey* 48:6 (2008), 1018–37.
8. Ardeth Maung Thawnghmung, *Behind the Teak Curtain: Authoritarianism, Agricultural Policies and Political Legitimacy in Rural Burma/Myanmar* (London: Kegan Paul, 2004).
9. Monique Skidmore, "Introduction: Burma at the Turn of the Twenty-first Century," in Monique Skidmore (ed.), *Burma at the Turn of the Twenty-first Century* (Honolulu, HI: University of Hawai'i Press, 2005), 1–18, p.6.
10. Kyaw Yin Hlaing, "Setting the Rules for Survival: Why the Burmese Military Regime Survives in an Age of Democratization," *Pacific Review* 22:3 (2009), 271–91, pp.275, 283.
11. Kyaw Yin Hlaing, "Power and Factional Struggles in Post-independence Burmese Governments," *Journal of Southeast Asian Studies* 39:1 (2008), 149–77, pp.171–3.
12. Alex M. Mutebi, "'Muddling through' Past Legacies: Myanmar's Civil Bureaucracy and the Need for Reform," in Kyaw Yin Hlaing, Robert H. Taylor and Tin Maung Maung Than (eds), *Myanmar: Beyond Politics to Societal Imperatives* (Singapore: ISEAS Publications, 2005), 140–60.
13. Neil A. Englehart, "Is Regime Change Enough for Burma? The Problem of State Capacity," *Asian Survey* 45:4 (2005), 622–44, pp.624–8. Alison Vicary, "The Relief and Reconstruction Programme following Cyclone Nargis: A Review of SPDC

Policy," in Nick Cheesman, Monique Skidmore and Trevor Wilson (eds), *Ruling Myanmar: From Cyclone Nargis to National Elections* (Singapore: ISEAS Publishing, 2010), 208–35.

14. Tin Maung Maung Than, "Myanmar: Preoccupation with Regime Survival, National Unity, and Stability," in Muthiah Alagappa, ed., *Asian Security Practice: Material and Ideational Influences* (Stanford, CA: Stanford University Press, 1998), 390–416.
15. Bruce Matthews, "The Present Fortune of Tradition-bound Authoritarianism in Myanmar," *Pacific Affairs* 71:1 (1998), 7–23, pp.14–15.
16. Ardeth Maung Thawnghmung, *Behind the Teak Curtain*, pp.211, 222.
17. Ardeth Maung Thawnghmung, *Behind the Teak Curtain*, p.2.
18. Cited in Human Rights Watch, *Human Rights Watch World Report 1992: Events of 1991* (New York, NY: Human Rights Watch, 1991), p.346.
19. Burma Library, "Section 5 of the Emergency Provisions Act" (unofficial translation). www.burmalibrary.org/docs6/Section_5_of_the_Emergency_Provisions_Act-en.pdf.
20. Amnesty International, *Myanmar: Justice on Trial*, ASA16/019/2003 (London: Amnesty International, 2003).
21. International Bar Association Human Rights Institute, *Prosperity versus Individual Rights? Human Rights, Democracy and the Rule of Law in Singapore* (No place: International Bar Association, 2008).
22. Nick Cheesman, "Thin Rule of Law or Un-Rule of Law in Myanmar?," *Pacific Affairs* 82:4 (2009–10), 597–613.
23. See Tin Maung Maung Than, "Myanmar," p.395.
24. Mary P. Callahan, *Political Authority in Burma's Ethnic Minority States: Devolution, Occupation, and Coexistence* (Washington, DC: East-West Center Washington, 2007), n.12.
25. Stephen McCarthy, *The Political Theory of Tyranny in Singapore and Burma: Aristotle and the Rhetoric of Benevolent Despotism* (Abingdon: Routledge, 2006).
26. Mikael Gravers, *Nationalism as Political Paranoia in Burma: An Essay on the Historical Practice of Power*, 2nd ed. (Richmond: Curzon Press, 1999).
27. Jennifer Leehey, "Writing in a Crazy Way: Literary Life in Contemporary Urban Burma," in Monique Skidmore, ed., *Burma at the Turn of the Twenty-first Century* (Honolulu, HI: University of Hawai'i Press, 2005), 175–205.
28. Ian Holliday, "National Unity Struggles in Myanmar: A Degenerate Case of Governance for Harmony in Asia," *Asian Survey* 47:3 (2007), 374–92.
29. *Working People's Daily*, "State LORC Declaration No. 1/90 of July 27, 1990," July 29, 1990.
30. Barbara Victor, *The Lady: Aung San Suu Kyi: Nobel Laureate and Burma's Prisoner* (Boston, MA: Faber and Faber, 1998). Justin Wintle, *Perfect Hostage: A Life of Aung San Suu Kyi* (London: Hutchinson, 2007).
31. Network for Democracy and Development, *The White Shirts*.
32. Mary Callahan, "Myanmar's Perpetual Junta: Solving the Riddle of the Tatmadaw's Long Reign," *New Left Review* 60 (Nov/Dec 2009), 26–63, p.29.
33. Amnesty International, *The Repression of Ethnic Minority Activists in Myanmar*, ASA 16/001/2010 (London: Amnesty International, 2010). Assistance Association for

Political Prisoners (Burma) and United States Campaign for Burma, *The Future in the Dark: The Massive Increase in Burma's Political Prisoners* (Mae Sot and Washington, DC: Assistance Association for Political Prisoners (Burma) and United States Campaign for Burma, 2008). Human Rights Watch, *Burma's Forgotten Prisoners* (New York, NY: Human Rights Watch, 2009).

34. Fink, *Living Silence in Burma*, pp.171–88.
35. Assistance Association for Political Prisoners (Burma), *The Darkness We See: Torture in Burma's Interrogation Centers and Prisons* (Mae Sot: Assistance Association for Political Prisoners (Burma), 2005).
36. Jane Perlez, "From a Burmese prison, a chronicle of pain in paint," *New York Times*, August 13, 2007.
37. Karen Connelly, *The Lizard Cage* (New York, NY: Spiegel & Grau, 2005).
38. The NLD had no online presence until a website (www.nldburma.org) was created by overseas party members and formally launched on January 30, 2011. Aung San Suu Kyi gained internet access at her home on January 20, 2011. Ko Htwe, "NLD website launched," *Irrawaddy*, January 31, 2011.
39. Kyaw Yin Hlaing, "Aung San Suu Kyi of Myanmar."
40. Khin Zaw Win, "2010 and the Unfinished Task of Nation-building," in Nick Cheesman, Monique Skidmore and Trevor Wilson (eds), *Ruling Myanmar: From Cyclone Nargis to National Elections* (Singapore: ISEAS Publishing, 2010), 19–31, p.23.
41. This was the evaluation made by Shari Villarosa, US chargé d'affaires in Yangon 2006–08, at the end of her tour of duty. US Department of State, "Continuing the pursuit of democracy in Burma," July 14, 2008. WikiLeaks US Embassy Cables, ref. 08RANGOON557.
42. Robert H. Taylor, "Burma's Ambiguous Breakthrough," *Journal of Democracy* 1:4 (1990), 62–72, p.70.
43. Fink, *Living Silence in Burma*, pp.83–6.
44. Human Rights Watch, *Crackdown: Repression of the 2007 Popular Protests in Burma* (New York, NY: Human Rights Watch, 2007), pp.23–7. Human Rights Documentation Unit, *Bullets in the Alms Bowl: An Analysis of the Brutal SPDC Suppression of the September 2007 Saffron Revolution* (No place: National Coalition Government of the Union of Burma, 2008), pp.32–6.
45. Perhaps the most common term is saffron revolution, designed to draw a parallel with color revolutions elsewhere in the world. However, since the monks who marched in Myanmar mainly wore maroon and never mobilized the general population, both parts of the designation are contested. Indeed, it may even be that uprising is stretching the point. Nevertheless, for ease of reference and since it is a term that has passed into the language, saffron uprising is used here. For a detailed account, see Hans-Bernd Zöllner, *Neither Saffron nor Revolution: A Commentated and Documented Chronology of the Monks' Demonstrations in Myanmar in 2007 and Their Background: Part I* (Berlin: Humboldt University, 2009).
46. Fink, *Living Silence in Burma*, p.103.

47. Kyaw Yin Hlaing, "Challenging the Authoritarian State: Buddhist Monks and Peaceful Protests in Burma," *Fletcher Forum of World Affairs* 32:1 (Winter 2008), 125–44. Andrew Selth, "Burma's 'Saffron Revolution' and the Limits of International Influence," *Australian Journal of International Affairs* 62:3 (2008), 281–97.
48. Julianne Pidduck, "Citizen Journalism in Burma and the Legacy of Graham Spry," *Canadian Journal of Communication* 35:3 (2010), 473–85.
49. Martin J. Smith, *Burma: Insurgency and the Politics of Ethnicity*, 2nd ed. (London: Zed Books, 1999). Zaw Oo and Win Min, *Assessing Burma's Ceasefire Accords* (Washington, DC: East-West Center Washington, 2007).
50. Martin J. Smith, "Ethnic Politics and Regional Development in Myanmar: The Need for New Approaches," in Kyaw Yin Hlaing, Robert H. Taylor and Tin Maung Maung Than (eds), *Myanmar: Beyond Politics to Societal Imperatives* (Singapore: ISEAS Publications, 2005), 56–85.
51. Paul Core, "Burma/Myanmar: Challenges of a Ceasefire Accord in Karen State," *Journal of Current Southeast Asian Affairs* 28:3 (2009), 95–105. Ken MacLean, "The Rise of Private Indirect Government in Burma," in Susan L. Levenstein, ed., *Finding Dollars, Sense, and Legitimacy in Burma* (Washington, DC: Woodrow Wilson International Center for Scholars, 2010), 40–52.
52. Ashley South, *Burma's Longest War: Anatomy of the Karen Conflict* (Amsterdam: Transnational Institute and Burma Center Netherlands, 2011), pp.4, 45.
53. Ashley South, *Ethnic Politics in Burma: States of Conflict* (Abingdon: Routledge, 2008).
54. Callahan, *Political Authority in Burma's Ethnic Minority States*, pp.2–3. Also see Tom Kramer, *The United Wa State Party: Narco-army or Ethnic Nationalist Party?* (Washington, DC: East-West Center Washington, 2007). And see Jane M. Ferguson, "Sovereignty in the Shan State: A Case Study of the United Wa State Army," in Nick Cheesman, Monique Skidmore and Trevor Wilson (eds), *Ruling Myanmar: From Cyclone Nargis to National Elections* (Singapore: ISEAS Publishing, 2010), 52–62.
55. Mark Duffield, "On the Edge of 'No Man's Land': Chronic Emergency in Myanmar," School of Sociology, Politics, and International Studies, University of Bristol Working Paper No. 01–08. www.bristol.ac.uk/spais/research/workingpapers/wpspaisfiles/duffield0108.pdf.
56. South, *Burma's Longest War*, p.12.
57. The Burma Campaign UK carries a large number of reports on its website. http://burmacampaign.org.uk.
58. Kei Nemoto, "Between Democracy and Economic Development: Japan's Policy towards Burma/Myanmar Then and Now," in N. Ganesan and Kyaw Yin Hlaing, eds, *Myanmar: State, Society and Ethnicity* (Singapore and Hiroshima: Institute of Southeast Asian Studies and Hiroshima Peace Institute, 2007), 96–108, p.104.
59. For a list of the major economic reforms from 1987 to 1996, see Koichi Fujita, Fumiharu Mieno and Ikuko Okamoto, "Myanmar's Economic Transformation after 1988," in Koichi Fujita, Fumiharu Mieno and Ikuko Okamoto (eds), *The Economic Transition in Myanmar after 1988: Market Economy versus State Control* (Singapore: NUS Press, 2009), 1–19, Table 2.

60. Stephen McCarthy, "Ten Years of Chaos in Burma: Foreign Investment and Economic Liberalization under the SLORC-SPDC, 1988 to 1998," *Pacific Affairs* 73:2 (2000), 233–62.
61. Ikuko Okamoto, "Transformation of the Rice Marketing System after Market Liberalization in Myanmar," in Koichi Fujita, Fumiharu Mieno and Ikuko Okamoto (eds), *The Economic Transition in Myanmar after 1988: Market Economy versus State Control* (Singapore: NUS Press, 2009), 216–45, p.240.
62. Okamoto, "Transformation of the Rice Marketing System," pp.219–21.
63. Koichi Fujita and Ikuko Okamoto, "Overview of Agricultural Policies and the Development in Myanmar," in Koichi Fujita, Fumiharu Mieno and Ikuko Okamoto (eds), *The Economic Transition in Myanmar after 1988: Market Economy versus State Control* (Singapore: NUS Press, 2009), 169–215.
64. Kyaw Yin Hlaing, "Power and Factional Struggles in Post-independence Burmese Governments," pp.175–6.
65. Mya Maung, *Totalitarianism in Burma: Prospects for Economic Development* (New York, NY: Paragon House, 1992). Callahan, "Myanmar's Perpetual Junta."
66. Dominic Faulder, "The big sleep: How a dream wedding illustrated the self-confidence of an elite at ease," *Irrawaddy* 14:12 (December 2006), 56–7, p.57.
67. MacLean, "The Rise of Private Indirect Government in Burma."
68. Richard M. Gibson and John B. Haseman, "Prospects for Controlling Narcotics Production and Trafficking in Myanmar," *Contemporary Southeast Asia* 25:1 (2003), 1–19. Martin Jelsma, Tom Kramer and Pietje Vervest (eds), *Trouble in the Triangle: Opium and Conflict in Burma* (Chiang Mai: Silkworm, 2005). Kramer, *The United Wa State Party*. Palaung Women's Organization, *Poisoned Hills: Opium Cultivation Surges under Government Control in Burma* (Mae Sot: Palaung Women's Organization, 2010).
69. Shan Herald Agency for News, *Show Business: Rangoon's 'War on Drungs' in Shan State* (No place: Shan Herald Agency for News, 2003). Shan Herald Agency for News, *Hand in Glove: The Burma Army and the Drug Trade in Shan State* (Chiang Mai: Shan Herald Agency for News, 2006).
70. Khin Maung Soe, *Trends of Development of Myanmar Fisheries: With References to Japanese Experiences* (Chiba: Institute of Developing Economies, Japan External Trade Organization, 2008).
71. H. C. Matthew Sim, *Myanmar on My Mind: A Guide to Living and Doing Business in Myanmar* (Singapore: Times Books International, 2001).
72. Eric Neumayer, "The Impact of Political Violence on Tourism: Dynamic Cross-national Estimation," *Journal of Conflict Resolution* 48:2 (2004), 259–81.
73. Andrea Valentin, "Citizen diplomacy through tourism?," Democratic Voice of Burma, February 18, 2011.
74. Ian Holliday, "The Yadana Syndrome? Big Oil and Principles of Corporate Engagement in Myanmar," *Asian Journal of Political Science* 13:2 (December 2005), 29–51.
75. Toshihiro Kudo and Fumiharu Mieno, "Trade, Foreign Investment and Myanmar's Economic Development in the Transition to an Open Economy," in Koichi Fujita, Fumiharu Mieno and Ikuko Okamoto (eds), *The Economic Transition in Myanmar*

after 1988: Market Economy versus State Control (Singapore: NUS Press, 2009), 103–27, Table 4.

76. Kudo and Mieno, "Trade, Foreign Investment and Myanmar's Economic Development in the Transition to an Open Economy," pp.111–16.
77. *International Herald Tribune*, "An industrial project that could change Myanmar," November 26, 2010.
78. Myat Thein, *Economic Development of Myanmar* (Singapore: Institute of Southeast Asian Studies, 2004), pp.235–6.
79. Ken MacLean, "Spaces of Extraction: Governance along the Riverine Networks of Nyaunglebin District," in Monique Skidmore and Trevor Wilson (eds), *Myanmar: The State, Community and the Environment* (Canberra: ANU E Press and Asian Pacific Press, 2007), 246–70. Nancy Hudson-Rodd and Sein Htay, "Farmers, Land and Military Rule in Burma," in Nick Cheesman, Monique Skidmore and Trevor Wilson (eds), *Ruling Myanmar: From Cyclone Nargis to National Elections* (Singapore: ISEAS Publishing, 2010), 147–67.
80. Kachin Development Networking Group, *Valley of Darkness: Gold Mining and Militarization in Burma's Hugawng Valley* (No place: Kachin Development Networking Group, 2007). EarthRights International, *Turning Treasure into Tears: Mining, Dams, and Deforestation in Shwegyin Township, Pegu Division, Burma* (Chiang Mai: EarthRights International, 2007). Karen Human Rights Group, *Development by Decree: The Politics of Poverty and Control in Karen State* (No place: Karen Human Rights Group, 2007). Mon Youth Progressive Organization, *In the Balance: Salween Dams Threaten Downstream Communities in Burma* (No place: Mon Youth Progressive Organization, 2007). Kachin Development Networking Group, *Damming the Irrawaddy* (No place: Kachin Development Networking Group, 2007). Ethnic Community Development Forum, *Biofuel by Decree: Unmasking Burma's Bio-energy Fiasco* (No place: Ethnic Community Development Forum, 2008). Kayan Women's Union, *Drowning the Green Ghosts of Kayanland: Impacts of the Upper Paunglaung Dam in Burma* (No place: Kayan Women's Union, 2008). Human Rights Foundation of Monland, *Laid Waste: Human Rights along the Kanbauk to Myaing Kalay Gas Pipeline* (Bangkok: Human Rights Foundation of Monland, 2009). Pa-O Youth Organization, *Robbing the Future: Russian-backed Mining Project Threatens Pa-O Communities in Shan State, Burma* (No place: Pa-O Youth Organization, 2009). Shan Sapawa Environmental Organization, *Roots and Resilience* (No place: Shan Sapawa Environmental Organization, 2009). Kachin Development Networking Group, *Resisting the Flood: Communities Taking a Stand against the Imminent Construction of Irrawaddy Dams* (No place: Kachin Development Networking Group, 2009). Kachin Development Networking Group, *Tyrants, Tycoons and Tigers: Yuzana Company Ravages Burma's Hugawng Valley* (No place: Kachin Development Networking Group, 2010). Pa-Oh Youth Organization and Kyoju Action Network, *Poison Clouds: Lessons from Burma's Largest Coal Project at Tigyit* (No place: Pa-Oh Youth Organization and Kyoju Action Network, 2011).
81. The ILO – Yangon website provides full details. www.ilo.org/yangon/lang--en/index.htm.

82. Duffield, "On the Edge of 'No Man's Land'," p.31.
83. Network for Democracy and Development, *The White Shirts.*
84. Raymond L. Bryant, "The Greening of Burma: Political Rhetoric or Sustainable Development?," *Pacific Affairs* 69:3 (1996), 341–59. Tun Myint, "Environmental Governance in the SPDC's Myanmar," in Monique Skidmore and Trevor Wilson (eds), *Myanmar: The State, Community and the Environment* (Canberra: ANU E Press and Asian Pacific Press, 2007), 189–217. United Nations Environment Programme, *National Sustainable Development Strategy: Myanmar.* www.rrcap.unep.org/nsds/brief/Myanmar%20brief.pdf.
85. Global Witness, *A Conflict of Interests: The Uncertain Future of Burma's Forests* (London: Global Witness, 2003). Global Witness, *A Choice for China: Ending the Destruction of Burma's Northern Frontier Forests* (London: Global Witness, 2005). Tint Lwin Thaung, "Identifying Conservation Issues in Kachin State," in Monique Skidmore and Trevor Wilson (eds), *Myanmar: The State, Community and the Environment* (Canberra: ANU E Press and Asian Pacific Press, 2007), 271–89. Global Witness, *A Disharmonious Trade: China and the Continued Destruction of Burma's Northern Frontier Forests* (London: Global Witness, 2009).
86. Matthew Smith, "Environmental Governance of Mining in Burma," in Monique Skidmore and Trevor Wilson (eds), *Myanmar: The State, Community and the Environment* (Canberra: ANU E Press and Asian Pacific Press, 2007), 218–45.
87. Images Asia and Pan Kachin Development Society, *At What Price? Gold Mining in Kachin State, Burm*a (Chiang Mai: Images Asia, 2004), cover page.
88. Arkar Moe, "Burmese gems for sale," *Irrawaddy*, June 24, 2009.
89. Fumiharu Mieno, "Characteristics of Capital Accumulation in Myanmar, 1988–2003," in Koichi Fujita, Fumiharu Mieno and Ikuko Okamoto (eds), *The Economic Transition in Myanmar after 1988: Market Economy versus State Control* (Singapore: NUS Press, 2009), 23–65, pp.29–31.
90. *Economist*, "The lion kings?," January 8, 2011, 70–1, p.70. In another story in the same issue, the magazine noted that "Global league tables are interesting, but not always reliable." *Economist*, "Wrong numbers," January 8, 2011, 58–60, p.58.
91. Fujita, et al., "Myanmar's Economic Transformation after 1988," Table 1.
92. Asia Society Task Force Report, *Current Realities and Future Possibilities in Burma/Myanmar: Options for U.S. Policy* (No place: Asia Society, 2010), pp.27–9.
93. Turnell, et al, "Burma's Economy 2009," p.633.
94. Turnell, et al, "Burma's Economy 2009," p.645.
95. Sean Turnell, Wylie Bradford and Alison Vicary, "Burma's Economy 2009: Disaster, Recovery … and Reform?," *Asian Politics and Policy* 1:4 (2009), 631–59, p.636.
96. UN Data, "Myanmar." http://data.un.org/CountryProfile.aspx?crName=MYANMAR.
97. Asia Society Task Force Report, *Current Realities and Future Possibilities in Burma/Myanmar*, p.24.
98. Turnell, et al, "Burma's Economy 2009," p.632.

99. Sean Turnell, "Finding Dollars and Sense: Burma's Economy in 2010," in Susan L. Levenstein, ed., *Finding Dollars, Sense, and Legitimacy in Burma* (Washington, DC: Woodrow Wilson International Center for Scholars, 2010), 20–39, p.20.
100. Turnell, et al, "Burma's Economy 2009," p.636.
101. Turnell, et al, "Burma's Economy 2009," p.655.
102. Human Rights Watch, *"I Want to Help My Own People,"* p.93. Also see Sean Turnell, "Recapitalizing Burma's Rural Credit System," in Nick Cheesman, Monique Skidmore and Trevor Wilson (eds), *Ruling Myanmar: From Cyclone Nargis to National Elections* (Singapore: ISEAS Publishing, 2010), 126–46.
103. Sean Turnell, *Fiery Dragons: Banks, Moneylenders and Microfinance in Burma* (Copenhagen: NIAS Press, 2009).
104. Purchasing power parity translates national income into the dollar equivalent for a person living in the US. Thus, Myanmar citizens face the kinds of challenge a US citizen would face if living on $1,596 a year, $133 a month, or $4.37 a day.
105. United Nations Development Programme, *Human Development Report 2010: The Real Wealth of Nations: Pathways to Human Development* (New York, NY: United Nations Development Programme, 2010), Table 1.
106. David I. Steinberg, *Burma: A Socialist Nation of Southeast Asia* (Boulder, CO: Westview Press, 1982), p.33.
107. Callahan, *Political Authority in Burma's Ethnic Minority States*, p.9.
108. Mary Callahan, "The Endurance of Military Rule in Burma: Not Why, but Why Not?," in Susan L. Levenstein, ed., *Finding Dollars, Sense, and Legitimacy in Burma* (Washington, DC: Woodrow Wilson International Center for Scholars, 2010), 54–76, p.60.
109. Emma Larkin, *Secret Histories: Finding George Orwell in a Burmese Teashop* (London: John Murray, 2004).
110. Matthews, "The Present Fortune of Tradition-bound Authoritarianism in Myanmar," p.15.
111. Network for Democracy and Development, *The White Shirts: How the USDA Will Become the New Face of Burma's Dictatorship* (Mae Sariang: Network for Democracy and Development, 2006), pp.18–19.
112. Aung San Suu Kyi, *Freedom from Fear; And Other Writings*, 2nd ed. (London: Penguin, 1995), pp.180–5. Skidmore, *Karaoke Fascism*, pp.33–57. Fink, *Living Silence in Burma*, pp.113–52.
113. Andrew Selth, *Burma's Armed Forces: Power without Glory* (Norwalk, CT: EastBridge, 2002). Maung Aung Myoe, *Building the Tatmadaw: Myanmar Armed Forces since 1948* (Singapore: Institute of Southeast Asian Studies, 2009). Andrew Selth, "Known Knowns and Known Unknowns: Measuring Myanmar's Military Capabilities," *Contemporary Southeast Asia* 31 (2009), 272–95.
114. Human Rights Watch, *"My Gun Was as Tall as Me": Child Soldiers in Burma* (New York, NY: Human Rights Watch, 2002). Human Rights Watch, *Sold to Be Soldiers: The Recruitment and Use of Child Soldiers in Burma* (New York, NY: Human Rights Watch, 2007). US Department of State, *Trafficking in Persons Report*, 10th ed. (Washington, DC: US Department of State, 2010), p.10.

115. Maung Aung Myoe, *Building the Tatmadaw*, pp.163–92.
116. Mary P. Callahan, "Burma: Soldiers as State Builders," in Muthiah Alagappa (ed.), *Coercion and Governance: The Declining Political Role of the Military in Asia* (Stanford, CA: Stanford University Press, 2001), 413–29, pp.424–5.
117. *Irrawaddy*, "Chronology of Burma's laws restricting freedom of opinion, expression and the press," May 1, 2004.
118. Reporters Without Borders, *World Report 2010: Burma* (No place: Reporters Without Borders, 2010).
119. Anna J. Allott, *Inked Over, Ripped Out: Burmese Storytellers and the Censors* (Chiang Mai: Silkworm, 1994).
120. Reporters Without Borders, *Freedom of the Press Worldwide in 2007: 2007 Annual Report* (Paris: Reporters Without Borders, 2007), pp.77–78.
121. Reporters Without Borders, *World Report 2010: Burma.*
122. Jennifer Leehey, "Writing in a Crazy Way: Literary Life in Contemporary Urban Burma," in Monique Skidmore (ed.), *Burma at the Turn of the Twenty-first Century* (Honolulu, HI: University of Hawai'i Press, 2005), 175–205. Fink, *Living Silence in Burma*, pp.209–25.
123. Human Rights Watch, *"I Want to Help My Own People": State Control and Civil Society in Burma after Cyclone Nargis* (New York, NY: Human Rights Watch, 2010), p.78, n.188. BBC Burmese, operating continuously since September 2, 1940, claims to be the leading external broadcaster with a weekly Myanmar audience of 8.4 million listeners. BBC Press Office, "BBC Burmese at 70: Roadshow in Thailand launches newsletter for Burmese migrants," September 1, 2010 press release.
124. Ko Htwe, "Burmese tuning in to events in Libya," *Irrawaddy*, March 23, 2011.
125. Centre for Peace and Conflict Studies, *Listening to Voices from Inside: Myanmar Civil Society's Response to Cyclone Nargis* (Phnom Penh: Centre for Peace and Conflict Studies, no date), p.187.
126. Many other sites, including the BBC, CNN, Google, Yahoo!, and YouTube, were banned.
127. Evgeny Morozov, *The Net Delusion: The Dark Side of Internet Freedom* (New York, NY: PublicAffairs, 2011).
128. In total, 37 countries were surveyed. Freedom House, *Freedom on the Net 2011: A Global Assessment of Internet and Digital Media* (Washington, DC: Freedom House, 2011).
129. Skidmore, *Karaoke Fascism*, pp.58–78.
130. David Steinberg, "The Union Solidarity and Development Association," *Burma Debate* IV:1 (Jan/Feb 1997). www.burmadebate.org/archives/janfebbttm.html#usda.
131. International Crisis Group, *Myanmar: The Role of Civil Society* (Bangkok/Brussels: International Crisis Group, 2001), p.i.
132. Network for Democracy and Development, *The White Shirts*, p.38.
133. Ashley South, "Political Transition in Myanmar: A New Model for Democratization," *Contemporary Southeast Asia* 26:2 (2004), 233–55.
134. Karl Dorning, "Creating an Environment for Participation: International NGOs and the Growth of Civil Society in Burma/Myanmar," in Trevor Wilson, ed., *Myanmar's*

Long Road to National Reconciliation (Singapore: Institute of Southeast Asian Studies, 2006), 188–217. Brian Heidel, *The Growth of Civil Society in Myanmar* (Bangalore: Books for Change, 2006). David Tegenfeldt, "More than Saving Lives: The Role of International Development Agencies in Supporting Change Processes in Burma/ Myanmar," in Trevor Wilson, ed., *Myanmar's Long Road to National Reconciliation* (Singapore: Institute of Southeast Asian Studies, 2006), 218–30.

135. Kyaw Yin Hlaing, "Associational Life in Myanmar: Past and Present," in N. Ganesan and Kyaw Yin Hlaing, eds, *Myanmar: State, Society and Ethnicity* (Singapore and Hiroshima: Institute of Southeast Asian Studies and Hiroshima Peace Institute, 2007), 143–71, p.167.
136. Centre for Peace and Conflict Studies, *Myanmar Civil Society's Response to Cyclone Nargis*. Emergency Assistance Team (Burma) and Johns Hopkins Bloomberg School of Public Health, *After the Storm: Voices from the Delta* (No place: Emergency Assistance Team (Burma) and Johns Hopkins Bloomberg School of Public Health, 2009).
137. Tripartite Core Group, *Post-Nargis Joint Assessment: A Report Prepared by the Tripartite Core Group Comprised of Representatives of the Government of the Union of Myanmar, the Association of Southeast Asian Nations and the United Nations with the Support of the Humanitarian and Development Community* (No place: Tripartite Core Group, 2008), p.29.
138. Chillingly, a June 2008 US Embassy cable reported that the number of Nargis deaths could be far higher: "On Saturday, June 7, [Vice Senior General] Maung Aye reportedly met with the regime's top crony, Tay Za, and told him the government calculated that approximately 300,000 people had perished in the cyclone, but that this number would be released to the public 'over his dead body'." US Department of State, "Burma: struggles at the top affecting relief effort," June 11, 2008. WikiLeaks US Embassy Cables, ref. 08RANGOON471.
139. Emma Larkin, *Everything Is Broken: The Untold Story of Disaster under Burma's Military Regime* (London: Granta, 2010). Vicary, "The Relief and Reconstruction Programme following Cyclone Nargis."
140. Human Rights Watch, *"I Want to Help My Own People,"* pp.52–3.
141. Centre for Peace and Conflict Studies, *Myanmar Civil Society's Response to Cyclone Nargis.*
142. Human Rights Watch, *"I Want to Help My Own People,"* p.84.
143. The figure comes from the Myanmar Information Management Unit, and is cited by the Three Diseases Fund. www.3dfund.org/index.php?option=com_content&view=article&id=4&Itemid=54.
144. Paung Ku, *Strengthening Civil Society in Myanmar* (No place: Paung Ku, 2010), pp.5–8.
145. Centre for Peace and Conflict Studies, *Listening to Voices from Inside: Ethnic People Speak* (Phnom Penh: Centre for Peace and Conflict Studies, 2010).
146. Matthews, "The Present Fortune of Tradition-bound Authoritarianism in Myanmar," pp.18–21. Stephen McCarthy, "Overturning the Alms Bowl: The Price of Survival and the Consequences for Political Legitimacy in Burma," *Australian Journal of*

International Affairs 62:3 (2008), 298–314. Julianne Schober, *Modern Buddhist Conjunctures in Myanmar: Cultural Narratives, Colonial Legacies, and Civil Society* (Honolulu, HI: University of Hawai'i Press, 2010).

147. J. A. Berlie, *The Burmanization of Myanmar's Muslims* (Bangkok: White Lotus Press, 2008). Fink, *Living Silence in Burma*, pp.236–41.

148. Martin J. Smith, *Burma: Insurgency and the Politics of Ethnicity*, 2nd ed. (London: Zed Books, 1999). Martin Smith, *State of Strife: The Dynamics of Ethnic Conflict in Burma* (Washington, DC: East-West Center Washington, 2007).

149. Amporn Jirattikorn, "Shan Virtual Insurgency and the Spectatorship of the Nation," *Journal of Southeast Asian Studies* 42:1 (2011), 17–38.

150. Human Rights Watch, *World Report 2007: Events of 2006* (New York, NY: Human Rights Watch, 2007), p.249.

151. Human Rights Watch, *World Report 2007*, p.250. Christian Solidarity Worldwide, "Deaf villager shot dead, Karen woman raped and murdered and thousands displaced in Burma Army offensive," *BurmaNet News*, May 24, 2007. Also see Stephen Hull, "The 'Everyday Politics' of IDP Protection in Karen State," *Journal of Current Southeast Asian Affairs* 28:2 (2009), 7–21.

152. Thailand Burma Border Consortium, *Internal Displacement and International Law in Eastern Burma* (Bangkok: Thailand Burma Border Consortium, 2008). Partners Relief and Development and Free Burma Rangers, *Displaced Childhoods: Human Rights and International Crimes against Burma's Internally Displaced Children* (Chiang Mai: Partners Relief and Development and Free Burma Rangers, 2010).

153. Josef Silverstein, "The Civil War, the Minorities and Burma's New Politics," in Peter Carey, ed., *Burma: The Challenge of Change in a Divided Society* (Basingstoke, Macmillan, 1997), 129–58. Christina Fink, "Militarization in Burma's Ethnic States: Causes and Consequences," *Contemporary Politics* 14:4 (2008), 447–62.

154. Callahan, *Political Authority in Burma's Ethnic Minority States*, p.25.

155. Tom Kramer, *Neither War nor Peace: The Future of the Cease-fire Agreements in Burma* (Amsterdam: Transnational Institute, 2009).

156. Emma Haddad, *The Refugee in International Society: Between Sovereigns* (Cambridge: Cambridge University Press, 2008). Also see Hazel J. Lang, *Fear and Sanctuary: Burmese Refugees in Thailand* (Ithaca, NY: Cornell Southeast Asia Program, 2002).

157. Shelby Tucker, *Among Insurgents: Walking through Burma* (London: Radcliffe Press, 2000). Zoya Phan with Damien Lewis, *Little Daughter: A Memoir of Survival in Burma and the West* (London: Simon & Schuster, 2009). Mac McClelland, *For Us Surrender Is out of the Question: A Story from Burma's Never-ending War* (Berkeley, CA: Soft Skull, 2010). Also see: Mike Tucker, *The Long Patrol: With Karen Guerillas in Burma* (Bangkok: Asia Books, 2003); Edith Mirante, *Down the Rat Hole: Adventures Underground on Burma's Frontiers* (Bangkok: Orchid, 2005); Phil Thornton, *Restless Souls: Rebels, Refugees, Medics and Misfits on the Thai-Burma Border* (Bangkok: Asia Books, 2006); Richard Humphries, *Frontier Mosaic: Voices of Burma from the Lands in Between* (Bangkok: Orchid, 2007). Sylvester Stallone's film *Rambo*, released in 2008, is crude and distorting.

158. Local people often use the terms Arakan Muslim or Rakhine Muslim rather than Rohingya. Berlie, *The Burmanization of Myanmar's Muslims.*
159. Irish Centre for Human Rights, *Crimes against Humanity in Western Burma: The Situation of the Rohingyas* (Galway: Irish Centre for Human Rights, 2010).
160. Human Rights Watch, *The Rohingya Muslims: Ending a Cycle of Exodus?* (New York, NY: Human Rights Watch, 1996). Médecins Sans Frontières-Holland, *10 Years for the Rohingya Refugees in Bangladesh: Past, Present and Future* (No place: Médecins Sans Frontières-Holland, 2002). Human Rights Watch, *Perilous Plight: Burma's Rohingya Take to the Seas* (New York, NY: Human Rights Watch, 2009).
161. Women's League of Burma, *Women in and from Conflict Areas of Burma* (No place: Women's League of Burma, 2000). Shan Human Rights Foundation and Shan Women's Action Network, *License to Rape: The Burmese Military Regime's Use of Sexual Violence in the Ongoing War in Shan State* (Chiang Mai: Shan Human Rights Foundation and Shan Women's Action Network, 2002). Karen Women's Organization, *Shattering Silences: Karen Women Speak Out about the Burmese Military Regime's Use of Rape as a Strategy of War in Karen State* (Mae Sariang: Karen Women's Organization, 2004). Karen Human Rights Group, *Dignity in the Shadow of Oppression: The Abuse and Agency of Karen Women under Militarisation* (No place: Karen Human Rights Group, 2006). Karen Women's Organisation, *State of Terror: The Ongoing Rape, Murder, Torture and Forced Labour Suffered by Women Living under the Burmese Military Regime in Karen State* (Mae Sariang, Karen Women's Organisation, 2007). Women's League of Chinland, *Unsafe State: State-sanctioned Sexual Violence against Chin Women in Burma* (No place: Women's League of Chinland, 2007). Women's League of Burma, *In the Shadow of the Junta: CEDAW Shadow Report* (Chiang Mai: Women of Burma, 2008). Karen Women Organization, *Walking amongst Sharp Knives: The Unsung Courage of Karen Women Village Chiefs in Conflict Areas of Eastern Burma* (Mae Sariang: Karen Women Organization, 2010).
162. Exhaustive human rights yearbooks, eventually running to more than 1,000 pages, were also released by the National Coalition Government of the Union of Burma. www.ncgub.net.
163. Benedict Rogers, *A Land without Evil: Stopping the Genocide of Burma's Karen People* (Oxford: Monarch, 2004). Guy Horton, *Dying Alive: An Investigation and Legal Assessment of Human Rights Violations Inflicted in Burma, with Particular Reference to the Internally Displaced, Eastern Peoples* (Chiang Mai: Images Asia, 2005).
164. Barbara Harff, "How to Use Global Risk Assessments to Anticipate and Prevent Genocide," *Politorbis* 47:2 (2009), 71–8, p.76. Yozo Yokota, "Challenge impunity in Myanmar," *Jakarta Post*, July 7, 2010.
165. Turnell, et al., "Burma's Economy 2009," p.638. Turnell, "Finding Dollars and Sense," p.22.
166. Fink, *Living Silence in Burma*, pp.196–200.
167. Turnell, et al, "Burma's Economy 2009," p.638. World Health Organization, *The World Health Report 2000: Health Systems: Improving Performance* (Geneva: World Health Organization, 2000).

168. In May 2008, Hlaing Aung was allowed to publish this opinion in *The New Light of Myanmar*: "In the early monsoon, large edible frogs are abundant. The people of the Ayeyarwady Division can survive with self-reliant efforts even if they are not given chocolate bars from [the] international community." Hlaing Aung, "Storm-hit areas will have been regenerated with thriving trees and crop plantations by next year," *New Light of Myanmar*, May 30, 2008, p.10. Cited in Human Rights Watch, *"I Want to Help My Own People,"* p.43.
169. Reporters Without Borders, *Press Freedom Index 2010* (No place: Reporters Without Borders, 2010).
170. Transparency International, *Corruption Perceptions Index 2010* (Berlin: Transparency International, 2010).
171. Institute for Economics and Peace, *Global Peace Index: 2010 Methodology, Results and Findings* (Sydney: Institute for Economics and Peace, 2010).
172. The Fund for Peace, *Failed States Index 2010*. www.fundforpeace.org/web/index.php?option=com_content&task=view&id=452&Itemid=908.
173. Freedom House, *Freedom in the World 2011: The Authoritarian Challenge to Democracy* (Washington, DC: Freedom House, 2011).
174. The Political Instability Task Force at George Mason University acts as a hub for several projects, all of which can be accessed through the main portal. http://global-policy.gmu.edu.
175. Anthony Ware and Matthew Clarke, "The MDGs in Myanmar: Relevant or Redundant?," *Journal of the Asia Pacific Economy* 16 (2011), forthcoming.
176. Duffield, "On the Edge of 'No Man's Land'."
177. Callahan, "Myanmar's Perpetual Junta," p.44.
178. Victor, *The Lady*. Wintle, *Perfect Hostage*.
179. Callahan, "Myanmar's Perpetual Junta," p.48. Robert H. Lieberman's 2011 film, *They Call it Myanmar: Lifting the Curtain*, presents striking images and voices from inside the country at the end of the junta period.
180. N. Ganesan, "Myanmar's Foreign Relations: Reaching out to the World," in Kyaw Yin Hlaing, Robert H. Taylor and Tin Maung Maung Than (eds), *Myanmar: Beyond Politics to Societal Imperatives* (Singapore: ISEAS Publications, 2005), 30–55.
181. Selth, "Burma's 'Saffron Revolution' and the Limits of International Influence," p.291.
182. US concern is visible in a 2009 cable sent by Larry M. Dinger, US chargé d'affaires in Yangon. US Department of State, "Burma: another conversation about Burma-DPRK," November 10, 2009. WikiLeaks US Embassy Cables, ref. 09RANGOON732. For a skeptical view, see Andrew Selth, "Burma and North Korea: Conventional Allies or Nuclear Partners?," *Australian Journal of International Affairs* 64:2 (2010), 145–65.
183. Maggie Lemere and Zoë West (eds), *Nowhere to Be Home: Narratives from Survivors of Burma's Military Regime* (San Francisco, CA: McSweeney's, 2011).
184. Selth, "Burma's 'Saffron Revolution' and the Limits of International Influence," p.283.

185. R. H. Taylor, "Political Values and Political Conflict in Burma," in Robert I. Rotberg, ed., *Burma: Prospects for a Democratic Future* (Washington, DC: Brookings Institution Press, 1998), 33–48. David I. Steinberg, "'Legitimacy' in Burma/Myanmar: Concepts and Implications," in N. Ganesan and Kyaw Yin Hlaing, eds, *Myanmar: State, Society and Ethnicity* (Singapore and Hiroshima: Institute of Southeast Asian Studies and Hiroshima Peace Institute, 2007), 109–42. McCarthy, "Overturning the Alms Bowl."
186. Kevin Bales, *Disposable People: New Slavery in the Global Economy* (Berkeley, CA: University of California Press, 1999).
187. Callahan, "Myanmar's Perpetual Junta."
188. Duffield, "On the Edge of 'No Man's Land'."

Chapter 4

1. Associates to Develop Democratic Burma, *Burma Alert* 10:3 (October 1992), 3–4.
2. Mary P. Callahan, "Burma in 1995: Looking Beyond the Release of Aung San Suu Kyi," *Asian Survey* 36:2 (1996), 158–64, p.160.
3. Tin Maung Maung Than, *State Dominance in Myanmar: The Political Economy of Industrialization* (Singapore: Institute of Southeast Asian Studies, 2007), p.343.
4. Human Rights Watch, *Burma: Events of 2008* (New York, NY: Human Rights Watch, no date).
5. Myanmar Ministry of Information, *Constitution of the Republic of the Union of Myanmar (2008)* (No place: Myanmar Ministry of Information, 2008), Article 441.
6. Article 50 prescribes Nay Pyi Taw as Union territory under direct administration of the President. Article 56 creates six self-administered areas for named ethnic groups: Naga, Danu, Pa-O, Pa Laung, Kokang, and Wa. Myanmar Ministry of Information, *Constitution of the Republic of the Union of Myanmar.*
7. Susanne Prager Nyein, "Expanding Military, Shrinking Citizenry and the New Constitution in Burma," *Journal of Contemporary Asia* 39:4 (2009), 638–48.
8. Transnational Institute and Burma Centrum Nederland, *Burma's 2010 Elections: Challenges and Opportunities* (Amsterdam: Transnational Institute and Burma Centrum Nederland, 2010).
9. Myanmar State Peace and Development Council, *Political Parties Registration Law*, SPDC Law No. 2/2010, para.10e. March 8, 2010.
10. Richard Horsey, "Preliminary Analysis of Myanmar's 2010 Electoral Laws," Conflict Prevention and Peace Forum Briefing Paper, March 31, 2010. Amnesty International, *Myanmar's 2010 Elections: A Human Rights Perspective*, ASA 16/007/2010 (London: Amnesty International, 2010).
11. Aung Zaw, "Suu Kyi gives Than Shwe a smart sidekick," *Irrawaddy*, March 25, 2010. *Irrawaddy*, "NLD says 'No' to election," March 29, 2010.
12. BBC News, "Burma upholds dissolution of Suu Kyi's NLD party," January 28, 2011. www.bbc.co.uk/news/world-asia-pacific-12307838.

13. Centre for Peace and Conflict Studies, *Listening to Voices from Inside: People's Perspectives on Myanmar's 2010 Election* (Phnom Penh: Centre for Peace and Conflict Studies, 2010).
14. Richard Horsey, "Myanmar: A Pre-election Primer," Conflict Prevention and Peace Forum Briefing Paper, October 18, 2010, pp.1–2.
15. Official population estimates (in millions) are: Shan State 4.75; Rakhine State 2.71; Mon State 2.43; Kayin State 1.45; Kachin State 1.25; Chin State 0.47; Kayah State 0.26. Myanmar Ministry of Hotels and Tourism, "The eight major national ethnic races in Myanmar." www.myanmar.gov.mm/ministry/hotel/fact/race.htm.
16. Richard Horsey, "Countdown to the Myanmar Elections," Conflict Prevention and Peace Forum Briefing Paper, August 25, 2010, Appendices 2, 3.
17. Horsey, "Countdown to the Myanmar Elections," p.3.
18. Transnational Institute and Burma Centrum Nederland, *Burma in 2010: A Critical Year in Ethnic Politics* (Amsterdam: Transnational Institute and Burma Centrum Nederland, 2010).
19. Horsey, "Myanmar: A Pre-election Primer," pp.3–4.
20. Transnational Institute and Burma Centrum Nederland, *Unlevel Playing Field: Burma's Election Landscape* (Amsterdam: Transnational Institute and Burma Centrum Nederland, 2010), p.4.
21. Network for Democracy and Development, *Burma: A Violent Past to a Brutal Future: The Transformation of a Paramilitary Organization into a Political Party* (No place: Network for Democracy and Development, 2010).
22. Horsey, "Myanmar: A Pre-election Primer," p.8.
23. Horsey, "Myanmar: A Pre-election Primer," p.2.
24. Transnational Institute and Burma Centrum Nederland, *Unlevel Playing Field*, p.4.
25. Horsey, "Countdown to the Myanmar Elections," p.6.
26. Horsey, "Countdown to the Myanmar Elections," p.7.
27. Assistance Association for Political Prisoners (Burma), *Silencing Dissent: The Ongoing Imprisonment of Burma's Political Activists in the Lead Up to the 2010 Elections* (Mae Sot: Assistance Association for Political Prisoners (Burma), 2010).
28. International Crisis Group, *Myanmar's Post-election Landscape* (Jakarta/Brussels: International Crisis Group, 2011), Appendix B.
29. Transnational Institute and Burma Centrum Nederland, *A Changing Ethnic Landscape: Analysis of Burma's 2010 Polls* (Amsterdam: Transnational Institute and Burma Centrum Nederland, 2010).
30. Derek Tonkin, "Myanmar after the elections," *Burmese Perspectives*, December 18, 2010, p.4. http://www.networkmyanmar.org/images/stories/PDF6/bp181210.pdf.
31. Thomas Fuller, "Parliament picks insider as president of Myanmar," *International Herald Tribune*, February 4, 2011.
32. *Irrawaddy*, "Misreading Burma's crisis," March 18, 2011.
33. International Crisis Group, *Myanmar's Post-election Landscape*, pp.5–8.
34. Kyaw Kyaw, "Burma's parliamentary system explained," *New Mandala*, April 1, 2011. http://asiapacific.anu.edu.au/newmandala/2011/04/01/burmas-parliamentary-system-explained.

35. *Irrawaddy*, "Misreading Burma's crisis."
36. W. B. Gallie, "Essentially Contested Concepts," *Proceedings of the Aristotelian Society* 56 (1955–56), 167–98.
37. David Held, *Models of Democracy*, 3rd ed. (Cambridge: Polity, 2006).
38. Joseph A. Schumpeter, *Capitalism, Socialism and Democracy* (London: Routledge, 1992).
39. Human Rights Watch, *"I Want to Help My Own People": State Control and Civil Society in Burma after Cyclone Nargis* (New York, NY: Human Rights Watch, 2010), p.58, n.130.
40. David Collier and Steven Levitsky, "Democracy with Adjectives: Conceptual Innovation in Comparative Research," *World Politics* 49:3 (1997), 430–51.
41. Enrique Krause, *Por una democracia sin adjetivos* (Mexico City: Joaquín Mortiz & Planeta, 1986).
42. Roman David and Ian Holliday, "International Sanctions or International Justice? Shaping Political Development in Myanmar," *Australian Journal of International Affairs* (2011), forthcoming.
43. Sheri Berman, "How Democracies Emerge: Lessons from Europe," *Journal of Democracy* 18:1 (January 2007), 28–41, p.28.
44. Seymour Martin Lipset, *Political Man: The Social Bases of Politics* (London: Heinemann, 1960). Gabriel A. Almond and Sidney Verba, *The Civic Culture: Political Attitudes and Democracy in Five Nations* (Princeton, NJ: Princeton University Press, 1963). Robert A. Dahl, *Polyarchy: Participation and Opposition* (New Haven, CT: Yale University Press, 1971).
45. Samuel P. Huntington, *The Third Wave: Democratization in the Late Twentieth Century* (Norman, OK: University of Oklahoma Press, 1991).
46. Francis Fukuyama, *The End of History and the Last Man* (New York, NY: Free Press, 1992).
47. The thesis was originally cast as liberal peace theory. See Michael W. Doyle, "Kant, Liberal Legacies, and Foreign Affairs," *Philosophy and Public Affairs* 12:3 (1983), 205–35.
48. Edward D. Mansfield and Jack Snyder, "Democratization and the Danger of War," *International Security* 20:1 (Summer 1995), 5–38. Edward D. Mansfield and Jack Snyder, "Democratization and War," *Foreign Affairs* 74:3 (1995), 79–97. Jack L. Snyder, *From Voting to Violence: Democratization and Nationalist Conflict* (New York, NY: Norton, 2000). Amy Chua, *World on Fire: How Exporting Free Market Democracy Breeds Ethnic Hatred and Global Instability* (New York, NY: Doubleday, 2003). Fareed Zakaria, *The Future of Freedom: Illiberal Democracy at Home and Abroad* (New York, NY: W. W. Norton & Company, 2003). Edward D. Mansfield and Jack Snyder, *Electing to Fight: Why Emerging Democracies Go to War* (Cambridge, MA: MIT Press, 2005).
49. Mansfield and Snyder, *Electing to Fight*, pp.18–19.
50. Seymour Martin Lipset, "Some Social Requisites of Democracy: Economic Development and Political Legitimacy," *American Political Science Review* 53:1 (1959), 69–105.

51. Barrington Moore, Jr., *Social Origins of Dictatorship and Democracy: Lord and Peasant in the Making of the Modern World* (Boston, MA: Beacon Press, 1966), p.418.
52. Dietrich Rueschemeyer, Evelyne Huber Stephens and John D. Stephens, *Capitalist Development and Democracy* (Chicago, IL: University of Chicago Press, 1992).
53. Adam Przeworski, Michael E. Alvarez, José Antonio Cheibub and Fernando Limongi, *Democracy and Development: Political Institutions and Well-Being in the World, 1950–1990* (Cambridge: Cambridge University Press, 2000).
54. Carles Boix and Susan Carol Stokes, "Endogenous Democratization," *World Politics* 55:4 (2003), 517–49.
55. Ronald Inglehart and Christian Welzel, *Modernization, Cultural Change, and Democracy: The Human Development Sequence* (New York, NY: Cambridge University Press, 2005).
56. Almond and Verba, *The Civic Culture.*
57. Robert D. Putnam with Robert Leonardi and Raffaella Y. Nonetti, *Making Democracy Work: Civic Traditions in Modern Italy* (Princeton, NJ: Princeton University Press, 1993), pp.183, 185.
58. Robert D. Putnam, *Bowling Alone: The Collapse and Revival of American Community* (New York, NY: Simon & Schuster, 2000).
59. Mansfield and Snyder, *Electing to Fight*, p.2.
60. Dahl, *Polyarchy.*
61. Mansfield and Snyder, *Electing to Fight*, pp.17–18.
62. Ian Holliday, "Voting and Violence in Myanmar: Nation Building for a Transition to Democracy," *Asian Survey* 48:6 (2008), 1038–58.
63. Mansfield and Snyder, *Electing to Fight*, p.266.
64. Carol Skalnik Leff, "Democratization and Disintegration in Multinational States: The Breakup of the Communist Federations," *World Politics* 51:2 (1999), 205–35.
65. Andrew Reynolds, Alfred Stepan, Zaw Oo and Stephen Levine, "How Burma Could Democratize," *Journal of Democracy* 12:4 (October 2001), 95–108.
66. Ashley South, *Burma's Longest War: Anatomy of the Karen Conflict* (Amsterdam: Transnational Institute and Burma Center Netherlands, 2011), p.47.
67. Kristin M. Bakke and Erik Wibbels, "Diversity, Disparity, and Civil Conflict in Federal States," *World Politics* 59:1 (2006), 1–50. Gerald Schneider and Nina Wiesehomeier, "Rules that Matter: Political Institutions and the Diversity-Conflict Nexus," *Journal of Peace Research* 45:2 (2008), 183–203.
68. Hale E. Henry, "Divided We Stand: Institutional Sources of Ethnofederal State Survival and Collapse," *World Politics* 56:2 (2004), 165–93.
69. Benjamin B. Smith, "Life of the Party: The Origins of Regime Breakdown and Persistence under Single-party Rule," *World Politics* 57:3 (2005), 421–51.
70. Guillermo O'Donnell and Philippe C. Schmitter, *Transitions from Authoritarian Rule: Tentative Conclusions about Uncertain Democracies* (Baltimore, MD: Johns Hopkins University Press, 1986), p.21.
71. O'Donnell and Schmitter, *Transitions from Authoritarian Rule*, p.38.
72. O'Donnell and Schmitter, *Transitions from Authoritarian Rule*, p.59.
73. O'Donnell and Schmitter, *Transitions from Authoritarian Rule*, pp.3, 62.

74. Michael McFaul, "The Fourth Wave of Democracy and Dictatorship: Noncooperative Transitions in the Postcommunist World," *World Politics* 54:2 (2002), 212–44.
75. Valerie Bunce, "Rethinking Recent Democratization: Lessons from the Postcommunist Experience," *World Politics* 55:2 (2003), 167–92.
76. McFaul, "The Fourth Wave of Democracy and Dictatorship."
77. Kyaw Yin Hlaing, "Setting the Rules for Survival: Why the Burmese Military Regime Survives in an Age of Democratization," *Pacific Review* 22:3 (2009), 271–91. Mary Callahan, "The Endurance of Military Rule in Burma: Not Why, but Why Not?," in in Susan L. Levenstein, ed., *Finding Dollars, Sense, and Legitimacy in Burma* (Washington, DC: Woodrow Wilson International Center for Scholars, 2010), 54–76.
78. Mark Duffield, "On the Edge of 'No Man's Land': Chronic Emergency in Myanmar," School of Sociology, Politics, and International Studies, University of Bristol Working Paper No. 01–08. www.bristol.ac.uk/spais/research/workingpapers/wpspaisfiles/duffield0108.pdf.
79. Ashley South, "Political Transition in Myanmar: A New Model for Democratization," *Contemporary Southeast Asia* 26:2 (2004), 233–55. Duffield, "On the Edge of 'No Man's Land'." Centre for Peace and Conflict Studies, *Listening to Voices from Inside: Myanmar Civil Society's Response to Cyclone Nargis* (Phnom Penh: Centre for Peace and Conflict Studies, 2009). CDA Collaborative Learning Projects, *Listening Project: Field Visit Report: Myanmar/Burma* (No place: CDA, 2009). Callahan, "The Endurance of Military Rule in Burma." Centre for Peace and Conflict Studies, *Listening to Voices from Inside: Ethnic People Speak* (Phnom Penh: Centre for Peace and Conflict Studies, 2010).
80. Zaw Oo and Win Min, *Assessing Burma's Ceasefire Accords* (Washington, DC: East-West Center Washington, 2007).
81. Wai Moe, "One blood, one voice, one command," *Irrawaddy*, June 27, 2008.
82. Maung Zarni, "An Inside View of Reconciliation," in Lex Rieffel (ed.), *Myanmar/Burma: Inside Challenges, Outside Interests* (Washington, DC: Konrad Adenauer Foundation/Brookings Institution Press, 2010), 52–76.
83. Aung San Suu Kyi, *Freedom from Fear; And Other Writings*, 2nd ed. (London: Penguin, 1995), pp.249–59. Maung Aung Myoe, "The National Reconciliation Process in Myanmar," *Contemporary Southeast Asia* 24:2 (2002), 371–84.
84. *New York Times*, """Myanmar dissident calls for change," November 14, 2010.
85. Movement for Democracy and Rights of Ethnic Nationalities, *2010 Elections: Stealing Democracy*, March 2010. http://humanrightshouse.org/Articles/13800.html.
86. "Open letter of Myanmar fraternal democratic parties to European Union regarding economic sanctions against Myanmar," March 11, 2011. www.networkmyanmar.org.
87. Centre for Peace and Conflict Studies, *Listening to Voices from Inside: Ethnic People Speak* (Phnom Penh: Centre for Peace and Conflict Studies, 2010), pp.5–6.
88. Reynolds and his colleagues hold Myanmar to be an unpromising environment for a pacted transition. Reynolds, et al, "How Burma Could Democratize," p.106.

89. Mikael Gravers (ed.), *Exploring Ethnic Diversity in Burma* (Copenhagen: NIAS Press, 2007). Ashley South, *Ethnic Politics in Burma: States of Conflict* (Abingdon: Routledge, 2008).
90. The Panglong Agreement is reproduced in Maung Maung, *Burma's Constutition*, 2nd ed. (The Hague: Martinus Nijhoff, 1961), pp.229–30.
91. Matthew J. Walton, "Ethnicity, Conflict, and History in Burma: The Myths of Panglong," *Asian Survey* 48:6 (2008), 889–910, p.889.
92. Ko Htwe, "Suu Kyi faces challenges in supporting second Panglong conference," *Irrawaddy*, November 22, 2010.
93. Aung San, February 2, 1947, cited in Walton, "Ethnicity, Conflict, and History in Burma," p.896.
94. Walton, "Ethnicity, Conflict, and History in Burma," p.901.
95. Walton, "Ethnicity, Conflict, and History in Burma," pp.903–7.
96. Walton, "Ethnicity, Conflict, and History in Burma," p.908.
97. Walton, "Ethnicity, Conflict, and History in Burma," p.910.
98. Katherine Glassmyer and Nicholas Sambanis, "Rebel-Military Integration and Civil War Termination," *Journal of Peace Research* 45:3 (2008), 365–84.
99. Martin J. Smith, *Burma: Insurgency and the Politics of Ethnicity*, 2nd ed. (London: Zed Books, 1999), pp.88–101.
100. Macartan Humphreys and Jeremy M. Weinstein, "Demobilization and Reintegration," *Journal of Conflict Resolution* 51:4 (2007), 531–67.
101. Barbara F. Walter, "Does Conflict Beget Conflict? Explaining Recurring Civil War," *Journal of Peace Research* 41:3 (2004), 371–88.
102. Paige Arthur, "How 'Transitions' Reshaped Human Rights: A Conceptual History of Transitional Justice," *Human Rights Quarterly* 31:2 (2009), 321–67.
103. Luc Huyse, "Justice after Transition: On the Choices Successor Elites Make in Dealing with the Past," *Law and Social Inquiry* 20:1 (1995), 51–78, p.52.
104. Stanley Cohen, "State Crimes of Previous Regimes: Knowledge, Accountability, and the Policing of the Past," *Law and Social Inquiry* 20:1 (1995), 7–50, pp.11–12.
105. Arthur Stinchcombe, "Lustration as a Problem of the Social Basis of Constitutionalism," *Law and Social Inquiry* 20:1 (1995), 245–73, p.246.
106. Cohen, "State Crimes of Previous Regimes," p.36.
107. Priscilla B. Hayner, *Unspeakable Truths: Facing the Challenge of Truth Commissions* (New York, NY: Routledge, 2002).
108. Roman David, "From Prague to Baghdad: Lustration Systems and Their Political Effects," *Government and Opposition* 41:2 (2006), 347–72.
109. James L. Gibson, *Overcoming Apartheid: Can Truth Reconcile a Divided Nation?* (New York, NY: Russell Sage Foundation, 2004). Audrey R. Chapman and Hugo van der Merwe (eds), *Truth and Reconciliation in South Africa: Did the TRC Deliver?* (Philadelphia, PA: University of Pennsylvania Press, 2008).
110. Robert I. Rotberg and Dennis Thompson (eds), *Truth v. Justice: The Morality of Truth Commissions* (Princeton, NJ: Princeton University Press, 2000).

111. Jean Hampton, "Forgiveness, Resentment and Hatred," in Jeffrie G. Murphy and Jean Hampton, *Forgiveness and Mercy* (Cambridge: Cambridge University Press, 1988), 35–87.
112. Jodi Halpern and Harvey M. Weinstein, "Rehumanizing the Other: Empathy and Reconciliation," *Human Rights Quarterly* 26:3 (2004), 561–83.
113. Jeremy Sarkin, "An Evaluation of the South African Amnesty Process," in Audrey R. Chapman and Hugo van der Merwe (eds), *Truth and Reconciliation in South Africa: Did the TRC Deliver?* (Philadelphia, PA: University of Pennsylvania Press, 2008), 93–115.
114. Carsten Stahn, "Accommodating Individual Criminal Responsibility and National Reconciliation: The UN Truth Commission for East Timor," *American Journal of International Law* 95 (2001), 952–66.
115. Roman David, "Lustration Laws in Action: The Motives and Evaluation of Lustration Policies in the Czech Republic and Poland (1989–2001)," *Law and Social Inquiry* 28:2 (2003), 387–439.
116. Roman David and Ian Holliday, "Set the Junta Free: Pre-transitional Justice in Myanmar's Democratization," *Australian Journal of Political Science* 41:1 (2006), 91–105.
117. Cohen, "State Crimes of Previous Regimes," p.26. Also see Roman David, "Transitional Injustice? Criteria for Conformity of Lustration to the Right to Political Expression," *Europe-Asia Studies* 56:6 (2004), 789–812. And see Yvonne Chiu, "Liberal Lustration," *Journal of Political Philosophy* 19 (2011), forthcoming.
118. Cohen, "State Crimes of Previous Regimes," p.44.
119. Maria Łoś, "Lustration and Truth Claims: Unfinished Revolutions in Central Europe," *Law and Social Inquiry* 20:1 (1995), 117–61. Tim Kelsall, "Truth, Lies, Ritual: Preliminary Reflections on the Truth and Reconciliation Commission in Sierra Leone," *Human Rights Quarterly* 27:2 (2005), 361–91. John Roosa, "How Does a Truth Commission Find Out What the Truth Is? The Case of East Timor's CAVR," *Pacific Affairs* 80:4 (2007–08), 569–80. Audrey R. Chapman and Patrick Ball, "Levels of Truth: Macro-truth and the TRC," in Audrey R. Chapman and Hugo van der Merwe (eds), *Truth and Reconciliation in South Africa: Did the TRC Deliver?* (Philadelphia, PA: University of Pennsylvania Press, 2008), 143–68.
120. Margaret Popkin and Naomi Roht-Arriaza, "Truth as Justice: Investigatory Commissions in Latin America," *Law and Social Inquiry* 20:1 (1995), 79–116.
121. Huyse, "Justice after Transition," p.78.
122. David and Holliday, "Set the Junta Free."
123. Richard Spitz with Matthew Chaskalson, *The Politics of Transition: The Hidden History of South Africa's Negotiated Settlement* (Oxford: Hart Publishing, 2000), p.31.
124. Rajeev Bhargava, "Restoring Decency to Barbaric Societies," in Robert I. Rotberg and Dennis Thompson (eds), *Truth v. Justice: The Morality of Truth Commissions* (Princeton, NJ: Princeton University Press, 2000), 45–67.
125. Amy Gutmann and Dennis Thompson, "The Moral Foundations of Truth Commissions," in Robert I. Rotberg and Dennis Thompson (eds), *Truth v. Justice:*

The Morality of Truth Commissions (Princeton, NJ: Princeton University Press, 2000), 22–44.

Chapter 5

1. Hugh Tinker, *The Union of Burma: A Study of the First Years of Independence*, 4th ed. (London: Oxford University Press, 1967), p.110.
2. William C. Johnstone, *Burma's Foreign Policy: A Study in Neutralism* (Cambridge, MA: Harvard University Press, 1963).
3. Ademola Adeleke, "The Strings of Neutralism: Burma and the Colombo Plan," *Pacific Affairs* 76:4 (2003–04), 593–610.
4. Donald M. Seekins, *Burma and Japan since 1940: From "Co-Prosperity" to "Quiet Dialogue"* (Copenhagen: Nordic Institute of Asian Studies, 2007), p.56.
5. David I. Steinberg, "Democracy, Power, and the Economy in Myanmar: Donor Dilemmas," *Asian Survey* 31:8 (1991), 729–42, p.741.
6. Chi-shad Liang, *Burma's Foreign Relations: Neutralism in Theory and Practice* (New York, NY: Praeger, 1990), pp.67–96.
7. Maureen Aung-Thwin and Thant Myint-U, "The Burmese Ways to Socialism," *Third World Quarterly* 13:1 (1992), 67–75, p.67. Also see Robert H. Taylor, "Burma's Ambiguous Breakthrough," *Journal of Democracy* 1:4 (1990), 62–72.
8. Mary Callahan, "The Endurance of Military Rule in Burma: Not Why, but Why Not?," in Susan L. Levenstein, ed., *Finding Dollars, Sense, and Legitimacy in Burma* (Washington, DC: Woodrow Wilson International Center for Scholars, 2010), 54–76.
9. John B. Haseman, "Destruction of Democracy: The Tragic Case of Burma," *Asian Affairs* 20:1 (1993), 17–26, p.17.
10. Gary Clyde Hufbauer, Jeffrey J. Schott, Kimberly Ann Elliott and Barbara Oegg, *Economic Sanctions Reconsidered*, 3rd ed. (Washington, DC: Pearson Institute for International Economics, 2007).
11. Morten B. Pedersen, *Promoting Human Rights in Burma: A Critique of Western Sanctions Policy* (Lanham, MD: Rowman and Littlefield, 2008).
12. Aung San Suu Kyi, *Freedom from Fear: And Other Writings*, rev. ed. (London: Penguin, 1995).
13. David I. Steinberg, "The United States and Myanmar: A 'Boutique Issue'?," *International Affairs* 86:1 (2010), 175–94.
14. Ashley South, *Burma's Longest War: Anatomy of the Karen Conflict* (Amsterdam: Transnational Institute and Burma Center Netherlands, 2011), p.48.
15. Michael Aung-Thwin, "Parochial Universalism, Democracy *Jihad* and the Orientalist Image of Burma: The New Evangelism," *Pacific Affairs* 74:4 (2001–02), 483–505.
16. Derek Tonkin's series of *Burmese Perspectives* convincingly makes this point. www.networkmyanmar.org.
17. David Kinley and Trevor Wilson, "Engaging a Pariah: Human Rights Training in Burma/Myanmar," *Human Rights Quarterly* 29:2 (2007), 368–402.

18. International Crisis Group, *Myanmar: New Threats to Humanitarian Aid*, Asia Briefing No.58, December 8, 2006 (Yangon/Brussels: International Crisis Group, 2006), p.3. Also see David Camroux and Renaud Egreteau, "Normative Europe Meets the Burmese Garrison State: Processes, Policies, Blockages and Future Possibilities," in Nick Cheesman, Monique Skidmore and Trevor Wilson (eds), *Ruling Myanmar: From Cyclone Nargis to National Elections* (Singapore: ISEAS Publishing, 2010), 267–93.
19. Asia Society Task Force Report, *Current Realities and Future Possibilities in Burma/ Myanmar: Options for U.S. Policy* (No place: Asia Society, 2010). Priscilla Clapp, "Prospects for Rapprochement between the United States and Myanmar," *Contemporary Southeast Asia* 32:3 (2010), 409–26. Priscilla Clapp, "Burma's Political Transition: Implications for U.S. Policy," in Nick Cheesman, Monique Skidmore and Trevor Wilson (eds), *Ruling Myanmar: From Cyclone Nargis to National Elections* (Singapore: ISEAS Publishing, 2010), 32–51.
20. European Union, "Council Decision 2011/239/CFSP of 12 April 2011 amending Decision 2010/232/CFSP renewing restrictive measures against Burma/Myanmar." *Official Journal of the European Union*, April 15, 2011, L 101/24.
21. Ian Holliday, "Beijing and the Myanmar Problem," *Pacific Review* 22:4 (2009), 479–500.
22. Woodman notes, for instance, that during imperial annexation "British policy in Upper Burma was geared to the calculations of what the Chinese would, or could do on their side." Dorothy Woodman, *The Making of Burma* (London: Cresset Press, 1962), pp.4–5. Also see pp.247–95.
23. J. K. Fairbank, "A Preliminary Framework," in J. K. Fairbank, ed., *The Chinese World Order: Traditional China's Foreign Relations* (Cambridge, MA: Harvard University Press, 1968), 1–19.
24. Johnstone, *Burma's Foreign Policy*, pp.56–7.
25. Donald M. Seekins, "Burma-China Relations: Playing with Fire," *Asian Survey* 37:6 (1997), 525–39.
26. Bertil Lintner, *The Rise and Fall of the Communist Party of Burma (CPB)* (Ithaca, NY: Cornell Southeast Asia Program, 1990).
27. International Crisis Group, *China's Myanmar Dilemma*, Asia Report No.177, September 14, 2009. Jürgen Haacke, "China's Role in the Pursuit of Security by Myanmar's State Peace and Development Council: Boon and Bane?," *Pacific Review* 23:1 (2010), 113–37.
28. Seekins, "Burma-China Relations," pp.531–3. Rosemary Foot, *Rights beyond Borders: The Global Community and the Struggle over Human Rights in China* (Oxford: Oxford University Press, 2000). Ming Wan, *Human Rights in Chinese Foreign Relations: Defining and Defending National Interests* (Philadelphia, PA: University of Pennsylvania Press, 2001). Lai-Ha Chan, Pak K. Lee and Gerald Chan, "Rethinking Global Governance: A China Model in the Making?," *Contemporary Politics* 14:1 (2008), 3–19.
29. EarthRights International, *China in Burma: The Increasing Investment of Chinese Multinational Corporations in Burma's Hydropower, Oil and Natural Gas, and Mining*

Sectors (Chiang Mai: EarthRights International, 2008). International Crisis Group, *China's Myanmar Strategy: Elections, Ethnic Politics and Economics*, Asia Briefing No.112, September 21, 2010.

30. Kachin Development Networking Group, *Damming the Irrawaddy* (No place: Kachin Development Networking Group, 2007). Kachin Development Networking Group, *Resisting the Flood: Communities Taking a Stand against the Imminent Construction of Irrawaddy Dams* (No place: Kachin Development Networking Group, 2009).
31. Bo Kong, "The Geopolitics of the Myanmar-China Oil and Gas Pipelines," in Edward Chow, Leigh E. Hendrix, Mikkal E. Herberg, Shoichi Itoh, Bo Kong, Marie Lall and Paul Stevens, *Pipeline Politics in Asia: The Intersection of Demand, Energy Markets, and Supply Routes* (Seattle, WA: National Bureau of Asian Research, 2010), 55–65, pp.57, 64.
32. Global Witness, *A Conflict of Interests: The Uncertain Future of Burma's Forests* (London: Global Witness, 2003). Global Witness, *A Choice for China: Ending the Destruction of Burma's Northern Frontier Forests* (London: Global Witness, 2005). Global Witness, *A Disharmonious Trade: China and the Continued Destruction of Burma's Northern Frontier Forests* (London: Global Witness, 2009).
33. EarthRights International, *China in Burma: The Increasing Investment of Chinese Multinational Corporations in Burma's Hydropower, Oil and Natural Gas, and Mining Sectors* (Chiang Mai: EarthRights International, 2008).
34. International Crisis Group, *China's Myanmar Dilemma*, pp.25–6. International Crisis Group, *China's Myanmar Strategy*, pp.14–15. Centre for Peace and Conflict Studies, *Listening to Voices from Inside: Ethnic People Speak* (Phnom Penh: Centre for Peace and Conflict Studies, 2010), pp.57–8.
35. David Bachman, "Domestic Sources of Chinese Foreign Policy after Deng," in Shalendra D. Sharma, ed., *The Asia-Pacific in the New Millennium: Geopolitics, Security, and Foreign Policy* (Berkeley, CA: Institute of East Asian Studies, University of California, Berkeley, 2000), 33–51, p.49.
36. Nicholas R. Lardy, "The Role of Foreign Trade and Investment in China's Economic Transformation," *China Quarterly* 143 (1995), 1065–82. S. Gordon Redding, *The Spirit of Chinese Capitalism* (Berlin: De Gruyter, 1990).
37. Ruben Gonzalez-Vicente, "China's Engagement in South America and Africa's Extractive Sectors: New Perspectives for Resource Curse Theories," *Pacific Review* 24:1 (2011), 65–87.
38. Eunsuk Hong and Laixiang Sun, "Dynamics of Internationalization and Outward Investment: Chinese Corporations' Strategies," *China Quarterly* 187 (2006), 610–34.
39. International Crisis Group, *China's Myanmar Dilemma*.
40. Holliday, "Beijing and the Myanmar Problem."
41. Renaud Egreteau, *Wooing the Generals: India's New Burma Policy* (New Delhi Authors Press, 2003).
42. Pavin Chachavalpongpun, *A Plastic Nation: The Curse of Thainess in Thai-Burmese Relations* (New York, NY: University Press of America, 2005).
43. Egreteau, *Wooing the Generals: India's New Burma Policy* (New Delhi: Authors Press, 2003).

44. John Bray, *Burma: The Politics of Constructive Engagement* (London: Royal Institute of International Affairs, 1995).
45. Jürgen Haacke, *Myanmar's Foreign Policy: Domestic Influences and International Implications* (Abingdon: Routledge, 2006), pp.41–60.
46. Lee Jones, "ASEAN's Albatross: ASEAN's Burma Policy, from Constructive Engagement to Critical Disengagement," *Asian Security* 4:3 (2008), 271–93.
47. Jürgen Haacke, "ASEAN and Political Change in Myanmar: Towards a Regional Initiative?," *Contemporary Southeast Asia* 30:3 (2008), 351–78.
48. Christopher Roberts, *ASEAN's Myanmar Crisis: Challenges to the Pursuit of a Security Community* (Singapore: Institute of Southeast Asian Studies, 2009). Jürgen Haacke, "The Myanmar Imbroglio and ASEAN: Heading Towards the 2010 Elections," *International Affairs* 86:1 (2010), 153–74.
49. Julio Santiago Amador III, "Community Building at the Time of Nargis: The ASEAN Response," *Journal of Current Southeast Asian Affairs* 28:4 (2009), 3–22. Jürgen Haacke, "Myanmar, the Responsibility to Protect, and the Need for Practical Assistance," *Global Responsibility to Protect* 1:2 (2009), 156–84.
50. Pavin Chachavalpongpun and Moe Thuzar, *Myanmar: Life after Nargis* (Singapore: ISEAS Publishing, 2009). ASEAN Secretariat, *A Humanitarian Call: The ASEAN Response to Cyclone Nargis* (Jakarta: ASEAN Secretariat, 2010).
51. Kazuo Tamayama and John Nunneley, *Tales by Japanese Soldiers: Of the Burma Campaign 1942–1945* (London: Cassell, 2000).
52. Michio Takeyama, *Harp of Burma* (Rutland, VT: Tuttle, 1966). Seekins, *Burma and Japan since 1940*, pp.47–51.
53. Seekins, *Burma and Japan since 1940*, p.59. Also see Patrick Strefford, "How Japan's Postwar Relationship with Burma was Shaped by Aid," *Asian Affairs* 41:1 (2010), 35–45.
54. Mikio Oishi and Fumitaka Furuoka, "Can Japanese Aid Be an Effective Tool of Influence? Case Studies of Cambodia and Burma," *Asian Survey* 43:6 (2003), 890–907, p.898.
55. David I. Steinberg, "Japanese Economic Assistance to Burma: Aid in the *Tarenagashi* Manner?," in Bruce M. Koppel and Robert M. Orr, Jr. eds, *Japan's Foreign Aid: Power and Policy in a New Era* (Boulder, CO: Westview, 1993), 135–62.
56. Seekins, *Burma and Japan since 1940*, pp.94–7.
57. Oishi and Furuoka, "Can Japanese Aid Be an Effective Tool of Influence?," p.899.
58. Seekins, *Burma and Japan since 1940*, pp.88–148.
59. Steinberg, "Japanese Economic Assistance to Burma," p.158.
60. Haacke, *Myanmar's Foreign Policy*, pp.83–95.
61. Tomás Ojea Quintana, "Human Rights Situations that Require the Council's Attention: Progress Report of the Special Rapporteur on the Situation of Human Rights in Myanmar," Human Rights Council, Thirteenth Session, March 10, 2010. A/HRC/13/48.
62. Australian Council for Overseas Aid, *Axe-handles or Willing Minions? International NGOs in Burma*, December 1997. Note ii lists the INGOs that went into Myanmar in the mid-1990s. www.ibiblio.org/obl/docs3/purcellpaper.htm.

63. 3DF is successor to the Global Fund for AIDS, Tuberculosis and Malaria, which withdrew from Myanmar in August 2005 following political pressure from activist groups and the US Congress. International Crisis Group, *Myanmar*, p.4.
64. International Crisis Group, *Myanmar*, p.4.
65. Karl Dorning, "Creating an Environment for Participation: International NGOs and the Growth of Civil Society in Burma/Myanmar," in Trevor Wilson, ed., *Myanmar's Long Road to National Reconciliation* (Singapore: Institute of Southeast Asian Studies, 2006), 188–217, pp.197–9.
66. UNOPS, *Myanmar Operations Centre (MMOC)*. www.unops.org/english/whatwedo/locations/asiapacific/myanmar-operations-centre/pages/myanmaroperationscentre.aspx.
67. The figures come from Myanmar Information Management Unit, and are cited by the Three Diseases Fund. www.3dfund.org/index.php?option=com_content&view=article&id=4&Itemid=54.
68. Alex de Waal, *Famine Crimes: Politics and the Disaster Relief Industry in Africa* (Bloomington, IN: Indiana University Press, 1997), p.1.
69. Sadako Ogata, *The Turbulent Decade: Confronting the Refugee Crises of the 1990s* (New York, NY: W. W. Norton and Company, 2005), p.25.
70. David P. Forsythe, *The Humanitarians: The International Committee of the Red Cross* (Cambridge: Cambridge University Press, 2005), p.171.
71. For a case study, see Save the Children in Myanmar, *Disaster Preparedness Program*, May 2009. www.hapinternational.org/pool/files/save-children-in-myanmar-disaster-preparedness-program-case-study-may-2009.pdf.
72. Back Pack Health Worker Team, *Chronic Emergency: Health and Human Rights in Eastern Burma* (No place: Back Pack Health Worker Team, 2006). Support for this work linking public health and human rights comes from a team at Johns Hopkins Bloomberg School of Public Health. An emblematic Mobile Obstetric Maternal Health Workers Project, or MOM Project, focuses on training maternal health-care workers in ethnic nationality areas. Cathy Shufro, "Borderline Health," *Johns Hopkins Public Health*, Fall 2008. http://jhsphmag.nts.jhu.edu/2008/Fall/features/borderline_health/.
73. Some outside agencies support local NGOs. Others such as HOPE International Development Agency have their own Myanmar offices. Still others such as the Centre for Peace and Conflict Studies in Phnom Penh operate across borders to promote conflict resolution inside Myanmar.
74. David Allan, "Positive Engagement in Myanmar: Some Current Examples and Thoughts for the Future," in Nick Cheesman, Monique Skidmore and Trevor Wilson (eds), *Ruling Myanmar: From Cyclone Nargis to National Elections* (Singapore: ISEAS Publishing, 2010), 236–66. Also see Trevor Wilson, "The Use of Normative Processes in Achieving Behaviour Change in Myanmar," in Nick Cheesman, Monique Skidmore and Trevor Wilson (eds), *Ruling Myanmar: From Cyclone Nargis to National Elections* (Singapore: ISEAS Publishing, 2010), 294–318.
75. Asia Society, *Current Realities and Future Possibilities in Burma/Myanmar: Perspectives from Asia* (No place: Asia Society, 2010).

76. DLA Piper Rudnick Gray Cary, *Threat to the Peace: A Call for the UN Security Council to Act in Burma* (Washington, DC: DLA Piper Rudnick Gray Cary, 2005).
77. International Crisis Group, *Myanmar's Post-election Landscape* (Jakarta/Brussels: International Crisis Group, 2011), p.3.
78. Asia Society Task Force Report, *Current Realities and Future Possibilities in Burma/ Myanmar.*
79. International Crisis Group, *China's Myanmar Dilemma.*
80. Renaud Egreteau, "India's Ambitions in Burma: More Frustration than Success?," *Asian Survey* 48:6 (2008), 936–57.
81. Stephen McCarthy, "Burma and ASEAN: Estranged Bedfellows," *Asian Survey* 48:6 (2008), 911–35.
82. Kyaw Yin Hlaing, "ASEAN's Pariah: Insecurity and Autocracy in Myanmar (Burma), in Donald K. Emmerson (ed.), *Hard Choices: Security, Democracy, and Regionalism in Southeast Asia* (Singapore: Institute of Southeast Asian Studies, 2009), 151–89.
83. Centre for Peace and Conflict Studies, *Listening to Voices from Inside: Myanmar Civil Society's Response to Cyclone Nargis* (Phnom Penh: Centre for Peace and Conflict Studies, 2009).
84. On the broad, critical issue of China's behavior as both a target and a sender of economic sanctions, see Tong Zhao, "Sanction Experience and Sanction Behavior: An Analysis of Chinese Perception and Behavior on Economic Sanctions," *Contemporary Politics* 16:3 (2010), 263–78.
85. In December 2009, a US diplomat reported the opinion of a UK counterpart: "the very robust domestic UK lobby on Burma hamstrings much of what the Foreign Office can do because it presses UK politicians very forcefully to maintain a strong, hard-edged line on Burma." US Department of State, "Burma: UK offers insight into EU position, thoughts on USG policy review," December 10, 2009. WikiLeaks US Embassy Cables, ref. 09LONDON2761.
86. Pedersen, *Promoting Human Rights in Burma.* On its website the State Department provides a full, though sometimes outdated, policy overview. US Department of State, *Background Note: Burma.* www.state.gov/r/pa/ei/bgn/35910.htm.
87. John F. Cady, *The United States and Burma* (Cambridge, MA: Harvard University Press, 1976), pp.17–18.
88. Matheo Falco, *Burma: Time for Change: Report of an Independent Task Force Sponsored by the Council on Foreign Relations* (Washington, DC: Council on Foreign Relations, 2003), pp.23–4.
89. Asia Society Task Force Report, *Current Realities and Future Possibilities in Burma/ Myanmar*, pp.61–2.
90. William J. Clinton, *Executive Order 13047 – Prohibiting New Investment in Burma.* May 20, 1997. *Federal Register*, 62:99, May 22, 1997.
91. *Burmese Freedom and Democracy Act of 2003*, US Public Law 108–61, July 28, 2003. George W. Bush, *Executive Order 13310 – Blocking Property of the Government of Burma and Prohibiting Certain Transactions.* July 28, 2003. *Federal Register*, 68:146, July, 30, 2003.

92. George W. Bush, *Executive Order 13448 – Blocking Property and Prohibiting Certain Transactions Related to Burma.* October 18, 2007. *Federal Register*, 72:204, October 23, 2007. George W. Bush, *Executive Order 13464 – Blocking Property and Prohibiting Certain Transactions Related to Burma.* April 30, 2008. *Federal Register*, 73:86, May 2, 2008.
93. *Tom Lantos Block Burmese Jade (Junta's Anti-Democratic Efforts) Act of 2008.* US Public Law 110–286, July 29, 2008.
94. Asia Society Task Force Report, *Current Realities and Future Possibilities in Burma/Myanmar.* Clapp, "Burma's Political Transition."
95. In 2007, Mitchell co-authored an article casting Myanmar as "Asia's forgotten crisis." Michael Green and Derek Mitchell, "Asia's Forgotten Crisis," *Foreign Affairs* 86:6 (2007), 147–58.
96. Roman David and Ian Holliday, "International Sanctions or International Justice? Shaping Political Development in Myanmar," *Australian Journal of International Affairs* (2011), forthcoming.
97. Human Rights Watch, "US: Act Now on Burma Commission of Inquiry," October 29, 2010. www.hrw.org/en/news/2010/10/29/us-act-now-burma-commission-inquiry.
98. Burma Campaign UK, "Burma Briefing: Support for a UN Commission of Inquiry," January 2011. http://burmacampaign.org.uk/images/uploads/7-support-for-un-commission-of-inquiry.pdf.
99. International Human Rights Clinic at Harvard Law School, *Crimes in Burma* (Cambridge, MA: International Human Rights Clinic at Harvard Law School, 2009).
100. These were Yokota's words: "During my period as UN special rapporteur on human rights in Myanmar, I received incontrovertible evidence that forced labor, the forcible conscription of child soldiers, torture and rape as a weapon of war are widespread and systematic in Myanmar." Yozo Yokota, "Challenge impunity in Myanmar," *Jakarta Post*, July 7, 2010.
101. Amnesty International, "No international compromise on human rights in Myanmar," March 12, 2011. www.amnesty.org.au/news/comments/25066.
102. Government of Canada, *Special Economic Measures (Burma) Regulations*, SOR/2007–285, December 13, 2007.
103. EUR-Lex 96/635/CFSP, *Common Position on Burma/Myanmar*, October 28, 1996.
104. European Union, "Council Decision 2011/239/CFSP."
105. Asia Society, *Current Realities and Future Possibilities in Burma/Myanmar: Perspectives from Asia* (No place: Asia Society, 2010), pp.9–23.
106. International Crisis Group, *Myanmar's Post-election Landscape* (Jakarta/Brussels: International Crisis Group, 2011), p.10.
107. Mark Duffield, "On the Edge of 'No Man's Land': Chronic Emergency in Myanmar," School of Sociology, Politics, and International Studies, University of Bristol Working Paper No. 01–08, p.17. www.bristol.ac.uk/spais/research/workingpapers/wpspais-files/duffield0108.pdf.
108. International Labour Organization, *Forced Labour in Myanmar (Burma)* (Geneva: International Labour Organization, 1998).

109. Asia Society Task Force Report, *Current Realities and Future Possibilities in Burma/Myanmar*, p.32.
110. Susan Banki, "Contested Regimes, Aid Flows, and Refugee Flows: The Case of Burma," *Journal of Current Southeast Asian Affairs* 28:2 (2009), 47–73, pp.52–5.
111. International Crisis Group, *Burma/Myanmar after Nargis: Time to Normalize Aid Relations* (Yangon/Brussels, International Crisis Group, 2008), p.15, n.68.
112. OECD, *Development Aid at a Glance 2011: Statistics by Region*. www.oecd.org/dac/stats/regioncharts.
113. Seekins, "Burma-China Relations," p.531.
114. Simon Roughneen, "Burma sanctions debate intensifies," *Irrawaddy*, March 9, 2011.
115. Stephen McCarthy, "Ten Years of Chaos in Burma: Foreign Investment and Economic Liberalization under the SLORC-SPDC, 1988 to 1998," *Pacific Affairs* 73:2 (2000), 233–62.
116. John R. Schermerhorn, "Foreign Investment in Burma: Contrasting Perspectives," *Asian Case Research Journal* 2 (1998), 117–32, pp.121–2.
117. H. C. Matthew Sim, *Myanmar on My Mind: A Guide to Living and Doing Business in Myanmar* (Singapore: Times Books International, 2001).
118. The Global Unions website archives letters sent to each company believed to have business links with Myanmar, together with any replies received. Occasionally companies respond by making a principled case for corporate engagement. www.global-unions.org/burma.
119. Ian Holliday, "Doing Business with Rights Violating Regimes: Corporate Social Responsibility and Myanmar's Military Junta," *Journal of Business Ethics* 61:4 (2005), 329–42.
120. National League for Democracy, "Economic analysis and vision of the NLD," January 4, 2011. National League for Democracy, "Sanctions on Burma," February 8, 2011. www.nldburma.org/media-press-release.
121. *Bangkok Post*, "Aung San Suu Kyi calls for trade boycott," June 4, 1989.
122. Aung San Suu Kyi, "Please Use Your Liberty to Promote Ours," *International Herald Tribune*, February 4, 1997.
123. After the NLD released its review of sanctions on February 8, 2011, *The New Light of Myanmar* published seven hostile critiques in seven days. Derek Tonkin, "Lost in translation," *Burmese Perspectives*, February 23, 2011, p.1. www.networkmyanmar.org/images/stories/PDF6/bp230211.pdf.
124. Marc Bossuyt, "The adverse consequences of economic sanctions on the enjoyment of human rights," working paper prepared for UN Commission on Human Rights, June 21, 2000. E/CN.4/Sub.2/2000/33. Paras 41–7.
125. Derek Tonkin, "The annual follies on Burma/Myanmar," *Burmese Perspectives*, March 14, 2011, p.3. www.networkmyanmar.org/images/stories/PDF6/bp140311.pdf.
126. Nick Mathiason, "Banks Bust Burma Trade Ban," *Observer*, January 18, 2004.
127. Alan Boyd, "Myanmar Boycott on Shaky Ground," *Asia Times*, December 13, 2003.
128. Toshihiro Kudo, "The Impact of U.S. Sanctions on the Myanmar Garment Industry," *Asian Survey* 48:6 (2008), 997–1017, p.998.
129. Kudo, "The Impact of U.S. Sanctions on the Myanmar Garment Industry," p.1008.

130. Kudo, "The Impact of U.S. Sanctions on the Myanmar Garment Industry," pp.1016–17.
131. David Lektzian and Mark Souva, "An Institutional Theory of Sanctions Onset and Success," *Journal of Conflict Resolution* 51 (2007), 848–71.
132. Susan Hannah Allen, "The Domestic Political Costs of Economic Sanctions," *Journal of Conflict Resolution* 52:6 (2008), 916–44.
133. Hufbauer, et al., *Economic Sanctions Reconsidered.*
134. David I. Steinberg, *The Future of Burma: Crisis and Choice in Myanmar* (Lanham, NY: University Press of America, 1990), p.91.
135. US Department of State, "Burma: the dialogue is dead," November 28, 2007. WikiLeaks US Embassy Cables, ref. 07RANGOON1148. US Department of State, "Burma's generals: starting the conversation," April 2, 2009. WikiLeaks US Embassy Cables, ref. 09RANGOON205.
136. International Crisis Group, *China's Myanmar Strategy*, p.11.
137. Asia Society, *Current Realities and Future Possibilities in Burma/Myanmar*, p.43.
138. Asia Society, *Current Realities and Future Possibilities in Burma/Myanmar*, p.105.
139. Steinberg, "The United States and Myanmar."
140. An August 2008 US London Embassy cable reported this breakdown of EU opinion: "in addition to the UK, the strong players on this issue are the Nordics – led by a forceful Danish position and then the Swedes and Finns, as well as the Czechs, Dutch and a strong and effective Irish approach. The French are in the middle, constrained primarily by their Total investments and concerns that financial sanctions could impact all of Total's operations in Burma … At the far end opposing sanctions are the Germans and Austrians – for legalistic reasons – and the Mediterraneans (Italy, Portugal), who are philosophically reluctant to believe that sanctions can have an impact." US Department of State, "UK doesn't expect strong new Burma sanctions from EU," August 8, 2008. WikiLeaks US Embassy Cables, ref. 08LONDON2070.
141. Pedersen, *Promoting Human Rights in Burma.*
142. Andrew Selth, "Even Paranoids Have Enemies: Cyclone Nargis and Myanmar's Fears of Invasion," *Contemporary Southeast Asia* 30:3 (2008), 379–402. Mary Callahan, "The Endurance of Military Rule in Burma: Not Why, but Why Not?," in Susan L. Levenstein, ed., *Finding Dollars, Sense, and Legitimacy in Burma* (Washington, DC: Woodrow Wilson International Center for Scholars, 2010), 54–76.
143. Charles McDermid, "Missing the point on Myanmar," *Asia Times Online*, July 4, 2009. www.atimes.com/atimes/Southeast_Asia/KG04Ae01.html.
144. National League for Democracy, "Sanctions on Burma."
145. Mark MacKinnon, "Aung San Suu Kyi on Egypt, sanctions and raising the megabyte," *The Globe and Mail*, February 18, 2011. In 1997, Aung San Suu Kyi wrote this: "Some would insist that man is primarily an economic animal interested only in his material well-being. This is too narrow a view of a species which has produced numberless brave men and women who are prepared to undergo relentless persecution to uphold deeply held beliefs and principles. It is my pride and inspiration that such men and women exist in my country today." Aung San Suu Kyi, "Please Use Your

Liberty to Promote Ours." Now, however, many compatriots feel she devotes too much attention to principle, and too little to pragmatic issues of daily survival.

146. *Straits Times*, "Sanctions must stay in place: Myanmar's Suu Kyi," March 23, 2011.
147. International Crisis Group, *Myanmar's Post-election Landscape* (Jakarta/Brussels: International Crisis Group, 2011), p.14.
148. "Open letter of Myanmar fraternal democratic parties to European Union regarding economic sanctions against Myanmar," March 11, 2011. www.networkmyanmar.org.
149. Centre for Peace and Conflict Studies, *Listening to Voices from Inside: Ethnic People Speak* (Phnom Penh: Centre for Peace and Conflict Studies, 2010), pp.188–204.

Chapter 6

1. David Miller, *Principles of Social Justice* (Cambridge, MA: Harvard University Press, 1999).
2. John Rawls, *A Theory of Justice* (Cambridge, MA: Belknap Press, 1971), p.8.
3. Nozick's utopia is a collection of states, minimal in the default position and more than minimal if unanimously endorsed by citizens. Robert Nozick, *Anarchy, State, and Utopia* (New York, NY: Basic Books, 1974).
4. Peter Singer, "Famine, Affluence, and Morality," *Philosophy and Public Affairs* 1:3(1972), 229–43.
5. As will be seen in this chapter and the next, Walzer has been both a key proponent of the communitarian focus on specific societies and cultures, and a leading analyst of just engagement across borders.
6. Michael N. Barnett, *The International Humanitarian Order* (Abingdon: Routledge, 2010), p.2.
7. Michael Barnett, "Evolution without Progress? Humanitarianism in a World of Hurt," *International Organization* 63:4 (2009), 621–63, p.623.
8. Samuel Moyn, *The Last Utopia: Human Rights in History* (Cambridge, MA: Harvard University Press, 2010).
9. Barnett, *The International Humanitarian Order*, p.1.
10. James D. Fearon, "The Rise of Emergency Relief Aid," in Michael Barnett and Thomas G. Weiss (eds), *Humanitarianism in Question: Politics, Power, Ethics* (Ithaca, NY: Cornell University Press, 2008), 49–72.
11. Boutros Boutros-Ghali, *An Agenda for Peace: Preventive Diplomacy, Peacemaking and Peace-keeping*, A/47/277 – S/24111 (1992). Also see William Shawcross, *Deliver Us from Evil: Warlords and Peacekeepers in a World of Endless Conflict* (London: Bloomsbury, 2000).
12. Boutros Boutros-Ghali, *Supplement to An Agenda for Peace: Position Paper of the Secretary-General on the Occasion of the Fiftieth Anniversary of the United Nations*, A/50/60 – S/1995/1, (1995). Panel on United Nations Peace Operations, *Report*, A/55/305 – S/2000/809 (2000).
13. International Commission on Intervention and State Sovereignty, *The Responsibility to Protect* (Ottawa: International Development Research Centre, 2001). UN General Assembly, *2005 World Summit Outcome*, A/RES/60/1 (2005), para. 139. Andrew

Cottey, "Beyond Humanitarian Intervention: The New Politics of Peacekeeping and Intervention," *Contemporary Politics* 14:4 (2008), 429–46.

14. United Nations Security Council, Resolution 1973, March 17, 2011. S/RES/1973 (2011).
15. Michael Barnett and Thomas G. Weiss, "Humanitarianism: A Brief History of the Present," in Michael Barnett and Thomas G. Weiss (eds), *Humanitarianism in Question: Politics, Power, Ethics* (Ithaca, NY: Cornell University Press, 2008), 1–48.
16. David P. Forsythe, *The Humanitarians: The International Committee of the Red Cross* (Cambridge: Cambridge University Press, 2005).
17. Stephen Hopgood, *Keepers of the Flame: Understanding Amnesty International* (Ithaca, NY: Cornell University Press, 2006).
18. Barnett and Weiss, "Humanitarianism."
19. David Chandler, "The Road to Military Humanitarianism: How the Human Rights NGOs Shaped a New Humanitarian Agenda," *Human Rights Quarterly* 23:3 (2001), 678–700.
20. Ann Marie Clark, *Diplomacy of Conscience: Amnesty International and Changing Human Rights Norms* (Princeton, NJ: Princeton University Press, 2001). Human Rights Watch was formed in 1988, following the creation of Helsinki Watch in 1978, Americas Watch in 1981 and Asia Watch in 1985.
21. Scott Jerbi, "Business and Human Rights at the UN: What Might Happen Next?," *Human Rights Quarterly* 31:2 (2009), 299–320.
22. United Nations Global Compact Office, *Corporate Citizenship in the World Economy* (New York, NY: United Nations, 2008).
23. Barnett, *The International Humanitarian Order*, p.2.
24. In 1988, before the Wall came down and the international humanitarian order became fully established, Judith N. Shklar focused on this distinction in the Storrs Lectures at Yale Law School. Judith N. Shklar, *The Faces of Injustice* (New Haven, CT: Yale University Press, 1990).
25. Jennifer M. Welsh, "Introduction," in Jennifer M. Welsh, ed., *Humanitarian Intervention and International Relations* (Oxford: Oxford University Press, 2004), 1–7, p.2. Also see Roberta Cohen and Francis M. Deng, *Masses in Flight: The Global Crisis of Internal Displacement* (Washington, DC: Brookings Institution, 1998).
26. Thomas Nagel, "The Problem of Global Justice," *Philosophy and Public Affairs* 33:2 (2005), 113–47.
27. Singer, "Famine, Affluence, and Morality," p.232.
28. Thomas Pogge, *World Poverty and Human Rights*, 2nd ed. (Cambridge: Polity Press, 2008), p.175.
29. Onora O'Neill, *Bounds of Justice* (Cambridge: Cambridge University Press, 2000), p.149.
30. Charles R. Beitz, *Political Theory and International Relations* (Princeton, NJ: Princeton University Press, 1979).
31. Henry Shue, *Basic Rights: Subsistence, Affluence, and U.S. Foreign Policy*, 2nd ed. (Princeton, NJ: Princeton University Press, 1996). Onora O'Neill, *Faces of Hunger: An Essay on Poverty, Justice and Development* (London: Allen & Unwin, 1986).

32. Simon Caney, *Justice beyond Borders: A Global Political Theory* (Oxford: Oxford University Press, 2005), pp.7–15. Hedley Bull, *The Anarchical Society: A Study of Order in World Politics* (New York, NY: Columbia University Press, 1977).
33. Chris Brown, *International Relations Theory: New Normative Approaches* (New York, NY: Harvester Wheatsheaf, 1992).
34. Michael Walzer, *Thinking Politically: Essays in Political Theory* (New Haven, CT: Yale University Press, 2007), p.220.
35. Walzer, *Thinking Politically*, p.221.
36. Walzer, *Thinking Politically*, pp.221–2.
37. David Miller, *National Responsibility and Global Justice* (Oxford: Oxford University Press, 2007), pp.124–6.
38. Miller, *National Responsibility and Global Justice*, p.80.
39. Miller, *National Responsibility and Global Justice*, pp.5–6.
40. Henry Shue, "Mediating Duties," *Ethics* 98:4 (1988), 687–704, p.688.
41. Robert H. Jackson, *Quasi-states: Sovereignty, International Relations and the Third World* (Cambridge: Cambridge University Press, 1990).
42. Thomas Pogge, *World Poverty and Human Rights*, 2nd ed. (Cambridge: Polity Press, 2008).
43. Pogge, *World Poverty and Human Rights*, pp.118–22, 202–21.
44. John Rawls, *The Law of Peoples: With "The Idea of Public Reason Revisited"* (Cambridge, MA: Harvard University Press, 1999).
45. Khin Nyunt's argument was that SLORC "has been accepted as [a military government] by the United Nations and the respective nations of the world." *Working People's Daily*, "State LORC Declaration No. 1/90 of July 27, 1990," July 29, 1990.
46. Richard M. Auty, *Sustaining Development in Mineral Economies: The Resource Curse Thesis* (London: Routledge, 1993). Paul Collier, *The Bottom Billion: Why the Poorest Countries Are Failing and What Can Be Done about It* (Oxford: Oxford University Press, 2007).
47. Richard W. Miller, *Globalizing Justice: The Ethics of Poverty and Power* (Oxford: Oxford University Press, 2010), p.1.
48. Miller, *Globalizing Justice*, pp.69–77.
49. Miller, *Globalizing Justice*, p.162.
50. Miller, *Globalizing Justice*, p.163.
51. Iris Chang, *The Rape of Nanking: The Forgotten Holocaust of World War II* (New York, NY: Basic Books, 1997).
52. John Breen (ed.), *Yasukuni, the War Dead and the Struggle for Japan's Past* (New York, NY: Columbia University Press, 2008).
53. In the mid-1950s, Collis noted that British colonialists themselves had a "change of view in the twentieth century, when we began to doubt whether empire building was as noble an occupation as we had conceived." Maurice Collis, *Last and First in Burma (1941–1948)* (London: Faber and Faber, 1956), p.291. Also see Mark Duffield, "On the Edge of 'No Man's Land': Chronic Emergency in Myanmar," School of Sociology, Politics, and International Studies, University of Bristol Working Paper No. 01–08,

pp.20–2. www.bristol.ac.uk/spais/research/workingpapers/wpspaisfiles/duffield0108.pdf.

54. Benjamin E. Goldsmith and Baogang He, "Letting Go without a Fight: Decolonization, Democracy and War: 1900–94," *Journal of Peace Research* 45:5 (2008), 587–611.
55. Maung Maung, *Burma's Constutition*, 2nd ed. (The Hague: Martinus Nijhoff, 1961), p.85. The introduction to *Burma's Fight for Freedom*, the official record of the independence process, included these sentences: "The title of this publication is perhaps a little misleading. Freedom has been won without a fight, a fact which testifies to Britain's wisdom and Burma's unity." Cited in Hugh Tinker, *The Union of Burma: A Study of the First Years of Independence*, 4th ed. (London: Oxford University Press, 1967), p.33, n.2.
56. Donald M. Seekins, *Burma and Japan since 1940: From "Co-Prosperity" to "Quiet Dialogue"* (Copenhagen: Nordic Institute of Asian Studies, 2007).
57. Miller, *Globalizing Justice*, pp.118–46. Also see Chalmers Johnson, *Blowback: The Costs and Consequences of American Empire* (New York, NY: Metropolitan Books, 2002).
58. Anthony Ware and Matthew Clarke, "The MDGs in Myanmar: Relevant or Redundant?," *Journal of the Asia Pacific Economy* 16 (2011), forthcoming.
59. Richard Lloyd Parry, "Aung San Suu Kyi meets ambassador for sanctions talks," *Times*, October 10, 2009.
60. For an account of just two episodes among many, see Donald K. Emmerson, "Critical Terms: Security, Democracy, and Regionalism in Southeast Asia," in Donald K. Emmerson (ed.), *Hard Choices: Security, Democracy, and Regionalism in Southeast Asia* (Singapore: Institute of Southeast Asian Studies, 2009), 3–56, pp.26–34, 40–50.
61. Janna Thompson, *Taking Responsibility for the Past: Reparation and Historical Injustice* (Cambridge: Polity Press, 2002).
62. Miller, *National Responsibility and Global Justice*, p.161.
63. O'Neill, *Bounds of Justice*, p.4.
64. Shue, "Mediating Duties," p.687.
65. Simon Caney, *Justice beyond Borders: A Global Political Theory* (Oxford: Oxford University Press, 2005), pp.232–3.
66. Richard A. Falk, Robert C. Johansen and Samuel S. Kim, "Global Constitutionalism and World Order," in Richard A. Falk, Robert C. Johansen and Samuel S. Kim, eds, *The Constitutional Foundations of World Peace* (Albany, NY: State University of New York Press), 3–12, pp.3–4.
67. Daniele Archibugi, *The Global Commonwealth of Citizens: Toward Cosmopolitan Democracy* (Princeton, NJ: Princeton University Press, 2008). Richard Falk, *On Humane Governance: Toward a New Global Politics* (University Park, PA: Pennsylvania State University Press, 1995). David Held, *Democracy and the Global Order: From the Modern State to Cosmopolitan Governance* (Stanford, CA: Stanford University Press, 1995). Andrew Kuper, *Democracy beyond Borders: Justice and Representation in Global Institutions* (Oxford: Oxford University Press, 2004). Anne-Marie Slaughter, *A New*

World Order (Princeton, NJ: Princeton University Press, 2005). Iris Marion Young, *Inclusion and Democracy* (Oxford: Oxford University Press, 2000).

68. O'Neill, *Bounds of Justice*, p.200.
69. Onora O'Neill, "Global Justice: Whose Obligations?," in Deen K. Chatterjee, ed., *The Ethics of Assistance: Morality and the Distant Needy* (Cambridge: Cambridge University Press, 2004), 242–59, p.252.
70. Caney, *Justice beyond Borders*, p.182.
71. Caney, *Justice beyond Borders*, p.264.
72. Walzer, *Thinking Politically*, p.237.
73. Walzer, *Thinking Politically*, p.238.
74. Walzer, *Thinking Politically*, p.257.
75. Walzer, *Thinking Politically*, p.238.
76. Walzer, *Thinking Politically*, p.251.
77. Miller, *National Responsibility and Global Justice*, p.197.
78. Miller, *National Responsibility and Global Justice*, pp.167–8.
79. Miller, *National Responsibility and Global Justice*, p.133.
80. Leif Wenar, "Why Rawls Is Not a Cosmopolitan Egalitarian," in Rex Martin and David A. Reidy (eds), *Rawls's Law of Peoples: A Realistic Utopia?* (Oxford: Blackwell, 2006), 95–113.
81. Rawls, *The Law of Peoples*, p.37.
82. Rawls, *The Law of Peoples*, pp..62–70, 90.
83. Rawls, *The Law of Peoples*, pp.37, 93.
84. Rawls, *The Law of Peoples*, pp.106–12.
85. Rawls, *The Law of Peoples*, p.111.
86. Daniel A. Bell, *Beyond Liberal Democracy: Political Thinking for an East Asian Context* (Princeton, NJ: Princeton University Press, 2006), pp.23–51. Torkel Brekke (ed.), *The Ethics of War in Asian Civilizations: A Comparative Perspective* (Abingdon, Routledge, 2006).
87. Bell, *Beyond Liberal Democracy*, pp.52–83.
88. Joanne R. Bauer and Daniel A. Bell, "Introduction," in Joanne R. Bauer and Daniel A. Bell, eds, *The East Asian Challenge for Human Rights* (Cambridge: Cambridge University Press, 1999), 3–23, p.4.
89. Amitav Acharya, *Constructing a Security Community in Southeast Asia: ASEAN and the Problem of Regional Order* (London: Routledge, 2001). William T. Tow, *Asia-Pacific Strategic Relations: Seeking Convergent Security* (Cambridge: Cambridge University Press, 2001). Jürgen Haacke, *ASEAN's Diplomatic and Security Culture: Origins, Development and Prospects* (London: RoutledgeCurzon, 2003). Donald E. Weatherbee, *International Relations in Southeast Asia: The Struggle for Autonomy*, 2nd ed. (Lanham, MD: Rowman & Littlefield, 2009).
90. Amitav Acharya, *Whose Ideas Matter? Agency and Power in Asian Regionalism* (Ithaca, NY: Cornell University Press, 2009), pp.137–8. Lee Jones, "ASEAN's Unchanged Melody? The Theory and Practice of 'Non-interference' in Southeast Asia," *Pacific Review* 23 (2010), 479–502.

91. The closest state prepared to impose economic sanctions on Myanmar is Australia.
92. John F. Cady, *A History of Modern Burma* (Ithaca, NY: Cornell University Press, 1958), p.154. Burman is used here in the standard colonial sense to embrace all ethnic groups.
93. John F. Cady, *The United States and Burma* (Cambridge, MA: Harvard University Press, 1976), p.16.
94. Lieutenant General Phone Myint, cited in David I. Steinberg, "Democracy, Power, and the Economy in Myanmar: Donor Dilemmas," *Asian Survey* 31:8 (1991), 729–42, p.735.
95. Centre for Peace and Conflict Studies, *Listening to Voices from Inside: Ethnic People Speak* (Phnom Penh: Centre for Peace and Conflict Studies, 2010), p.195.
96. Lucian W. Pye, *Asian Power and Politics: The Cultural Dimensions of Authority* (Cambridge, MA: Belknap Press, 1985). Cited in Stephen McCarthy, *The Political Theory of Tyranny in Singapore and Burma: Aristotle and the Rhetoric of Benevolent Despotism* (Abingdon: Routledge, 2006), p.12.
97. William C. Johnstone, *Burma's Foreign Policy: A Study in Neutralism* (Cambridge, MA: Harvard University Press, 1963). Chi-shad Liang, *Burma's Foreign Relations: Neutralism in Theory and Practice* (New York, NY: Praeger, 1990).
98. Aung San Suu Kyi, "Please use your liberty to promote ours," *International Herald Tribune*, February 4, 1997.
99. Michael Aung-Thwin, "Parochial Universalism, Democracy *Jihad* and the Orientalist Image of Burma: The New Evangelism," *Pacific Affairs* 74:4 (2001–02), 483–505.
100. *International Herald Tribune*, "Confirmation hearing of Condoleezza Rice," January 18, 2005. David I. Steinberg, "The United States and Myanmar: A 'Boutique Issue'?," *International Affairs* 86:1 (2010), 175–94.
101. Inge Brees, "Burmese Refugee Transnationalism: What Is the Effect?," *Journal of Current Southeast Asian Affairs* 28:2 (2009), 23–46.
102. Shklar, *The Faces of Injustice*, p.115.
103. Aung San Suu Kyi, *Freedom from Fear: And Other Writings*, rev. ed. (London: Penguin, 1995).
104. Centre for Peace and Conflict Studies, *Listening to Voices from Inside: Myanmar Civil Society's Response to Cyclone Nargis* (Phnom Penh: Centre for Peace and Conflict Studies, 2009), pp.vi, 2.
105. Centre for Peace and Conflict Studies, *Ethnic People Speak*, p.25.
106. CDA Collaborative Learning Projects, *Listening Project: Field Visit Report: Myanmar/Burma* (No place: CDA, 2009), p.11.
107. Caney, *Justice beyond Borders*, p.238.
108. CDA Collaborative Learning Projects, *Myanmar/Burma*, p.7.
109. CDA Collaborative Learning Projects, *Myanmar/Burma*, p.19.
110. Caney, *Justice beyond Borders*, pp.238–9.

Chapter 7

1. Ian Holliday, "When Is a Cause Just?," *Review of International Studies* 28:3 (2002), 557–75. Ian Holliday, "Ethics of Intervention: Just War Theory and the Challenge of the 21st Century," *International Relations* 17:2 (2003), 115–33.
2. Catherine Lu, *Just and Unjust Interventions in World Politics: Public and Private* (Basingstoke: Palgrave Macmillan, 2006), p.11.
3. Lu, *Just and Unjust Interventions in World Politics*, p.4.
4. Michael Barnett and Jack Snyder, "The Grand Strategies of Humanitarianism," in Michael Barnett and Thomas G. Weiss (eds), *Humanitarianism in Question: Politics, Power, Ethics* (Ithaca, NY: Cornell University Press, 2008), 143–71, pp.145–6.
5. In 1995, Andrew Rigby used three criteria to construct a typology of non-violent intervention: location, style and objective. Andrew Rigby, "Unofficial Nonviolent Intervention: Examples from the Israeli-Palestinian Conflict," *Journal of Peace Research* 32:4 (1995), 453–67.
6. The ICRC is a classic mixed-zone humanitarian agency. "The ICRC … is neither, strictly speaking, nongovernmental nor intergovernmental; it is in a category by itself because states provide the bulk of its resources and also give it a particular mandate – to develop, protect, and disseminate international humanitarian law – but individual citizens, and not states, are members." Michael Barnett and Thomas G. Weiss, "Humanitarianism: A Brief History of the Present," in Michael Barnett and Thomas G. Weiss (eds), *Humanitarianism in Question: Politics, Power, Ethics* (Ithaca, NY: Cornell University Press, 2008), 1–48, p.14.
7. Thomas J. Volgy, Elizabeth Fausett, Keith A. Grant and Stuart Rodgers, "Identifying Formal Intergovernmental Organizations," *Journal of Peace Research* 45:6 (2008), 837–50.
8. Adam Watson, *Diplomacy: The Dialogue between States* (London: Methuen, 1982), p.226.
9. R. P. Barston, *Modern Diplomacy*, 2nd ed. (London: Longman, 1997).
10. Watson, *Diplomacy*.
11. Patrick M. Regan, Richard W. Frank and Aysegul Aydin, "Diplomatic Interventions and Civil War: A New Dataset," *Journal of Peace Research* 46:1 (2009), 135–46.
12. Boutros-Ghali, *An Agenda for Peace*, para 20.
13. Norrie MacQueen, *Peacekeeping and the International System* (Abingdon: Routledge, 2006). Paul F. Diehl, *Peace Operations* (Cambridge: Polity, 2008). Alex J. Bellamy and Paul D. Williams with Stuart Griffin, *Understanding Peacekeeping*, 2nd ed. (Cambridge: Polity, 2010).
14. Boutros Boutros-Ghali, *An Agenda for Peace: Preventive Diplomacy, Peacemaking and Peace-keeping*, A/47/277 – S/24111 (1992), para 46.
15. Steven R. Ratner, *The New UN Peacekeeping: Building Peace in Lands of Conflict after the Cold War* (Basingstoke: Macmillan, 1997), p.2.
16. Pak K. Lee, Gerald Chan and Lai-Ha Chan, "China in Darfur: Humanitarian Rule-maker or Rule-taker?," *Review of International Studies* 37 (2011), forthcoming.

17. Nick Butler, "Companies in International Relations," *Survival* 42:1 (Spring 2000), 149–64. William H. Meyer, *Human Rights and International Political Economy in Third World Nations: Multinational Corporations, Foreign Aid, and Repression* (Westport, CT: Praeger, 1998).
18. Arne Tostensen and Beate Bull, "Are Smart Sanctions Feasible?," *World Politics* 54:3 (2002), 373–403. Meghan L. O'Sullivan, *Shrewd Sanctions: Statecraft and State Sponsors of Terrorism* (Washington, DC: Brookings Institution, 2003).
19. Gary Clyde Hufbauer, Jeffrey J. Schott, Kimberly Ann Elliott and Barbara Oegg, *Economic Sanctions Reconsidered*, 3rd ed. (Washington, DC: Pearson Institute for International Economics, 2007), p.3.
20. Hufbauer, et al., *Economic Sanctions Reconsidered*, pp.44–5.
21. Steve Chan and A. Cooper Drury, "Sanctions as Economic Statecraft: An Overview," in Steve Chan and A. Cooper Drury, eds, *Sanctions as Economic Statecraft: Theory and Practice* (Basingstoke: Macmillan, 2000), p.3.
22. David Cortright and George A. Lopez, *The Sanctions Decade: Assessing UN Strategies in the 1990s* (Boulder, CO: Lynne Rienner, 2000).
23. Thomas G. Weiss, "Sanctions as a Foreign Policy Tool: Weighing Humanitarian Impulses," *Journal of Peace Research* 36:5 (1999), 499–509.
24. Hufbauer, et al., *Economic Sanctions Reconsidered*. Kern Alexander, *Economic Sanctions: Law and Public Policy* (London: Palgrave Macmillan, 2009).
25. The definition comes from L. Oppenheim's *International Law*. It is cited in Yoram Dinstein, *War, Aggression and Self-defence*, 4th ed. (Cambridge: Cambridge University Press, 2005), p.5.
26. Leslie C. Green, *The Contemporary Law of Armed Conflict*, 2nd ed. (Manchester: Manchester University Press, 2000), pp.54–5, 71.
27. Michael Howard, "When Are Wars Decisive?," *Survival* 41:1 (Spring 1999), 126–35, p.126.
28. I. William Zartman and J. Lewis Rasmussen (eds), *Peacemaking in International Conflict: Methods and Techniques* (Washington, DC: United States Institute of Peace Press, 1997). Tom Woodhouse, Robert Bruce and Malcolm Dando (eds), *Peacekeeping and Peacemaking: Towards Effective Intervention in Post-Cold War Conflicts* (Basingstoke: Palgrave Macmillan, 1998). Andrew Cottey, "Beyond Humanitarian Intervention: The New Politics of Peacekeeping and Intervention," *Contemporary Politics* 14:4 (2008), 429–46.
29. The International Military Intervention dataset is a comprehensive resource. Jeffrey Pickering and Emizet F. Kisangani, "The International Military Intervention Dataset: An Updated Resource for Conflict Scholars," *Journal of Peace Research* 46:4 (2009), 589–99.
30. Steven Simon and Daniel Benjamin, "America and the New Terrorism," *Survival* 42:1 (Spring 2000), 59–75, p.66. Also see Daniel Benjamin and Steven Simon, *The Age of Sacred Terror: Radical Islam's War against America* (New York, NY: Random House, 2002).
31. Lu, *Just and Unjust Interventions in World Politics*.

32. United Nations General Assembly, "Strengthening of the Coordination of Humanitarian Emergency Assistance of the United Nations', A/RES/46/182 (1991). Nicholas Hopkinson, *The United Nations in the New World Disorder* (London: HMSO, 1993). Larry Minear and Thomas G. Weiss, *Humanitarian Action in Times of War: A Handbook for Practitioners* (Boulder, CO: Lynne Rienner, 1993). World Conference on Religion and Peace, *The Mohonk Criteria for Humanitarian Assistance in Complex Emergencies* (New York, NY: World Conference on Religion and Peace, 1994). International Federation of Red Cross and Red Crescent Societies, *The Code of Conduct for the International Red Cross and Red Crescent Movement and Non-Governmental Organisations (NGOs) in Disaster Relief* (No place: International Federation of Red Cross and Red Crescent Societies, 1994). John Harriss, ed., *The Politics of Humanitarian Intervention* (London: Pinter/Save the Children, 1995).
33. Frederick H. Russell, *The Just War in the Middle Ages* (Cambridge: Cambridge University Press, 1975). James Turner Johnson and John Kelsay, eds, *Cross, Crescent, and Sword: The Justification and Limitation of War in Western and Islamic Tradition* (Westport, CT: Greenwood, 1990). John Kelsay, and James Turner Johnson, eds, *Just War and Jihad: Historical and Theoretical Perspectives on War and Peace in Western and Islamic Traditions* (Westport, CT: Greenwood, 1991). James Turner Johnson *The Holy War Idea in Western and Islamic Traditions* (University Park, PA: Pennsylvania State University Press, 1997). Michael Walzer, *Just and Unjust Wars: A Moral Argument with Historical Illustrations*, 3rd ed. (New York, NY: Basic Books, 2000). John Kelsay, *Arguing the Just War in Islam* (Cambridge, MA: Harvard University Press, 2007).
34. Robert L. Phillips and Duane L. Cady, *Humanitarian Intervention: Just War vs Pacifism* (Lanham, MD: Rowman and Littlefield, 1996). Oliver Ramsbotham and Tom Woodhouse, *Humanitarian Intervention in Contemporary Conflict: A Reconceptualization* (Cambridge: Polity Press, 1996). Stephen A. Garrett, *Doing Good and Doing Well: An Examination of Humanitarian Intervention* (Westport, CT: Praeger, 1999). Nicholas J. Wheeler, *Saving Strangers: Humanitarian Intervention in International Society* (Oxford: Oxford University Press, 2000). Simon Chesterman, *Just War or Just Peace? Humanitarian Intervention and International Law* (Oxford: Oxford University Press, 2001). International Commission on Intervention and State Sovereignty, *The Responsibility to Protect* (Ottawa: International Development Research Centre, 2001). Brian D. Lepard, *Rethinking Humanitarian Intervention: A Fresh Legal Approach Based on Fundamental Ethical Principles in International Law and World Religions* (University Park, PA: Pennsylvania State University Press, 2002).
35. Jean Bethke Elshtain, *Just War against Terror: The Burden of American Power in a Violent World* (New York, NY: Basic Books, 2003). Michael Walzer, "Terrorism and Just War," *Philosophia* 34 (2006), 3–12. Steven P. Lee, ed., *Intervention, Terrorism, and Torture* (Dordrecht: Springer, 2007).
36. Walzer, *Just and Unjust Wars.*
37. Today theorists point to a third set of concerns with *jus post bellum*, focused on the notion of a just peace. Brian Orend, "Justice after War," *Ethics and International Affairs* 16:1 (2002), 43–56. Brian Orend, "*Jus Post Bellum*: The Perspective of a Just-War Theorist," *Leiden Journal of International Law* 20:3 (2007), 571–91.

38. Jeff McMahan, "War and Peace," in Peter Singer, ed., *A Companion to Ethics* (Oxford: Blackwell, 1991), 384–95, p.388.
39. Richard Norman, *Ethics, Killing and War* (Cambridge: Cambridge University Press, 1995), p.119.
40. Brien Hallett, *The Lost Art of Declaring War* (Urbana, IL: University of Illinois Press, 1998).
41. Compare International Commission on Intervention and State Sovereignty, *The Responsibility to Protect*, which implicitly made this exclusion by drawing on only six just war principles.
42. Norman, *Ethics, Killing and War.*
43. A. J. Coates, *The Ethics of War* (Manchester: Manchester University Press, 1997), p.147.
44. Duane L. Cady, "Just War," in Donald A. Wells, ed., *An Encyclopedia of War and Ethics* (Westport, CT: Greenwood Press, 1996), 255–9.
45. For a full analysis, see Judith N. Shklar, *The Faces of Injustice* (New Haven, CT: Yale University Press, 1990).
46. Martha Finnemore, *The Purpose of Intervention: Changing Beliefs about the Use of Force* (Ithaca, NY: Cornell University Press, 2003).
47. Michael Walzer, *Just and Unjust Wars: A Moral Argument with Historical Illustrations*, 2nd ed. (New York, NY: Basic Books, 1992), p.xviii.
48. It cannot be assumed that humanitarian intentions are uniformly right, and all others uniformly suspect. Alain Finkielkraut, *In the Name of Humanity: Reflections on the Twentieth Century* (New York, NY: Columbia University Press, 2000). Tony Vaux, *The Selfish Altruist: Relief Work in Famine and War* (Sterling, VA: Eartscan, 2001).
49. United Nations Department of Public Information, *The United Nations and Somalia, 1992–1996* (New York, NY: United Nations, 1996).
50. David Rohde, *Endgame: The Betrayal and Fall of Srebrenica, Europe's Worst Massacre since World War II* (Boulder, CO: Westview, 1998). Netherlands Institute for War Documentation, *Srebrenica: A "Safe" Area: Reconstruction, Background, Consequences and Analyses of the Fall of a Safe Area* (Amsterdam: Netherlands Institute for War Documentation, 2002).
51. Hufbauer, et al., *Economic Sanctions Reconsidered.*
52. John S. Dryzek, *Deliberative Democracy and Beyond: Liberals, Critics, Contestations* (Oxford: Oxford University Press, 2000), p.1.
53. Dryzek, *Deliberative Democracy and Beyond*, p.1.
54. Ian O'Flynn, *Deliberative Democracy and Divided Societies* (Edinburgh: Edinburgh University Press, 2006).
55. James S. Fishkin, *When the People Speak: Deliberative Democracy and Public Consultation* (Oxford: Oxford University Press, 2009).
56. Ethan J. Leib and Baogang He (eds), *The Search for Deliberative Democracy in China* (New York, NY: Palgrave Macmillan, 2006). Baogang He, "A Deliberative Approach to the Tibet Autonomy Issue: Promoting Mutual Trust through Dialogue," *Asian Survey* 50:4 (2010), 709–34.

57. John S. Dryzek, *Deliberative Global Politics: Discourse and Democracy in a Divided World* (Cambridge: Polity, 2006).
58. UN Security Council, "Security Council Fails to Adopt Draft Resolution on Myanmar, Owing to Negative Votes by China, Russian Federation," SC/8939 (2007).
59. The Group comprises 14 countries. At its first meeting, representatives came from Australia, China, France, India, Indonesia, Japan, Norway, Portugal, Russia, Singapore, Thailand, the UK, the US, and Vietnam. The EU's rotating presidency subsequently generated marginal membership changes. On the idea of a coordinated approach embracing ASEAN, China, India, Japan and the US, see Michael Green and Derek Mitchell, "Asia's Forgotten Crisis," *Foreign Affairs* 86:6 (2007), 147–58.
60. Richard Falk, *Predatory Globalization: A Critique* (Cambridge: Polity, 1999). For a skeptical view, see Neera Chandhoke, "The Limits of Global Civil Society," in Marlies Glasius, Mary Kaldor and Helmut Anheier, eds, *Global Civil Society 2002* (Oxford: Oxford University Press, 2002), 35–53.
61. Ian Holliday, "Doing Business with Rights Violating Regimes: Corporate Social Responsibility and Myanmar's Military Junta," *Journal of Business Ethics* 61:4 (2005), 329–42.
62. William Sabandar, "Cyclone Nargis and ASEAN: A Window for More Meaningful Development Cooperation in Myanmar," in Nick Cheesman, Monique Skidmore and Trevor Wilson (eds), *Ruling Myanmar: From Cyclone Nargis to National Elections* (Singapore: ISEAS Publishing, 2010), 197–207.
63. Christina Fink, *Living Silence in Burma: Surviving under Military Rule*, second edition (London: Zed Books, 2009). In non-sensitive sectors, social research is increasingly possible. Myanmar Marketing Research & Development employs more than 160 full-time staff, including 100 interviewers, in 13 offices around the country. Building on standard market research commissioned by companies for years, it is now starting to undertake corporate social responsibility projects with clear social dimensions. www.mmrdrs.com.
64. Myanmar Information Management Unit is an outstanding online hub, providing a shared data exchange service for humanitarian agencies through information coordination, collection, processing, analysis and dissemination. www.themimu.info.
65. The 2005 study commissioned by Václav Havel and Desmond Tutu is an example of this kind of dossier. DLA Piper Rudnick Gray Cary, *Threat to the Peace: A Call for the UN Security Council to Act in Burma* (Washington, DC: DLA Piper Rudnick Gray Cary, 2005).
66. Fareed Zakaria, *The Post-American World* (New York, NY: W. W. Norton & Co., 2008).

Chapter 8

1. Michael Green and Derek Mitchell, "Asia's Forgotten Crisis," *Foreign Affairs* 86:6 (2007), 147–58.
2. US Department of State, "PRC/Burma: A/S Campbell's meeting with Asian Affairs DG Yang Yanyi," October 14, 2009. WikiLeaks US Embassy Cables, ref.

09BEIJING2868. Lauren Dunn, Peter Nyers and Richard Stubbs, "Western Interventionism versus East Asian Non-interference: Competing 'Global' Norms in the Asian Century," *Pacific Review* 23:3 (2010), 295–312.

3. Just one example among many is an Ottawa Declaration issued by a number of eminent exiles in August 2007. Lalit K. Jha, "Ottawa Declaration: Convene multi-party talks on Burma," *Irrawaddy*, August 31, 2007.
4. DLA Piper Rudnick Gray Cary, *Threat to the Peace: A Call for the UN Security Council to Act in Burma* (Washington, DC: DLA Piper Rudnick Gray Cary, 2005).
5. Amartya Sen, "New pressure can oust Burma's generals," *Financial Times*, November 21, 2010.
6. Arne Tostensen and Beate Bull, "Are Smart Sanctions Feasible?," *World Politics* 54:3 (2002), 373–403. Derek Tonkin, "Into the unknown," *Burmese Perspectives*, November 4, 2010, p.2. www.networkmyanmar.org/images/stories/PDF5/bp041110x.pdf.
7. Guy Horton, *Dying Alive: An Investigation and Legal Assessment of Human Rights Violations Inflicted in Burma, with Particular Reference to the Internally Displaced, Eastern Peoples* (Chiang Mai: Images Asia, 2005). International Human Rights Clinic at Harvard Law School, *Crimes in Burma* (Cambridge, MA: International Human Rights Clinic at Harvard Law School, 2009). Physicians for Human Rights, *Life under the Junta: Evidence of Crimes against Humanity in Burma's Chin State* (Cambridge, MA: Physicians for Human Rights, 2011).
8. Burma Campaign UK, "Burma Briefing: Support for a UN Commission of Inquiry," January 2011. http://burmacampaign.org.uk/images/uploads/7-support-for-un-commission-of-inquiry.pdf.
9. Roman David and Ian Holliday, "International Sanctions or International Justice? Shaping Political Development in Myanmar," *Australian Journal of International Affairs* (2011), forthcoming.
10. United Nations Security Council, Resolution 827, S/RES/827, May 25, 1993. United Nations Security Council, Resolution 955, S/RES/955, November 8, 1994.
11. United Nations, Rome Statute of the International Criminal Court, A/CONF.183/9*.
12. United Nations General Assembly, Resolution 57/228, "Khmer Rouge trials," A/RES/57/228, December 18, 2002.
13. Diane F. Orentlicher, "Settling Accounts: The Duty to Prosecute Human Rights Violations of a Prior Regime," *Yale Law Journal* 100:8 (1990–91), 2537–615. Naomi Roht-Arriaza, "Combating Impunity: Some Thoughts on the Way Forward," *Law and Contemporary Problems* 59:4 (Autumn 1996), 93–102. Payam Akhavan, "Beyond Impunity: Can International Criminal Justice Prevent Future Atrocities?," *American Journal of International Law* 95 (2001), 7–31. Dominic Raab, "Evaluating the ICTY and Its Completion Strategy: Efforts to Achieve Accountability for War Crimes and Their Tribunals," *Journal of International Criminal Justice* 3:1 (2005), 82–102. Judith Armatta, *Twilight of Impunity: The War Crimes Trial of Slobodan Milosevic* (Durham, NC: Duke University Press, 2010).
14. Minna Schrag, "Lessons Learned from ICTY Experience," *Journal of International Criminal Justice* 2:2 (2004), 427–34. Michelle Sieff and Leslie Vinjamuri,

"Prosecuting War Criminals: The Case for Decentralisation," *Conflict, Security and Development* 2:2 (2002), 103–13.

15. Akhavan, "Beyond Impunity."
16. Martha Minow, "The Hope for Healing: What Can Truth Commissions Do?," in Robert I. Rotberg and Dennis Thompson (eds), *Truth v. Justice: The Morality of Truth Commissions* (Princeton, NJ: Princeton University Press, 2000), 235–60.
17. Orentlicher, "Settling Accounts." Gary Jonathan Bass, *Stay the Hand of Vengeance: The Politics of War Crimes Tribunals* (Princeton, NJ: Princeton University Press, 2000), p.310. Roman David and Susanne Y. P. Choi, "Getting Even or Getting Equal? Retributive Desires and Transitional Justice," *Political Psychology* 30:2 (2009), 161–92.
18. Schrag, "Lessons Learned from ICTY Experience." Antonio Cassese, "The ICTY: A Living and Vital Reality," *Journal of International Criminal Justice* 2:2 (2004), 585–97. Raab, "Evaluating the ICTY and Its Completion Strategy."
19. James Meernik, "Justice and Peace? How the International Criminal Tribunal Affects Societal Peace in Bosnia," *Journal of Peace Research* 42:3 (2005), 271–89.
20. Schrag, "Lessons Learned from ICTY Experience."
21. International Criminal Court, "Warrant of Arrest for Omar Hassan Ahmad Al Bashir," ICC-02/05–01/09, March 4, 2009.
22. Neil MacFarquhar and Marlise Simons, "Bashir defies war crimes arrest order," *New York Times*, March 6, 2009, p.A10.
23. Marlise Simons, Lydia Polgreen and Jeffrey Gettleman, "Arrest is sought of Sudan leader in genocide case," *New York Times*, July 15, 2008, p.A1.
24. Seth Mydans, "Myanmar's leading dissident reunites with youngest son," *International Herald Tribune*, November 23, 2010.
25. One good example is a five-minute audio address sent by Aung San Suu Kyi to the January 2011 World Economic Forum in Davos. World Economic Forum, *Aung San Suu Kyi Addresses World Economic Forum Annual Meeting in Davos*, January 28, 2011. www.weforum.org/news/aung-san-suu-kyi-addresses-world-economic-forum-annual-meeting-davos?fo=1.
26. Transnational Institute and Burma Centrum Nederland, *Unlevel Playing Field: Burma's Election Landscape* (Amsterdam: Transnational Institute and Burma Centrum Nederland, 2010). "Open letter of Myanmar fraternal democratic parties to European Union regarding economic sanctions against Myanmar," March 11, 2011. www.networkmyanmar.org.
27. Centre for Peace and Conflict Studies, *Listening to Voices from Inside: Myanmar Civil Society's Response to Cyclone Nargis* (Phnom Penh: Centre for Peace and Conflict Studies, 2009). CDA Collaborative Learning Projects, *Listening Project: Field Visit Report: Myanmar/Burma* (No place: CDA, 2009). Centre for Peace and Conflict Studies, *Listening to Voices from Inside: Ethnic People Speak* (Phnom Penh: Centre for Peace and Conflict Studies, 2010). Centre for Peace and Conflict Studies, *Listening to Voices from Inside: People's Perspectives on Myanmar's 2010 Election* (Phnom Penh: Centre for Peace and Conflict Studies, 2010).

28. Ashley South, "Political Transition in Myanmar: A New Model for Democratization," *Contemporary Southeast Asia* 26:2 (2004), 233–55, p.234.
29. Duffield, "On the Edge of 'No Man's Land'," p.6.
30. Charles McDermid, "Missing the point on Myanmar," *Asia Times Online*, July 4, 2009. www.atimes.com/atimes/Southeast_Asia/KG04Ae01.html.
31. Callahan, "The Endurance of Military Rule in Burma," p.72.
32. Centre for Peace and Conflict Studies, *Listening to Voices from Inside: Myanmar Civil Society's Response to Cyclone Nargis* (Phnom Penh: Centre for Peace and Conflict Studies, 2009). CDA Collaborative Learning Projects, *Listening Project: Field Visit Report: Myanmar/Burma* (No place: CDA, 2009). Centre for Peace and Conflict Studies, *Listening to Voices from Inside: Ethnic People Speak* (Phnom Penh: Centre for Peace and Conflict Studies, 2010).
33. Mark Duffield, "On the Edge of 'No Man's Land': Chronic Emergency in Myanmar," School of Sociology, Politics, and International Studies, University of Bristol Working Paper No. 01–08, p.24. www.bristol.ac.uk/spais/research/workingpapers/wpspais-files/duffield0108.pdf.
34. US Department of State, "PRC/Burma."
35. Duffield, "On the Edge of 'No Man's Land'," p.34.
36. Duffield, "On the Edge of 'No Man's Land'," p.6.
37. Ashley South, "Political Transition in Myanmar: A New Model for Democratization," *Contemporary Southeast Asia* 26:2 (2004), 233–55, p.235.
38. Details of these activities are provided on the NLD's website. www.nldburma.org.
39. Metta Development Foundation, www.metta-myanmar.org.
40. Shalom (Nyein) Foundation, http://shalom2.elizaga.net.
41. James A. Wall, Jr. and Michael Blum, "Community Mediation in the People's Republic of China," *Journal of Conflict Resolution* 35:1 (1991), 3–20. Nam Hyeon Kim, James A. Wall, Jr., Dong-Won Sohn and Jay S. Kim, "Community and Industrial Mediation in South Korea," *Journal of Conflict Resolution* 37:2 (1993), 361–81. Ronda Roberts Callister and James A. Wall, Jr., "Japanese Community and Organizational Mediation," *Journal of Conflict Resolution* 41:2 (1997), 311–28. James A. Wall, Jr. and Ronda Roberts Callister, "Malaysian Community Mediation," *Journal of Conflict Resolution* 43:3 (1999), 343–65. Ronda Roberts Callister and James A. Wall, Jr., "Thai and U.S Community Mediation," *Journal of Conflict Resolution* 48:4 (2004), 573–98.
42. A full decade ago in 2001, the total number of publications was put at well over 500. James A. Wall, Jr., John B. Stark and Rhetta L. Standifer, "Mediation: A Current Review and Theory Development," *Journal of Conflict Resolution* 45:3 (2001), 370–91.
43. Ronald J. Fisher, "Interactive Conflict Resolution," in I. William Zartman and J. Lewis Rasmussen (eds), *Peacemaking in International Conflict: Methods and Techniques* (Washington, DC: United States Institute of Peace Press, 1997), 239–72.
44. J. Michael Greig, "Moments of Opportunity: Recognizing Conditions of Ripeness for International Mediation between Enduring Rivals," *Journal of Conflict Resolution* 45:6 (2001), 691–718. James A. Wall, Jr. and Daniel Druckman, "Mediation

in Peacekeeping Missions," *Journal of Conflict Resolution* 47:5 (2003), 693–705. Garance Genicot and Stergios Skaperdas, "Investing in Conflict Management," *Journal of Conflict Resolution* 46:1(2002), 154–70.

45. Siobhán McEvoy, "Communities and Peace: Catholic Youth in Northern Ireland," *Journal of Peace Research* 37:1 (2000), 85–103. Ifat Maoz, "An Experiment in Peace: Reconciliation-aimed Workshops of Jewish-Israeli and Palestinian Youth," *Journal of Peace Research* 37:6 (2000), 721–36. Deepak Malhotra and Sumanasiri Liyanage, "Long-term Effects of Peace Workshops in Protracted Conflicts," *Journal of Conflict Resolution* 49:6 (2005), 908–24.
46. Jodi Halpern and Harvey M. Weinstein, "Rehumanizing the Other: Empathy and Reconciliation," *Human Rights Quarterly* 26:4 (2004), 561–83.
47. Baogang He, "A Deliberative Approach to the Tibet Autonomy Issue: Promoting Mutual Trust through Dialogue," *Asian Survey* 50:4 (2010), 709–34.
48. Frances McLernon, Ed Cairns, Miles Hewstone and Ron Smith, "The Development of Intergroup Forgiveness in Northern Ireland," *Journal of Social Issues* 60:3 (2004), 587–601. Miles Hewstone, Ed Cairns, Alberto Voci, Juergen Hamberger and Ulrike Niens, "Intergroup Contact, Forgiveness, and Experience of 'The Troubles' in Northern Ireland," *Journal of Social Issues* 62:1 (2006), 99–120. Tania Tam, Miles Hewstone, Jared B. Kenworthy, Ed Cairns, Claudia Marinetti, Leo Geddes and Brian Parkinson, "Postconflict Reconciliation: Intergroup Forgiveness and Implicit Biases in Northern Ireland," *Journal of Social Issues* 64:2 (2008), 303–20.
49. Saw Yan Naing, "Is Than Shwe seeking military advice in Sri Lanka?," *Irrawaddy*, November 12, 2009.
50. Kumar Rupesinghe, "Ethnic Conflicts in South Asia: The Case of Sri Lanka and the Indian Peace-keeping Force (IPKF)," *Journal of Peace Research* 25:4 (1988), 337–50. John Stephen Moolakkattu, "Peace Facilitation by Small States: Norway in Sri Lanka," *Cooperation and Conflict* 40:4 (2005), 385–402.
51. Camilla Orjuela, "Building Peace in Sri Lanka: A Role for Civil Society?," *Journal of Peace Research* 40:2 (2003), 195–212.
52. Patrice C. McMahon, *Taming Ethnic Hatred: Ethnic Cooperation and Transnational Networks in Eastern Europe* (Syracuse, NY: Syracuse University Press, 2007).
53. Susan Dicklitch and Doreen Lwanga, "The Politics of Being Non-political: Human Rights Organizations and the Creation of a Positive Human Rights Culture in Uganda," *Human Rights Quarterly* 25:2 (2003), 482–509. Also see Aili Mari Tripp, *Museveni's Uganda: Paradoxes of Power in a Hybrid Regime* (Boulder, CO: Lynne Rienner, 2010).
54. Centre for Peace and Conflict Studies, *Myanmar Civil Society's Response to Cyclone Nargis*, p.49.
55. Centre for Peace and Conflict Studies, *Myanmar Civil Society's Response to Cyclone Nargis*, p.165.
56. Centre for Peace and Conflict Studies, *Myanmar Civil Society's Response to Cyclone Nargis*, p.122.
57. Centre for Peace and Conflict Studies, *Myanmar Civil Society's Response to Cyclone Nargis*, p.123.

58. Centre for Peace and Conflict Studies, *Ethnic People Speak*, p.188.
59. Centre for Peace and Conflict Studies, *Ethnic People Speak*, p.194.
60. CDA Collaborative Learning Projects, *Listening Project*.
61. Aung San Suu Kyi, "Empowerment for a Culture of Peace Development." Address to a meeting of the World Commission on Culture and Development, Manila, November 21, 1994. Cited in International Crisis Group, *Myanmar: The Role of Civil Society* (Bangkok/Brussels: International Crisis Group, 2001), p.21.
62. Caroline A. Hartzell and Matthew Hoddie, *Crafting Peace: Power-sharing Institutions and the Negotiated Settlement of Civil Wars* (University Park, PA: Pennsylvania State University Press, 2007). Gerald Schneider and Nina Wiesehomeier, "Rules that Matter: Political Institutions and the Diversity-Conflict Nexus," *Journal of Peace Research* 45:2 (2008), 183–203. Svensson, "Who Brings Which Peace?."
63. Brett D. Schaefer (ed.), *ConUNdrum: The Limits of the United Nations and the Search for Alternatives* (Lanham, MD: Rowman & Littlefield, 2009).
64. The international community established a long-term partnership with the Afghan government through the Afghanistan Reconstruction Trust Fund. Since early 2002, the Fund has drawn total contributions of more than $3 billion from about 30 states headed by the UK, Canada and the US. Its Management Committee, which meets regularly in Kabul, consists of the World Bank (as administrator), the Islamic Development Bank, the Asian Development Bank, and the UN. World Bank, *Afghanistan Reconstruction Trust Fund*. http://siteresources.worldbank.org/INTAFGHANISTAN/Resources/Afghanistan-Reconstructional-Trust-Fund/ARTF_information.pdf.
65. Stephen Hopgood, "Saying 'No' to Wal-Mart? Money and Morality in Professional Humanitarianism," in Michael Barnett and Thomas G. Weiss (eds), *Humanitarianism in Question: Politics, Power, Ethics* (Ithaca, NY: Cornell University Press, 2008), 98–123.
66. Alex de Waal, *Famine Crimes: Politics and the Disaster Relief Industry in Africa* (Bloomington, IN: Indiana University Press, 1997), p.221.
67. De Waal, *Famine Crimes*, p.xv. Also see pp.65–85.
68. De Waal, *Famine Crimes*, p.5.
69. De Waal, *Famine Crimes*, p.xvi.
70. Dambisa Moyo, *Dead Aid: Why Aid Is Not Working and How There Is a Better Way for Africa* (New York, NY: Farrar, Straus, and Giroux, 2009). Also see R. Glenn Hubbard and William Duggan, *The Aid Trap: Hard Truths about Ending Poverty* (New York, NY: Columbia University Press, 2009), and Linda Polman, *The Crisis Caravan: What's Wrong with Humanitarian Aid?* (New York, NY: Metropolitan Books, 2010).
71. Fiona Terry, *Condemned to Repeat? The Paradox of Humanitarian Action* (Ithaca, NY: Cornell University Press, 2002).
72. David Rieff, *A Bed for the Night: Humanitarianism in Crisis* (New York, NY: Simon & Schuster, 2003).
73. William Easterly, *The Elusive Quest for Growth: Economists' Adventures and Misadventures in the Tropics* (Cambridge, MA: MIT Press, 2001). William Easterly,

The White Man's Burden: Why the West's Efforts to Aid the Rest Have Done So Much Ill and So Little Good (New York, NY: Penguin, 2006).

74. Jeffrey D. Sachs, *The End of Poverty: Economic Possibilities for Our Time* (New York, NY: Penguin, 2005).
75. Amartya Sen, *Development as Freedom* (New York, NY: Knopf, 1999). Paul Collier, *The Bottom Billion: Why the Poorest Countries Are Failing and What Can Be Done about It* (Oxford: Oxford University Press, 2007).
76. Easterly, *The White Man's Burden*, p.5.
77. Amartya Sen, "The Man without a Plan: Can Foreign Aid Work?," *Foreign Affairs* 85:2 (2006), 171–7, pp.177, 172.
78. Sen, "The Man without a Plan," p.172.
79. Sen, "The Man without a Plan," p.174.
80. Greg Mortenson and David Oliver Relin, *Three Cups of Tea: One Man's Mission to Promote Peace… One School at a Time* (New York, NY: Penguin, 2006). Greg Mortenson, *Stones into Schools: Promoting Peace through Education in Afghanistan and Pakistan* (New York, NY: Penguin, 2010).
81. Ian Holliday, "The Yadana Syndrome? Big Oil and Principles of Corporate Engagement in Myanmar," *Asian Journal of Political Science* 13:2 (December 2005), 29–51.
82. World Bank, *Globalization, Growth, and Poverty: Building an Inclusive World Economy* (New York, NY: World Bank/Oxford University Press, 2002). Jay R. Mandle, *Globalization and the Poor* (Cambridge: Cambridge University Press, 2003). Jagdish Bhagwati, *In Defence of Globalization* (New York, NY: Oxford University Press, 2004). Martin Wolf, *Why Globalization Works* (New Haven, CT: Yale University Press, 2004). Thomas L. Friedman, *The World Is Flat: A Brief History of the Twenty-first Century* (New York, NY: Farrar, Straus and Giroux, 2005). C. K. Prahalad, *The Fortune at the Bottom of the Pyramid: Eradicating Poverty through Profits* (Upper Saddle River, NJ: Wharton School Publishing, 2005). Hubbard and Duggan, *The Aid Trap*.
83. Andre Gunder Frank, *Capitalism and Underdevelopment in Latin America: Historical Studies of Chile and Brazil* (Harmondsworth: Penguin, 1971).
84. Andrew Crane, Abagail McWilliams, Dirk Matten, Jeremy Moon and Donald S. Siegel (eds), *The Oxford Handbook of Corporate Social Responsibility* (Oxford: Oxford University Press, 2008).
85. David Allan, "Positive Engagement in Myanmar: Some Current Examples and Thoughts for the Future," in Nick Cheesman, Monique Skidmore and Trevor Wilson (eds), *Ruling Myanmar: From Cyclone Nargis to National Elections* (Singapore: ISEAS Publishing, 2010), 236–66, pp.256–7.
86. Holliday, "The Yadana Syndrome?."
87. EarthRights International and Southeast Asian Information Network, *Total Denial* (No place: EarthRights International, 1996). EarthRights International, *Total Denial Continues: Earth Rights Abuses Along the Yadana and Yetagun Pipelines in Burma* (No place: EarthRights International, 2000). Burma Campaign UK, *Totalitarian Oil – Total Oil: Fuelling the Oppression in Burma* (London: Burma Campaign UK, 2005).

88. Collaborative for Development Action, *Corporate Options: Constructive Engagement in Conflict Zones: Field Visit: Yadana Gas Transportation Project* (Cambridge, MA: Collaborative for Development Action, 2002). Collaborative for Development Action, *Second Visit: Yadana Gas Transportation Project* (Cambridge, MA: Collaborative for Development Action, 2003). Collaborative for Development Action, *Third Visit: Yadana Gas Transportation Project* (Cambridge, MA: Collaborative for Development Action, 2004). Collaborative for Development Action, *Yadana Gas Transportation Project: Fourth Visit* (Cambridge, MA: Collaborative for Development Action, 2005). Collaborative for Development Action, *Report of Fifth CDA/CEP Visit to the Yadana Pipeline* (Cambridge, MA: Collaborative for Development Action, 2008).
89. Total, *Total in Myanmar: A Sustained Commitment* (No place: Total, 2005), p.56.
90. Bernard Kouchner, "Report on a Trip to Myanmar and the Discovery of a Silent Industry" (2003), p.19. http://birmanie.total.com/en/publications/bk_report.pdf.
91. Ariel Colonomos and Javier Santiso, "Vive la France! French Multinationals and Human Rights," *Human Rights Quarterly* 27:4 (2005), 1307–45.
92. Joe Palazzolo, "China criminalizes foreign bribery," *Wall Street Journal* blog, March 2, 2011. http://blogs.wsj.com/corruption-currents/2011/03/02/china-criminalizes-foreign-bribery.
93. Gerald F. Cavanagh, "Global Business Ethics: Regulation, Code, or Self-restraint," *Business Ethics Quarterly* 14:4 (2004), 625–42.
94. Oliver F. Williams, ed., *Global Codes of Conduct: An Idea Whose Time Has Come* (Notre Dame, IN: University of Notre Dame Press, 2000).
95. S. Prakash Sethi, *Setting Global Standards: Guidelines for Creating Codes of Conduct in Multinational Corporations* (Hoboken, NJ: Wiley, 2003), p.xi.
96. S. Prakash Sethi and Oliver F. Williams, *Economic Imperatives and Ethical Values in Global Business: The South African Experience and International Codes Today* (Dordrecht: Kluwer, 2000), p.392.
97. Ian Holliday, "Doing Business with Rights Violating Regimes: Corporate Social Responsibility and Myanmar's Military Junta," *Journal of Business Ethics* 61:4 (2005), 329–42.
98. Ian Maitland, "The Great Non-Debate Over International Sweatshops," *British Academy of Management Annual Conference Proceedings*, September 1997, 240–65. Peter A. Voyer and Paul W. Beamish, "The Effect of Corruption on Japanese Foreign Direct Investment," *Journal of Business Ethics* 50:3 (2004), 211–24.
99. Jürgen Rüland, "Burma Ten Years after the Uprising: The Regional Dimension," in Robert H. Taylor, ed., *Burma: Political Economy Under Military Rule* (London: Hurst, 2001), 137–58.
100. John R. Schermerhorn, "Foreign Investment in Burma: Contrasting Perspectives," *Asian Case Research Journal* 2:2 (1998), 117–32, p.121.
101. United Nations Environment Programme, *National Sustainable Development Strategy: Myanmar*. www.rrcap.unep.org/nsds/brief/Myanmar%20brief.pdf.
102. Caux Round Table, *Principles for Business*. www.cauxroundtable.org/index.cfm?menuid=8.

103. Calvin M. Boardman and Hideaki Kiyoshi Kato, "The Confucian Roots of Business Kyosei," *Journal of Business Ethics* 48:4 (2003), 317–33.
104. CSR Asia provides a wealth of general information on the topic. www.csr-asia.com.
105. Holliday, "Doing Business with Rights Violating Regimes."
106. Allan, "Positive Engagement in Myanmar," p.237.
107. Lawrence Sáez and Crystal Chang, "The Political Economy of Global Firms from India and China," *Contemporary Politics* 15:3 (2009), 265–86.
108. Norman Bowie, "The Moral Obligations of Multinational Corporations," in Steven Luper-Foy (ed.), *Problems of International Justice* (Boulder, CO: Westview, 1988), 241–53.
109. Heinrich Böll Foundation (ed.), *Active Citizens under Political Wraps: Experiences from Myanmar/Burma and Vietnam* (Chiang Mai: Heinrich Böll Foundation, 2006).
110. Ardeth Maung Thawnghmung, *Behind the Teak Curtain: Authoritarianism, Agricultural Policies and Political Legitimacy in Rural Burma/Myanmar* (London: Kegan Paul, 2004).

Conclusion

1. Aung San Suu Kyi, *The Voice of Hope: Conversations with Alan Clements with Contributions by U Kyi Maung and U Tin U* (London: Penguin, 1997), p.9.
2. Mary Callahan, "The Endurance of Military Rule in Burma: Not Why, but Why Not?," in Susan L. Levenstein, ed., *Finding Dollars, Sense, and Legitimacy in Burma* (Washington, DC: Woodrow Wilson International Center for Scholars, 2010), 54–76.
3. Timothy Garton Ash, "Beauty and the beast in Burma," *New York Review of Books*, May 25, 2000.
4. David I. Steinberg, "'Legitimacy' in Burma/Myanmar: Concepts and Implications," in N. Ganesan and Kyaw Yin Hlaing (eds), *Myanmar: State, Society and Ethnicity* (Singapore: Institute of Southeast Asian Studies, 2007), 109–42, p.110.
5. Maung Htin Aung, *A History of Burma* (New York, NY: Columbia University Press, 1967), p.310.
6. Kyaw Zwa Moe, "Burma's 2011: A look ahead," *Irrawaddy*, December 9, 2010.
7. James M. Buchanan and Gordon Tullock, *The Calculus of Consent: Logical Foundations of Constitutional Democracy* (Ann Arbor, MI: University of Michigan Press, 1962).
8. Bruce Bueno de Mesquita, Alastair Smith, Randolph M. Siverson and James D. Morrow, *The Logic of Political Survival* (Cambridge, MA: MIT Press, 2003).
9. Kyaw Yin Hlaing, "Setting the Rules for Survival: Why the Burmese Military Regime Survives in an Age of Democratization," *Pacific Review* 22:3 (2009), 271–91.
10. Paul Collier, *The Bottom Billion: Why the Poorest Countries Are Failing and What Can Be Done about It* (Oxford: Oxford University Press, 2007).
11. Christian Davenport, "State Repression and the Tyrannical Peace," *Journal of Peace Research* 44:4 (2007), 485–504.

12. Matthias Basedau and Jann Lay, "Resource Curse or Rentier Peace? The Ambiguous Effects of Oil Wealth and Oil Dependence on Violent Conflict," *Journal of Peace Research* 46:6 (2009), 757–76.
13. Charles Tilly, *The Politics of Collective Violence* (Cambridge: Cambridge University Press, 2003).
14. Francisco Herreros, "'The Full Weight of the State': The Logic of Random State-sanctioned Violence," *Journal of Peace Research* 43:6 (2006), 671–89.
15. Richard McGregor, *The Party: The Secret World of China's Communist Rulers* (New York, NY: HarperCollins, 2010).
16. Teresa Wright, *Accepting Authoritarianism: State-Society Relations in China's Reform Era* (Stanford, CA: Stanford University Press, 2010).
17. Martin King Whyte, *Myth of the Social Volcano: Perceptions of Inequality and Distributive Injustice in Contemporary China* (Stanford, CA: Stanford University Press, 2010).
18. Tina Rosenberg, "Revolution U: What Egypt Learned from the Students Who Overthrew Milosevic," *Foreign Policy*, February 16, 2011. www.foreignpolicy.com/articles/2011/02/16/revolution_u?print=yes&hidecomments=yes&page=full.
19. Gene Sharp, *From Dictatorship to Democracy: A Conceptual Framework for Liberation* (Boston, MA: Albert Einstein Institution, 2002).
20. *Irrawaddy*, "Gene Sharp: Why Burmese resistance has failed so far," March 22, 2011.
21. Mikael Gravers (ed.), *Exploring Ethnic Diversity in Burma* (Copenhagen: NIAS Press, 2007). Ashley South, *Ethnic Politics in Burma: States of Conflict* (Abingdon: Routledge, 2008).
22. Paul Collier and Anke Hoeffler, "Resource Rents, Governance, and Conflict," *Journal of Conflict Resolution* 49:4 (2005), 625–33.
23. Michael L. Ross, "What Do We Know about Natural Resources and Civil War?," *Journal of Peace Research* 41:3 (2004), 337–56. James D. Fearon, "Primary Commodity Exports and Civil War," *Journal of Conflict Resolution* 49:4 (2005), 483–507. Silje Aslaksen, "Oil and Democracy: More than a Cross-country Correlation?," *Journal of Peace Research* 47:4 (2010), 421–31.
24. Basedau and Lay, "Resource Curse or Rentier Peace?."
25. Svante E. Cornell, "The Interaction of Narcotics and Conflict," *Journal of Peace Research* 42:6 (2005), 751–60.
26. Hideyuki Takano, *The Shore beyond Good and Evil: A Report from inside Burma's Opium Kingdom* (Reno, NV: Kotan, 2002). Ko-Lin Chin, *The Golden Triangle: Inside Southeast Asia's Drug Trade* (Ithaca, NY: Cornell University Press, 2009). Pierre-Arnaud Chouvy, *Opium: Uncovering the Politics of the Poppy* (London: I. B. Tauris, 2009). Bertil Lintner and Michael Black, *Merchants of Madness: The Methamphetamine Explosion in the Golden Triangle* (Chiang Mai: Silkworm, 2009).
27. Martin Smith, *State of Strife: The Dynamics of Ethnic Conflict in Burma* (Washington, DC: East-West Center Washington, 2007).
28. James D. Fearon, "Why Do Some Civil Wars Last So Much Longer than Others?," *Journal of Peace Research* 41:3 (2004), 275–301.

29. Amartya Sen, "Violence, Identity and Poverty," *Journal of Peace Research* 45:1 (2008), 5–15. Ole Magnus Theisen, "Blood and Soil? Resource Scarcity and Internal Armed Conflict Revisited," *Journal of Peace Research* 45:6 (2008), 801–18.
30. Karl R. de Rouen, Jr. and David Sobek, "The Dynamics of Civil War Duration and Outcome," *Journal of Peace Research* 41:3 (2004), 303–20. Lars-Erik Cederman, Halvard Buhaug and Jan Ketil Rød, "Ethno-nationalist Dyads and Civil War: A GIS-based Analysis," *Journal of Conflict Resolution* 53:4 (2009), 496–525.
31. Nils B. Weidmann, "Geography as Motivation and Opportunity: Group Concentration and Ethnic Conflict," *Journal of Conflict Resolution* 53:4 (2009), 526–43. Nils B. Weidmann, Jan Ketil Rød and Lars-Erik Cederman, "Representing Ethnic Groups in Space: A New Dataset," *Journal of Peace Research* 47:4 (2010), 491–9.
32. Halvard Buhaug, Scott Gates and Päivi Lujala, "Geography, Rebel Capability, and the Duration of Civil Conflict," *Journal of Conflict Resolution* 53:4 (2009), 544–69. Idean Salehyan, "Transnational Rebels: Neighboring States as Sanctuary for Rebel Groups," *World Politics* 59:2 (2007), 217–42.
33. Ashley South, *Burma's Longest War: Anatomy of the Karen Conflict* (Amsterdam: Transnational Institute and Burma Center Netherlands, 2011), pp.4, 33.
34. Guy Lubeigt, "Industrial Zones in Burma and Burmese Labour in Thailand," in Monique Skidmore and Trevor Wilson (eds), *Myanmar: The State, Community and the Environment* (Canberra: ANU E Press and Asian Pacific Press, 2007), 159–88.
35. Baogang He, "A Deliberative Approach to the Tibet Autonomy Issue: Promoting Mutual Trust through Dialogue," *Asian Survey* 50:4 (2010), 709–34, p.734.
36. Desirée Nilsson, "Partial Peace: Rebel Groups inside and outside of Civil War Settlements," *Journal of Peace Research* 45:4 (2008), 479–95.
37. Mary P. Callahan, *Political Authority in Burma's Ethnic Minority States: Devolution, Occupation, and Coexistence* (Washington, DC: East-West Center Washington, 2007).
38. Charles King, "The Benefits of Ethnic War: Understanding Eurasia's Unrecognized States," *World Politics* 53:4 (2001), 524–52. Also see: Scott Pegg, *International Society and the* De Facto *State* (Aldershot: Ashgate, 1998); and Pål Kolstø, "The Sustainability and Future of Unrecognized Quasi-states," *Journal of Peace Research* 43:6 (2006), 723–40.
39. South, *Ethnic Politics in Burma*.
40. Jalal Alamgir, "Against the Current: The Survival of Authoritarianism in Burma," *Pacific Affairs* 70:3 (1997), 333–50. Kyaw Yin Hlaing, "Setting the Rules for Survival." Robert H. Taylor, *The State in Myanmar* (Honolulu, HI: University of Hawai'i Press, 2009). Mary Callahan, "The Endurance of Military Rule in Burma."
41. James L. Gibson, *Overcoming Apartheid: Can Truth Reconcile a Divided Nation?* (New York, NY: Russell Sage Foundation, 2004). James L. Gibson, "The Contributions of Truth to Reconciliation: Lessons from South Africa," *Journal of Conflict Resolution* 50:3 (2006), 409–32.

42. Karen Brounéus, "The Trauma of Truth Telling: Effects of Witnessing in the Rwandan Gacaca Courts on Psychological Health," *Journal of Conflict Resolution* 54:3 (2010), 408–37.
43. Laurel E. Fletcher, Harvey M. Weinstein and Jamie Rowen, "Context, Timing and the Dynamics of Transitional Justice: A Historical Perspective," *Human Rights Quarterly* 31:1 (2009), 163–220.
44. Michael H. Bernhard and Ekrem Karakoç, "Civil Society and the Legacies of Dictatorship," *World Politics* 59:4 (2007), 539–67.
45. Centre for Peace and Conflict Studies, *Listening to Voices from Inside: Myanmar Civil Society's Response to Cyclone Nargis* (Phnom Penh: Centre for Peace and Conflict Studies, 2009), p.v.
46. Centre for Peace and Conflict Studies, *Myanmar Civil Society's Response to Cyclone Nargis*, p.39.
47. Centre for Peace and Conflict Studies, *Myanmar Civil Society's Response to Cyclone Nargis*, p.144.
48. Centre for Peace and Conflict Studies, *Myanmar Civil Society's Response to Cyclone Nargis*, p.100.
49. Robert A. Dahl, *Who Governs? Democracy and Power in an American City* (New Haven, CT: Yale University Press, 1961).
50. Harold D. Lasswell, *Politics: Who Gets What, When, How* (New York, NY: Peter Smith, 1950).
51. Stephen G. Brooks and William C. Wohlforth, *World Out of Balance: International Relations and the Challenge of American Primacy* (Princeton, NJ: Princeton University Press, 2008). David P. Calleo, *Follies of Power: America's Unipolar Fantasy* (New York, NY: Cambridge University Press, 2009). Carla Norloff, *America's Global Advantage: US Hegemony and International Cooperation* (Cambridge: Cambridge University Press, 2010).
52. A March 2010 Asia Society task force report on options for US policy in the wake of the September 2009 Obama administration policy review is cast in this context. Asia Society Task Force Report, *Current Realities and Future Possibilities in Burma/ Myanmar: Options for U.S. Policy* (No place: Asia Society, 2010), p.8.
53. Martin Jacques, *When China Rules the World: The Rise of the Middle Kingdom and the End of the Western World* (New York, NY: Allen Lane, 2009). Stefan Halper, *The Beijing Consensus: How China's Authoritarian Model Will Dominate the Twenty-first Century* (New York, NY: Basic Books, 2010). Elizabeth C. Economy, "The Game Changer," *Foreign Affairs* 89:6 (2010), 142–52.
54. Lai-Ha Chan, Pak K. Lee and Gerald Chan, "Rethinking Global Governance: A China Model in the Making?," *Contemporary Politics* 14:1 (2008), 3–19.
55. Richard N. Haass, "The Age of Nonpolarity," *Foreign Affairs* 87:3 (2008), 44–56. Jeffrey Henderson, "China and Global Development: Towards a Global-Asian Era?," *Contemporary Politics* 14:4 (2008), 375–92.
56. Peter Beinart, *The Icarus Syndrome: A History of American Hubris* (New York, NY: HarperCollins, 2010).

57. Charles A. Kupchan, *How Enemies Become Friends: The Sources of Stable Peace* (Princeton, NJ: Princeton University Press, 2010).
58. James Traub, *The Freedom Agenda: Why America Must Spread Democracy (Just Not the Way George Bush Did)* (New York, NY: Farrar, Straus and Giroux, 2008).
59. T. J. Pempel, "How Bush Bungled Asia: Militarism, Economic Indifference and Unilateralism Have Weakened the United States across Asia," *Pacific Review* 21:5 (2008), 547–81. Simon S. C. Tay, *Asia Alone: The Dangerous Post-Crisis Divide from America* (Singapore: John Wiley, 2010).
60. Bill Emmott, *Rivals: How the Power Struggle between China, India and Japan Will Shape Our Next Decade* (London: Allen Lane, 2008).
61. For an analysis of how a hypothetical collapse of central authority in Myanmar might be handled, see Alain Guilloux, "Myanmar: Analyzing Problems of Transition and Intervention," *Contemporary Politics* 16:4 (2010), 383–401.
62. Zarni, "Sanctions aren't the problem," *Irrawaddy*, January 4, 2011. International Crisis Group, *China's Myanmar Dilemma*, Asia Report No.177, September 14, 2009. David Arase, "Non-traditional Security in China-ASEAN Cooperation: The Institutionalization of Regional Security Cooperation and the Evolution of East Asian Regionalism," *Asian Survey* 50:4 (2010), 808–33.
63. Robert M. Gates, "Helping Others Defend Themselves," *Foreign Affairs* 89:3 (2010), 2–6.
64. Steven R. David, *Catastrophic Consequences: Civil Wars and American Interests* (Baltimore, MD: Johns Hopkins University Press, 2008).
65. In January 2008, US Chargé d'affaires Shari Villarosa hosted the Chinese Ambassador for lunch, and reported that China shared a desire to see stability, development and democracy in Myanmar. While that is probably true, a key point of difference is the ordering of these objectives. US Department of State, "Chinese losing patience with Burma," January 18, 2008. WikiLeaks US Embassy Cables, ref. 08RANGOON44.
66. Stephanie Kleine-Ahlbrandt and Andrew Small, "China's New Dictatorship Diplomacy," *Foreign Affairs* 87:1 (2008), 38–56.
67. Alastair Iain Johnston, *Social States: China in International Institutions, 1980–2000* (Princeton, NJ: Princeton University Press, 2008).
68. Pak K. Lee, Gerald Chan and Lai-Ha Chan, "China in Darfur: Humanitarian Rule-maker or Rule-taker?," *Review of International Studies* 37 (2011), forthcoming.
69. Ethan Bronner and David E. Sanger, "Arab League endorses no-flight zone over Libya," *International Herald Tribune*, March 12, 2011.
70. Donald K. Emmerson (ed.), *Hard Choices: Security, Democracy, and Regionalism in Southeast Asia* (Singapore: Institute of Southeast Asian Studies, 2009).
71. S. D. Muni, *India's Foreign Policy: The Democracy Dimension* (New Delhi: Foundation Books, 2009). Rajiv Sikri, *Challenge and Strategy: Rethinking India's Foreign Policy* (New Delhi: Sage, 2009). Evan A. Feigenbaum, "India's Rise, America's Interest," *Foreign Affairs* 89:2 (2010), 76–91. Admiral Raja Menon and Rajiv Kumar, *The Long View from Delhi: To Define the Indian Grand Strategy for Foreign Policy* (New Delhi: Academic Foundation, 2010). Robert D. Kaplan, *Monsoon: The Indian Ocean and the Future of American Power* (New York, NY: Random House, 2010).

72. Ian Holliday, 'Japan and the Myanmar Stalemate: Regional Power and Resolution of a Regional Problem', *Japanese Journal of Political Science* 6:3 (2005), 393–410. Ian Holliday, 'Extending a Hand in Myanmar', *Dissent* 58:2 (Spring 2011), 14–18.
73. Kent E. Calder, *Pacific Alliance: Reviving U.S.-Japan Relations* (New Haven, CT: Yale University Press, 2009).
74. James P. Muldoon, Jr., JoAnn Fagot Aviel, Richard Reitano and Earl Sullivan (eds), *The New Dynamics of Multilateralism: Diplomacy, International Organizations, and Global Governance* (Boulder, CO: Westview, 2010).
75. Hillary Clinton, "Leading through Civilian Power," *Foreign Affairs* 89:6 (2010), 13–24.
76. Anne-Marie Slaughter, *A New World Order* (Princeton, NJ: Princeton University Press, 2004). Anne-Marie Slaughter, "America's Edge: Power in the Networked Century," *Foreign Affairs* 88:1 (2009), 94–113.
77. William H. Overholt, *Asia, America, and the Transformation of Geopolitics* (New York, NY: Cambridge University Press, 2008).
78. Cemil Aydin, *The Politics of Anti-Westernism in Asia: Visions of World Order in Pan-Islamic and Pan-Asian Thought* (New York, NY: Columbia University Press, 2007).
79. The White House, "Remarks by the President on a New Beginning," Cairo University, June 4, 2009. www.whitehouse.gov/the-press-office/remarks-president-cairo-university-6–04-09.
80. Barack H. Obama, "Nobel Lecture: A Just and Lasting Peace," December 10, 2009. http://nobelprize.org/nobel_prizes/peace/laureates/2009/obama-lecture_en.html.
81. Catherine Ashton, "Listening to the revolution," *International Herald Tribune*, February 26–27, 2011, p.6.
82. Charles McDermid, "Missing the point on Myanmar," *Asia Times Online*, July 4, 2009. www.atimes.com/atimes/Southeast_Asia/KG04Ae01.html.
83. Margaret E. Keck and Kathryn Sikkink, *Activists beyond Borders: Advocacy Networks in International Politics* (Ithaca, NY: Cornell University Press, 1998).
84. Thomas Risse, Stephen C. Ropp and Kathryn Sikkink, eds, *The Power of Human Rights: International Norms and Domestic Change* (Cambridge: Cambridge University Press, 1999).
85. Tobias Böhmelt, "The Effectiveness of Tracks of Diplomacy Strategies in Third-party Interventions," *Journal of Peace Research* 47:2 (2010), 167–78.
86. Daniel Lieberfeld, "Evaluating the Contributions of Track-two Diplomacy to Conflict Termination in South Africa, 1984–90," *Journal of Peace Research* 39:3 (2002), 355–72. Ronald J. Fisher, "Assessing the Contingency Model of Third-party Intervention in Successful Cases of Prenegotiation," *Journal of Peace Research* 44:3 (2007), 311–29.
87. Amanda Murdie and Tavishi Bhasin, "Aiding and Abetting: Human Rights INGOs and Domestic Protest," *Journal of Conflict Resolution* 55 (2011), forthcoming.
88. Amanda A. Licht, "Coming into Money: The Impact of Foreign Aid on Leader Survival," *Journal of Conflict Resolution* 54:1 (2010), 58–87.

89. Amanda Murdie and David R. Davis, "Problematic Potential: The Human Rights Consequences of Peacekeeping Interventions in Civil Wars," *Human Rights Quarterly* 32:1 (2010), 49–72.
90. Timothy Garton Ash, "Technology lets us peer inside the Burmese cage, but not unlock its door," *Guardian*, December 15, 2010.
91. Zarni, "Sanctions aren't the problem."
92. Steven E. Finkel, Aníbal S. Pérez Liñan and Mitchell A. Seligson, "The Effects of U.S. Foreign Assistance on Democracy Building, 1990–2003," *World Politics* 59:3 (2007), 404–40.
93. International Crisis Group, *China's Myanmar Dilemma*, Asia Report No.177, September 14, 2009.
94. Amitav Acharya, *Whose Ideas Matter? Agency and Power in Asian Regionalism* (Ithaca, NY: Cornell University Press, 2009).
95. Jason Brownlee, "Can America Nation-build?," *World Politics* 59:2 (2007), 314–40.
96. Wright, *Accepting Authoritarianism.*
97. Jürgen Haacke, *Myanmar's Foreign Policy: Domestic Influences and International Implications* (Abingdon: Routledge, 2006).
98. Acharya, *Whose Ideas Matter?*, pp.31–41.
99. Chen Jian, "China and the Bandung Conference: Changing Perceptions and Representations," in See Seng Tan and Amitav Acharya (eds), *Bandung Revisited: The Legacy of the 1955 Asian-African Conference for International Order* (Singapore: NUS Press, 2008), 132–59, p.134.
100. Richard Wright, *The Color Curtain: A Report on the Bandung Conference* (New York, NY: World Publishing Company, 1956), p.12.
101. Rahul Mukherji, "Appraising the Legacy of Bandung: A View from India," in See Seng Tan and Amitav Acharya (eds), *Bandung Revisited: The Legacy of the 1955 Asian-African Conference for International Order* (Singapore: NUS Press, 2008), 160–79, p.168.
102. Amitav Acharya reports that a Chinese proposal to create a permanent regional organization was discussed at Bandung by three leaders: Zhou, Nehru and Nu. Acharya, *Whose Ideas Matter?*, p.77.
103. U Nu, *U Nu: Saturday's Son* (New Haven, CT: Yale University Press, 1975), pp. 225–85.
104. Cited in Acharya, *Whose Ideas Matter?*, p.45.
105. World Economic Forum, *Aung San Suu Kyi Addresses World Economic Forum Annual Meeting in Davos*, January 28, 2011. www.weforum.org/news/aung-san-suu-kyi-addresses-world-economic-forum-annual-meeting-davos?fo=1.
106. Daniel A. Bell, *China's New Confucianism: Politics and Everyday Life in a Changing Society* (Princeton, NJ: Princeton University Press, 2008). Anand Giridharadas, *India Calling: An Intimate Portrait of a Nation's Remaking* (New York, NY: Times Books, 2011).

Index

Note: Name changes decreed mainly in 1989 mean that any analysis of recent history will capture many people and places under two different terms: Arakan and Rakhine, Rangoon and Yangon, and so on. In this index, all cases of split identity are listed separately.